Joan Priest

SCHOLARS AND GENTLEMEN

A Biography of the Mackerras Family

BOOLARONG PUBLICATIONS

By the same author

VIRTUE IN FLYING
OUTBACK AIRMAN (with H. Purvis)
THE THIESS STORY

First published in 1986
by Boolarong Publications,
24 Little Edward Street, Spring Hill, Brisbane. Qld.

Copyright © Joan Priest

This book is copyright. Apart from any fair dealing for the purposes of private study, research, criticism or review, as permitted under the Copyright Act, no part may be reproduced by any process without written permission. Inquiries should be addressed to the Publishers.

All rights reserved.

National Library of Australia
Cataloguing-in-Publication data

   Priest, Joan, 1920- .
     Scholars and gentlemen.

   Includes index.
   ISBN 0 86439 013 0

    1. Mackerras family. 2. Australia — Genealogy.
   I. Title.

994.04

BOOLARONG PUBLICATIONS,
24 Little Edward Street, Spring Hill, Brisbane, Qld.
Design, reproduction and photo-typesetting by Press Etching Pty. Ltd., Brisbane.
Printed by Poly-Graphics Pty. Ltd., Brisbane.
Bound by Podlich Enterprises Pty. Ltd., Brisbane.

Acknowledgments

We wish to thank the editors of the following publications for use of material: Sydney Morning Herald, Daily Telegraph, Sydney; The Age, Melbourne; The Courier-Mail; Brisbane: The Australian, Australian Financial Review and The Bulletin.

Author's Note

There are a number of remarkable families who have made their mark on Australian life in the 20th century — Street, Kent-Hughes, Bonython, Cilento, Durack, Mackerras — are some that spring instantly to mind. It has been my purpose to illustrate this by tracing the diverse careers of the Mackerras family and assessing the contribution they have made to the development of this country.

The work could not have been undertaken without the assistance of the Literature Board of the Australia Council. I also wish to thank the Mitchell Library and the University of NSW Library for the use of their resources, the Mackerras family themselves, their colleagues and the many distinguished community leaders who gave of their time. Their reminiscences and opinions were invaluable.

My special thanks go to Alastair Mackerras for checking the entire manuscript for any error in fact, and to Neil Mackerras, the genealogist of the family, for supplying the family tree and many useful papers.

I thank also my husband Eric Priest who gave unstinting assistance throughout, and my daughter Helen O'Reilly for her constructive ideas and suggestions.

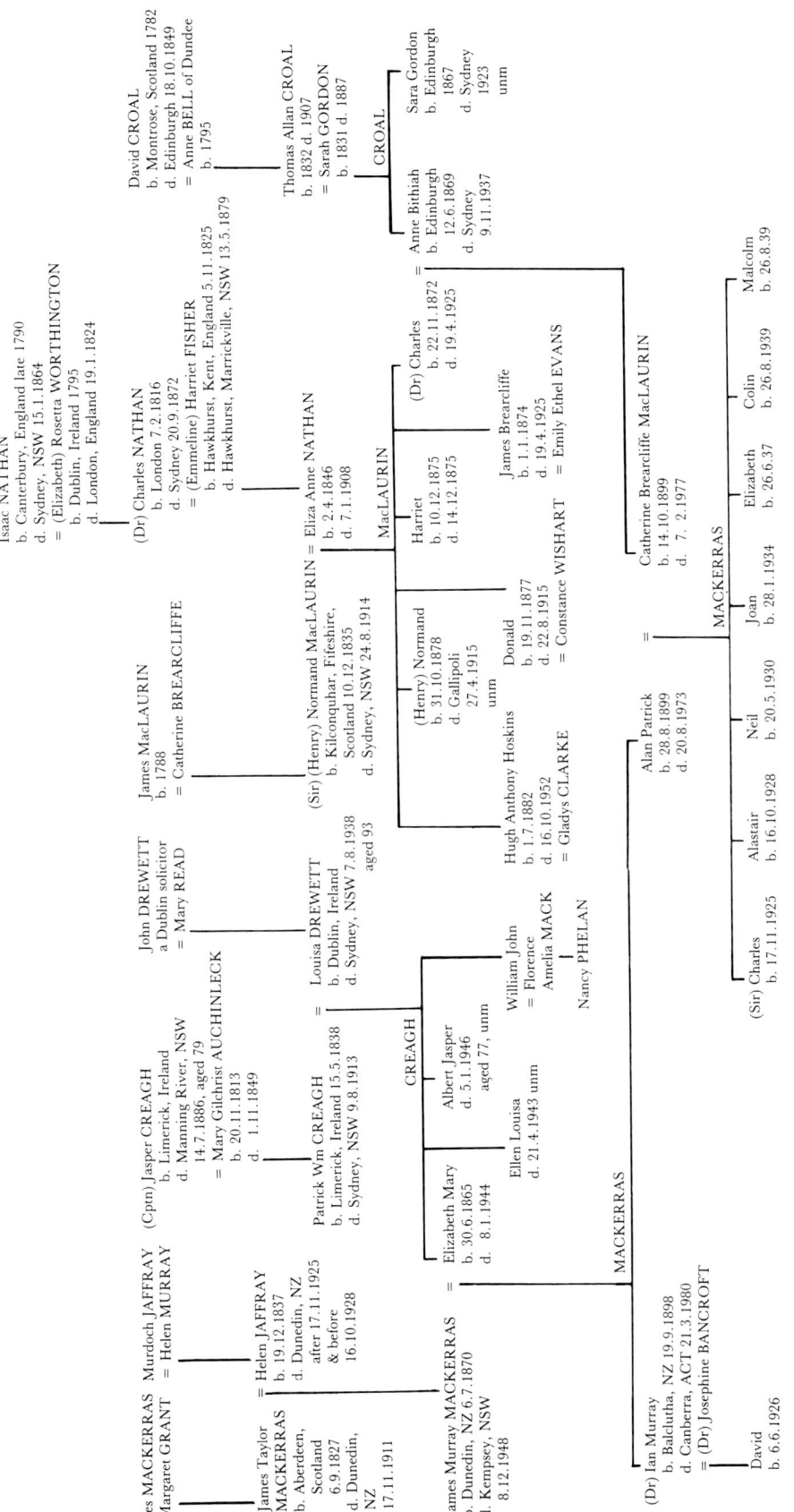

> . . . . *Brothers all*
> *In honour, as in one community,*
> *Scholars and Gentlemen.*
>
> (Wordsworth)

Catherine —

> *I agree with no man's opinions. I have some of my own.*
>
> (Turgenev)

CONTENTS

Author's note	iv
Family tree	v
Catherine and Alan (I)	1
Early Years of Marriage	38
Family at Turramurra	53
Charles	88
Alastair	125
Neil	171
Joan and Elizabeth	202
Colin	233
Malcolm	270
Catherine and Alan (II)	302
Index	321

Chapter 1

Catherine and Alan (I)

Outside the house in Bayswater Road, Rushcutters Bay, a sulky passes briskly and a cable car clangs along its black ribbon route over the hills to the city. But it is to the crashing of gears of one of Sydney's first cars on this summer morning of 1904 that the exultant trio lurch forward, mother and four year old child swathed in motoring veils, father, wearing a neat Edwardian beard under his panama, resolute behind the wheel.

The child, perched bright-eyed and expectant between her parents, is Catherine MacLaurin. A picnic basket and a large canvas bag with bathing costumes lie at her feet as they set off on this first major venture in motoring for a swim at Cronulla. Life is a great adventure. And so, for this only offshoot of a family belonging to both the intellectually and socially elite of a very much stratified society, it will continue to be. Precociously aware, she is probably conscious even at this early stage that the joys of her privileged little existence are paid for by responsibilities of a similar order. And joys, it is swiftly brought home on this balmy day, are tempered with hazards.

On this and many subsequent occasions, setting out for beach or bush and quiet willow-hung creek by which to laze and boil the billy, the trials of early motoring beset them. The temperamental vehicle, like all its counterparts from Perth to New York, frequently rebelled at hills and could be coaxed over them only by disgorging the passengers, enlisting the aid of bystanders, turning the car about and with the help of the strong reverse gear pushing it backwards to the crest. The mortification of trudging uphill with her mother in the wake of her father, the central figure in this spectacle, the car a conspicuous bright red, was doubled for Catherine by the glee of the local urchins who gathered to hurl insults. The memory rankled, for, fifty years later, she recalls in her memoirs these 'mocking guttersnipes'.

Her father, Dr Charles MacLaurin, was a graduate of the great medical school at Edinburgh, as his Scots father before him, but he had been sent there in preference to Sydney University for another and very specific reason. A talented student with a retentive memory, a capacity for sustained study, a taste for literature and gifted musically, he had excelled throughout his years at Sydney Grammar School in both mathematics and the classics. At the same time he suffered from a most unfortunate affliction.

As a small somewhat nervous child, he was locked by his nurse for some minor misdemeanour in a dark cupboard on the top floor of his father's tall Victorian slate-roofed house in Macquarie Street. The wretched girl went off down the long narrow staircase, became absorbed in a novel, and left him there for two terrifying hours. When he was released he was speechless with fear and never spoke again without a prolonged and distressing stammer.

In Edinburgh in the 1890s there was an eminent physician and speech therapist, who, it was hoped, would cure him. He took an exacting course to no effect and was desperately lonely in that far off university in the fogs and bitter winds. A good all rounder, his sports were tennis and sailing, he wrote of his longing for 'the white yachts dotting Sydney harbour and the long wash of Australasian seas on Manly beach' and also consoled himself writing stories inspired by his studies, sad tales of students with consumption and women dying in childbirth. This interest in authorship deepened and later bore fruit. But the turning point in his life occurred during the summer vacation when he went searching for the ancestral places of the clan Laurin and at the small village of Strathyre fell instantly in love with a Scottish girl, Anne Croal, he saw walking with her sister on an old stone bridge crossing the river Balvaig. The pair, later that day, met and were engaged within a month, though he was only 19 and had four years of his medical course to complete.

They waited five long years to marry. The Croal household of eleven, meanwhile, became a second home for him. Thomas Croal, a civil servant and journalist, had a wide circle of friends with literary interests — one of whom had been Robert Louis Stevenson before he set forth for his Pacific island — and he was welcomed by them. He graduated in 1896 and returned to Sydney to establish a career, with the promise by Croal that his daughter would join him in a year 'if things turned out'. Anne's farewell present, inscribed in her flowing hand, was a volume of Longfellow's poems. She marked in black the lines —

> Sail on, nor fear to breast the sea
> Our hearts, our hopes are all with thee.

Things 'turned out'. A year later a small figure, with a tartan scarf up to her ears, waved from a deck of the P & O steamer, *China*, to her anxious father who had pressed into her hand as he kissed her goodbye a return ticket 'in case'. He never saw her again. However, long affectionate letters assured him of her happiness at the far end of the world. The Bank of New South Wales converted her return fare and the money furnished their first drawing room at Rushcutters Bay.

This was in a small mid-Victorian terrace house in a street known as Roslyn Gardens. Sydney was a thriving city of half a million and this was considered a quietly prosperous harbourside suburb. There were beautiful views, in no way impaired by the larger houses on the hillside whose gardens ran down to the water's edge, many with boat sheds and private swimming baths. Charles had set up practice there on his return and quickly became established.

The pair married on one hundred and fifty pounds a year, paying five shillings a week, a quite considerable portion of it, in order to keep a maid. Such were the standards of the day. A successful doctor's wife did not expect to do housework. She helped with the making of the big double bed, washed her best china herself, dusted the drawing room and ordered the meals. She was then free to visit, to write, to practise her Scottish ballads, to arrange musical evenings and concert-going for the talented husband whom she adored.

It was 1897, Queen Victoria's jubilee year, the height of the power and prestige of the British Empire. The doctor and his friends and colleagues were ardent Imperialists, modelling their lives on the British. The daily life of the MacLaurins was different in only one major respect, apart from the benefits of climate, from that which Anne had known in Scotland and from that of the big majority of church-going late Victorians. Charles was a radical with a strong anti-religious bias, a supporter of the evolutionist theories of Darwin and Huxley, Spencer and Mill. Religion he regarded as superstition and wanted no talk of it in his home. He discouraged his wife from the Sunday attendances and bible reading which had been obligatory in the Croal family in Edinburgh. She compromised on this and once a month took herself off to St Andrew's Scots Church, Rose Bay, where they had married. On other Sundays there were outings, friends visiting and her husband at the piano playing Chopin and Schumann.

He was, in many ways, a man of contradictions. Inflexible in his anti-religious attitude, a rabid teetotaller who would not allow a drop of alcohol in the house even for medicinal purposes, he was yet described by friends as genial, generous and hospitable. To his colleagues he was always Charlie, and had their affection; he was a man quick to quarrel and fiery in argument, but also quick to forgive. There can be no doubt that his combativeness was worsened by the fact of his difficulty with speech. But he was making a reputation as a surgeon, rising rapidly in the profession, and he never allowed his distressing impediment to stand in the way of the social life he shared with his young wife. They moved to a home at Bayswater Road with large grounds and a stable where he could house sulky and horse which he used for his rounds, and he now employed a groom to look after both.

Catherine was a much longed for and awaited child, an only one, born within weeks of the turn of the century, in October 1899, as the first rumblings of discord with the established order of things manifested itself in South Africa with the outbreak of the Boer War. But at Bayswater Road there was rejoicing and within a few months a nursemaid for the baby joined the household. This girl, Ellen, who was to stay for seven years, winning the parents' trust and the child's affection, was a devout Anglican but sworn to silence by the doctor on the subject of religion.

Ellen daily wheeled her charge off in her pram to the cool haven of Rushcutters Bay Park at the foot of the hill, close to the moored boats, stretching sails and life of the harbour. There she chatted frequently with another nurse wheeling the infant, Alan Mackerras. He was a few months older, and propped, like Catherine, in embroidered garments on fine linen covers, for his daily dose of fresh air at this lovely place with its great flourishing oaks, planted with only half-hearted hopes of success by homesick Englishmen half a century before. His elder brother, Ian, usually trotted beside the small cavalcade. The boys were nephews of Charles MacLaurin's close friend, the highly idiosyncratic but fine lawyer, William John Creagh, with whom he had been at university. Creagh lived still at the patriarchal mansion at nearby Elizabeth Bay with other members of his family, including, at this point, his sister, the boys' mother, Elizabeth Mackerras, whom Charles had attended for the birth of Alan. Both men were expert yachtsmen and Saturdays found them sailing with the Royal Sydney Yacht Squadron. Music, interest in the first wind-up gramophones, and a catholic taste in literature, were other bonds and the families were frequently in touch. The MacLaurins had now built a new home along Bayswater Road, sold the horse and buggy, and acquired the car.

Catherine, four years old, was about to widen her horizons again. The ideas of the mid-nineteenth century German educationalist, Friedrich Froebel, founder of the Kindergarten movement, had now been implemented in Australia and a Kindergarten Training College formed in Sydney. Free kindergartens were envisaged but more practical training was needed. At Rushcutters Bay, an auxiliary centre, known as Froebel House, was set up and with it a Kindergarten to act as a model for those proposed. The objective was 'early training for individual development'. Catherine was promptly enrolled.

The big majority of children at Froebel House belonged to far less radical households. It was after all a Christian, and predominantly Protestant, society in which they lived and they took for granted the recital of the Lord's Prayer each morning. They had been repeating it at bedtime after their nurses since they were able to speak. Catherine had never heard it. She decided to question her father on this mystery and went in search of him. It was a scene she never forgot. She found him gluing a tiny leather hinge on the door of a doll's house he was making for her. About him, as

Catherine, aged about 4

Her mother, Anne MacLaurin

ever in those days, there hung the faint aroma of chloroform and disinfectant.

She began, precipitately, as was her way, with her questions, bending over at the same time to examine the intricate work. His beard brushed her cheek and he began breathing rather hard. He was not, he assured her, 'Our Father'. That was God and it was a prayer and if he told her what he felt about the matter her mother would be angry. He suggested she talk to her. When approached, her mother was evasive; she would 'understand later', but she resolved herself that from then on the child would accompany her to the festive Christmas service and at least come to know the carols. Ellen would not comment but was scandalised when she asked if the notice on the boatshed at the park: 'Trespassers will be prosecuted', was also a prayer. She consulted other booted and buttoned tots at Froebel House and one offered the suggestion that the 'Lord' of the prayer was probably God. That was the end of the matter for the time being. But she was aware of feeling unsatisfied and there seems little doubt that the deliberate shutting out of the subject had a deep-seated effect on her and also, contrary to plan, spurred her curiosity and interest.

Meanwhile, there were exciting visits to 155 Macquarie Street, the home of her grandparents, Sir Normand and Lady MacLaurin. The doctor was the eldest of their family of five sons and was deeply devoted to his father whom Catherine was taught to revere. This was scarcely necessary. Sir Normand was a patriarch of austere, commanding presence who automatically inspired respect, a leading public figure in medical,

Dr Charles MacLaurin's first car, outside 155 Macquarie Street, the home of his parents, Sir Normand and Lady MacLaurin.

parliamentary, university and business circles, with an extraordinary record of achievement. As the son of a dominie (schoolmaster) in Fifeshire, this gaunt, determined Scot had begun his tertiary studies at 15, walking, frock-coated, seven miles to attend his lectures at St Andrew's University and home again. He graduated M.A. with high distinction in mathematics and classics, then M.D. at Edinburgh University, and subsequently became an assistant surgeon in the Royal Navy. His future was decided when his ship visited Sydney in 1871. He met at this same house, 155 Macquarie Street, the then owner, Dr Charles Nathan, whose bevy of beautiful daughters, embroidery to hand, together with their mother and brothers, were grouped around the big drawing room to entertain the ship's officers.

The young surgeon, in conversation with Dr Nathan, learnt that the latter was the honorary consulting surgeon to St Vincent's Hospital, had introduced the use of anaesthetics to Australia and was proud to have been awarded an Honorary F.R.C.S. for his services. The challenges and opportunities waiting to be grasped right there in Sydney seemed enormous. Next, he was captivated when the elegant, dark-haired eldest daughter, Eliza, played and sang some Scottish airs. Her father, in jovial mood, then sang a Mozart aria. It was a congenial atmosphere the serious Scot could hardly have dreamed of finding. The path ahead was suddenly clear. He resigned his commission and married Eliza, who walked on her father's arm to the lovely old St James Anglican Church nearby, while the waiting bridegroom called silently on his covenanting Scots ancestors for forgiveness. After some preliminary months with Dr Nathan, they moved to Parramatta where he set up practice.

Just a year later, the popular Nathan, at the height of his career, aged only 56, died of septicaemia; he had scratched his finger while operating on a bad case. It was the classic death of the pre-antiseptic surgeon. Sydney mourned. Not only the carriages of the distinguished citizenry followed the dark-plumed, horse-drawn hearse along Macquarie Street but, on foot, a line of hundreds of the more humble whom he had attended so devotedly.

His widow asked her son-in-law to move into 155 Macquarie Street and take over his practice. This he did and the couple spent the rest of their days there; all their children were born in the big front bedroom, five sons and a daughter who, sadly, survived only a few days. During these years he was appointed to the Board of Health and took strong measures to curb an outbreak of typhoid in the city, became a parliamentarian and a member of the Legislative Council, where as a minister in Sir George Dibbs' government, he conceived the legislation which mitigated the bank smash of 1893. He was a director of the Bank of NSW, MLC (later chairman), CSR and other companies, and on the board of Trustees of Sydney Grammar School. He was appointed Vice-Chancellor of Sydney University in 1893, Chancellor in 1896 and knighted in King Edward VII's coronation honours for his services. The University was his first love and under him were built the Medical School, the Russell School of Engineering, the Fisher Library and, by a financial master stroke, a building for the Universtiy Union to which he had directed the Challis Bequest. He had, as his granddaughter observed, very strong opinions about everything on earth and made many enemies. The students objected

Dr Charles Nathan, as a young man.

His daughter, Eliza (later Lady MacLaurin).

Catherine's grandfather, Sir Normand MacLaurin, Chancellor of Sydney University in the early 1900s.

Main Building Sydney University

to his interference in day to day matters after he had become Chancellor and it was no longer his province. They retaliated with various pranks, the most upsetting of which was the ordering of several funeral directors to the house, saying that he had died. He took an unpopular and misplaced stand against Federation on financial grounds and in 1899 *The Bulletin* took great delight in publishing a caricature satirising this with the caption:'Fully 29s.6d. per head per annum extra taxation if Queensland is invited in.'

Portraits of him show a strained, rather worried expression on the fine craggy features, which is hardly surprising in view of his responsibilities, which, unfortunately, his wife added to, rather than minimised. She had never had very much confidence in herself, had grown very stout, was afflicted with deafness, and found her role as official hostess at the University extremely taxing. She took refuge in the fine sherries and wines that were always on hand and eventually became an alcoholic. This, no doubt, was the reason why her son Charles would have no alcohol in his own house.

On the early visits as a child to 155 Macquarie Street, Catherine was not at all inhibited by her grandfather. Firstly, there was the pleasure of pulling the big polished brass DAY bell and hearing its sweet extended chimes reverberating through the house. Then, having greeted him and deposited a kiss on the august cheek, she would brush impatiently aside the huggings of her grandmother, burdened with her big awkward silver ear trumpet, and race up the steep narrow steps to her father's old nursery on the top floor, kneel on the window sill, grasp the bars and gaze with never ending fascination at the ships and sights of the harbour right out to South Head and beyond.

She was a self-sufficient child; she had learnt to be. Sir Normand had said to her mother soon after her arrival in Sydney, and before her marriage, 'Have you ever met an *old* man who stammers?' She said she had not and he asked her why she thought this was. 'I suppose,' said Anne, 'because they get better as they get older.' 'No, my dear,' the old man told her, 'they die.' The clear inference that such an affliction does not make for longevity had haunted Anne and made her concentrate, more than was usual, all her gentle attention on her husband. Catherine never remembered hearing a harsh word between them. Her mother had a quick, apt turn of phrase, one of the qualities which had drawn her husband to her, and one which was never used against him. It was a love match which never faltered and Catherine was aware of always coming second, never first, in their affections.

The question now for the MacLaurins was a choice of school for their child. The doctor would not have a church school where she might imbibe 'dogma or superstition', or a state school, for it might worsen her 'Australian accent' which already alarmed him. A compromise was made with the small progressive school, *Shirley*, at Edgecliff, run by two fine women educationalists from England, Margaret Hodge and Harriet Newcombe. The former was an historian with a great gift for teaching, the latter a specialist in elementary education. Innovative teachers, they were much ahead of their time and used pictures, songs, improvised acting and practical projects, as well as reading aloud literary and historical pieces with exquisite articulation in an inspired jovial fashion'. They returned to England after two years to plunge into politics and the Votes for Women movement and Catherine lamented. Of her five years at the school, it was the first two, under their tuition, which undoubtedly set her ahead and spurred her quick imagination.

In 1908, Lady MacLaurin died. She, poor woman, had suffered a lingering stroke and had sat propped, deaf and speechless, for months at her window. Catherine was filled with remorse, for she had been particularly hateful to her, not only pushing away from her embraces, but scarcely pausing to thank her for the beautiful presents which she frequently gave her. She had found her embarrassing and somehow sensed her inadequacy. Now, in the great gloomy bedroom, as she watched her mother sort out the silks and velvets, the feather boas and mantles and French kid gloves, and saw the trinkets and netted purses which lay in a drawer and had never been used, because 'grandfather disapproved', she felt for her grandmother. She thought, belatedly, of the interesting things. How she could actually remember the last corroborees of the Sydney aborigines in the Botanical Gardens opposite, and the tales of her grandfather, Isaac Nathan, the first professional musician to migrate to Australia, who had studied their chants and made a part song of the Aboriginal call 'cooee'. Catherine looked at a charming, silver-framed photograph of the dark-haired young bride her grandmother had been, leaning so elegantly on the chiffonier, and longed to ask her mother never to grow old and fat and grey and die. She refrained. Such talk, she knew, would be dismissed by her practical parent as 'morbid imagination'.

One of the MacLaurins' five sons, Donald, now lived in Scotland, but four were in Sydney; J.B., Henry Normand, the father's tall handsome namesake who was a barrister and had a commission in the Scottish Rifles (a militia regiment), Charles, and Hugh, who was still at university and living at No. 155. But it was to Charles that Sir Normand turned now, asking him to move in with his family so that the home could continue to run smoothly. Reluctantly, but never able to refuse his father anything, he agreed and for the next five years their lives were dominated by him.

It was a heavily intellectual household for a child. International politics and finance were the most frequent topics at all meals in the long, sombre dining room which was hung with family portraits. At breakfast, the men sat with their newspapers propped in front of them 'munching their toast and making acid comments on the articles'. The Labor Party and the Roman Catholic Church, she knew by the time she was ten, were things to be avoided. After breakfast, silence was mandatory while the great man attended to his official papers, and later in the day Catherine was weighed down by the sight of her father's and grandfather's patients sitting so gravely in a circle in the waiting room. She imagined them all to be desperately ill. There was nowhere to play so she took to her room and read, or, driven by both curiosity and need, haunted the servants' quarters and the big kitchen down in the basement with its arrow-marked, convict-built walls. The old house was one of the last to be built after transportation ceased.

These were the days of what was often termed *the Protestant ascendancy* in Australia. Roman Catholics in the community, predominantly Irish, were mainly of the servant class and regarded as disloyal to the Empire and

Catherine, aged about 9, when she lived at 155 Macquarie St.

155 Macquarie St. — Sir Normand leaves for an appointment.

Britain. Sir Normand, nevertheless, had found them honest and hardworking and the four servants in the house, parlourmaid, pantrymaids and cook were invariably Irish and Catholic. It was better, he said, to have all of a kind. Catherine was fascinated with their stories of Ireland, also by the sentimental holy pictures and tinsel altars which adorned their rooms, and the medals they wore around their necks. It was something which was all pervasive and mysterious. She asked question after question of the perspiring cook at the great fuel stove until she was chased away; the preparation of meals was a serious business and they must be produced on time. Sir Normand had had a small lift installed in the pantry to save the maids carrying the heavy trays up the dark, uneven kitchen stairs to the dining room, and Catherine always returned in time to peer down the little lift well, watch the pulleys at work, and the family meal emerge.

The other daily ritual which enthralled her, as it had her father before her, was the breaking of the flag, on the stroke of 8 a.m., at the Royal Navy's Australian Station ships in Farm Cove and the thrilling bugle calls sounding the Royal Salute. Further out in the harbour too, merchant ships, mostly British, frequently rode the tide, while from her eyrie she had the whole lovely vista out through the Heads to the ocean beyond and rarely missed the excitement of an approaching or departing passenger liner. She knew by name those of P & O, Funnel, Aberdeen, Union and Orient lines, just as her father had known both steamships and the great clippers such as *Cutty Sark* and *Sir Lancelot* coming and going to England or America. But, as with him, there was nothing like the glamour of the British naval ships, the *Men o'War*, for they were the very symbol of security for Australia. Sir Normand harboured, like most Scots, some feeling against the ruling class of England and spoke tersely of 'butcher Cumberland' and English landlords, but like her father he was an ardent Imperialist. The narrow hallways of No. 155 were hung with prints of naval battles and an enormous painting of the Death of Nelson. Britain had dominated the seas since Trafalgar and seemed likely to do so forever. Imperialism reigned supreme. At school they sang Miss Hodge's Empire Song—

> From the icy northern regions
> Southward where the sun flames high
> Britain draws her willing legions
> Bound for her to do or die.
> Other Empires have existed
> And have crumbled in decay
> But this Union close cemented
> It shall never pass away.

Catherine, uneasy at this, muttered instead, 'May it never pass away'.

On Sundays, while her father played Beethoven's more sombre music and added Wagner to his repertoire on the Steinway grand which had recently arrived from America, Catherine was required to accompany her grandfather, bible in hand, and in godly silence, to austere St Stephen's Presbyterian church, not many doors away. He had become a rationalist but believed still in the virtues of Christian observances, 'Protestantism and Teutonic liberty', on which, he observed, the great American University, Yale, had been founded. She sat beside him in the high old-fashioned gallery, in the pew marked with his name, and even with the diversion of hymns and the collection plate, found the services unutterably long and dreary. In contrast, in her mind, were the lovely bells that sounded from St Mary's Cathedral and the staff from No. 155 hurrying towards them, not only on Sundays but often during the week to this mysterious 'Mass' of which they spoke. On hot summer evenings when she knelt at her window for coolness, and to watch the lights of the harbour and the North Shore, she heard often the practising of the bellringers at the cathedral, and the 'solemn, yet joyful peals clashing irregularly, sweet and melodious'.

So, everything compounded to stimulate the mind and emotions of this remarkable and far too solitary child in the forbidden realm of the Roman Church. Next, she caught an early tram to school one morning, and greatly daring, and of course strictly forbidden to alight anywhere but the school stop, got off at St Mary's. She pushed open the heavy leather door and walked out of the bright sunshine into the cool depths of the great church. There were a number of people kneeling before the white marble altar. She fled in panic but an indelible impression remained. It was to be greatly reinforced by experiences on the forthcoming trip abroad which had now been arranged.

Meanwhile, they received a visit from her mother's sister, Sally, an admirably spirited woman who had broken away from the enclave of maiden aunts in Edinburgh, paid for advanced piano lessons for herself by governessing for a German nobleman in Stuttgart, and settled to teach in Greenwich. She gave Catherine her first piano lessons and generally won her heart by engaging wholeheartedly in every new and invigorating pursuit possible. She took enthusiastically to motoring and picnicking with the family, and especially loved the surf. She had herself fitted out with a neck to knee costume and flung herself into the bracing, frothing water with the same delight as Catherine. On their summer holiday at Palm Beach she took joyously to the sailing skiff Charles MacLaurin launched for them in the broad expanse of the Pittwater, while in the Blue Mountains she cheerfully scaled hundreds of steps with her niece. Noting this accord, the doctor decided that now was the time to go to Edinburgh and study for his F.R.C.S. Sally, whom presumably he helped financially, could accompany them, take charge of Catherine, and so leave him and Anne free to tour Italy together *en route*. This had an unexpected side-effect.

Catherine was naturally wild with delight at the prospect, a delight that was only temporarily dampened by imagined disaster when a street singer below No. 155 the night before they sailed sang in mournful tones:

Many brave hearts are asleep in the deep,
 So beware!   beware!

The journey, of course, was a joy and the highlight of her young life. "Civilisation at last!" said her father as they passed through Suez and sighted the Mediterranean, for here, he told her, was the cradle of it all. He and Anne disembarked at Naples, Catherine and her aunt at Marseilles, with arrangements to meet later in Paris. The fact that Aunt Sally was a practising Anglo-Catholic had been kept from Catherine as something of a disgrace, and Sally herself had been asked to remain silent on the subject at Macquarie Street. Now, Catherine found herself taken to the church of sailors, Notre Dame de La Gard, high on the cliff at Marseilles, where her aunt lit a candle and offered thanks for their safe voyage. Catherine, in spite of her curiosity, had known nothing but rationalism and a smattering of strict Presbyterianism and was appalled to find herself 'in the midst of all this idolatry and burning candles'. She told her aunt that her parents wouldn't like it. Sally was unrepentant and lighthearted and later took her to early Mass at a church in Lyons.

This was to be another glowing and formative memory in the critical course of action which she later pursued. 'It was all mysterious silences interrupted with tinkling bells. Shadowy passing up and down. All very strange.' When they came out 'the golden Madonna statue shone above the cupola on the Romanesque tower of the Basilica, for it was now day and five hundred feet below the ancient city of Lyons was still half-wrapped in the mists of early morning'. Nothing ever effaced in all the years 'the impression of solemn mystery in that early Mass at Notre Dame Fourviere'. And so to Paris and the heady heights of Montmartre and Sacré Coeur, accompanied by her enthusiastic aunt. She was overcome by it all; a fact she did not mention when her parents joined them.

The other comment on this journey which must be made is the strong effect the household of tight-bunned, sharp-tongued Presbyterian maiden aunts in Edinburgh had upon her. She was the only grandchild of Thomas Croal's family of nine — the last of the vigorous Scots left their blood in the new world it has often been said — and she was at first made much of. She was not only lively and intelligent, but a lovely looking child, with enormous blue eyes and an abundance of fair hair, and it must have been a pleasure to take her to see the sights.

A weekend visit to Peebles to her father's brother Donald, who had settled there, was another pleasure; to find small cousins to play with was a rare treat. But when her parents went on to a medical conference in London and the stay with her aunts extended for months, she became very unhappy. The atmosphere changed and the cumulative result of their unbending attitude made a deep mark on her. She grew clumsy and nervous; she fidgeted at the interminable services at the bare and ugly Christ Kirk on the Tron. She overheard the aunts remark to each other — 'The child has been dragged up in the colonies.' Everyone who called seemed old and about to die. Conversation was punctuated with much shaking of heads and pursing of mouths as they took tea and munched shortbread and oatcakes by the fire. The crunch came one dank morning when Catherine's natural exuberance reasserted itself at the sight of a plate of sizzling sausages. She was told coldly, 'It's a sin to love your food.' This dour, Calvinistic, killjoy attitude she never forgot. It was later to be a factor pointing her in a very different direction.

Home again at last, Sydney's expanses of blue and warmth enfolded her, and extended to Sir Normand's welcome, unsaid but felt. She asked him to read to her each night again. They got through 'great chunks of the Odyssey and Aeneid which he read with beautiful rhythm and then translated rapidly from Greek or Latin, with equal ease in either'. He introduced her to the works of Sir Walter Scott, lent her the Waverley novels in turn, taking them down from the great glass-fronted bookcase which held his special books. He showed her the most precious one, which he had bought in Edinburgh, of the original manuscript of a most illustrious collateral ancestor, the 18th century mathematician, Colin MacLaurin, after whom the MacLaurin theorem was named. This ancestor, he told her, became Professor of Mathematics at Aberdeen University at the very early age of 19, and six years later was given the chair at Edinburgh on the recommendation of Sir Isaac Newton.

She won as a school prize a sentimental life of Marie Antoinette and showed it to him. He smiled and took down Carlyle's *French Revolution*, reading aloud to her the famous passage on the death of Louis — 'sumptuous Versailles burst asunder like a dream, into void immensity; Time is done, and all the scaffolding of Time falls wretched with hideous clangour round thy Soul'. That night, she tossed and turned with the terrifying words and could not sleep. It was strong meat for an eleven year old.

Anne MacLaurin had also seen the effect of the prolonged Edinburgh stay on Catherine and now felt that the exclusively adult atmosphere at Macquarie Street was too much. She persuaded her husband to build at Rose Bay. But before Catherine's days at No. 155 ended, and the carefree ones at *Balvaig* began, with friends to play and a host of new interests, several other events occurred which left undelible memories of her remarkable grandparent. The most dramatic was the demonstration staged by students outside the house in 1912 to protest against his forbidding

Catherine and her mother with the formidable array of Presbyterian maiden aunts in Edinburgh, 1910.

them their procession because of bad behaviour. They came in hansoms and taxis, beating drums, blowing horns, stuffed the mailbox with letters addressed to *The Horrible Sir Normand MacLaurin* and generally mocked the Chancellor. Watching it all, Catherine was filled with rage and shame. The Proctorial Board felt likewise and recommended strong action to him. He took none. Youth must have its say. Memories of his own were his one vulnerable spot. Catherine discovered this when playing and singing an old Scottish air that had taken her fancy—

> Oh Rowan tree, oh Rowan tree,
> thou'll aye be dear to me,
> Entwined thou art with many ties
> of home and infancy.

He loomed suddenly in the drawing room. "Cease," was his request, "it is too painful to me." A portrait of his father as a young headmaster hung in pride of place in the same room, and below it, on the mantelpiece, stood the Austrian Castle Clock his Scottish pupils had given their 'dominie'. Catherine ceased her song. But it was Sir Normand who restored the balance after her father had taken her to a visiting European opera company's performances of *Lohengrin* and *Tristan* and she had found Wagner overwhelming. "We'll go and hear some real music," he told her, and took her off to Mozart and *The Marriage of Figaro*.

Predominant also, were memories of him on ceremonial occasions at the University, in the magnificent central Edmund Blacket building, its delicate Gothic Revival-style, inspiring then, as now — 'advancing slowly and majestically down the aisle of the Great Hall, a splendid and commanding figure in his black and gold silk robes'. Then, in the role of host, of the old world courtly variety, he made a lasting impression on his grandchild. He invited to dine with him, in turn, at Macquarie Street the heads of the University colleges, with other distinguished guests such as the eminent lawyer, Patrick Creagh, of the grey imperial beard, clear blue eyes, and aristocratic tread. This was the grandfather of Alan Mackerras.

Alan's early background held more drama and less happiness than Catherine's. His mother, Elizabeth, was the third of Patrick and Louisa Creagh's family of two sons and two daughters; she was the beauty, spoilt and indulged. They lived at *The Peel*, the end house of a Dutch terrace, *Tamworth Mansions*, at Elizabeth Bay and all was starched, formal and ordered.

Patrick Creagh, spare and hardworking, with a strongly imbued sense of duty, had quickly made a name for himself in Sydney after his family's immigration there and married a lively blue-eyed young Irish girl of sixteen whose father had been a solicitor in Dublin. Louisa was small, warm, indiscreet, full of Irish wit, insouciance, quirks and anti-Catholic prejudices. She seems to have been mildly astonished to find herself married to such an august personage, whom she always addressed as *Mr Creagh*, and also to have produced accomplished, rather formidable and very distinctly, Creagh offspring. Certainly, she taught her two daughters, Lillian and Elizabeth, the art of exquisite embroidery and fine lace-making and they sat at this by the hour, but they had an aloofness that rather alarmed her. Her own idiosyncrasies, recalled by her younger son's second daughter, Nancy Phelan (Creagh), were rather endearing. She was given

Patrick Creagh, lawyer and yachtsman, grandfather of Ian and Alan Mackerras.

His daughter, Elizabeth Creagh, mother of Ian and Alan Mackerras.

to sucking humbugs and frequently drew from her small plump bosom the exquisite enamel watch which hung there, murmuring as she opened the catch, 'I wonder what o'clock it is?' She relished visitors, particularly the clergy, for whom she reserved her raciest barbs.

Her husband and sons, Albert, an austere man who was to remain a bachelor, and the effervescent Willie, who had yearned for the navy but, duty-bound, had followed his father and brother into the law, were rarely to be seen. They were either in the substantial legal offices of Creagh & Creagh in the city or with their father turning intricate woodwork in his magnificent workroom where the glistening tools lay in cased and ordered rows, or out on the harbour with him, sailing. Patrick was an outstanding yachtsman and one of the first at Royal Sydney Yacht Squadron to introduce the centre-board yacht. His sons were both enthusiasts and excelled at the sport. The family yacht, *Bettina*, painted a daring white (black was then usual), had figured prominently in the exciting centenary Anniversary Regatta in 1888, the annual event, first raced in 1835, which was to stay very much part of the Creagh family tradition. Such then, was the household at *The Peel* around 1897.

Elizabeth had suffered an unhappy love affair and was now thirty-one years old. Her sister, Lillian, a spinster, whether by inclination or otherwise is not known, cosseted her even more. Then there appeared on the scene a New Zealander, some five years her junior, James Murray Mackerras, the only son of a Dunedin business friend of her father. Patrick had met the young man's father, an enterprising Scots merchant, James Taylor Mackerras, in the latter's earlier years in Australia. It seems likely that Mackerras senior, after settling in the southern island of New Zealand, wrote to Creagh for advice on a protracted legal matter. He had formed a partnership, Mackerras & Hazlett, and the case was over the siting of a railway depot vital to the firm's distribution of merchandise — principally wine, spirits, tea and tobacco — throughout both islands. The friendship and correspondence with Patrick Creagh continued and young Mackerras, when visiting Sydney, was invited to *The Peel*. He promptly fell in love with Elizabeth and proposed to her during his stay.

Apart from the difference in age, their were many factors to be considered. He was without any specific qualifications, had no desire to go into his father's extensive merchandising business, and intended to 'set up in farming outside Dunedin'. To Patrick and even the comparatively flighty Louisa, the pitfalls of this prospect, for such a one as Elizabeth, were very clear indeed. They advised against it but to no avail. James Mackerras was both personable and persuasive, and a salve to her pride. She threw all caution aside and accepted him. *The Peel* was thrown into a great flurry from which even the men did not escape. Carriages came and went with the Anglican Bishop, other members of the clergy, uncles, aunts and friends. All was a mêlé of scurrying servants, tradesmen, dressmakers, milliners. gifts, gowns, plans and portmanteaux. So Elizabeth married her somewhat impulsive New Zealander and steamed off across the Tasman. It was the one precipitate action of her life. Posterity can only be glad of it, though she was to have different views on the matter.

First impressions were good. Dunedin is a beautiful city on the southeast coast of the southern island overlooking Otago Harbour, and the Mackerras house was a substantial double-storeyed weatherboard on a hilltop with a view of harbour and ocean. She was welcomed by James Mackerras senior and his wife, Helen, both with strong highland Scots accents. She felt about them something of the reassuring substantial atmosphere to which she was accustomed. He was a member of the Harbour Board, the Chamber of Commerce, a director of the Railway and Coal Company, an elder of the Knox Church, a horticulturist, and very genial with it all. She walked with the pair in their garden with its profusion of roses which were his specialty. She found their six daughters, of whom only one was married, congenial, and as skilled in fine needlework as herself. But the 'setting up of a farm outside Dunedin' was the real matter in hand and could not be deferred. An apple orchard, some sixty-five kilometres south at Balclutha, was decided upon.

The farmhouse was hardly what she had expected but it was there that she must now make a home and it was there that her first son, Ian, was born in September, 1898. The following year, when she found herself pregnant again, still with a babe-in-arms, she could no longer face the rigours of farm life and the extreme cold. She wrote plaintively to her family. They sent her sister Lillian to New Zealand to bring her back to the comfort of the household at Elizabeth Bay, to await her next confinement. Her second son, Alan, was born at *The Peel* in August, 1899.

As her family had been well aware, she was not of the stuff of which pioneers are made, and it was not until the new century was well under way that she was persuaded to return with her two infant sons to their father at Balclutha. In 1902 a drought of unprecedented proportions struck the south island of New Zealand. On the high slopes above the Mackerras farm, the snow melted and an avalanche ruined the orchard and James's

James Murray Mackerras, father of Alan and Ian.

His parents, James Taylor and Helen Mackerras.

The Mackerras family home, 'Rosemount', Dunedin, N.Z.

Alan and Ian Mackerras as infants in New Zealand.

prospects as a farmer. In the resulting chaos, Elizabeth returned with the children to her family in Sydney. James asked her father for some financial assistance and once again the old patriarch complied, but this time the separation of the pair remained permanent, and since divorce was considered a disgrace in those days, that was the way matters were left.

A nursemaid was at once employed, and with a household of servants assuming all other practical responsibilities, she simply retired with her sister to the drawing-room and exquisite needlework as before. She became cold and withdrawn, and seems to have moved in a trance through the next misfortune which befell the family.

Patrick Creagh's partner died suddenly and it was found that he had been dipping into a major trust account held by the firm. This was in the days before the Solicitors' Fidelity Fund. A man of the most impeccable integrity himself, Patrick saw no other option than to pay the debt back in full. He sold *The Peel*, moved to a smaller house, *Wychwood*, at Glebe Point and proceeded to do just that. Every penny was eventually repaid. Fewer staff were employed but otherwise the family continued in their usual style of living.

The small boys, Ian and Alan, the former a handsome, lively outgoing child, the latter, red-headed, Scottish and shy, spent the rest of their childhood there. Close in age, very different in temperament but extremely devoted to each other, both showed early promise scholastically. A natural extrovert, Ian probably missed less than Alan any demonstration of affection or interest from their mother, while the attention given to them by their grandmother, Louisa, would have been far too spasmodic to be a substitute. It seems certain that Alan, like most shy children, would have needed badly some warmth of response in those closest to him. This was not to be. Their mother had turned completely inward since her disastrous marriage; no doubt, as she had brought the disaster upon herself. Their father was well aware that they were being cared for by the Creagh family and showed no active interest in them. Both boys felt this at the time.

James Mackerras does deserve sympathy for the impossible situation in which he was left. He subsequently met a widow with two children, made a new life for himself, migrated to the central coast of New South Wales, went into business successfully there and brought up a family of seven who found him consistently kind and devoted. One of the widow's two children was to say later that she was sure that he moved to Australia so that he could feel in some sort of contact with his first two sons and hear something of their progress. They, however, were unaware of his interest, and when, very much later, he felt pride in their achievements and expressed it, they were unable to respond.

However, at Glebe Point with the Creaghs around 1910, life was very full and far from gloomy. Their grandfather and uncles ensured that. The boys learnt to hoist a jib as naturally as they learnt to read and were also often to be found hammering away in the workshop. When Willie Creagh was about, there was invariably music and the piano resounded with everything from Mozart to the popular Gilbert & Sullivan airs which they soon knew by heart. His much used bookshelves held everything from the Latin poets and Shakespeare to Baudelaire and Mark Twain. At the same time his Irish humour was as lively as their grandmother's. Their other uncle, Albert, was kind but much less outgoing and the difference was most apparent when they went sailing. Both were expert, but Uncle Willie sang sea shanties as they tacked out through Middle Harbour and allowed everything from bananas to fruitcake aboard to fuel his crew. With Uncle Albert, the only sound other than the swish of water and the wind in the sails was the call of *Steady about!* and he allowed only neat packets of sandwiches for lunch, no peel, no crumbs. Alan followed this uncle's example, the preference being inherent in him. It was a factor which was to become more vital than it deserved to be.

The boys were taken each week to St John's Church of England at Glebe and were greatly influenced at the time by the gifted Canon Cranswick who was the rector there. It was an association which lasted for two generations, in spite of a radical change in their views. It was often

Alan and Ian Mackerras as small boys in Sydney.

to take Alan across Bass Strait when the son of the former Canon became Bishop of Tasmania, and was the sort of long term loyalty to a relationship which was basic to him.

In 1913 the man from whom he undoubtedly inherited this quality, the fine, talented founder of the Creagh family fortunes in Australia, Patrick, collapsed. The family was summoned. Willie had now married and was living in Mosman, while Albert was at Tamworth where a branch of Creagh & Creagh was thriving. Patrick's sister, who had been educated by the Sacré Coeur in Paris and had become a nun in Sydney, persuaded them to call a priest. Their father did not regain consciousness. The last rites were performed and, ironically, the originator of the Protestant branch of the Australian Creaghs, was buried in the Catholic section of Waverley cemetery. Louisa, with her changeable views, based often on the twist of the conversation of the moment, probably did not mind this unduly. The sad fact was simply that her matchless *Mr Creagh* had gone from her.

She now moved with Lillian, Elizabeth and the two boys to Mosman and a hilltop house, *Beechworth*, within reasonable distance of Willie's high harbourside home above Chinaman's Beach. Ian had already started at Sydney Grammar School and Alan was now ready to go; their uncles undertook the payment of fees. So Alan also donned suit and Grammar School hat and the pair took the ferry across to the city each morning. At school it became clear that both would find their careers in one branch or another of the scientific field.

Catherine, meanwhile, was enjoying life at *Balvaig*, where her father had had a tennis court carved out on their land which sloped down to the harbour; there was a new car, a new school — Westwood, Point Piper — and she lost all her 'sadness and depression'. Her father was happy doing experimental work in brain surgery. A fine cartoon of the time by Lionel Lindsay depicts him, tennis racquet in hand, winding up to serve a ball labelled 'craniotomy'. This was 1914 and by August the world was at war.

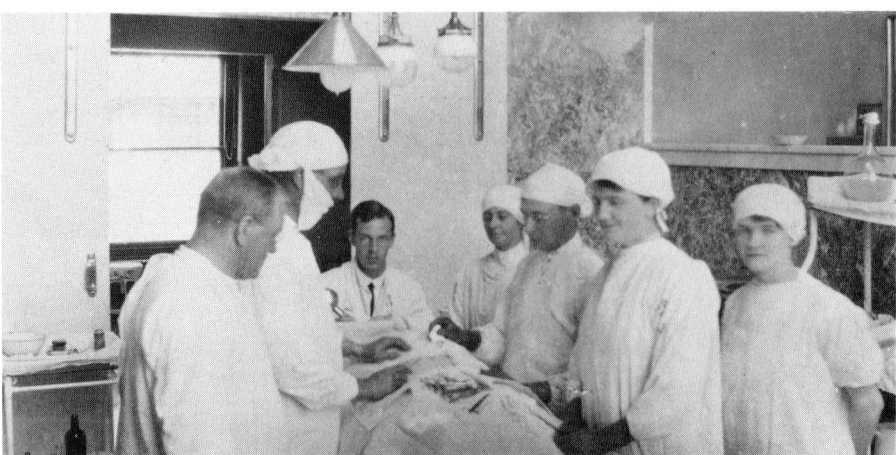

Dr Charles MacLaurin operating at Prince Alfred Hospital, Sydney about 1914

Cartoon of Dr Charles MacLaurin by Lionel Lindsay (1914)

Normand MacLaurin, already trained in the Scottish Rifles, was swiftly in uniform and appointed officer commanding the Australian First Brigade. Before they embarked for Suez and the Turkish battlefield, that great old patriarch, Sir Normand, who had been able to build so much during all the years of peace, was stricken at 78 with his final illness.

An operation was performed and Catherine was taken to visit him in hospital. Sir Normand, aware that he was dying, held her hand and asked her to remember that her second name — Brearcliffe — was after his mother. Insulated in her youthful self-revolving cocoon, she felt no emotion that day. In the waiting room was her Uncle Normand, that chief object of the old man's pride, resplendent in his colonel's uniform. It was he who, a few days later, took her to see her grandfather lying in his coffin in the big drawing room at Macquarie Street. It was her first sight of death. She was shaken. She found 'his stern and noble face awe-inspiring in its marble stillness'.

Tributes poured in from all sections of the community. The press listed his extraordinary achievements and the *Sydney Morning Herald* summed them up by saying that his death would be felt by all Australians, for 'our great men are citizens of not one city only but of the whole country'. *The Bulletin*, commenting on the passing of 'that fine old New South Wales citizen (doctor, knight, Chancellor Sydney University), who stood for most of the things which this paper abhors — foreign trade, the State Rights gospel and vehement Toryism,' concluded, 'but his political honesty was as transparent as his commercial and social probity . . . the kindliest and most courteous of opponents'.

A vast cortége formed along the historic street for his funeral, some taxis, but mostly 'the soft clattering and shuffling of horse-drawn carriages'. There was a galaxy of distinguished mourners, from Vice-Royalty and the judiciary, to parliamentarians, members of all the professions, directors of the great business houses of the city and the president of the Students Representative Council, Herbert Vere Evatt, later to make his own mark in Australian history. As the dark-plumed horses drawing the hearse moved from No. 155, the home he had lived in since 1872, Catherine realised she was witnessing the end of an era. Her own private tribute was to hear again the sonorous Latin and the patient translations as, night after night, he read to her the classic poets.

He was buried in the family vault which he had built when his wife died; this was at Waverley cemetery, on the high windswept cliff overlooking the ocean. Catherine went with her parents later to inspect the inscription her father had ordered for the coffin. These were the sad words, written he said, on many a Roman tombstone, *Sit Terra Tibi Levis* (may the earth rest lightly on you). She was astonished as she walked in the vault to see, beside the beautiful Celtic cross in dark green polished granite that her grandfather had imported from Scotland to rest on his wife's coffin, the famous words of the twenty-fourth psalm, 'Yea, though I walk through the valley of the shadow of death . . . ' She asked her mother why Sir Normand, by then an unbeliever, had had that inscription. Her grandfather and father, she was told 'were not very consistent on these things'. She was glad to hear it.

A few weeks after this, just before the house itself was sold, the family assembled at No. 155 for the last time to farewell her uncle before his embarkation for the front. He lifted and hugged her 'in strong reassuring arms'. It was a moment she never forgot. Six months later, as she sat with her parents at dinner at *Balvaig*, the old Presbyterian minister of St Stephen's came heavily down the path to tell her father that her uncle had been killed in action at Gallipoli and buried there by his troops at midnight on 28th April, 1915. He had been promoted in the field to Brigadier-General.

Catherine left her stunned parents and went outside, around the terrace to the stone steps above the tennis court and the garden, and looked out at the harbour. There was no reassurance there that night. The old poem on Sir John Moore's death 'They buried him darkly at dead of night' whirled like a dervish in her head. It was so impossible to come to terms with the fact that the strong, handsome uncle of a few months before 'lay dead on a wild hillside in Gallipoli, shot by a Turkish sniper'. Within a year, she herself was to be within earshot of the guns on the battlefields of France.

His brother's death profoundly affected her father. He enlisted as a medical officer and sailed on a troopship with 500 troops and 50 nurses; since the families of doctors were allowed to travel over with them, Catherine and her mother accompanied him. She was 15 years old and the experience fired her with a tremendous pride in the unity of the British race and the Empire. At Suez they watched the young, cheerful troops disembark on to lighters which were towed ashore. They were all destined for Gallipoli and the majority were not much older than herself. At

Brigadier General Normand MacLaurin, son of Sir Normand, killed in action at Gallipoli, 1915.

Marseilles there were young officers of the Indian Army waiting on wives and children who had boarded the ship in Aden; they accompanied them to Calais. In the train, *en route* at Amiens, they could hear the booming of the guns and the carriage trembled under them at the station. Most of the young Indian Army men were dead by Christmas in the shocking battle of Loos which was then in progress.

During the Channel crossing they had a destroyer either side, and when they reached Aunt Sally at Greenwich there was a Zespelin raid. She remembered that during her piano student days in Stuttgart, Count Zeppelin and his daughter had come to tea, and he had seemed to her then a genial, elderly gentleman with a friendly handshake. Now, as they peered through a window of her tall Regency house, with its exquisite *objets d'art*, at the small bright cigar in the sky — the genial Count's invention engaged in dropping bombs — she murmured, "All the perfumes of Araby will not wash the stain from this little hand". This was Catherine's sixteenth birthday.

Dr Charles MacLaurin, as Lieut. Colonel, A.M.C., A.I.F., on active service in France, 1916.

She went to an Anglican school, St Felix, run by two feminist friends of her aunt. It was 'unspeakably cold, with driving white sleet' and she longed for Sydney. Her father was sent to the 2nd Australian Casualty Clearing Station in the spring of 1916; troops there were on the way to the battle of the Somme where 60,000 men were killed in one day on the first offensive. He wrote to her that the noise of the guns was 'like all the kettle drums of the Queen's Hall going *forte fortissimo*'. His operations on Australian and New Zealand wounded were, he said, 'dreadfully bloody, and almost butchery, for I get all the worst cases'. He came home on leave, they took a cottage in the country and Catherine began to fall in love with England. She was preparing for Oxford Senior examination at St Felix, but her parents, sensing danger on the east coast, sent her to a small private school, St Margaret's, at Harrow on the Hill. There she revelled in the history classes and one day the visiting lecturer — on Australia — turned out to be Miss Hodge who embraced her warmly. She was inspiring in her lecture, mentioning the heroic Australian action at Gallipoli. "When you see that word girls, never forget the Australian graves there, 6,000 of them, and each the grave of a volunteer." She climaxed this with a stirring verse from her Empire song and Catherine, remembering her uncle, wept.

Meanwhile, there was a report in the Sydney press from her father in his role as Lieutenant Colonel, A.M.C., A.I.F., Surgical Staff No. 3, London General Hospital. He commented that full x-ray reports could be made available in under half an hour and there was no problem in pathology or treatment that could not be solved with authority. He said he had 'gone to school again with the Chief of Surgery Staff, Sir Alfred Pearce Gould', and was finding it 'of inestimable value'. He commented that he could not lay too much stress 'upon the deadly nature of all bone operations in wounds which have healed slowly, with much sepsis', and added, 'most of the surgical deaths in hospitals are in these cases'.

The strain was beginning to tell on him now and he was invalided home. Catherine and her mother followed, sailing on the now weather-beaten ship on which they had gone over in December 1916, on the day the Asquith government had resigned and the forceful Lloyd George had taken over the reins of the embattled nation. This was the last voyage on which women and children were allowed to travel by sea on British ships, principally because of the increasing intensity of submarine warfare and the number of U-boat sinkings. The ship went via the Atlantic and Cape Town, where they saw in the New Year, 1917.

It would be interesting to know if the vessel on which Charles MacLaurin was invalided back happened to be the one on which Alan Mackerras's brother, Ian, as a member of the Army Medical Corps, A.I.F. was serving as a laboratory attendant. It must have seemed astonishing to Alan, with his much more conservative approach to life, that his brother, after matriculating in 1915, should want to advance his age by a year and join the forces. But this is precisely what he did, managing to talk their mother into consenting to it — a feat in itself. The ship on which he served was ITS *Karoola* which plied between Australia and the United Kingdom repatriating sick and wounded from the battle zones; he later transferred to the 13th Field Artillery Brigade and was badly gassed in action at Villiers Bretonneux.

During this time, Alan continued his studies at Sydney Grammar, played a cornet in the School band and generally formed a strong attachment to the School. Early in his matriculation year, at the peak of summer, he spent one Saturday out sailing all day and suffered a severe case of sunstroke which put him out of action for months. This necessitated a repeat of the year. He matriculated in 1918 and went the following year, with the continued support of the Creagh uncles, to study Mechanical and Electrical Engineering at Sydney University. There he met again the daughter of their old family friends, the MacLaurins, and they struck up a firm friendship.

Catherine was doing Arts, majoring in history and, like Alan, was an extremely serious-minded student, more so than was usual. They were observed by the hour, day after day, in earnest discussion on a seat they had discovered near the entrance to the cloisters from the quadrangle, with its busy flow of students. A particularly charming friend and contemporary of Catherine, Louise Hutchinson, then Wilson, frequently noticed the pair, as her architecture lectures took her close by their chosen spot. She had known Catherine all her life, for her father was Professor of Anatomy at the University and a longtime colleague of Dr MacLaurin.

"Why they chose the quad with everyone rushing past, I don't know!" she remarked with a gleam of amusement. She added that they were segregated in those days, not allowed into each other's colleges and although it was possible to have lunch at the men's Union, it was always very crowded, noisy — and expensive.

This first glimpse of Catherine and Alan as a pair, talking so long and hard — they also gravitated towards each other at parties and dances — is particularly interesting in view of the problems of communication which were later to afflict them. Catherine regarded herself as a sceptic at this stage, which is also significant. Alan would undoubtedly have told her that his mind was more and more inclined to agnosticism, that he disliked dogma and that his study of physics had given him a deep interest in the marvels of astronomy and in observing the planets, the stars and their constellations. He had, in fact, made himself a telescope, grinding the mirrors from slabs of glass, and the planet Saturn and its rings were his first gratifying sight. But history, we can be sure, was their main topic; for one thing it was inexhaustible, for another it was Catherine's all consuming interest.

She was studying the subject with the big, hearty, liberal-minded Professor Arnold Wood who was much appreciated by his students and had survived trouble earlier in his career over his pro-Boer stance. Catherine never ceased to be grateful for his brilliant teaching. She noted that the 'great American Union was bought at the cost of a million dead', that the French Revolution 'ended in a blood bath', and the century of material progress which followed culminated in the horrors of World War I — of which she had such surprisingly close first-hand knowledge. She lost hope 'in every political and social theory to alleviate the sorrows of mankind'. The professor's vivid account of the Industrial Revolution caused her to investigate the Labor movement. She went to several lectures at the Trades Hall, met the editor of *The Australian Worker*, and contributed some non-political verse to that journal.

Catherine, aged about 18.

Professor Wood chose Seeley's *The Expansion of England* as a text. Its theme was that England had ceased regarding the colonies as possessions and was now promoting the concept of a Greater Britain, of other 'Englands' scattered throughout the globe, united by Protestantism and the bond of the English race; the dissident Irish Catholics were the problem. Catherine subsequently heard a lecture by the rector of the University's Catholic College, Dr O'Reilly, in which he quoted Gladstone and the historian Lecky on 'the sorrowful history of relations between Ireland and the British government'. This was 1919 and there were strong anti-Catholic feelings abroad, for during the war there had been many accusations of disloyalty, fanned by Melbourne's Archbishop Mannix and his anti-conscription rallies. O'Reilly was received in stony silence, but he spurred Catherine's interest. She read Gladstone, Lecky and all she could find on the subject, and found herself in sympathy with the Irish. She was clearly a rebel. Feminism never at any time appealed to her, but now she had discovered a cause and she threw herself into it with all the confidence that her background and intellect gave her.

She had bitter arguments with her father on the subject. He dismissed what he called her 'socialist phase' as affectation, but was still very mortified to see her setting off for the Trades Hall and the MacLaurin name appearing in *The Australian Worker*. He was even more deeply disturbed at her adopting the Irish Catholic cause. Their wrangling was so severe, and her excited fluency provoked him to such irritation, that her mother feared some sort of paroxysm in his battle for speech and pleaded in her soft voice for peace. She spoke separately with Catherine, discussing woman's role in life as she saw it. She told her that by far the most effective way of endeavouring to implement her ideals was to concentrate on her studies now, then marry, have children and nurture their talents. "You would then," she said, "be able to lead your sons to positions of importance and influence in the community." These words made an impression on Catherine, remained with her and were to some degree formative, but they did not deter her from her present course of action, and for some time she continued to give what she called 'practical support to the oppressed'.

Her father had given up medicine now, since inheritance from both his father and brother had made him financially independent, and was devoting himself to writing. It was a great relief to express his ideas flowingly on paper, away from the need for verbal battle, and released all his pent up frustrations.

Combining his medical and historical knowledge, he wrote a brilliant series of articles for the Medical Journal on the general thesis that the effects of illness on the famous have altered history. Joan of Arc, Henry

Dr Charles MacLaurin during his later years as an author.

VIII, Elizabeth I, Henri Quatre, Emperor Charles V and Phillip II of Spain all came in for clinical observation. He was dismayed when people wrote to him saying he had destroyed their faith, but nevertheless continued the series. He wrote reviews for literary journals, charming or terse as the occasion demanded. A title, *Combat is the Salt of Life*, came under the latter category: 'The idea that war is a biological necessity is a fallacious perversion of Darwinism. Man's natural enemies are germs, which destroy his body and insects which destroy his crops and not his fellow-man.' Catherine admired her father's style but they were very frequently at odds on the content. She found him 'fiercely anti-clerical'. When he engaged a tutor for her in second year French and tried to persuade her to continue reading rationalist Anatole France, she acknowledged his classic style and wit but read instead Bourget's *The Disciple* with its opposing religious themes. When he wrote under a pseudonym in *The Bulletin* on the virtues of paganism, freedom of the instincts and 'the new sexual morality', she was appalled. Norman Lindsay paintings appeared on the walls at *Balvaig* and she told him that she saw no virtue in 'unclad nymphs of an uncertain age and Roman soldiers prancing round together in far from graceful attitudes'. She argued with their tennis guests, however erudite, and these included the scholarly new minister at St Andrew's Scots Church, Rose Bay, John Edwards, and the theologian Professor Angus, who had the chair of New Testament and History Theology at St Andrew's College. Both of these, she decided, were Platonists at heart. The latter was partially forgiven, for when the light went early at tennis one winter afternoon and they trooped up to tea by the fire, he introduced her to *Paradise Lost* —

> Now came still evening on
> and Twilight grey. . .

However, she continued her argument with John Edwards. Her mother persuaded her to attend several of the quarterly communion services at St Andrew's and when she discovered that raspberry syrup was substituted for wine, on teetotalitarian principles, she refused to go again. The rector called at *Balvaig* to discuss the matter and pointed out that the communion practice was symbolic, therefore it was of no consequence what was used. Catherine argued that by substituting syrup for wine, the Presbyterian Church was casting a moral judgment on God, manifested as Christ, and on the Last Supper itself.

Some of these things must have formed part of her discussions with Alan but he still could hardly have suspected the powderkeg of religious contention within her. Furthermore, he would certainly never have provoked her, as, for instance, her father constantly did, to the support of opposites.

At this point, Dr MacLaurin was advised by speech therapists to study singing. Catherine was a member of the Conservatorium Choir and she persuaded him to join it. They sang side by side, his voice found perfect articulation, and both admired greatly the remarkable first director of the Conservatorium, Henri Verbrugghen. Unfortunately, his impediment returned again when he spoke, but the months of intensive rehearsal they had together for a performance of the Beethoven *Missa Solemnis* were their most companionable ever and they were agreed upon its great sense of mystery and beauty.

Ever since her childhood she had spent wonderful summer weeks at the Blue Mountains, where she rode a great deal and became very adept at the reins of a sulky, and at Palm Beach at the home of Dr Gordon Craig whose daughter Helen was her closest friend. A pattern was set during school and university years of mixed and chaperoned groups holidaying together at these places — young friends, such as Norman Cowper, who were also frequent tennis guests at *Balvaig*. The lively *Logs* Catherine kept at Palm Beach, with contributions of nonsense verse, *Letters to the Editor*, pastel sketches and photographs of the group, are a delight. Apart from swimming, there was sailing, fishing, and walking in the enchanting bushland, interspersed with their light-hearted literary diversions. Alan joined them for the first time in 1920 at Craig's *Cabin* in this veritable little paradise. His sailing expertise was very much appreciated. Each one of the group had a suitable literary tag and his, from Thackeray, was —

> He vexed no quiet neighbour — no
> useless conquest made
> But by the laws of pleasure — his
> peaceful realm he swayed.

To which someone had added —

> See, at his feet some little plan or chart
> shaped by himself with newly dreamed art.

Catherine's was Shakespeare and very much to the point —

> Farewell the tranquil mind
> Farewell content.

She obviously relished the role of stirrer in all their spirited talk, for it was one she continued to play all her life.

Alan now had the companionship of Ian once again at home at Mosman; something which both of them valued. Ian, who had received an ex-servicemen's grant to do a medical course at Sydney University, discovered early that he wanted to become a zoologist and had taken on medicine and science simultaneously. This was 1919, Alan's first year engineering, and with maths and physics overlapping, they shared some of the plethora of textbooks. Any spare time found them out on the harbour or, at night, Alan in the garden with his telescope and Ian at this desk with microscope and slides.

Their mother still remained in seclusion. The trauma she had experienced in the years of their birth and infancy seemed to have left her incapable of forming a warm relationship with them, or, for that matter, establishing any sort of real communication. They had become used to this and were aware that it did not preclude feeling on her part. For one thing, she had had a gold and enamel locket made enclosing two cameos, one of each boy in his infancy, and this she wore almost constantly. Nevertheless, she and her sister stirred to life only for the visits of their brother, the boys' Uncle Albert, from Tamworth.

Alan and Ian's sharp-eyed young cousin, Nancy, Uncle Willie's daughter, observed that both her Creagh aunts and their mutual grandmother, Nan Tay (Louisa Creagh), had now exalted Uncle Albert into some kind of divinity. His mere presence lifted them out of themselves, the household was geared to his slightest wish while he stayed, and they hung on his words. For them, he had certainly taken the role of Patrick, while for Alan he was also a father figure; the Creagh children were given the polite fiction that Alan and Ian's own father had 'gone off and died in the war'.

Nancy (now Phelan), in her delightful book, *A Kingdom by the Sea*, in which she recalls these years of her childhood, gives a fresh glimpse of Alan out under the stars one clear, cold night, giving 'turns' at his telescope to her, to Sheila (her elder sister) and their young brother, John. This was accompanied by vivid explanations so that they alternately gazed and listened to the lovely litany of names — Betelgeuse, Aldebaran, Bellatrix, Antares . . . 'the most beautiful star in the sky', he told them, 'the red eye of Scorpio'. They found to their joy that they were able to identify this constellation in the shape of a scorpion right above their house 'Standing upside-down with his tail curving over his head.' They plied him with questions and he told them, 'If the earth were closer or further away from the sun life as we know it could not exist'. "But who put us here?" they asked. "It just happened. It is," he replied. They were rather overcome at this, though young Nancy felt that the heavens were so beautiful, the miracle was to be alive, to be there in the crisp, lovely night able to drink it all in.

Alan joined the New South Wales branch of the British Astronomical Association in 1920 and two years later went with them to Stanthorpe, a town just over the Queensland border, to witness the total eclipse of the sun (August, 1922). He gives a magnificent description of this in an article he contributed to Catherine's 1922 *Log*, the highlights of which are as follows — 'The expected shadow of the moon gradually appeared in the west . . . its transparent murky darkness in wonderful contrast to the glorious golden orange light when the outer sunshine was seen on the northern and southern horizon . . . The curious shadow-bands, a well-known feature of total eclipses, were then seen wherever there was a light background. The true cause of these rapidly moving bands of alternate light and shade is unknown; but they are without doubt an atmospheric effect . . . Then came a sudden cold blast of wind as the moon completely covered the sun. At this instant we photographed the flash spectrum, a curious optical phenomenon only seen at the beginning and ending of totality. It was now quite dark, but the light was so even and diffused that we could see our instruments perfectly. The light was weird, and it was an uncanny sight to see men hurriedly operating their cameras which looked like infernal machines directed against the sun . . . When I raised my eyes (from my reflector) I saw the dead black moon surrounded by the bright silvery cream corona, set in a transparent blue black sky. There were 4 vertical streamers, 2 up and 2 down, making 2 nearly straight lines which touched the moon's edge. The left-hand pair were longer, the lower streamer extending for some three diameters of the sun, over 2½ million miles. The upper left-hand streamer was like a bird's wing; its outer edge was a most beautiful curve, thrown into relief by a dark rift continuing almost to the moom. The short polar rays extended horizontally in curves which exactly resembled magnetic lines of force. The corona in its unique setting was by far the most impressive sight I have ever seen; it utterly defies description or reproduction. Most of the pictures (taken) give the idea that these are faint streamers, extending from a bright circular inner corona, that the lines are hard and the divisions clear cut. Nothing could be further from the truth. The inner corona, comparable in brightness with the surface of the full moon, imperceptibly merged into invisibility at their ends and sides. There was only distinct line — the beautiful bird's wing curve, convex near the moon, and concave higher up and it served to emphasise the superb gradations of tone which were the chief beauty of this magnificent sight . . . Suddenly a bright speck appeared at the bottom of the moon, and in the twinkling of an eye the sun burst forth; totality was over, and my heart sank. It had lasted just 3½ minutes.'

After the eclipse, they were 'exhausted with wonder and tried to say a thousand things which could never be expressed in words'. He did nevertheless make an excellent fist of doing just that. They were 'entertained in the evening at a grand dinner where we took it in turns with our hosts to pay elaborate compliments' and discovered during the course of the night that they all had somewhat different ideas of what they had seen. This was to be expected, but the press version was hopelessly inaccurate. Alan commented, with the easy humour for which he was already known amongst his friends, 'It certainly revolutionised our ideas of astronomy!! One perfectly temperate member of the party, after reading the account of the lecture he had given, asked, *Was I really as far gone as that?*' But Stanthorpe was kind to them, giving them perfect weather, for even a few clouds could have ruined it. 'It was,' he commented, 'a wonderful experience and there is a moral to be drawn from it: never rest satisfied with a partial eclipse of the sun if you can possibly see its total . . . . a total solar eclipse is the sight of a lifetime, but it must be total for only then can the wonderful corona be seen'.

At this point, Catherine was abroad with her parents. She had completed her Arts degree, and was *proxime accessit* with Victor Windeyer (later Sir Victor, of the High court of Australia) for the University's history medal. Interestingly, her much admired Professor Wood had admitted quite casually to her the discriminatory attitude (usual at that time) which he had adopted in coming to his decision. "Your paper was as good as his," he told her, "but I gave it to him because it's much more useful for a man." Catherine never forgot the remark but had no time to brood over it, for her father had been invited by Sydney University to be its delegate to Padua University's 700th anniversary celebration and she and her mother were preparing to accompany him.

In the midst of all the mediaeval splendour, Catherine noted that it was where the great Giotto painted, observed that it was one of the few old universities not founded by the church and that there was a great collection of agnostics present. She got into conversation with a German American professor who was interested to talk religion and 'the ultimates' with her. For her father, it was the last real pleasure of his life. He wrote a very lively article for the *Sydney Morning Herald* describing the week's celebrations; the angry dissension when German delegates were classed with Czecho-slovaks — 'fierce gentlemen shaking their fists and leaping in wrath' — and the Irish request not to be classed with the English but with Brittany 'as they also spoke a Celtic language!' He concluded the article by saying— 'the whole show was the most brilliant exhibition of mediaeval pomp and glory that I have seen — academic procession with banners and robes and the Paduans were rather touched at a delegate from so far as Sydney and the name Australia received thunderous applause'. For her part, Catherine was moved to watch the ceremony on the final day when her father, with all official delegates attending, had an Hon. LLD conferred.

The other highlight of this trip for Catherine was in Dorchester in England, when her mother suggested that she accompany her father, instead of herself, in a visit to Thomas Hardy whom both father and daughter considered the greatest of English novelists. She was astonished to find the 82 year old novelist looking barely 70, walking briskly, fixing bright blue eyes upon them and talking in a very 'cheerful, animated manner' which the 'general melancholy of his works' had not led her to expect. He questioned them about Australia, the changed seasons, the different aspects of the stars; spoke of decay in England, the picturesque rural customs 'killed by the railway and motor car', of his admiration for Jane Austen, and finally of Nelson and Trafalgar. Catherine, genuinely overcome at sitting at the tea-table with the great writer, had quickly recovered her tongue and seems to have answered a good share of the questions. She then asked one of her own. Was he related to Captain Hardy of the *Victory* and Trafalgar? He was and it was even said that he resembled him.

Before their return her father arranged with Jonathan Cape for the publication of his series of historical essays under the title of *Post Mortem*. It was subsequently received very well in both London and New York. The review which Catherine remembered was by Hilaire Belloc in the *New Statesman*. Belloc considered it 'a delicious and highly readable volume' and went on to quote from the Joan of Arc essay. 'I hate to suggest', MacLaurin had written, 'that these spectres before the eyes may have been the result of toxaemia from the intestines, induced by confinement and terror'. Belloc comments, 'Mr MacLaurin hates nothing of the kind, on the contrary he is delighted with his rationalistic theory!' Catherine herself wrote, 'My father's style was lucid, charming and distinguished. Its brightness often concealed its seriousness of purpose. I have thought it strange that a man so warm, affectionate and generous should have chosen for his literary models the coldly mocking Gibbon, the cynical, profoundly disillusioned Anatole France. He was never far from his chief preoccupation, the *Riddles of Existence*. He never found it.'

Back in Sydney, she found Alan in the throes of his final examinations. Soon there were holidays at Palm Beach and Craig's *Cabin* with all their university crowd. To have Catherine back, to be out sailing with her, to have finished his course, spurred Alan to his most light-hearted behaviour ever. He took a photograph of her at the tiller of his skiff and scribbled an eleven stanza nonsense verse, *The Photograph*, which went, in part —

Cameras have been all the rage
And photos in profusion,
A damsel sweet a face she had

Catherine and Alan Sailing, Palm Beach, 1922

> A Youth he wished to take it
> How do I look the damsel said,
> I want to look my best,
> The youth he placed her here and there
> She faced now East, now West.
>
> The youth he uttered *Wait*,
> To get this photo quite correct
> We'll have to go about!

Catherine, who was herself given to writing quantities of romantic, strongly felt, high-toned verse, heavily larded with classical allusion, was highly amused — and touched — and placed the verse, the photograph itself, together with another she had taken of Alan sailing, in her 1922 *Log*, with the inscription —

> Youth at the prow,
> pleasure at the helm.

As soon as his results were out, they announced their engagement and a paragraph appeared in the *Sydney Morning Herald* social pages commenting on it as '. . . a romance of old standing, for they were at Sydney University together where both did brilliantly in the schools . . .'

Alan had now to establish a career. He began looking at once for something in electrical engineering which had emerged as his predominant interest. In both this and his voyage into the future with Catherine, he was supremely confident. They were very much in love; any reefs that might lie ahead, they would negotiate as they came. If Catherine was aware that these were already surfacing in her mind, she gave no indication of it. Subtlety was not in her nature, but here, as with other women in love, she displayed it.

Chapter 2

Early Years of Marriage

A long sixteen months wait now lay ahead for the two. Catherine seized the opportunity to exercise her considerable literary flair and knowledge. The editorial staff of *The Bulletin* had been featuring articles by her father for many years and the name MacLaurin was familiar to them. She wrote some trial book reviews and soon had acceptance slips, both from *The Bulletin* and a now defunct journal, *The Pacific*. But the primary concern was the launching of Alan's career in electrical engineering and this began in April that year, 1923, with his appointment to the Electricity Undertaking of the Municipal Council of Sydney, which some years later, became the Sydney County Council.

At home, he saw somewhat less of Ian now, for he too had his sights set on matrimony, having met and become engaged to a young Queensland woman who had enrolled as a post-graduate student in second year Medicine. This was Josephine (Jo) Bancroft, a member of the third generation of a family of distinguished scientists whose work in medicine and zoology was already known to him. They had a common interest in research and seem to have paired off immediately, doing a great deal of joint investigative work even in their university years, such as taking blood smears from fish they caught off North Head in his skiff and peering through their microscopes at the results until all hours of the night.

The young Creagh cousins, Nancy and her sister and brother, found it incomprehensible that the handsome, outgoing Ian and the good-looking, lively Catherine had not chosen one another. The quieter Alan and the straight-haired, bespectacled Jo seemed much more of a piece to them. In fact, the latter was one of those women whom the years suit, and she and Ian adored each other to the end of their lives; while if Catherine, as Nancy observed, were going to make a difficult wife for any man, how much more so for the volatile Ian than the more peaceable Alan. He, meanwhile, oblivious to such undercurrents, sailed on, happy and immersed in his work. He determined that when they were married, he would seek leave from the council to work in America and apply there to the General Electric Company where the most valuable experience in his field was to be had.

Catherine covered a lot of ground in her reviews, achieving *The Bulletin's* Red Page with a fine article on women novelists, their limitations, but also their ability to capture emotion. She reviewed a new edition of Dumas'

Monte Cristo and commented, 'His fairy tale Count moving with such fell purpose among the Parisian *nouveaux riches* of the 1830's is the creation of a master hand . . . as immortal (though not so immoral) as the *Arabian Nights*, to which it owes much of its inspiration'. She did demanding batches of criticisms for *The Bulletin's* Brief Notices column. For another journal, an in-depth comment on Strachey's *Queen Victoria*, a monarch 'who depended first to last upon some man . . . Lord Melbourne . . . . the Prince Consort . . . Disraeli, and understood nothing of the significance of the great movements that were stirring England to its heart'. Then, most telling, she reviewed for *The Pacific*, D.H. Lawrence's *Kangaroo* which had just reached Australia. She conceded that 'though many of us may dislike Mr Lawrence as an author . . . he has caught and imprisoned in word the elusive charm of Sydney . . . has described it with marvellous insight that has never before been approached . . . .but were it not for splendid word-pictures, it would not be worthy of much attention, for it is one of the neurasthenic products typical of our day. Altogether a queer, neurotic book, very characteristic of its author; but one which no Australian can afford to leave unread'. Her basic disapproval of Lawrence is very much in character — as is her appreciation of his magnificent literary gift.

In the summer, the old university crowd went back again to Craig's *Cabin* at Palm Beach and Catherine joined them. It was the last holiday that she and Alan were to share with them and there is a delightful photograph of the pair sitting together on the bank gazing out reflectively over the Pittwater. Catherine captured their lyrical feeling when she scribbled on the back of the photograph just one evocative word — *Velvet*.

Both the brothers married in April, 1924. Ian, having graduated with First Class Honours in Zoology and taken out the University Medal, sold a microscope in order to get himself up to Jo's home town of Eidsvold in Queensland. There an amiable but rather surprised clergyman conducted the wedding ceremony under a river-gum on the banks of the Burnett River.

Catherine and Alan married several weeks later at St Andrew's Scots Church, Rose Bay, as Charles and Anne MacLaurin had before them and they gave the fortunate pair, as a wedding present, a house at Vaucluse. The demure young woman in her chosen 'velvet', face framed in Limerick lace, must have seemed a far cry to the minister, John Edwards, from his fierce debating partner on symbolism, raspberry syrup and the Last Supper. But his beautiful resonant voice rang resolutely through the old church as he led them through the service, there is no record that he faltered on the word 'obey', and he joined them at *Balvaig*, where the charming terraces had been made festive for the reception. Elizabeth Mackerras not only attended her son's wedding, most elegantly gowned, but, altogether stirred by memories of *The Peel*, was photographed happily with the MacLaurins in the wedding group for the occasion.

Catherine and Alan left within a matter of weeks for the United States. Alan's plan had come to fruition and he was to spend the next three years in the Central Station Engineering Department of the General Electric Company in Schenectady, a city set amongst farmlands in the State of New York. They went via Vancouver, sailing on the Canadian-

Catherine and Alan leave St Andrew's Scots Church, Rose Bay on their wedding day in April, 1924.

The wedding group, Dr and Mrs MacLaurin on Alan's right, Mrs Mackerras beside Catherine.

Guests on the terrace at Balvaig.

Catherine and Alan looking out over the Pittwater, 1923.

Australasian Royal Mail Liner, *Niagara*. The feelings of Catherine and her parents that morning as they said goodbye can be imagined. For as long as she could remember, Sir Normand's words of warning to her mother had been with them. Charles MacLaurin himself knew, although it did not occupy his thoughts unduly, that he was unlikely to make old bones. He was now fifty-one; constant stress must tell. He had shared with his daughter, in spite of all their contention, his love of music and literature, motoring, sailing, golden afternoons on the tennis court, and journeys abroad both in war and in peace. It was hard to see her go. Catherine concealed her own feelings with an excited flow of talk. When the ship pulled out of its berth at Darling Harbour, it was, for once, a tourist deck from which she waved. She would swiftly be coming to terms with some very practical living.

During the first year, while Alan threw himself into his work and enlarged his professional horizons, Catherine kept house with the help of a young Spanish girl, Juanita, and observed the American lifestyle. There was a great boom in the U.S., she noted, and even office girls at General Electric were gambling on the Stock Exchange. There seemed to be a conviction everywhere that American prosperity would go on forever. She was absorbed still in her pursuit of 'truth' and in that engineering city she found people 'so much impressed with the obvious triumphs of science that their minds were virtually closed to metaphysics'. Also, the social situation was exactly the same as in Sydney. She met no Catholics. Catholics in America were 'servant girls or labourers on roads and immigrants from Italy or Poland, yet in that great country they were already reckoned in so many millions'. Their upwardly mobile movement through the universities and colleges and their entry into academic circles would soon occur in both countries, thus, she observed later, 'breaking down the social separation'.

Meanwhile, she contented herself with belonging to a discussion group and thrashing out all manner of subjects with her very articulate American peers. As it happened, early in 1925, whether at her instigation or not, they spent a very fruitful evening discussing 'Aspects of Truth'. She wrote to her father at some length on this. A few weeks later his reply crossed a letter from Catherine telling her parents she was expecting her first child. Before either letter was received, one quiet Sunday evening at home at *Balvaig* with his wife, he collapsed and died.

No warning over the years mitigated the anguish of Anne MacLaurin. Of the tributes that were paid him when the press reported his achievements as Macquarie Street specialist, surgeon and author, the phrase 'His scalpel may have been skilled, his pen was inspired', somehow helped her through the days. Catherine, when the cable came, was filled with overwhelming and conflicting emotions, one of which, inevitably, was remorse; not for the fact that she had pitted herself so vehemently against him in argument, but for her impatience with his speech. She clung to the memory of their singing together in the Beethoven Mass. She was sad that he had not known of her expected child and that he had died within days of the publication of his new book. But she was filled with pride when the prestigious *New York Times Book Review* published, with a fine photograph of him, a feature article — *Dr MacLaurin's Last Sally in Medical Biography*, with the sub-heading *Publication of "Mere Mortals" Precedes His Death by a Few Days*, and a favourable review.

Then the letter he had written to her arrived. He spoke of seeing the Harbour Bridge foundation stone laid, of coming to visit them the following year, and commented, 'I notice that you had a discussion on Truth the other night, that good old subject that men have wrangled over since the Greeks . . . To my mind there is only one truth and that is objective truth. So called inner truth, that sways so many people, especially religious people and mystics, is not truth at all.' He had left her then, as she said, 'with the old confused empiricism', whereas she was concerned with 'the absolute and that which is external to the human mind'. She liked to think that he who wrote so much about arterio-sclerosis and its effects on character, revealed, in his increasing hatred of religion that warping of the judgment of which he often wrote in others — for it was of a thrombosis that he died . . .'

Her close friend, Helen Craig, wrote to her from Sydney— 'He felt your going away dreadfully, but it has meant that he and your mother have been, if that were possible, even more to each other this last year than they have ever been'. She went on to comment on how she must feel to have been born of such a marriage. Catherine set arrangements under way immediately for her mother to visit them.

Alan had been in touch with well-known astronomers across the U.S., and it was now decided that, with annual leave due, he would visit them and their observatories *en route* to the west coast to meet his mother-in-law at Seattle. Catherine was not sufficiently interested to make the long train trip; there was also the matter of her pregnancy. He planned his itinerary meticulously, cost and hour-wise and wrote to her almost daily on his three weeks journey. A quite extraordinary peculiarity is displayed in these letters; there is no greeting of any kind, no endearment, no signature, simply the date. The fact of his writing was, for him, enough. For any young wife, married little more than a year, the lack of even the briefest and simplest endearment must have seemed strange beyond measure. Many non-effusive intellectuals, the other extreme from the Bernard Shaws and Brownings of the world, have found means of expressing, with some telling word, some brief salute and goodbye, their need and love for the other. Some deep reserve within Alan, exacerbated, as we have seen, in his childhood, made him incapable of this sort of articulation. Catherine, warmly articulate herself, away from her own country, with a child expected, would have been looking for and needing such confirmation of his caring. Nevertheless, these letters, together with one to Ian, are in other ways revealing and it is interesting to follow the highlights and his reactions to both life and scientific technology in the U.S. at the time.

He was stunned to find Chicago 'a dark, dirty, noisy hole, where every second building has either been burned down, has fallen down or is being knocked down . . . 90% of its people look like cut-throats, mostly negroes and low class Europeans'. A visit to Dearborn Observatory at a university there compensated, and even more so, another to Yerkes Observatory, a few hours bus ride away on the high northern side of Lake Geneva. There, shown about by the eminent Dr Frost and his colleagues, he was able to see the then famous 24" reflector, '. . . of the Newtonian construction . . . .a very beautiful instrument, used for photography'. He was able to *use* their 12" refractor, viewing Saturn and Jupiter, the latter his best ever of that planet; whilst he found the 40" refractor in the western dome, 'a wonderful instrument . . . mounted on the rising and falling floor . . .' It was used that evening for taking spectrographs for the determination of 'radial velocity and absolute magnitude'. In the midst of many more technical details, he mentioned that a visiting friend of a staff member was an Italian opera singer and delighted them all by singing the Toreador song from *Carmen* in the southern dome; whilst next day, 'in borrowed swimming suits', they joined the staff for their daily summer swim in Lake Geneva with its pleasing quota of sails.

On the bus drive back to Chicago he struck 'a party of shopgirls who powdered their faces without intermission'. At the 'bright, clean city of Denver' he was downcast to find no letters. The Santa Fe trail, running along the foot of the Rocky Mountains and on to Flagstaff and the Lowell Observatory on Mars Hill, revived him. He allowed himself an overnight run out to the Grand Canyon where he was amazed that the huge distances could appear so short 'from the rim to the bottom seemed but a step, yet mules looked smaller than ants'.

At Los Angeles he was met by the manager of General Electric who showed him two radically different types of sub-station. Then came another highlight, two days at the nearby Mt Wilson Observatory where a 100" reflector was located; this was the largest in the world at the time. He was shown around by the mathematician, Dr Stromburg, with whom he sat up until 1 a.m. 'discussing Einstein and all the latest developments and theories'. At 1.30 a.m. he went off to Signal Point, close to the observatory, to a sight so impressive that, for him, it was 'second only to the 1922 eclipse'. There, as he emerged from the darkness, were the 'thousands of lights of Pasadena, Los Angeles and 60 other towns and cities all glittering below'. He never forgot this thrilling evidence of mankind's achievement in the particular field of science which was to be his life's work. After these high flights, he permitted himself an afternoon sightseeing at 'a sort of Wonderland City on a pier on the ocean front where he found some 'extraordinary and amusing things' and walked round chuckling to himself, chiefly at the antics of people. Then it was the gorgeous granite cliffs of the Yosemite Valley and a night in a canvas cabin; on to the Lick Observatory in San José, *en route* to which, he told Catherine, it was 'as hot as Hades . . . in the train the red liquid was pouring out at the top of the thermometer . . ., the worst that I have ever endured'.

San Francisco he took to his heart, and even enjoyed experiencing a minor earthquake there. He was taken under the wing of the director of the Academy of Science Museum, who escorted him also to the Museum of Antiquities and the Art Gallery. There, at last, he found an ocean view which rivalled those of Sydney and Broken Bay. He supposed it was his 'insanity for the sea and ships' but he was 'more impressed by the magnificent sight from the Legion of Honour building in Lincoln Park, back through the Golden Gate than by the Grand Canyon'. Spurred by it all, he bought his mother a necklace (still carefully costed) and sent it across the ocean to his own great stretch of sea.

Arriving in Seattle, which had many of the things that appealed to him, 'water, boats and snowclad mountains', he summed up his feelings in a letter to Ian, 'So you see, I have had a most splendid trip and (*mirabile dictu*) less expensive than I had anticipated. I count the astronomical side as the most successful . . . to have had contact talks with all these famous astronomers . . . all most kind and friendly, they have promised to keep in touch with me when I get back to Sydney . . . and keep me in touch with the latest works of these big observatories'.

After meeting Mrs MacLaurin, Alan loosened the tight financial rein he had kept on himself throughout. They swept back across the country with sleepers and all the comforts he could find for her. As charming as ever, with her gentle Scots accent, graceful in everything she did, it was a pleasure for him to look after her. Catherine was overjoyed to have her in that engineering city, which she was never likely to take to her heart, and her mother stayed for her confinement in November.

Catherine gives an amusing description of her conversation with the attending doctor. 'There I was, sitting in the bed, very miserable, and he said, *How's the courage?* I thought of my great-grandfather, Charles Nathan, who had given his very young wife the first anaesthetic in Australia when she was having her first child. She had gone on to have sixteen children, most of whom survived. I said, *My great-grandmother had sixteen so I suppose I can have one.*' In due course then, on that November day in Schenectady, 1925, their son, Alan Charles, was born and there was much rejoicing.

In 1926 Alan wrote a paper which was published in two issues of the authoritative journal *General Electric Review* on *Calculation of Single Phase Short Circuits by the Method of Symmetrical Component*. He was later gratified to find that conceptual engineers Wagner and Evans, of Westinghouse Electric Corporation, quoted it in their text book on the subject which was published in London and New York. It was, in fact, to survive the challenges of more than half a century. The eminent Sydney scientist, Dr Harley Wood, says of this particular paper, 'Many regard it as classical, it did a great deal to make this powerful analytical method available to practising engineers and is still acknowledged in the main reference books'. A well-known colleague of Alan, T.J. (Tom) Keating, commented, 'It was 28 pages long. Thick text books have been written on symmetrical components since then; but this article gives in simple terms all that is necessary for the application of the method to a very large class of problems.'

In 1927 Alan and Catherine, with their 18 months old son, known always as Charles or Charlie, returned via the Cape of Good Hope to their much loved Sydney, and to the house high on the hilltop at Vaucluse which had been her parents' wedding gift to them. There they were startled to see the arches of the bridge well under way, or as Catherine put it, 'Sydney Harbour Bridge beginning to fling its proud arch across the water'. They could hear the hammering of the rivets from their home, something that stayed as the earliest memory of the incipient young musician, Charles, who also found an infant cousin, Ian's son David, with whom to play while their fathers compared scientific notes. Ian had already made an impact in his special field of medical zoology, 'that area of medicine', as he said, 'which involves both man and other animals', and Alan and he had much to discuss. Catherine noted that conditions generally were very much the same as in the U.S. — still on the crest of the post-war boom.

Alan was appointed Assistant Engineer when he resumed duties with the Municipal Council of Sydney. He became keenly interested in economic problems associated with the electricity supply industry, and was also active in the Institute of Engineers where he made the acquaintance of a gifted engineering student, David Myers, who was to have a formative influence on his later career. At meetings of the British Astronomical Association he spoke on his experiences in the United States and displayed a latent gift for lecturing, for, as former colleagues and associates have remarked, 'He had a fine voice, an excellent delivery and could express himself very clearly, explaining complex issues in the simplest possible terms'. He also had the necessary ability on this sort of occasion to leaven an address with humour.

He now designed and built his own 27 footer, *Maricita*, and weekends found the Mackerrases and the Willie Creagh family out sailing together. "Catherine was a great sailor in those days," Nancy recalls, "and my father was very fond of her. They both had a rather 18th century feeling for literature and he greatly admired her writing." Their exchanges must have been something to hear in that carefree atmosphere, with each flinging apposite quotes from the classics at the other, spiked on one side with the well-timed Creagh humour. Catherine used also to cap his snatches of song and Gilbert & Sullivan airs, something which Alan might have done — anywhere but sailing. He had recordings from all the operas and also knew them off by heart; they were part and parcel of the family tradition. Catherine's restlessness of spirit seems to have been temporarily in abeyance, life went along smoothly, and in 1928 their second son, Alastair, was born.

About this time, finding the Presbyterian church 'rent with modernism', as she rather sweepingly put it, and herself at odds with St Andrew's minister, John Edwards, she went occasionally to the Anglican church, St Michael's, Vaucluse, taking young Charles with her. It was here that he made his well-known remark that the hymn *Onward Christian Soldiers* reminded him of *The Gondoliers*; since both were composed by Sir Arthur Sullivan, Catherine was decidedly impressed. Her mother's remark about having young sons to lead towards productive careers flashed into her mind. This was certainly something that must be fostered. In the meantime, she sent him off to the kindergarten at the Anglican girls' school, Kambala, which was close at hand; there he found one other small boy and settled in happily. His mother's Anglican phase however, was brief; she found no inspiration at St Michael's and instead noticed the big flock of people spilling out of the Roman Catholic Church of St Mary Magdalene. There, numbers alone spoke to her.

In 1929 the Great Depression hit. Catherine and Alan themselves were not troubled financially; her inheritance from her father was in trust and securely invested and Alan's career was secure, but these years had a very strong effect on her. Initially, she simply observed the situation, noting how it affected her mother and her contemporaries 'with all their props failing them . . . Labor politicians attacking the Bank of England . . .the social system itself almost tottering under the stress of the times'. Then, by 1930, beggars became a common sight in Sydney. Artists covered pavements with gaudy pictures, and she noticed that 'bootblacks' stools were everywhere, sellers of matches appeared in droves, and men out of work called incessantly at the door'. She felt for them.

Charles, aged 4.

Catherine with Charles and Alastair at Vaucluse, 1929

In May of that year, as her third confinement approached, Catherine sent young Charles to stay with her mother as she had done also when Alastair was born. On that first occasion, he had discovered in the drawing room at *Balvaig* the big wind-up gramophone and its cabinet beneath filled with Dr MacLaurin's collection of records. "Although the electrical recording had been invented when I was a little boy," he recalls, "my grandmother hadn't bought one and she played these old non-electric records. There was a complete set of Gilbert & Sullivan which still sound quite good, some Beethoven — conducted by Weingartner I noticed later — and lots of Wagner selections. When I stayed with her she let me use this funny old wind-up gramophone myself and I was forever fiddling round with it. I got to know a great deal of music, particularly my Wagner, and I suppose it was then that I began to realise I was musical."

He returned home to meet his new brother, Neil, and to find his mother exceedingly busy, so that he and Alastair often romped in the garden of their close friends, the Parkinson family, who lived a few doors along. Their small son, now Sydney psychiatrist John Parkinson, reveals that Charles showed his boisterous rather than musical side at the Parkinson home. "My mother used to tell us," he recalled, "that the earliest interest he displayed in music at our home was jumping on top of our grand piano, and my mother by no means fostered this by ordering him off immediately!" Alastair and John were the same age and a friendship began which has remained lifelong. "As three year olds," he said, "we used to fantasize lions and tigers in the garden. And there was some basis to reality in it, because although we didn't actually see any, my mother pointed out that there were still native cats at Vaucluse, a striped or spotted species."

He remembered Catherine's warmth and responsiveness to the very young and his own pleasure one day in the Mackerras drawing room when he and Alastair had wandered in and were investigating the bookcase and a particular row of cream-coloured titles. "Those are French books," he told Alastair, having had something similar drawn to his attention at home. Catherine stopped what she was doing and called to him, "What an intelligent child!" This strongly supportive attitude with the young was now to become her outstanding attribute. "She was," said John Parkinson, "the most marvellous encouragement to her children right from the early years."

The rebel, however, was still on hand, spurred this time by the worsening of the Depression. She saw almost every day some evidence of human suffering and later observed, 'The unemployed who knocked at my door at Vaucluse became almost threatening when speaking of the inequalities and injustices of the world. Some attacked the churches for being tools of the capitalists, some merely thought them useless, some, more intelligent, voiced theories on the nationalism on which I had been reared'. She had a very distinctive voice, richly timbred, clear-cut and decided, and striking blue eyes; she must have made a strangely compelling figure, with her cluster of children, arguing at the front door with these unfortunates and trying to offer them some hope, since she was unable to make small paid tasks go round. One particularly vociferous man, to whom she defended Christianity, said bitterly, "It's all very well for you". She began to feel oppressed by human suffering, as during the war, and

Alastair, aged 1.

Neil and Alastair as small boys.

THE GROWING FAMILY AT VAUCLUSE

Catherine with Neil.

Charles and Alastair, 1932.

decided to 'examine Christianity with an open mind, not too influenced by inherited prejudices'.

So, as Alan went off to his meetings and lectures, she plunged into the *Confessions of St Augustine*, contrasted them with the 'splendid but decaying Roman world observed by Walter Pater's *Marius the Epicurean*'; then read Newman's *Apologia Pro Vita Sua*, which she had spurned at university; she now felt that it contained 'the perfect balance between emotion and intellect, reason and passion'. The next step was compulsive and formative.

'In 1930,' she wrote, 'I entered St Mary's Cathedral for the first time since I fled from it in my childhood — I was attracted yet repelled. Pushing open the heavy leather door and seeing once more the same sight, the people kneeling silently in front of the great marble altar, with the world outside hurrying by on its futile occupations. There was a rack of pamphlets near the door and I took one . . . I have lost the pamphlet, but I remember that Father Cyril Martindale, S.J., wrote it, and I am not likely to forget its thesis, which was that the Church was the upholder of the human reason. Here, then was the starting point to Catholic Theology; that the human reason was a valid instrument for the discovery of Truth, not only the empirical Truth revealed by microscopes and other instruments of research into the sensory world but the absolute metaphysical Truth. In all my reading I had missed the point that to deny the possibility of attaining by reasoning to the knowledge of ultimate realities, is to deny the competence of reason in its most important search, the search for God . . . I knew that I stood on the brink of the great Religion of Affirmation. I had escaped from confusion and was at last approaching order, the majestic order of Catholic theology'.

This is a particularly revealing passage. Until that day generations of intellectual libertarians were warring in her mind, together with a strong sense of the forbidden, such as she had felt as a child at Notre Dame Fourviere, Lyons, with her aunt. Now, the phrase 'upholder of the human *reason*', removed her inhibitions. She could proceed. Even so she was still very unsure of herself and she left the matter unspoken with Alan, who, given the fact of her wide tastes in reading, had not thought it particularly strange to find the writings of St Augustine beside Walter Pater on the bedside table. If she had a *confidante* at all at this stage it would have been her mother who knew something of her daughters crusade, for she had herself rejected, in her mild way, what Catherine called 'the melancholy scepticism of her husband and father'. Like all crusades, Catherine's seemed to have something of the romantic in it. On Christmas eve 1931, she announced her intention of attending the midnight Mass at St Mary Magdalene, Rose Bay. It was the festive season, the season of good will. It would be an experience.

It is doubtful if Alan felt more than a mild unease at this, for he had no reason to believe that they were not still basically as one in their thoughts. As it was, the 'immense and silent crowd pressing forward to receive Holy Communion' affected her strongly — 'Surely here was the Spirit.' Next she began wrestling with the belief in Christ as the Son of God, since there was 'a leap from the statement that God exists, to the statement that he had been revealed'. Finally, she felt, 'Christianity is not a statement of belief only, it must warm the heart as well as satisfying the reason'.

It was that much tried man, John Edwards, the minister of St Andrew's, who had married them and with whom she had had so much spirited discussion, who now provided the catalyst. He called on her early in 1932 and they had their final fiery argument. He admitted, with his devastating honesty, that he no longer believed in the Resurrection and felt that the greatest teaching of Christianity is embodied in the Sermon on the Mount and not in the creeds of the Roman Catholic Church. All her pent up feelings poured out. She accused him of apostasy, of being a witness to the Church's decay, and predicted that Presbyterianism would soon be dead 'for the very reason of its discarding of the Roman Church's basic creeds'. He upheld his faith in the essentially gentle Jesus. She charged back, 'Was he so gentle? He used whips to the money changers, called the Pharisees extortioners and adultresses, prophesied that blood would flow. He said that He came to cast fire on the earth, to divide families — it's a picture of the Catholic Church. But He was gentle to those who admitted they were sinners, to them He brought not a sword, but peace'. John Edwards made his own peace with her and left quietly. It was five years before she saw him again.

If all this fire and brimstone was too much for that liberal-minded, gentle Scot, how much more so for the one with whom she lived? She was set on her course now, and attended a series of lectures at the Town Hall by Father W. Lockington S.J., who is described by that fine Loreto convent educationalist, Mother Borgia, of the Sydney family, Tipping, and later a friend of Catherine, as 'a splendid exponent of his themes when bigotry needed to be fought'. His subject was *What Catholics Believe*. Catherine omitted to mention this final step in her journal, perhaps because of the over-simplistic title of the lectures, which would certainly have included an address on the *Apologetics* — the five reasons for belief in God — and a great deal more theological exposition. It seems to have satisfied her. She sought advice, underwent instruction at the Sacré Coeur Convent, Rose Bay, began the process of being received into the Roman Catholic Church and confronted Alan with the situation.

His reaction to this sudden complete change of direction, for that is what it seemed to him, and for that matter to their circle of friends when they heard it, bordered on shock and despair. The former, because never in all their long and deep discussions on history in their student days and since, even when reporting arguments with her father over his extreme anti-clerical views, had she given any indication that her mind and heart were not set, as ever, on the same broad, analytical path which both had accepted, together with a shared belief in Christian ethics. Despair, because creed and dogma were anathema to him. And behind it all, stood that most revered figure of his childhood, grandfather Patrick Creagh, who in spite of belonging to a famous Catholic Irish family, one of whose ancestors had been Primate of all Ireland, had yet seen fit to leave the Roman Church, which could only have been because of rigidity of some aspects of dogma or excesses in regard to images. He wanted nothing to do with the rescinding of that decision made so long ago. He stated this clearly, but underlying it must also have been an actual fear of being dragged backwards in time and away from the clear light of scientific thinking. He would never follow her.

Now there was the complex question of the children; Catherine said she must promise that they be brought up in the faith. He insisted on a compromise. They could have their primary education at Catholic schools, their secondary education at Sydney Grammar School, and if they should have a daughter, then the secondary schooling must also be non-Catholic. As young adults they could then make up their own minds. The priests agreed with this solution and young Charles was sent off to St Aloysius College at Milsons Point and received his early training there with the Jesuits, as did the others in turn. Mother Borgia commented, ". . . A tangled skein. I could never express adequately my respect for Mr Mackerras . . .for his honour. He was a true Scot. A gallant gentleman. There was to be no break in the family — the children would make decisions when they found truth."

"Alan never spoke of it to us," said his cousin Nancy, who had a great affection for both Alan and Catherine, "it would have been against his code, he had that sort of absolute integrity and loyalty. But I am sure that when Catherine became a Catholic it completely negated the things that had drawn them together. She said so later herself. Their strong mutual interest in history now became a battleground — in any discussion she would take one side and Alan the other. Catholicism split them down the middle in that sense. Then, because of the children, Catherine had gradually to give up sailing, so that the only thing they still shared was their great love of music. And of course, the family."

Certainly, to see her at the piano with the children in the early evening, playing the songs and rounds which were the musical counterpart of the stories she read them — Dick Whittington, the Pied Piper and many others — must have been a deeply needed respite for Alan. She was not given to tact, and since the subject of her conversion obsessed her at this time, she rarely let it rest. The difficulty of coming to terms with it all was made worse for him by the fact that Ian had moved with his family to Canberra where he was heading a research programme with the newly formed Council for Scientific and Industrial Research. Alan missed their companionship and scientific talk badly, and also the lightheartedness and humour he was able to share with him. Even the children missed their uncle's infectious laugh. They noticed that there now appeared in their father's study a photograph of him with his microscope, slides and a funnel-web spider under close observation.

The gradual coming together of the arches of the Harbour Bridge, which Alan had photographed and the family had watched from their Vaucluse hilltop, was now complete. In May 1932, after the drama of the official opening by Premier Lang, the small Mackerras boys, Charles and Alastair, were consumed with excitement at the magnificent fireworks and allowed to climb on their roof to watch the display. The somewhat insecure, chubby, four-year-old Alastair, was glad of his older brother up there in their lofty perch and clutched him for safety as they watched the dazzling multi-coloured rockets shoot into the sky. It was their last strong memory of their years at Vaucluse.

Ian Mackerras at work with his microscope, slides and a funnel web spider.

Now, with the North Shore opened up, and also another child expected, their parents decided to move there. They found a half acre of land at Turramurra and engaged an architect and builder. Alan looked forward to the quieter, rural atmosphere and to the extra space for the children. Catherine, as she prepared for the move, was aware of the change in her relationship with him and had some doubts about her own action which had precipitated it. Yet she could not regret it, for as she reiterated, in one way or another, to her mother and then wrote in her journal, 'In the Catholic Church I had found that which satisfies the restless enquiries of the mind and the persistent cravings of the heart'.

Chapter 3

Family at Turramurra

The Mackerrases moved home in two stages and lived at Wahroonga for some months in order to keep an eye on the home that was taking shape in Warrangi Street, Turramurra, amongst a myriad of trees. There were figs, camphor laurels, bottle brush and eucaplypts on the half acre of land which sloped gently down to the willow-hung creek on the far boundary.

Catherine planted a liquid amber, a plum, a peach, and along the sloping driveway, a row of poplars; they named the house *Harpenden* after an English village which had appealed to her. It contains a good share of the memories people have of the Mackerrases as a distinctive clan. It is double-storeyed, gabled, stuccoed white, with arched entrance, spacious drawing room, a long dining room with the low ceiling to which architects were given at the time, French windows opening on to a terrace with a large study for Alan, while upstairs there were bedrooms, nursery and sleepout verandah. This, then, was the setting for their markedly happy, noisily companionable, music and debate-filled childhood.

The family was augmented early in 1934 by a daughter, Joan, who was to have the dark, Italianate good looks of brother Neil; in 1937 by the slender-framed, auburn-haired Elizabeth who delighted her father's heart and was photographed by him at all stages of tottering and toddling; and in 1939 by the highly individual twins, Colin and Malcolm. All of them were born in their mother's large airy bedroom at *Harpenden*. They were fed, contrary to the beliefs of the time, on demand; Catherine pronounced the strict Karitane four-hourly method 'rubbish'. She also told friends that she intended to follow her present course and always make time for talk with her children. This she assuredly did. Her personality thrived and expanded amongst the gifted brood, as did theirs. She spurred them to precocious articulateness and generally eclipsed the qualities which they might otherwise have appreciated in their father.

"He was a quiet man," said Alastair, who, like Neil and Colin inherited his mathematical ability. " He was much better in a one to one situation than in a group. And mother was a very noisy person. She just dominated the whole place and took over any discussion that was going on. He couldn't stand the noise, he used to go off to his study and work. We were all too boisterous for him. Also we were awful. We wouldn't go and look through his telescope — it was cold out there at night. And we didn't like

'Harpenden', Turramurra, the Mackerras family home for 32 years.

sailing. I don't happen to like the salt air anyway, and he was very strict in the boat. We used to call it *Going to Church*. Then, at home, we were always playing Wagner full bore. All these screeching sopranos. He liked Mozart and chamber music.''

It was ironic that they so frequently played, at full volume, music that caused him to come from his study to the drawing room with his fingers stuffed in his ears and the plea, '*I wonder if you'd turn it down*', for he had put together their first electrical gramophone. "He went and got all the valves and everything necessary," said Alastair, "and actually manufactured this thing himself, and it was a very good gramophone. He was constantly refining and improving it, so that in our youth we had far better what is now called *sound equipment* than most other people." Doubly a pity then, that Alan's tastes and temperament so frequently worked against him within the family.

Yet there were many moments when his particular brand of humour came to the fore and passed into family legend. *Let's Depart, Dignified and Stately*, was one of his sayings when putting on coat and hat of a morning or after rounding up a straggler for some family outing, and the children immediately began the chorus of peers from *Iolanthe* and added a line or two. Again, if a dab of iodine was needed for a grazed knee, or a first tooth was hanging by a thread and needed to be pulled, his remark would be, "If you're going to do it, do it *bravely*."

It was extremely disappointing, to say the least, that the children did not take naturally to sailing as he had in his youth, and also were not

Alan sailing his yacht, Maricita, on Sydney Harbour about 1935. North Head in background.

particularly interested in astronomy. On the other hand, the high position and clear, unpolluted air at Turramurra was ideal for his observations and nothing could take from his own affinity with the stars or the sea. He now kept his yacht, *Maricita*, at The Spit in a rough but adequate shed known as Griffin's, and later, as John O'Rourke's and became a foundation member of the Middle Harbour Yacht Club. The young Creaghs, particularly Nancy, often sailed with him, as well as several friends and an occasional reluctant offspring. Charles, in fact, later developed a liking for sailing but was at this time put off by his father's *'don't do this, don't do that'* strictures; he was also frightened, as he peered out under a large pith helmet designed to protect his fair skin, at the odd sortie Alan made through the Heads where the sea seemed very big and the boat very small indeed.

In the first days at Turramurra, Catherine found the three boys scrapping and issued an edict which was to have a profound effect. ''Don't tell me whose fault it is, it's everybody's fault,'' she told them. ''There is one rule in this family, *you must not quarrel*, and believe me, when you're older you'll find that your own flesh and blood will stick to you when nobody else will.'' All three vouch for the fact that thereafter they obeyed this rule as did the younger ones as they grew up. Although it is true that in the days of big families, children did quarrel less, this remains remarkable testimony to her influence over them.

''It's a fact,'' said Alastair, ''none of us did fight with each other at all. I can't remember a single family fight. The result is, if I have a row with somebody, I feel bad for about a month. We're all like that. No good at fighting.'' This seems to have been the only legacy of the prohibition, for each had to battle daily simply to be heard in the noisy flow of talk and music in the house, so that both their confidence and competitiveness emerged unimpaired.

One of the first tasks for the heavily pregnant Catherine after their move to the North Shore, was to arrange music lessons for Charles; she took him to the convent at Pymble to learn the violin. He found the elderly nun who taught him too severe, so, although he liked the instrument, he gave it up and took piano lessons instead. He did not fare much better as a piano student at the convent, for that Sister was also the 'finger rapping type', so he persuaded a conservatorium student who lived nearby to teach him. "But the nuns were marvellous in many ways," he remarked. "Most of the professional musicians of Australia, the real Australians, started at the convents."

Meanwhile, he startled Catherine by taking an enormous copy of *The Messiah*, lying on his tummy on the floor with it, and checking the statement *You don't have consecutive fifths or octaves* which he had overheard at the convent. He found it was correct. He then took to sitting about composing music for poems he was learning at school. "Do you know how the music will sound?" his mother asked him. "Of course I do," he told her, "I'm going to be a musician." Then, a little later, he told her he seemed to have been born knowing harmony, and she really began to wonder what lay before him. Next, he tried his hand at some very basic theatre.

"Charlie started running puppet shows out of an old fruit box," said Neil. "It had a curtain and a sort of superstructure on top that Dad made. He christened it with *Rumpelstilzchen* — we called it 'stiltskin' — for my birthday." So he developed an early taste for an audience and the flexible voice which later was to switch with remarkable ease from one language to another in Europe as demanded, and in lighter moments indulge in excellent mimicry, had some early practice with Kings and Queens, deformed dwarfs and other characters from folktale. When he tired of that, he borrowed his mother's valuable set of libretti, in English, of Wagner's four Ring operas with magnificent illustrations by Arthur Rackham, and made an attempt at a puppet version of *Siegfried*, using their own records for sound. Then he began some composing.

Alan's mother seems to have been drawn out of her silences by all this early enterprise. which was further reinforced when Catherine took Neil to the nearby convent for a first taste of school and it was discovered that he could already read and write. "We got tired of hearing about the brilliant Mackerras children from my aunt," Nancy recalls. "The eldest of the clan, Charlie, is now a very charming man but I have to admit he was rather awful when he was about ten. He was obsessed with his music but we didn't believe him when he talked about the concertos he was writing. We were quite wrong of course." Fortunately, a very lively sense of humour, which enabled him to see things in perspective and was to be as much part of him as his musical ability, was not far below the surface, as a review in the school magazine, *The Aloysian*, in 1937, testifies.

The school's very well staged Gilbert & Sullivan presentations at the Conservatorium each year were manna to the young Mackerrases. Boys' and girls' schools did not combine in casting as they now do, and one of

Charles' first appearances on stage was with wig and wings as an unlikely, freckle-nosed fairy in *Iolanthe* in 1936. The following year he was given the fully-fledged role of Ko-Ko in *The Mikado*, while Alastair was one of the thirty-eight schoolboys playing the Chorus of Schoolgirls; it was a superbly dressed production. The set and some of the costumes were borrowed from the country's top professional company, J.C. Williamson Ltd., and it was played before a very distinguished audience which included the Apostolic Delegate to Australia. As Lord High Executioner, Charles seems to have wielded his snickersnee and wooed the ancient Katisha with equal aplomb —

> Are you old enough to marry, do you think?
> Won't you wait till you are eighty in the shade?
> There's a fascination frantic
> In a ruin that's romantic
> Do you think you are sufficiently decayed?

He was reported to have stolen the show. 'And this,' said the reviewer, 'implies no blame whatever. Whether on or off the scene his brilliant presentation of Ko-Ko vitalised the whole piece. He seemed really to grasp the exquisite humour of the Gilbertian situation and his cool and confident acting, while it overshadowed none, brought out the best in all that played with him. At one time I thought that the excitement had been too much for him and that his voice had gone — three minutes later he sang Tit-Willow perfectly. Never once did his antics distract the audience from the

Charles as Ko-Ko and Alastair as one of the Chorus of Schoolgirls in the St Aloysius College 1937 production of The Mikado.

Alastair as a dragoon and Neil as a love-sick maiden in Patience.

scene to himself, and the applause he received was a spontaneous tribute to his really fine work.' In embryo, there were all the qualities that were to make the conductor.

Catherine and Alan were, for once in a while, equally delighted and the former, with her flair for high moments in the life of their young, had a photograph taken of Charles and Alastair together in their costumes. The pair had, in fact, displayed some joint sang-froid in the final dress rehearsal when the cast's Yum Yum, having had a tooth knocked out in the afternoon's football, was unable to appear and Charles, between scenes, coached his sharp-memoried, unflappable young brother to play the leading lady for the interim. There were other memorable productions for the Mackerrases, with different combinations of the brothers — Alastair as one of the chorus of dragoons and Neil as a love-sick maiden in *Patience* — but the 1937 Mikado remained the highlight. It was Charles' last year at primary school and *The Aloysian* also records the gratifying fact that he topped English and Latin examinations; it was the last occasion he could be persuaded to knuckle down to any subject other than music.

Later that year, a heavy blow fell. Anne MacLaurin had had few health problems, she was slight and fit and frequently had the boys to stay at *Balvaig*, particularly when Catherine was busy with a new baby; they have memories of the long tram ride from Rose Bay and the little ferry they took across to school at Milson's Point. The old wind-up gramophone had provided Charles with the first realisation of his feeling for music, and he photographed the Wagner recordings in his musical memory, as did Alastair. Their grandmother was very much part of their lives; to Catherine she was most precious. There had always been love, companionship, little criticism, no friction. She was the gentle person who gave her life continuity. Anne was now sixty-eight, no great age, and the Croals were a long-lived family. She told Catherine that she had several troublesome teeth and her dentist advised having them all extracted. Catherine was naturally distressed for her but not unduly alarmed. After the operation, she tucked her into bed at *Balvaig* and set off on the long tram and train journey across the city to Turramurra, secure in the knowledge that a doctor would see her next morning and check her condition. When she returned later in the week, with the three year old Joan, to visit her, she found her mother sitting up in bed looking very flushed and with orders to stay there. She died of blood poisoning a few days later.

Catherine was anguished. Her friend, Louise Hutchinson, who had known her since university days and was now living close by at Pymble with her husband and young family, said of this, "It never, never should have happened. It absolutely bit into Catherine's soul." She did, indeed, seem destined to feel remorse as well as grief when those closest to her died. This time she blamed herself badly for not getting a second opinion initially, for not ensuring the best possible attention. Why hadn't this doctor acted more quickly? She tortured herself with these questions. The grave, beautiful voice of John Edwards, who conducted the service at Scots Church, and the majestic flow of English words (she was now well accustomed to the Latin) overwhelmed her further. Afterwards, she stood in the family vault where her mother now lay beside her much loved husband and Catherine's grandparents, then wandered along the high cliffs at Waverley Cemetery in the breezes blowing straight from the immensity of ocean and was comforted by the beauty of the place. She remembered a text she had seen on a wall at the Croals' home in Edinburgh and asked the attendant to have inscribed on her mother's coffin — *And underneath are the everlasting arms.*

Alan felt Anne MacLaurin's death also; he had had a deep affection for her, admiring the way in which she had combined wit and purpose with her quiet and gentle charm. As well, he appreciated her involvement with his children, especially at times of crisis, which were frequent enough, with four of them and now the baby, Elizabeth. There was the irony of his own mother, aunt and grandmother — now aged 92 — living their very much more cloistered lives at Mosman with a family retainer employed by Uncle Albert to look after them. It was an irony which Catherine did not allow to go unremarked. When Louisa died the following year, Alan arranged for his mother to move to *Rothermere* at Turramurra to be closer to them. Catherine, however, frowned upon the kind of overtures she made to the children, giving them sweets and suddenly unburdening herself of what Neil describes as 'a great fund of disaster stories, such as the wreck of the *Dunbar* just outside Sydney Harbour'. Catherine, perhaps with good reason, could not forgive her for that 'household without affection' in which Alan had grown up.

The Mackerras children were allowed an unusual amount of freedom by their parents. Catherine believed in developing independence in the young, something which Alan did not dispute, so that apart from doing all the things that children do, such as playing in the creek, catching tadpoles, climbing the big loquat tree in the garden, gorging themselves on the fruit, catching and dismembering cicadas, complaining about bindy-eyes, playing rowdy games — particularly one called *Walls* in which they attacked each other at play, thereby neatly circumventing the 'no fighting' rule — they were allowed to go off alone to such things as the Royal Easter Show. They also went on long bike rides and train trips unaccompanied. Alastair and Neil, as ten and eight-year-olds, with Joan very soon accompanying them, used to take train excursions for sixpence each on a Saturday or school holiday to somewhere like Mt Colah or Cronulla. On arrival, they would perhaps see a children's film, such as *The Wizard of Oz*, or just go for a walk. On the way back, they used to memorise the station stops, talk about everything to do with trains, what sort of engines drove them, how many carriages they usually had, and so on, until they became quite expert on the subject. As a friend of Neil from those early days at St Aloysius and onwards, Sydney magistrate, John Goldrick, remarked, "It was part of the Mackerras mystique. Railway tickets had magical properties — they had two enlarged and put on one of the walls at home. 'They'll take you anywhere in the world,' they said. As schoolboys in those days, we used to have big pocket watches which you could buy at Selfridges or Woolworths for five shillings. They'd suddenly pull theirs out of their pockets, say about 3.15 in the afternoon, and announce, 'The north-west mail is now leaving Wee Waa'! — or wherever it was leaving. At any given moment they could do this sort of thing!"

Joan shared this interest and recalls from her home in Suffolk, England, now, 'those lovely train trips' with her brothers. She remarked, "Of course, the other thing about Alastair and Neil was that they were frightfully good at school. Both extremely clever, although they didn't make much fuss about it — prizes for best at mathematics and top or near top of the class. And later on they always seemed to be quoting at you in Latin and Neil could reel off long lists of statistics, lists of American presidents and everything you could think of." All this unrestrained ebullience, plus the fact that each learnt a musical instrument as soon as he or she was old enough — Alastair the flute, Neil the clarinet, Joan the violin — caused people to remark that the noise level in the Mackerras household was quite unbelievable. John Goldrick summed it up, "It was extraordinary — all the commotion, the shouting and the music. The father in the background. And in the foreground the all pervasive Mrs Mackerras — a presence."

Charles, aged 14, with his flute, in Sydney Grammar School uniform.

Charles was by now at Sydney Grammar School, not at all interested in anything but music, and had begun learning the flute from an acquaintance of his father, an electrical engineer, Gordon Foster, who lived nearby and was one of those amateur musicians who are of professional standard. A fortunate chance occurred which was to be of considerable help to him in his career. "I just bought a flute from a fellow I knew," he recalled. "It was a magnificent instrument and I couldn't understand why he'd sold it to me so cheaply. I showed it to Mr Foster and he said, 'Well, the reason is, it's high-pitched'. It was *old high pitch*, which wasn't in use any more in England or Australia. So, I had this flute that was about half a tone out with the piano, and it meant that I had to transpose. It taught me. I became perfectly at home transposing. It was a very lucky accident." He was now able to understand easily the whole theory about transposing instruments and the fact that some are written differently from the way they sound. "For instance," he said "the trumpet and the clarinet — B flat instruments — are written a tone higher than they sound, others, the E flat instruments, a sixth higher and so on." His sharp-pitched flute which gave him immediate understanding of these things, remains a grateful memory.

He now began taking piano lessons from Ramsay Pennicuick at the Conservatorium, going straight there after school. This meant missing sport but that didn't worry him. "I was always there," he said, "whether I had a lesson or not. I just played truant from sport." He was completely obsessed with music and although Catherine and Alan still firmly believed that he must first of all complete an academic course at school and then university, both were prepared to help him in every way to develop his musical talent.

He persuaded them to ask their friends to a concert he intended giving at *Harpenden*. Professor David Myers, (then Engineering Faculty, University of Sydney) recalled the occasion. "Alan was a family friend, he knew my wife's family and mine and we always remained on terms of close friendship. He invited us this night to hear a performance by a children's orchestra, conducted by his eldest son Charles, playing some of his own compositions. He had two or three of his brothers or sisters in the orchestra. It was an interesting performance and his composition was clearly influenced by Mozart." So, three years on from his talk of writing concertos, Charles could really be taken seriously as a young musician of exceptional promise and his father clearly had as much confidence in him as did his mother.

It is interesting to pause here and look at Alan's career. He had been appointed Assistant Distribution Engineer to the Electricity Undertaking of the Municipal Council of Sydney in 1935. The Distribution Superintendent at the time was Charles J. Craggs, a very able and distinguished engineer and something of a personality. He was well-known for giving the impression that he was not concentrating — looking out windows, tossing keys in the air — then coming up with a solution that went swiftly to the heart of the complicated matter on hand. Alan, who was known as Mac or A.P.M. at the Council, had a similar ability and in the early days was often referred to as *'Charlie Craggs' slide rule'*.

"He was, of course, much more than that," said his former colleague, Tom Keating. "He not only fleshed out the skeletons of ideas thought out by C.J.C., but he usually supplied part of the skeleton too. I had been on the staff of the Bunnerong Power Station which was under construction at this time, but my tastes were for work of a more academic kind and in 1937 I was given the opportunity of serving as assistant to A.P.M. This was an extraordinary piece of good fortune. I had been for some years furthering my knowledge of mathematics and electrical engineering theory and A.P.M. had, even then, the reputation of being something of a wizard. Shortly before the war, an Austrian refugee of Jewish extraction, Dr Walter Diesendorf, who later became a close friend, joined our small group, and I am proud to have been associated with these two brilliant men. Walter went on to become a very senior engineer in the Snowy Mountains Authority and Alan in the Electricity Commission, but in these years, A.P.M., and Walter and myself, the junior partner, formed a team which, I think I can say, left its mark on the Municipal Council, the Sydney County Council and their electricity undertakings." He added "A.P.M. was a reserved rather than outgoing person. . . . a born teacher with the ability to reduce a problem to its fundamentals . . . the same approach necessary in presenting a new subject to students . . . there is evidence of this in his various reports and published articles . . . He was kindly, helpful . . . and very easy to get along with. I never once saw him angry or heard him raise his voice. He was always cheerful."

This rounded assessment not only throws light on Alan professionally and dispenses with any sort of dour Scot image, but points to the direction his career was later to take, which was to the academic. His reserve, and somehow it was palpable enough to prevent the use of his Christian name by his colleagues, seems to have warred with a very real need to teach, to help and inform. In his own home, in spite of the growing family, this need was frustrated; it was not in him to compete with Catherine for the attention of the children, and with her overwhelmingly forceful personality and equally fine intellect, she simply monopolised the teaching role. The only occasions the family remember him rebuking their mother for talking too much were on what they called '*Astronomy Nights*', when he had invited friends, and she began introducing extraneous subjects. However, musical evenings predominated, sometimes with recordings, sometimes with Catherine at the piano and instrumentalists or singers; then there was no holding her in all the noisy, knowledgeable talk between items or at supper. It was a pity that, once again, that strange inhibition which trapped Alan within himself with those he most cared for — as we have seen in his letters to her in America — prevented him from telling her of his pride in her playing or at least in letting it be seen. She was an excellent accompanist and would take on anything, a Mozart or Beethoven concerto, Handel, or whatever was required.

It was unfortunate also that Catherine's insensitive streak seemed to manifest itself more frequently with Alan than with anyone else. She was very well-off herself, and engineers were not paid large salaries in those days. It was her money which had provided the big, substantial house and many of the things which adorned it, such as the Persian rugs and antiques — about which she was also knowledgeable — and she never let Alan forget the fact. She frequently mentioned it in front of friends or acquaintances, and always referred to *Harpenden* as 'my house'. She managed her own business affairs and they went their separate ways on financial matters. Since they never discussed the subject, neither knew what the other had; Alan simply met day to day expenses. This was at a time when men were regarded very much as the providers, and he was a conventional man. The situation would therefore have been difficult enough for him if Catherine had been a quiet, tactful woman; as it was, he found the references she made to her major financial contribution to their style of living, very nearly as hard to bear with as her conversion to Catholicism. He was also as frugal as she was generous, a fact which the upbringing of each had heightened, and he could not restrain himself from an occasional, 'It's all very well for you'.

In spite of these things, they managed to rub along, the children were extremely happy and quite unaware of undercurrents. It was Alan who bought their first family car, a Hillman, in 1938 and took them all driving, the fair, year old Elizabeth, who was to continue to be his chief joy, perched on her mother's knee. Both Catherine and Alan could have been termed conservationists, though the word was not then in use, and he drove them to the beautiful Burragorang Valley, which was soon to be flooded to make way for a Sydney Water Supply dam, and lamented that this lovely place was to have its face irreparably changed in the name of progress. Next, one of his New Zealand aunts died and left him a small legacy, the equivalent of about $650, with which, very enterprisingly, he managed to buy a cottage at Leura in the Blue Mountains. It was certainly very rough and ready but it was to provide the setting for May, and sometimes August, school holidays for the family.

The other notable event of that sesqui-centenary year of 1938 for the Mackerrases, was the winning of the Anniversary Day Regatta by Alan and his crew in *Maricita*. "It was a southerly buster that day," said Alastair, "and I was one of the crew. *Maricita* was a good old-fashioned yawl, a comfortable old thing, she went very, very well in heavy weather and it's a handicap race." His cousin, Ian's son David, who was at boarding school at Shore at the time and often went sailing with Alan, added that in those conditions they used to take down the mainsail and sail on the jib and the mizzen. Alastair has kept the medal which testifies that he was a member of the crew that won the Anniversary Regatta in 1938, but is quite unrepentant that he did not do more sailing with his father. "He was a mild-mannered man," he said, "but when he got in a boat he was a martinet. If you brought a grain of sand on with you there was trouble, and if you talked too much there was trouble." So the problem remained. The young Mackerrases were not prepared to take any sport seriously; they preferred to do other things with their time, a pattern which also remained. Nevertheless, Charles was sufficiently interested at this point to invest his pocket money in a share in a Vaucluse junior skiff with another Grammar School boy and for a brief time did a little sailing, a passing enthusiasm which caught up with him again some thirty years later in Europe.

In 1939, with tensions in Europe rapidly mounting and talk in the household, as everywhere, of the grim possibility of war, Catherine awaited impatiently the birth of twins. For one so eager to talk and expound on everything under the sun, she was strangely inhibited about discussing the whys and wherefores of reproduction with her children and left them all uninformed on the subject. Alan was certainly not the one to fill the gap. Therefore, in spite of their mother's enormous size, Alastair and Neil, who had been spending the August holidays at Leura, were astonished on their return to be introduced to week-old twin brothers, "This is Colin Patrick. This is Malcolm Hugh."

It was the 3rd September, and after the excitement of meeting the new members of the household had subsided, they were told that, this very day, Europe had once again become a battlefield, Hitler's troops had invaded Poland, and Australia, as a Commonwealth country, had followed Great Britain with a declaration of war against Germany. They listened to the grave voice of the new Prime Minister, R.G. Menzies, on their radio; then the general hubbub of the family reigned again.

It was, however, brought home very substantially only a few months later when their Uncle Ian called, spent an hour with their father in his study, then emerged to say goodbye to them. Ian, at 41, had enlisted once again in the Medical Corps of the A.I.F., feeling that his experience and the knowledge he could provide in his particular field of study could be put to best use in this way. Besides, as David remarked, "He would also be where he most wanted to be — over there in the thick of it all."

He left Sydney with the rank of Major, in the first convoy out of Australia in January 1940, and gave valuable service in the Western Desert in the prevention of enteric infections. Later, after Japan entered the war, he was transferred to the Pacific area and in New Guinea made a major contribution organising the study and control of malaria, dengue fever and scrub typhus; he was twice Mentioned in Despatches.[1]

Catherine now issued another of her edicts. She was tired after the birth of the twins, and domestic help, to which she was totally accustomed, was impossible to get because of the exodus of women to the services and munitions factories. She clearly could not cope single-handed. Charles had all his extra-curricular musical activities, which she had recently stepped up considerably, arranging for him to have lessons in harmony, counterpoint and the organ at St Mary's Cathedral with a Spanish priest, musician and composer, Father Alftred Muset, who was a refugee from Franco's Spain. He was learning a great deal from this gifted man, but of course it also meant that he was seldom at home. Alastair and Neil must step into the breach and assist with the rearing of the twins.

It was a formative time. Charles, at fourteen, escaped practical responsibilities in order to get on with his career. Alastair, at eleven, with an admixture of his father's calm and his mother's positiveness, accepted them. Neil, on the other hand, remembers feeling 'rather bad-tempered about it', and was relieved to find his older brother prepared to shoulder

---

1. Ian Murray Mackerras 1898 — 1980, a bibliographical monograph by K.R. Norris (Historical Records of Australian Science, Vol. 5 No. 2) gives a full account of his very distinguished career and publications.

Family at Turramurra 65

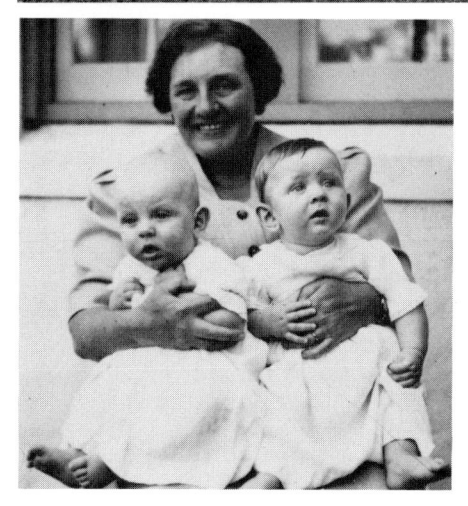

Joan, aged 3 with the baby, Elizabeth.

Elizabeth meets the calf at Harpenden, Catherine hovers.

THE FAMILY
NOW COMPLETE

Catherine with the twins, Colin and Malcolm.

the major responsibility. So it happened that Alastair found himself bathing and feeding his young brothers, cleaning up their messes, and learning to concentrate on mathematics, or whatever textbook was on hand, with one or other of them crawling over him, and even enjoying this nurturing role which had been thrust upon him. It seems likely that Neil's partial abnegation had something of frustration in it, for it was obvious that Alastair, two years his senior, would have the edge in efficiency and responsibility in any case. The middle role in any family is difficult enough; it is no wonder that Neil, with two gifted elder brothers to measure up to, and two younger sisters, each with her special niche in the family — Joan much in her mother's mould, Elizabeth, her father's pride and joy — viewed the prospect of physically caring for these demanding new twins with a marked lack of enthusiasm. The family were never consciously competitive in relation to one another but Neil seems to have had an inner struggle to make his specific mark, as some temperamental instability during his academic career was to indicate, and also the peculiarly intense attitudes he adopted which precipitated the many dramas that were to attend him over the years.

Charles, at this time, read in the *Sydney Morning Herald* that there was a scarcity of oboe, horn and bassoon players in the city and decided to switch from the flute to the oboe, for he was determined to be a professional musician and saw a quick way of getting into an orchestra. He took lessons after school with Jan Brinkman, a Dutchman who had come out with one of the opera companies and was a fine musician. He also studied piano at the Conservatorium and was constantly there, not only for lessons, but listening to and talking with the other students. He told his parents he had definitely made up his mind to become a professional musician. They did not argue too vehemently; if he still felt that way after he had finished secondary school and taken a university degree, as they felt he must as a matter of course, then so be it. Meanwhile, he composed a dramatic cantata, in Handelian style, based on the Greek legend of *Marysas*, the musician who challenged the god Apollo to a musical duel. Catherine wrote the libretto and he persuaded a group of student friends to perform it at the Conservatorium.

During these years the Marckerrases had formed a friendship at Turramurra with a Melbourne family, Dr Harold Wilson, his wife, Margaret, and their young children, who spent some seven years in Sydney. They were to remain lifelong friends; Alan later sailed with Dr Wilson on Port Phillip Bay, while his wife found Catherine tremendously stimulating company. But it was their small son, John, now also a doctor in Melbourne, who developed a special relationship with Alan. It is a measure of his feeling of isolation within his own family, that Alan used to call on the Wilsons quite frequently on his way home. "From my very early childhood," John Wilson recalled, "while my mother prepared dinner, Mr Mackerras sat with me talking of engines and yachts. He drew careful diagrams of how to set and gybe a spinnaker. Once he gave me a beautiful book on building a schooner. On another visit, a book on the building of the Sydney Harbour Bridge. He was gentle, patient, and slow, and made sure I understood. He was an ideal visitor for a young boy, and fired my enthusiasm for sailing." They moved to Melbourne in 1940 and thereafter each family stayed with the other when visiting their respective cities.

At *Harpenden*, the war years were marked by Catherine making maximum use of their half acre of land. She had a part-time gardener, a retired dairyman, known to all as Mr Boorman, who helped her run hens, keep a Jersey cow, and grow a few vegetables. Now, with wartime shortages and a family of seven with the vast, healthy appetites of the growing young, she doubled her efforts. She bought another Jersey, more hens, some ducks, and since, to her, books were the obvious source of knowledge, guidebooks on everything from vegetable growing and duck rearing to *How to make Your Own Bread*, and proceeded to implement them.

"My mother enthusiastically grew spinach, broccoli, cucumbers, potatoes and sweet corn," said Joan, who was particularly close to her. "The sweet corn was the real thing we all liked from the garden. We used to make pigs of ourselves and pour lashings of melted butter over it. We ate a lot of eggs and drank a lot of milk. It used to be brought up with brimming buckets to the kichen door in the evening where it would all be processed and mother would set the milk and skim the cream off and we'd have this lovely thick cream quite often." This era of practical self-sufficiency, apart from being quite wonderful for the children, was remarkble in itself, given Catherine's background, and the fact that at the same time she kept up with her reading and was in demand as a public speaker. Her friend, the educationalist, Mother Borgia, recalls a fine speech she made about this time at Loreto convent, Kirribilli, on the theme, *Women in History*. She took four outstanding women, concentrated on St Margaret of Scotland, and made a memorable impression 'as one steeped in history and literary allusion'.

Between Christmas and New Year in 1941, Alastair and Neil were invited by family friends, Sydney physician Dr David Adcock and his wife, who had a nephew about their age, to drive up with them for a week's holiday at their grazing property, *Merilba*, outside Armidale. The two had a wonderful time discovering the joys of country life, while at the same time the Adcocks shared their interest in music and chess and also taught them to play bridge. Neil, in particular, fell in love with the countryside. For the following six years, until the doctor sold the property, they returned for a similar holiday and Neil's liking for this northern New South Wales district was to be very formative in his later career.

During the height of the war in the Pacific, in May 1942, with an actual fear of invasion in Australia, the Battle of the Coral Sea raging, and Japanese submarines in Sydney Harbour, Catherine took the younger children to the cottage at Leura for some weeks. There she took over the boys' task of getting the big log fires going, coped with the usual wood stove cooking, rough bathing arrangements and the lightless outdoor lavatory which, the children remember, was inhabited by rather terrifying spiders. At night, they clustered round the fire while she read them such things as Kipling's *Just So Stories*. It is a picture that stays in the mind, for it captures her essential spiritedness and total devotion as a mother and is without that stridentness which was also part of her. Her own mother she never ceased to miss and often longed still to be able to talk to her.

At Turramurra, Alan, with a good friend, their family doctor Frank Lawes, had donned Air Raid Warden garb and, like with many other professional men in all the big Australian cities, went out at night to check the strict black-out regulations, inspect the sand-bagged shelters and man the First Aid Post. When Catherine returned, food shortages were worsening as a result of the great influx of American servicemen, and butter and meat joined petrol and clothing among rationed items; they were doubly glad of their home-grown products. Otherwise, life for the family went on much as usual and John Goldrick has a very distinct memory of a holiday with Neil and Alastair at Leura about this time which points up rather well the norm for the young generally, as distinct from the Mackerras norm. "I'd been to Cadet Camp," he recalled, "and I'd bought the Boomerang Songster No. 46 — it contained such hits of the day as *Chattanooga Choo Choo, Don't Sit Under the Apple Tree with Anyone Else But Me, Till the Boys Come Marching Home*, that sort of thing, and Alastair remarked, 'You have the most curious musical tastes!'"

Alastair was now in second class at Sydney Grammar and Charles' propensity for cutting across the Domain from the School to the Conservatorium had got out of hand. It was clear that his total absorption in music would preclude him from satisfactorily completing normal academic studies, which, for both parents, automatically meant matriculation and a university degree. They were also worried about the sort of company he was keeping at the Conservatorium and decided to send him to The King's School, Parramatta, as a boarder. After arrangements had been made and his parents were driving him to King's, he said, "I know you mean this for the child's good, but it's no good to *me*." He was right. The move was quite disastrous; he would not be regimented and disliked boarding school intensely. The one thing he enjoyed there was organ lessons, which replaced those he had had with Father Muset, and this organist was also not only gifted, but helpful to him personally. He still went into the city to Jan Brinkman for his oboe lessons but, even so, fretted constantly at being out of daily touch with other musicians which, formerly, proximity to the Conservatorium had made possible.

"So," he recalls cheerfully, "I misbehaved very badly and got myself chucked out of the school." Although he deliberately precipitated this, the fact still rankles a little and the remark from schooldays he likes most to remember was that of Sydney Grammar's elderly headmaster, kindly F.G. (Sandy) Phillips, who, realising that his heart would never be in academic work, had written in his final report — *Ars longa, vita brevis*.

Alan's reaction is recalled vividly by his colleague, Tom Keating, for he entered his office about this time to find there a very young man with red hair who was about to leave — "A.P.M. said to me, 'This is Charlie'. And after he'd gone he added, 'I'm very worried about Charlie. He's left school and enrolled at the Conservatorium of Music. He says he's going to be a conductor.' I replied that it was better to be a good conductor than a mediocre engineer or something of that sort. A.P.M., after a moment's thought, said, 'You may have something there'."

Catherine also resigned herself to the inevitable, and, as always when any of the family convinced her that they were serious about something, became supportive. She sat up till all hours of the night discussing the future and the possibilities with him. A few days later he had his first job — playing at the Gilbert & Sullivan Opera Co. at the old Theatre Royal in Castlereagh Street. The conductor, Leo Packer, created a very pleasant atmosphere there and Charles regaled the family at dinner with stories of happenings at the theatre and long Gilbertian quotes for them to cap. He also discovered at this point that the copyright on Sullivan's music would expire in 1951 and made a resolution that as soon as it did, he would step in quickly and arrange some of the delightful melodies in some other form. This was to prove very fruitful.

Meanwhile, some aspects of living at home began to be irksome. His own room was close to the drawing room where the family did most of their practising, often early in the morning, and he was pulled from sleep by the sound of a sharp instead of a natural or a major key instead of a minor. Again, one of his tasks was to teach Joan theory of music. "Poor Charlie became frightfully frustrated with me," she recalls, "it was all second nature to him and he just couldn't understand what I found difficult about it." His patient care on all matters musical did not extend to teaching the young. But above all, at that time, he wished he were not required to account for the hours he came in at night. He was very much the young man about town and had begun to take a decidedly positive interest in girls — Macquarie Place, with its monument to the first landing, another to a First Fleet ship, a Victorian drinking fountain, and in those days, a seat and square of lawn, holds memories for him of his first romantic moments. So, all in all, he decided, with Catherine's blessing, to leave home and take a small flat at Kings Cross. He was just sixteen when he made this very independent move. Predictably, like the young before and since, he returned frequently — for meals, laundry and talk.

About this time, he orchestrated Mozart's early operetta, *Bastien and Bastienne*, from a piano score — Mozart's own orchestration was now unavailable — and it was recorded and broadcast by the ABC. A little later, he wrote a fugue on *Waltzing Matilda* which was also broadcast, and in which he managed to interest the visiting conductor, Eugene Ormandy, who ran through it for him during a rehearsal at the Sydney Town Hall.

It is interesting to see the emerging schoolmaster in Alastair over these years. A longtime friend of Catherine, Kate Wilson, who especially enjoyed her skill as a pianist, knew them all well and had a particular fondness for Alastair, said of him, "Even at Turramurra, you'd see him walking along with a whole stream of children behind him, and he'd coach any who needed it. All his life he's been the Pied Piper!"

The same thing is expressed in a different way by Dr John Parkinson who moved from Cranbrook to Sydney Grammar in his mid-teens and renewed their early friendship. "He'd become a sort of foster parent to his young brothers by then, "he recalled. "I used to wonder, when he was working for his matriculation, how ever he managed it in that large household. But he always maintained he got so used to it he couldn't work unless children were clambering over him. I remember him in the playground, when he was in Sixth Form, surrounded by a crowd of younger boys, helping them with their mathematics and talking about music. He was never without an *entourage* of people with whom he was

The twins, Colin (L.) and Malcolm with Joan (L) and Elizabeth in the garden at Harpenden, 1944.

Alastair and Joan with the twins, about 1948.

involved." He added with a smile, "When Sandy Phillips was retiring as headmaster, I also remember, we were speculating who would succeed him. A senior Mathematics Master, who was also the Master of the Lower School, an important position at Grammar, was mentioned and Alastair said, 'Oh, he'd never be a headmaster, he's not enough of a hypocrite for that!'"

John Parkinson was one of those who appreciated the hospitality of the Mackerrases, particularly of Catherine. "I was the only child of divorced parents and without a proper sort of family of my own. I visited them frequently, stayed with them in their house in the country and found them the most warm-hearted and wonderful family."

Alastair has a particular memory of his mother's inventiveness in the conversational stakes at this time. A young son of a family friend came to spend a mid-term weekend with them. "He was mouthing all sorts of conventional schoolboy things," he recalled, "and mother started up an anti-British argument. Although she was in fact herself very pro-British, she gave about fifty good reasons why you should be anti-British. She was a terrific stirrer. She just used to throw in these remarks. Very provocative." *Indeed*, her long suffering spouse would surely have added; but it is clear what an extraordinary stimulus she provided for the young.

She also badly needed to get away from them occasionally, and managed to combine this with the religious exercise of a week's retreat at the Dominican Friary at Wahroonga. On these occasions, Alastair took over the reins of the household, and garbed in a large apron, learnt to cook roast dinners, grills and huge piles of chipped potatoes and greens for the family, developing a proficiency which was to stand him in good stead later as a bachelor. Catherine left quantities of her home-made ice-cream, for which many have a long and nostalgic memory, and they managed to get by, in spite of the fact that their father never thought, like most men of his generation and upbringing, to lend a hand. Alastair, from these early days, was quite notorious for his sweet tooth and woe betide anyone who left a plate of meringues beside him at a party, for he would demolish them without a second thought.

Elizabeth, who was now at the convent at Pymble, had added a pony to the ménage, which also included their mother's cat, Tolstoy, and she eventually became quite a young equestrienne. Catherine, a good rider in her youth, loved the pony but pronounced that she was too fat and old to try it out, and declared the same about a subsequent one which tempted her more, a fiery dappled grey, named Pepper, which Neil managed to subdue. She was, in fact, overweight and clearly agreed with the psalmist who not only praised the Lord for the bread which strengtheneth man's heart but for the wine which maketh it glad — the full-blooded red met with her particular approval. She also introduced the occasional sherry and glass of beer to the previously abstemious household, all of which helped to keep her remarkable energies from flagging.

"Mother worked like a Trojan in those days," Elizabeth remarked. "She used to iron until about midnight in spite of quite awful varicose veins and get through great piles of shirts — talking to people all the time. She also had to carry everything, there was just no petrol for shopping." This is a general reflection of households with families in the 1940s for even after the war came to an end in 1945, petrol rationing remained for some time. Catherine's problems were, of course, greater, for the number to be looked after at *Harpenden* were considerably larger than most.

Neither of the girls at this time was interested scholastically and they therefore acquitted themselves very badly at examinations. There was much hilarity at the dinner table when Joan came home with the news that she had received 8 for Arithmetic, 15 for Geography and come second bottom in the class. She made up for it in other respects, practised her violin assiduously, and with a flair for organisation akin to Charles, put together each year a Nativity Play which they performed at *Harpenden*. She had her sister play an angel and Elizabeth's close friend, Janie Lemann (Breden), the Virgin Mary, while the twins were shepherds. The performances became more elaborate and they put the play on outdoors; with Janie mounted on Elizabeth's pony and led by Colin as Joseph, they wound their way through the garden to Bethlehem, the Inn and the manger. They sang delightful Christmas carols, the familiar ones, together with the oldest and most esoteric Joan could find in the Oxford Book of Carols. So, as Elizabeth remarked, "Our happy childhood just ticked along, a great deal happening but nothing particularly eventful — a big house, lots of children and animals and music and noise and food."

Her father sometimes asked her to read to him at night, ostensibly to improve her reading, which was in need of it, but partly because it was such a pleasure to look at the slight, fair child who bore some resemblance to him, and to listen to her voice which was gentler than her brothers and sisters. At bedtime, as the two girls appeared in their gowns to wish everyone goodnight, he used often to make one of his Gilbertian quotes, 'So very incompletely dressed!' This, from the evergreen *Pirates of Penzance*, has remained in the collective family memory, together with the charming image of the pair.

Alan had sold *Maricita* now and bought a smaller yacht which he named *Bettina*, after his grandfather's. He developed a reputation as an excellent single-handed yachtsman, and spent all his spare time for four years at the drawing board in his study designing, perfecting and making parts for the 27' sloop of which he dreamed. When it came to fruition, he named it for the red star, *Antares*, which he had pointed out to his young Creagh cousins on that cool, crystal night in their youth. So it came about that Elizabeth often found herself sitting with her father in his study of an evening, balancing on a knife edge cardboard cut-outs of his designs, so that he could check his calculations. He depended very much now on this young daughter for some companionship, for he and Catherine had grown further apart, to the extent that the older members of the family began to notice that they now rarely addressed each other.

Catherine, taking Joan for violin lessons to Loreto convent at Normanhurst, with the twins in tow and their football to kick about, used often to pace the grounds there talking with Mother Borgia, for she was still plagued by doubts over her conversion and worried by the divisive effect it had had, particularly in the widening rift between Alan and herself. There were many things, however, which she did not mention. Importantly, the fact that despite their substantial family, produced over a period of fourteen years, and their initial happiness, there was a degree of sexual incompatibility. Certainly, sexuality did not develop between them as a solace and cornerstone of marriage as it could have done. It was never furthered and explored, for itself, as a deepening bond within their relationship. The streak of puritanism in Catherine, as seen in the prudish attidute she had adopted in her university days to her father's essays on 'the new sexual morality', and her terse comments on his Lindsay paintings, remained and was reinforced by her new beliefs. The sanctioning by the Roman Catholic Church of all the good things of life, good food, good wine, good company, but the repression of the sexual side except for the purpose of procreation, suited her thoroughly. Alan's early transports were probably quashed as much by this quality in her as his own difficulty in letting her see the strength of his feelings, and were more and more trampled by the sharpness of her tongue. Not only was she excessively voluble, but she could also be very scathing and this happened too frequently with him. They no longer shared a bed as at Vaucluse; he made his way at night from his study to the big sleepout verandah which adjoined her room and there was no physical closeness to help. There can be no doubt that both had the potential for the strengthening of the sexual tie, Catherine for her very warmth of temperament, Alan in his strong need for affection, which was to continue to find means of expression. Meanwhile, the remoteness grew, and although probably responsible for a certain remoteness in every day relationships inherent in the family, seems not otherwise to have had any effect on the exuberant household.

Charles had graduated, via playing the piano in a show band for the State picture theatre, to oboe in Jack Davey's *Calling the Stars* orchestra and plagued them on the nights he was at home by playing, repeatedly, popular records such as the *Warsaw Concerto* and *Bolero*, and songs such as *Smoke Gets in your Eyes* and *Alexander's Ragtime Band* in order to take down the orchestration for Davey's show. Alastair, Neil and Joan were the chief sufferers, while Catherine supplied him with coffee for as long as he could stay awake. "Charles had this skill for arranging tunes, it was one of the ways he became prominent," said Alastair. "During the war, you couldn't get music with full parts for orchestra and he was able to listen to a record, hear each instrument separately, and write down the music. And to do that, you have to play it back, and back again . . . " They were kept awake at night for a week by the Warsaw Concerto and hoped never to hear it again, although Joan consented to earn pocket money by drawing bar lines for him in black ink 'on enormous pages of manuscripts with dozens and dozens of lines for the orchestral score'. Anything to do with Charles was guaranteed to be fun. "We were all very mercenary," she said, "as the young usually are, and he used to haggle with me — 3d a page if no smudges, 2d a page if he found a smudge. It was amusing, all this assessing. He could also persuade me quite easily to clean his shoes for 2/-, he'd make it 2/3d if they looked really good and 2/6d if you could see your face in them!" These minutiae are characteristic; he was to continue to bargain in this practical way and be amusing in the process.

During this period he stayed in close touch at the Conservatorium with Jan Brinkman, kept a watchful eye on the possibility of getting into the Sydney Symphony Orchestra, and decided, by listening to records, that he liked the 'newer sound of the newer style of oboe playing that was being done in England by Leon Goossens'. This was the situation when he turned eighteen late in 1943.

There was the question of service in the armed forces. He did not consider volunteering, being quite certain that his full abilities were being best employed as they were. However, he was soon called up by the Australian Army. He was physically examined and since he was exceedingly thin at the time, his chest expansion was not considered sufficient, and he was classified 'physically unfit for military service' and referred to Manpower, who ordered him, to his great satisfaction, to the Sydney Symphony Orchestra as an oboist. In 1944, however, the United States Army, discovering that he was American-born and still technically an American citizen, re-called, examined him and declared him 'physically fit' for war service. Just at this time, he was made Professor of Oboe at the Conservatorium, following the retirement of Brinkman, and he scarcely paused to answer communications from the United States Embassy in Canberra and the Australian authorities in regard to transfer of papers. His uncle, Ian Mackerras, briefly in Sydney from New Guinea where he was presently serving as a major in the Medical Corps of the A.I.F., remonstrated with him. He told him it was his duty to enlist, let alone wait till the matter of the call-up was sorted out officially, if ever. But military service was furthest from Charles' mind as he worked round the clock with the Sydney Symphony Orchestra and at the Conservatorium, and his uncle was unable to persuade him differently. Catherine and Alan did not intervene; they knew very well their eldest son's single-minded, headstrong passion for music.

So the *status quo* remained; Charles continued teaching at the Conservatorium and was also appointed principal oboist with the Sydney Symphony Orchestra. He himself does not regret the decision, although some doubts emerged when the full realisation of the effects of military invasion were brought home to him in Czechoslovakia in 1948, and he remembered that in 1944 that situation existed in South East Asia where the Allied offensive was just beginning to be effective.

Meanwhile, he visited them at *Harpenden* frequently that year and often brought with him friends from the musical world. His sister Joan has a particular recollection of a wonderful evening with the violinist, Beryl Kimber. "She played part of the Beethoven Violin Concerto for us and Charlie sat down at the piano and played from memory the orchestral part," she recalled, and also her own mortification after this lovely performance to be asked, as a violin student of only 18 months, to perform herself. Charles was spurred by the visit of the distinguished guest conductor Eugene Ormandy, in 1944, to take on the violin himself. Ormandy made the orchestra sound very different and he remembered that other greats, such as Toscanini and Barbirolli, had first been string players and decided that he had better learn the violin to further equip himself for conducting. It didn't work out, since he was 'mentally very advanced as a professional instrumentalist but physically just couldn't play the thing'. He spent far too long tuning up in order to satisfy his ear and then couldn't get his fingers to do what he wanted. So, he stayed with the oboe.

He had a great flair as a raconteur and kept the family highly amused with the inside stories of rehearsals, usually under the reliable baton of Sir Bernard Heinze, so that when they all went off to concerts at the Town Hall to hear the Sydney Symphony Orchestra, and Charles in its midst, playing Beethoven or Haydn or Berlioz, they knew the personality traits of the conductor and players and all the *contretemps* along the strenuous rehearsal road. One memorable night at performance he became the unenviable centre of drama when, playing a solo passage in a Brahms work, his oboe reed split. Fortunately, that fine flautist, well-known to all Sydney concert-goers, Neville Amadio, stepped swiftly into the breach and played the solo line. A long friendship thus ensued.

Catherine swiftly restored open house and nights of music at *Harpenden* in the immediate post-war years. They played recordings of Strauss, Wagner, or whatever the mood called for, and there were shouts of "Horn!", "Clarinet!", "Trombone!" over the music as Charles and his friends — Richard Merewether, Richard Farrell and others — identified the instruments for the young. The family revelled in it but the noise level often brought Alan from his study once again with the plea, accompanied by the rather tense mannerism he had acquired of stretching his neck and chin forward as he spoke, "I wonder if you'd turn it down, please." A few years later, Colin recalls, he had really lost patience. When the family themselves were assembled, and the loud music disturbing his concentration, he would emerge with arms sweeping as though to actually give effect himself to an exasperated and peremptory, "Turn that frightful noise *down*!!"

There is an interesting glimpse of him professionally in 1945 from John Sproule, the present System Development Engineer of the Electricity Commission of New South Wales, who was then a student and about to undertake six months practical experience in industry. "Turning up at the Sydney County Council at the start of a six-week strike," he said, "I was sent to Bunnerong Power Station and found myself up one end of the large turbine house reading meters, etcetera. Every so often I met in the middle of the building with a red-haired gentleman doing the same thing at the other end. He introduced himself as Alan Mackerras, and startled me by asking what was a very revealing question, whether students were taught the 'physical significance of the complementary function and particular integral solution of the differential equation?'" He realised just how much engineering science would be applied in the S.C.C. and even more so when Alan invited him, and several other students he had met during the strike, to call at his office and explained to them some of the plans for development of the S.C.C. distribution system. "He had a fine, sonorous speaking voice," he added, "and could express himself very clearly, explaining complex issues in the simplest terms and he also enjoyed the company of these young people."

Alan had now developed a particular interest in the economic aspect of his subject and had written a widely recognised paper on *Allocation of Costs of an Electricity Supply Undertaking*. Several years later, John Sproule joined his staff and found that he was well-known for his 'pleasant, happy and jocular manner, according to the occasion' — and for the analogies he used when explaining a technical point to a layman. Many of them were from Gilbert & Sullivan and the junior staff were highly entertained when they heard these explanations issuing over his office partition, together with the occasional whistling of tunes, in paricular, 'a very fine rendition of parts of the Archduke Trio'.

In 1944 his mother died, having suffered for some time from the lingering effects of a stroke. Ian flew down from New Guinea where he was implementing anti-malarial measures, and after the service and the gathering of the Creagh family, the pair spent long satisfactory hours in Alan's study talking on scientific matters. Alan also enjoyed the companionship of their younger Creagh cousins. Nancy, returning about this time from some years in England, remarked, "Catherine always complained that at parties at *Harpenden* Alan would carry my sister and me off to his study. He would put in an appearance for a while and then retreat, taking us with him if he could. The truth was, of course, he could never get a word in amongst his own family." He had also developed the habit of calling on the Creaghs at Mosman on the way home from sailing — the redoubtable Uncle Willie welcomed all talk on wind and tide and sail, doubly so after losing his only son, John, as a result of conditions suffered as a prisoner of war in Ethiopia. John, like Charles, had shown exceptional musical promise and at the time of his death was in the United States on the advice of the singer, Lawrence Tibbett. There was much to talk about and as Nancy added, "Alan never stopped talking when he was with us . . . "

She herself had a great affection for Catherine; they had many bonds, an affinity with Europe, a love of literature and of travel, though Nancy upbraided her in an amused fashion for her unabashed snobbishness which sprang from an elitist attitude to the professions *('Common', Catherine? What do you mean by that? My aunts used to say, 'Not out of the top drawer!' What is the 'top drawer'?)*. At the same time, she was fond of Alan and understood him. "He had become very withdrawn at home," she said, "it had reached the stage where he simply put on a cloak when he came into the house." He had also been driven by the loud, full-scale orchestral music that so frequently filled the house, to seek the chamber music he loved, outside, and Nancy often met him, a solitary figure, at Musica Viva concerts. Yet, if there was no companionship at home, there was still much pride in the family's achievements.

In 1947, Alastair was in second year in the Arts Faculty at Sydney University, studying Mathematics and Classics, having matriculated, to their delight, with a maximum pass which meant First Class Honours in Mathematics and A's in all his subjects; Neil had completed school with excellent results and both had left their names on Honour Boards at Sydney Grammar. This was particularly gratifying to Catherine and Alan, for, already there, were members of their own families, Alan's brother and Catherine's father on the World War I Memorial, and amongst those killed in action, Catherine's uncle, Normand MacLaurin, whose death at Gallipoli had affected her so strongly in her own youth.

Charles, at twenty-one, had now come to a vital decision. His ability to compose and arrange music was extremely useful to him; he had written part of the music for Charles Chauvel's film, *The Rats of Tobruk*, and the music for a film on the Aboriginal painter, *Namatjira*. The latter he had found particularly interesting, conducting and recording it himself with friends at Burwood Studios. Nevertheless, he felt he was not sufficiently original or creative in that field and was now certain that he would direct his ambition towards conducting. Catherine applauded this and he discussed his immediate course of action with her. He wanted to train in Australia and be an Australian musician. "Don't be ridiculous, Charles," she told him, and recalled her words with great satisfaction some thirty years later, "you've got to go abroad to succeed, you simply must, whether you want to or not." Her early travels had given her a strong sense of Europe as the centre of all cultural development and she would have preferred to live there herself for that reason. Australia, she admitted, had provided her with a wonderful life but she did not have any real feeling for the country, as Alan very definitely did, and regarded it as a cultural backwater.

Charles sought the advice also of Eugene Goossens, who was just about to take up his appointment as resident conductor of the Sydney Symphony Orchestra. He agreed that there were more opportunities for an ambitious young musician in England and offered him an introduction to his brother, the London oboe player, Leon Goossens.

Arrangements were soon under way. Charles had saved some money, and Catherine went at once to look into the legal aspect of her father's will which the trustees agreed could be interpreted as allowing the withdrawal of capital for the furthering of her sons' and daughters' education. She withdrew a share which she thought would be equitable for Charles and thereafter did so for each of the others when the occasion arose. As soon as this vital matter was arranged, he was off.

They stood disconsolately at the wharf, where officialdom was also solemnly arrayed to farewell the Duchess of Gloucester taking leave from vice-regal duties, and waved him goodbye. They were to miss him sadly, all his lively talk, his music, his friends, the games of chess at which he had set the pace. As Joan put it, "Somehow there was a sudden hush over

Charles, at 21, just before leaving for England.

the house." He also missed the warmth of the close-knit family; the return to their usual high-spritedness was helped by the long amusing letters he wrote to them which Catherine read aloud at the dinner table. The first of these told them that the ship, the *Rangitiki*, was diverted to call at Pitcairn Island, which was largely inhabited by descendants of the mutineers of the *Bounty*, so that the Duchess could pay an official visit, presumably, he supposed, 'as a sort of official pardon for the Mutiny!' He was interested to note also that the Islanders sang *God Save the King* to a late 18th century version, with embellishments.

At this point, there was a near tragedy in the family. As part of their bargain for helping with the rearing of the twins, now eight years old and at St Aloysius College, Alastair and Neil often carried them off at the weekends in Catherine's car, a little Hillman she had bought after the war, to a cottage at Kiama or in the country. Often with them on these expeditions was Alastair's university friend, Tony Melville, whose father, Sir Leslie, was a friend and university comtemporary of Alan. Young Melville became very interested in Colin and the precocious flair for mathematics he had begun to display. "He was very indulgent to me," said Colin. "When he discovered that I knew such things as the square root of 1024 at that age without having to work it out, he began teaching me mathematics. He even thought I could fill in for a game of bridge — but I couldn't manage that, I'm afraid I ruined it for them . . . " They were all in the lovely Kangaroo Valley on this occasion and one morning, while swimming in the Kangaroo River, Colin got into a current and found himself in serious trouble. Instead of the usual cry of "Help!", he called out "To the rescue! To the rescue!" and they imagined he was joking. Tony Melville realised ahead of the others that the child was in fact close to drowning, swam out, reached him just as he was disappearing and brought him to the bank. He himself went to Cambridge, stayed in England and became headmaster of Persse School, Cambridge, but it is certain that if it had not been for his quick action, the Mackerras family would have been sadly depleted and Australia without one of its most eminent China watchers.

Joan and Elizabeth now fulfilled their father's side of their parent's educational compromise and attended PLC (Presbyterian Ladies College) at Pymble. Joan gives a revealing glimpse of how the twins, encouraged by laughter from their mother and the family, exacerbated the state of affairs with their father — "There was a tremendous amount of hilarity at the table, with the twins telling us exaggerated tales of what happened in the classroom and the rude things they said to their teachers. Father was rather shocked at this flippant attitude and didn't take part in these hilarious talks. He would get up and say he had more useful things to do and go away to his study. But it always happened that it was at the end of the meal when the talk became serious and there were really interesting discussions about the young priests and faith and sanctity and such things. And on nights when father went to give lectures at the WEA or to the Sydney Observatory, or his Astronomical Association meetings, we were able to say what we liked about religion because he wasn't there to be irritated or annoyed. I also remember feeling a resentment because he would not allow me to make my first communion . . . " So, inevitably, he grew away from them.

Young John Wilson arrived early in 1949 on school holidays from Melbourne and described *Harpenden* as a house of contrasts — "Inside, a ship's lamp hung on the dark panelling at the foot of the stairs, it was mostly dark but with a shaft of bright sunlight on a table — Catherine was as dominating and breathless as Alan was retiring and reserved. It was a warm and open house with much loud discussion, reciting of timetables of trains, singing of Gilbert & Sullivan, practising of musical instruments, and excitement over tennis or cricket." The latter was clearly some interest

Alan sails his yacht, Antares, on Sydney Harbour, 1949.

in the national euphoria in the post-war restoration of Davis Cup and Test Cricket matches for they had little personal interest in sport, though Elizabeth, and later Malcolm, played some tennis. The visitor was astonished to find that the Mackerras children either actively disliked or had no real interest in sailing. Malcolm did go out occasionally with his father, but also described it, as the older ones had done, as *going to church*.

"Indeed, there was something sacred about *Antares* and her skipper's relationship with her," Dr Wilson remarked. "In designing her, he had combined his love for Sydney sailing with his skill as an engineer to produce this Stradivarius among yachts. She is a lovely 27′6″ sloop with a beautiful classical counter stern, and nice sheer and flare, built at The Spit of oregon planks on spotted gum timbers. Alan carefully explained to me the Metacentric Shelf principle of yacht design by which the underwater surfaces of the hull are balanced at all angles of heel. One weekend he took me sailing from Jim O'Rourke's shed at The Spit to Quarantine Cove, where we camped overnight. It was sheer magic, and casts a powerful spell still on my life. Everything was perfect; the sun, the sand, the sea, the bright varnish, the quiet evening, the harbour lights, the primus stove, the cot bunks and amongst all these things Mr Mackerras, moving slowly, carefully, gently doing everything perfectly and very kindly." So speaks a man whom Alan inspired to a lifetime's love of sailing.

Ian was now doing his sailing on Moreton Bay, for he had been appointed director of the newly established Queensland Institute of Medical Research in Brisbane. His son David, after war service in which he took part in the repatriation of prisoners of war from Changi, was at Sydney University — ironically, he was the one of the family to pursue electrical engineering as a career. He often visited them at *Harpenden*, principally to talk with Alan and to go sailing with him, though he also joined enthusiastically in the musical evenings. His visits prompted Alan to suggest that Neil drive the twins to Brisbane to see something of their Uncle Ian, whom they hardly knew. This was very rewarding, for, as Nancy remarked, 'Ian had an enchanting personality. It was a pleasure to be with him and Jo (*his scientist wife*), also I must say, just to see the way their eyes rested on each other.' The twins, of course, were too young to observe all these subtleties but they enjoyed their visit, as did Neil, and Catherine had some respite from the constant round of daily responsibilities which often wore her down. At the same time, she was beginning to feel a mounting tension at the badly deteriorating relationship between Alan and herself.

"I sometimes feel I will have to go," she told Nancy, who replied, "Why don't you?" Nancy herself felt that Catherine and Alan were prisoners of their times and upbringing in the stiff upper lip, Anglo-Saxon attitude they adopted towards their thoroughly incompatible marriage. "No," replied Catherine, "I made a vow and I intend to keep it. He is a good man but I simply don't understand him."

Fortunately, there was little time to brood, for she was totally involved in the burgeoning careers and problems of their family. Neil, after so much early promise, had become restless and spasmodic in his attitude to study, failed a subject in his final year Arts, and wanted to break away from intellectual pursuits. He had greatly enjoyed himself each year at the Adcocks' property, *Merilba,* and decided now that he wanted to go on the land. As a dairy farm was more within the realm of practicality than a property, he wanted to get some experience in dairying. Through university contacts of Alan, it was arranged that he spend six weeks on a progressively run Jersey stud farm near Casino. His parents found his behaviour extremely hard to understand but thereafter, for many weekends, with the real possibility of a dairy farm ahead, Catherine drove about looking for land. If the Trust money could be stretched sufficiently, she would see that he had his own farm, if that was what he wanted.

Then she considered the prospects before Alastair, who had graduated with distinction and was teaching Mathematics at Trinity Grammar School, Sydney. It seemed to her that he should have some time at Cambridge in order to go further. She would go over and see what could be done, also see Charles and meet his wife, Judy. She was on a ship on her way to London and a much needed break, leaving Alastair in charge of the household, before anyone had time to collect their thoughts on the subject. "I didn't have a scholarship," said Alastair, "but mother went over there and badgered all the tutors until two colleges offered me a place." A somewhat modest assessment but he was, in fact, quite happy as he was, enjoying being financially independent and having great splurges buying such things as a complete recording of the St Matthew Passion, Bach cantatas and generally adding to their collection.

Catherine returned several months later, having been in London for the birth of her first grandchild, and also having spent some time travelling in Spain where she revelled in seeing the many glorious works of art inspired by the Church. She brought home with her a blue tile from Toledo cathedral which she had set into the whitewashed wall at the front entrance of *Harpenden* to remind her of the beauty of the place and the masterpieces of El Greco which had profoundly impressed her. But she also indulged her essential femininity, buying all sorts of interesting knick-knacks which made the opening of her suitcases from her sorties abroad an enormous amount of personal fun and pleasure for everyone. She was greatly invigorated, and also triumphant in regard to her Cambridge mission. Alastair quickly resigned himself to being catapulted abroad for a further degree. As Elizabeth remarked, "Mother was very good at throwing us out of the nest." Her own turn was not far off.

It is necessary from this point to follow the careers of the various members of the family separately, but before doing so, there are some vignettes of life at Turramurra needed to complete the picture over the years. One is provided by a young cousin of Catherine, Venetia Nathan (Nelson), a contemporary of the twins, who describes the somewhat daunting Mackerras parties for the young. "They didn't dance," she said. "They didn't do ordinary things like that, they had party games — like playing charades and such things which I used to hate. And they used to all sing at the top of their voices and stand in front of you conducting! It was just somehow typical Mackerras. They didn't go in for social graces." Her husband, Jeremy Nelson, senior English master at Sydney Grammar and a recently published poet, added, "They have a family culture, you know. To be a Mackerras is a sub-culture!"

Joan tells of a special relationship she developed with Neil at this time. They had both signified very early their intention of joining the Roman Catholic Church and had done so as soon as the agreement with their father allowed. Joan had also had some difficulty settling to study, and he chose her as a correspondent while he was on the farm at Casino. He was aware that both his parents and Alastair, though sympathetic towards him, found even a temporary turning away from the intellectual life extremely strange, if not inexplicable. "I remember how much I enjoyed getting these long personal letters," Joan recalled. "Neil told me all about the dairy, but also all his thoughts on life. I was still at school and I thought he was a wonderful brother to write to me in this way." It was part of the catharsis. He returned, decided, after all, to complete his course at the university and the pair found time for some companionable hours together in the late afternoons listening to recordings of such things as 'the Sibelius Fifth Symphony and the Brahms Violin Concerto'.

Joan had become a keen student at PLC and made a lasting friendship with a fine scholar, Helen Granowski, who was also a violinist and had had a schoolgirl crush on Charles which she had expressed in extravagant, well-turned verse; she later became headmistress of St Hilda's School at Southport, Queensland and subsequently, principal of Canberra Girls Grammar School. She is still in touch with the Mackerrases. Friendships such as these, made at Turramurra and earlier, as with John Parkinson, were formative in many ways.

"I was so strongly influenced by Catherine Mackerras in those days," Dr Parkinson recalled, "that I gave up my high Anglican Church — I used to attend Christ Church St Lawrence in the city — and became a convert to Catholicism for a time." This was also probably in temporary youthful rebellion against his own background. "My aunt was that somewhat strange woman, Una de Burgh," he said, "very high Anglican and rather predatory, of whom Patrick White lived in terror when he was a twelve-year-old, as he recalled in his memoirs recently. She was in charge of the choristers at St James and asked his mother, *When are we going to have him for the choir?* in tones which made him pray that his voice would crack immediately! She was, in fact, notorious for saying very sharp things about people and Mrs Mackerras expected her to be very nasty indeed to her after my conversion. But she was not, she was nice to her and referred to her as being a very warm-hearted person. I mention this because it is the strongest possible testimony to that warmth which she did indeed have, in spite of the hardness which she also had and the ability to be critical."

This is reinforced by David Mackerras' wife, Hilary, a young school teacher who shared his enthusiasm for sailing and his fondness for Alan, but found the Mackerrases extremely high-powered and the effort of standing up for yourself, so that you weren't completely swamped, difficult indeed. "I liked Aunt Catherine but she was such a brilliant woman, I felt I couldn't measure up to her," she said. "Somehow she seemed to sense these things, and every now and then, she'd see you were there and have a gentle touch for you — she had real kindness."

The fact that this warmth and gentleness was so conspicuously lacking in her relationship with Alan led to another Mackerras phenomenon, known as 'father's gems'. Alan genuinely liked women and particularly enjoyed the company of gentle, pretty girls amongst the family friends. When one of them visited, he would encircle her with an arm and remark, "Isn't she a gem?" They were often asked sailing. "Janie Lemann was one of Dad's gems," said Alastair, "and so were several of Frank Lawes' daughters — Mary and Janny — he loved them. We were all far too noisy for him." Elizabeth agreed, "Yes, something went wrong. We were all too overwhelming. He was a very peaceful sort of person and that's how he would have liked it to be."

Amidst all these complexities, practical things of a formative nature also occurred. Neil, with just one subject to complete his Arts degree, found time on his hands and since he was actively interested in the Liberal Party, applied for and received a job as one of Billy Hughes' two secretaries. There followed a remarkable three weeks in a particularly beautiful, cloudless, autumn-leafed April in Canberra. It was 1950, just following the election of Menzies and the Liberal-Country Party Government. "Billy was actually a much more important person before the 1949 election when the Chifley Government was in power and he was a member of the Opposition," said Neil. "When I was with him, he was really just an elder statesman. I got on very well with him, but I never knew what I was supposed to be doing and consequently didn't last long — none of his secretaries did. They had the same problem." He worked again on a dairy farm to earn some money, and Catherine, as a shareholder in MLC, contacted that company and found that there was an opening for him. He became a fulltime member of their staff and the General Manager, A.F. (now Sir Frederick) Deer, suggested to him, after he had completed his Arts course, that he take another degree. He chose Law.

Meanwhile, young Malcolm was spurred to an intense interest in politics by Neil's studying of election figures and discussions with him on dramatic happenings such as the 1951 double dissolution of parliament when the Labor-controlled Senate blocked the Menzies government's Commonwealth Bank Bill. By 1953, both Malcolm and Colin were at Sydney Grammar, with the latter a year ahead and being taught Mathematics by Alastair who, on his return with his Cambridge degree, had been appointed to the staff of the School. In May that year a separate election for half the Senate was held. Neil, who was a member of the Liberal Party, went to Mr Menzies' election meeting in North Sydney, and, at Malcolm's urging, took the 12 year old twins with him. Catherine had the knack of imbuing confidence in them all and Malcolm had his very good share, with a manner which increasingly resembled her own, though physically he resembled his father. After the Prime Minister's speech, Malcolm, nervous but determined, stood up and asked, "If the government loses the Senate election, sir, will you arrange for a sitting of parliament before June 30 so that you can get your bills through?" "It's not a bad idea," replied Mr Menzies smiling, "but unfortunately it can't be done. There's a Coronation." He was later introduced to the Prime Minister who told him, "You remind me of myself at your age." This was reported in the press in the morning in an article entitled *Schoolboy's Advice for Mr Menzies* and he thus made quite an auspicious start to his innovative and controversial career in political commentary.

Alan, together with a longtime colleague, Jack Rollo, had the distinction at this time of being seconded to the newly formed Electricity Commission of NSW, set up to plan an integrated high-voltage transmission system in the State. "For the first time several large power stations were being constructed on the coalfields some distance from the main Sydney load centre," commented John Sproule who received an appointment to Alan's staff, "and also the Snowy Mountains Scheme was being started." The principal aim of the latter was to utilise the water resources of the Snowy Mountains area for electricity production and for irrigation along the Murray and Murrumbidgee Rivers. Alan concentrated most of his work in the Sydney area and on transmission from the Snowy Mountains Scheme. He had tried frequently over the years to interest his children in power stations and the generation of electricity and had at last struck a chord with young Malcolm who enjoyed being taken about the sub-stations and had therefore become, for a time, a little closer to him than his other sons, though he took great pride in Alastair's ability in mathematics and his appointment at Sydney Grammar. Certainly, on this occasion, all the younger members of the family enjoyed being taken by him to the Snowy Mountains for the opening of the first stage of that great engineering enterprise.

Alan Mackerras at Harpenden about 1957.

Colin's comment on his relationship with his father at this early point was that he felt that he somehow mistrusted him. It seems likely that Alan, seeing the formidable young intellect grow, together with an overall capacity and exuberance very much allied to that of Catherine, with whom Colin had a close bond, probably felt himself outside.

Elizabeth's friend, Janie Lemann (Breden), has vivid memories of the younger members of the family in those days. She shared with Elizabeth a dislike of school but they made up for it with their extra-curricular actitivies which ranged from running tennis tournaments on the Lemann court to performances of the various shorter ballets in the Lemann drawing room, to which, with the sublime confidence of the young, they invited the neighbourhood. "We were probably awful," she observed, "but we had enormous fun. Malcolm was captain of the gramophone — an old wind-up one with 78s which he was always having to turn and change. Our best effort was *Invitation to the Dance* — Spectre de la Rose — with Colin as the rose. He was tremendously funny. He had a high spiritedness, a freshness of spirit somehow . . . " So their happy creativity continued, and Colin also, around this time, used to ride Elizabeth's pony across the district for piano lessons with the eminent Sydney musician and teacher, Dorothy White.

As the twins grew, Alan was gratified to find one or other of them quite frequently appearing at his side by the telescope in the garden; they would then listen to his explanations and try themselves to pick the constellations he pointed out. Both were to retain an interest in astronomy and Malcolm later actually bought a telescope himself.

Nevertheless, at *Harpenden*, Catherine remained the dynamo, the engine that drove the family, as their friend, Tim Yates, who shared their love of music and was a frequent visitor, aptly remarked. She presided over the household with enormous zest. She dissected Shelley and Keats, Shakespeare and Dickens over the vegetable peelings, somewhere on hand a glass of sherry or red wine — white she dimissed as not wine at all. *Was Hamlet mad or was he pretending to be mad?* Joan would ask, and she'd launch into the subject with gusto, with a separate dissertation on the character of Polonius and a dash outside to see the state of affairs for the night's number at dinner. Alan had made for them a device which was hung at the door, with the names of the various members of the family, three holes against each and a peg which they pushed into place as they left in the morning to indicate whether they would be IN, OUT or LATE for dinner.

In the midst of all this, Catherine wrote fine articles with a literary flavour for various journals, but principally the *Catholic Weekly*. She discoursed on everything from the collaboration of Lord Byron with her own ancestor, the musician Isaac Nathan, to *Beethoven in the Light of his Letters* and found the latter 'violent and uncharitable to his friends, ungrateful to his patrons, dishonest with his publishers, and self-righteous'! It is interesting to note that she was not exempt from the sudden doubts and loss of confidence which afflict most writers and often turned to Nancy for reassurance when in the throes of her articles, and later, books. During these years she also studied Thomas Aquinas and undertook Daily Devotional broadcasts for the ABC in which she was able to make authoritative comments on such things as St Francis de Sales' *Introduction*

Catherine, author and matriarch.

to a Devout Life, declaring that 'he was not only a great master of the spiritual life, but a master of French prose as well.'

"She used to get your ideas out and wring them by the neck," remarked Rodney Knock, a teaching colleague of Alastair at Sydney Grammar. The present Master of the Lower School there, John Sheldon, contemporary and friend of Colin, commented, "She was an outstanding intellectual woman of her time. Just to hear her talking was an education"; and the Headmaster of Edgecliff Prep School, Peter Harwin, while commenting on the essential stabilising effect of Alan on the family, said, "She had a sort of electricity in her — she affected so many lives and had this great love for the young." "A fascinating woman," Tim Yates summed up and went on to describe her reigning at the table, where, if her cat hopped up on the sideboard and tucked into the roast lamb, she didn't notice, kept on with her engrossing talk and was likely to ask later "Would you care for some more lamb?"

He remembered also their 'Passion night' each year, to which Joan invited people — "They played the St Matthew Passion from beginning to end, with about thirty people crammed into the lovely sitting room, some sitting on the floor, some on arms of chairs, all draped around the room and Catherine in the middle of everything. Some had scores, some didn't. She'd have made marvellous things to eat. Great nights. Other times I'd visit and we'd sit and talk and she'd dispense great steins of beer — she loved to slosh these around herself." A Rabelaisian touch which somehow fits her in these years. This friend, who also admired Alan very much and sailed with him occasionally — 'bobbing about with his little thermos and basket, well organised, a gentle character with a nice sense of humour' — felt that he had more influence over Catherine than was realised. He added, "To live in that house you really needed ear plugs and the temperament of a saint not to get trampled to death. Marvellous people, but it was like living at a railway station." He was a particular friend of Joan and Neil — "Both enormously musical. I remember Neil being terribly amused about the first three or four notes of the overture of *Figaro* — that anyone should have thought of starting with such a funny little phrase! I've never forgotten it — an intellectual musical thing — it just tickled hell out of Neil. Great fun. A very knowledgeable man."

Amongst the assembled family at this time Elizabeth provides us with a glimpse of Catherine in her lioness role. She was a recalcitrant pupil at PLC, Pymble, not interested in things scholastic and longing to devote her time to ballet for which she had formed a passion. The headmistress had a word with Catherine on the subject, suggesting that it would be better for Elizabeth to leave school than to continue with her present difficult attitude towards it and towards authority. "She is a happy child at home, very good," Catherine told her, adding with magnificent illogical partisanship, "so, if she is not good at school, then there is something wrong with the school." She withdrew Elizabeth from the school forthwith and sent her to the one available full-time ballet school in Sydney. Alastair, on hearing of the fracas with the headmistress. demurred, "That was not right." And it was not, but it filled Elizabeth with confidence, spurred her to work and set her on the path she was thereafter to take.

Similarly, several years later, when Colin, who had repeated his Leaving Certificate because he had been too young for acceptance at the university the first year he'd passed, amassed First Class Honours in French and German, Second Class Honours in Maths I and II and A's in all subjects, while Malcolm managed 3 A's and 3 B's, Catherine remarked to him, "Oh, how disappointing not to get First Class Maths," and to his twin, "Malcolm, your pass was very good, very good indeed." This conversation still brings a somewhat wry smile to Colin's face — he was close to his mother and wanted her approval — but she classified Malcolm, accurately, as 'a late developer', and it was he who needed encouragement.

Her instinct for her children, whatever came, the ability to influence events and set them on the right course, was infallible. The turning to Catholicism, which had had such a disruptive effect on the marriage, led to varying decisions by the children, as we shall see, but was enriching more than divisive.

So, we leave the combined family to look at the separate pursuits of each, with Alan on the eve of a new development in his own career, highly regarded professionally, president of the British Astronomical Association, a board member of Visitors of the Sydney Observatory, a greatly respected yachtsman who never carried a protest flag, and his extraordinary wife, in full matriarchal sail.

Chapter 4

Charles

Charles arrived in London in the English spring of 1947, oboe to hand, eager as always to get quickly on with his life and was able to persuade the director of Sadler's Wells Opera to take him on as second oboist. The company was about to go on tour and extra musicians were needed. This appointment was to prove crucial to his whole career as was the tour itself to his personal life.

Amongst the orchestra, his eye fell upon the first clarinettist, a fair-haired young Englishwoman, named Judy Wilkins, with whom he promplty fell in love. It was a 13-week tour and they travelled to Southsea, Bournemouth, Leicester, Manchester, Liverpool, Belfast — a veritable litany of historic names and places. "We got to know each other as well in that time as we would have in six months otherwise," Judy remarked, but was also probably swept off her feet by the lively Australian whose musical talents had always been accompanied by an infectious zest for living. In turn, it seems likely that the pleasantly rounded Judy, with her incisive voice, firm opinions and warm, direct personality, appealed to him instinctively; these were qualities he knew and appreciated.

When they reached Gloucestershire, she took him to her home at Cheltenham to meet her family and they discovered that her sister, who had been a WREN during the war and had visited Australia, remembered Charles as an oboist with the Sydney Symphony Orchestra. He was greeted warmly. By the end of the tour they had decided to marry and Charles put a call through to Sydney to introduce Judy to his family. Catherine's excitement and exclamations as she 'met' her prospective daughter-in-law were, however, tempered with some misgiving. It did seem precipitate and he was still very young. She immediately got in touch with a Croal relative in London, asking her, Charles recalls, 'to give Judy the once over, so to speak'. Fortunately for Catherine's peace of mind and harmony generally, she received glowing accounts and the prospective bride emerged with flying colours.

During those formative summer months, Charles' other vital step was the undertaking of repetiteur work and conducting backstage. The Sadler's Wells organisation was complex. The original Sadler's Wells Theatre had had the ballet company with such names as Robert Helpmann and Margot Fonteyn, and although it had now moved to Covent Garden it was still called Sadler's Wells Ballet. However, there was another more junior company, known as Sadler's Wells Theatre Ballet, which worked in conjunction with Sadler's Wells Opera, doing ballet within opera as required in such productions as *The Bartered Bride* and *Die Fledermaus*. The theatre ballet also put on separate performances, particularly on long provincial tours, which meant that two orchestras were needed and a great many orchestral players, which, together with his ex-Professor of Oboe status, was the reason that the young Australian had been able to get in at once. "Then," he remarked, "I'd always been told that the right way to go about becoming a conductor was to get into an Opera House and be a dogsbody and slowly work your way up. So that's what I did. I told the director, Norman Tucker, that I was joining Sadler's Wells in order to help fulfil my ambition to become a conductor. And I did all this rehearsing and backstage work." He also took private lessons from the conductor, Michael Mudie.

During the tour, lunching one day in a café, he met a Czech who mentioned to him that applications were currently being invited by the British Council and the Czechoslovakian Government for a scholarship, available for a year's study in Prague in any one of the arts or the Slavonic languages. He put in an application and did not think much more about it, since he was aware that there would be competitors of considerable standing from all over the British Commonwealth.

When they returned, he and Judy were married at Bishop's Cleeve church, the little Anglican church in North Cheltenham to which her family belonged. Charles, unlike the majority of his brothers and sisters, had not been strongly influenced personally by Catherine's conversion and his early years at the Jesuit school, St Aloysius, and had not become a Catholic. "The old Jesuit saying, 'Give me a boy till he's seven' was right with the others, though not in my case," he commented. "But I was very affected by the artistic side of it. The fact of my mother becoming a Catholic meant that I understood the Catholic view on art, particularly music — the Mozart Masses, the Schubert Masses, Verdi's Requiem, the religious scenes in the Verdi operas — all Catholic biassed — these things have had an influence on me." So it seems that Catherine's search for spiritual fulfilment, and the controversial religious issue within the family which had taken its toll on her marriage, served, with this eldest son, to increase his understanding and appreciation of some of the world's great music.

They had been married only a matter of weeks when he learnt that he had won the scholarship to Czechoslovakia and was to study conducting at the Prague Academy of Music under the famous Vaclav Talich, conductor of the Czech Philharmonic Orchestra. He was jubilant. But there was a major snag. The British Council did not take at all kindly to the fact that here *Came two young lovers lately wed*. The scholarship consisted of a living allowance — the tuition itself was free — and it was not meant to include two. "There was a terrible fuss when I wanted to take my wife," he recalls. "The British Council had arranged this with the Czechoslavakian authorities and they didn't want me to have the impediment of a wife, which they imagined would fritter away the allowance."

However, *omnia vincit amor*, and the two were determined not to spend a year apart. Judy wrote to the Prague Academy of Music under her maiden name and enrolled as a student of clarinet. She was accepted, the authorities were not fooled, but nothing further was said. Before they left, an aunt of Judy's introduced them to a Czechoslovakian friend, Eva Hustoles, who was studying in London and she arranged accommodation. This was a boon, for immediate post-war conditions there were very difficult, as in all European countries, and any sort of housing was at a premium. They were fortunate to find the Hustoles family friend, Mrs Hoftichova, whose flat they took in Prague, very friendly, but also non-English speaking. They set about learning the language immediately. There was no time for sightseeing for the pair — it was straight off to their respective courses at the Academy of Music.

In Sydney, the enterprising ABC was now encouraging young musicians such as Geoffrey Parsons and Richard Bonynge, while the twenty year old Joan Sutherland, a secretary, was two years away from her first Sun Aria and Mobil Quest wins and was beginning to enchant the musical societies of elegant suburbia. The success of the twenty-one year old Mackerras, whom the ABC had launched on his career, made headlines — PRAGUE SCHOLARSHIP FOR YOUNG MUSICIAN — and in the music magazine *Tempo*, Curt Prerauer commented: 'We never had any doubt about Mackerras's talent, but we thought his conducting last year of Mozart's *Bastien* was not in keeping with the demands of the work. We are looking forward to Mackerras's achievements after he has finished his studies . . . (for they) will put his talent into the right light.'

Nobody was more aware of this need than Charles himself and he flung himself into his studies with Talich; at the same time, by immediate chance, he developed an intense interest in the works of the Czech composer, Leos Janacek. On his arrival, one of the first people he met at the Academy was a fine young oboist, Jiri Tancibudek, who urged him to go and see the Janacek opera, *Katya Kabanova*, which Talich was currently conducting. It was a revelation. "I was absolutely bowled over by this marvellous music that I'd never dreamt existed," he recalled. "I hardly knew the composer's name . . . "

It was another key point in his career; he determined to make a particular study of Janacek's works during his stay in Prague. Talich considered Janacek's unusual method of orchestrating, in which he paid little attention to the balance of instruments against each other and in relation to the singers, too primitive, and had re-orchestrated the opera before performing it. This whetted Charles' appetite further. He spent long hours poring over these highly distinctive scores, including the appallingly scratched about, crookedly written, difficult to decipher originals; he also examined the different editions of the works. The composer had died in 1928, and from 1919 had been Professor of Composition at Brno (Brünn) Conservatory, so that there were many of his pupils still in Prague who were only too happy to talk to the Australian about him, for he had been a strong creative force in their lives. It must be said that for non-musicians, becoming acquainted with Janacek's music is like plunging into some wild mountain stream. There is an elemental quality which there is no escaping; the mood and taste for it has to be acquired. It was manna to Charles. What was more he had an inbuilt love for exploring orchestral scores and the instincts of a musicologist were as strong in him as those impelling him towards conducting.

He was working for as many hours as he could cram into the days and nights and his weight had dropped to nine stone which was precisely that of Judy. Food rationing was still very much in force and conditions generally made him realise just how grim they must have been under the Germans during the war. "It was my first taste of what you could call 'real life'," he told an interviewer later, "I simply had not realised the situation during the war in Australia." A doctor recommended extra milk coupons but the real salvation came from Eva Hustoles and her family who had a big farm outside Prague and invited the pair to spend Christmas with them. "My mother loved entertaining and my father was a great lot of fun too," said Eva, "and we had a distillery and made our own *slivovice* — plum brandy. So, although there were shortages, we managed very well."

When Eva's mother saw Charles, she threw her hands in the air and exclaimed, "Oh, this Charlies, he ees so skinny — more cream — we must feed him up!" This she proceeded to do. They had a wonderful Christmas which was also shared by the big, square-cut, lively Czech whom Eva was about to marry, Frank Plodr, who says, "He is a good scout, Charles. He enjoyed the beer, and a little wine and music, and parties and the plum brandy. We were young and he really got to know us, the Czech people, very well. It was after the war and before the communists came and for a short time we were happy — we were free." He went on to speak of the Slavonic uninhibitedness in the Czech character, a sharing of laughter, tears, song and dance. "It is all reflected in our music," he added, "and he understood that. He saw the country start to bloom . . . " Eva agreed that Charles was able at this time to capture the Czech spirit. The four sometimes saw the dawn in together in Prague, with the help of the home-brewed *slivovice*, and they have a standing joke from those days of the confusion between the Czech word for 'cheers' — *Nadrazi*! — and 'railway station' — *na zdravi*. Charles initially found some difficulty in distinguishing between the two, and has always since greeted them, tongue in cheek, in their language, with "Railway station!"

The light-heartedness which generated these things was brief indeed. The Communist *coup* occurred before Charles had finished his studies and the whole pattern of life changed. Vaclich Talich did not meet with the favour of the new authorities but continued to give lessons privately to the young Australian and several other pupils at his villa outside Prague. The Hustoles family suffered severely; their farm was taken over by their employees and they were banished to a small attic. Mrs Hoftichova, with whom the Mackerrases lived in Prague and of whom they had grown very fond, found it almost impossible to eke out the rations. "You'd find," said Charles, "that if you didn't get up at 6 o'clock and stand in a queue to get milk and bread and such things, you just didn't get anything." It was the first and only time in his life that he took to early rising, for, like most musicians, he is not given to communicating with the outside world before 9.30 or more in the morning.

They returned to London in the autumn of 1948 and he received an appointment at Sadler's Wells as assitant conductor and coach to the opera singers. As the settling in process began, a letter arrived from Eva Plodr. She and Frank had married, escaped across the border and arrived at the German refugee camp at Eschau. They had only the clothes they stood up in, there was very little food, and they would be glad of any help. Judy made up a clothes parcel — prominent amongst the items in the collective memory of the Plodrs being a pair of women's green corduroy slacks in which Eva lived for the long months, mounting almost to a year, it took to get permission for them to emigrate to Queensland. The friendship, forged in such unusual circumstances has remained, as has that with the fine oboist, Jiri Tancibudek, whom they also assisted — his playing subsequently delighted Melbourne concert-goers and now enriches the musical life of Adelaide where he helped form the Adelaide Wind Quintet. The Mackerras musical engagements in Czechoslovakia over many years have ensured the renewal of friendship with Mrs Hoftichova, the Hustoles family, and other friends of their student days.

Towards the end of 1948, at Sadler's Wells, Charles was given an unexpected opporunity to conduct a performance of Strauss's *Die Fledermaus*. He received an approving notice and from then on, working at the operatic repertoire, was occasionally brought to the attention of the critics. But more was needed.

They were living at Notting Hill Gate in an upper floor maisonette and Judy was expecting their first child, when Catherine arrived on her Cambridge mission on Alastair's behalf in 1949. She and Judy found an immediate *rapport*, and she helped them through a very difficult time. "I was still working when she arrived," said Judy, "and then my baby was born prematurely. Our daughter, Fiona, had this very perilous start to life and had to be kept in a nursing home for weeks. The fees were high, something like five pounds a week. It came to about eighty pounds, a huge sum then and we didn't have any money to spare at all in those days." Catherine, in her swift, generous way, covered this expense for them, shared their concern, lightened their worries and went on her way. "An amazing lady," said her grateful daughter-in-law. Indeed, the role of wellspring of the family was natural to her, but her great virtue was that she was not intrusive with it.

The following two years were crucial. Charles had yet to make his real impact and circumstances were conspiring towards just that. A useful preliminary was his first television appearance with an engagement by the BBC to conduct their opera orchestra in a performance of *La Bohême* with Australia's 'singing policeman', Kenneth Neate, who had leapt to fame in New York and Italy in the role of Rudolph.

Then, importantly, for it was 1950, the year before the expiration of the Gilbert & Sullivan copyright, he began to put into operation his long-held idea of arranging some of the exhilarating music from the opera in a new form. He saw the opportunity which presented itself at Sadler's Wells, with the opera and ballet companies housed in the same theatre, and the fact that the Sadler's Wells Ballet at Covent Garden was doing all the classics — *Swan Lake, Coppelia, Giselle* and the other big ballets — while Sadler's Wells Theatre Ballet was invariably looking round for smaller

Charles conducts at Sadler's Wells, 1948.

His wife, Judy, about this time.

things to do — preferably new English ballet. He had got to know the ballet people, in particular, the Theatre Ballet's director, Peggy van Praagh. Furthermore, the gifted South African, John Cranko, had just begun to work with them as a choreographer. "There we were," Charles commented, "the South African and the Australian, and Peggy van Praagh brought us together — for which I am eternally grateful." This was, in fact, one of the many formative influences of Peggy van Praagh (later Dame Peggy, artistic director, Australian Ballet), on Australians in the world of the arts, and there were many, including the young Charles Lisner, then dancing with Sadler's Wells Ballet at Covent Garden and soon to found the Queensland Ballet Company, who had reason to be grateful for her practical encouragement.

Charles immediately began work with Cranko and the pair, who shared a similar verve and humour, created the ballet, *Pineapple Poll*, based on

John Cranko, choreographer

Charles with Elaine Fifield, checks the score of 'Pineapple Poll'

Gilbert's *The Bumboat Woman's Story* from the Bab Ballads and a selection of Sullivan music from a number of the operas.

Judy is unlikely to forget the Cranko-Mackerras duo in their creative sessions at the Notting Hill Gate maisonette. "By then," she said, "we had a second daughter, Catherine, named for her grandmother, and somehow the children slept happily through it all. John Cranko used to dance around our sitting room while Charles played extracts from the operas, with John saying, 'Now, I need another ten bars of this sort of music to finish off this idea . . . ' They just developed the thing together, Charles at the keyboard and John literally trying things out. It went on till all hours of the night." So the light-hearted confection which has delighted so many was born. They presented it that summer of 1951 at Sadler's Wells, with Charles conducting an orchestra of fifty, the décor and costumes by Osbert Lancaster, and with Australian dancer, Elaine Fifield, as the sailor-infatuated Poll. It was an immediate success, rated the most amusing ballet for years, and is now one of the staples of ballet repertoire. Columbia did a recording of 'the new Sadler's Wells favourite', and *The Observer's* critic commented, 'Musically, this is an English *Boutique Fantasque*: an unexpectedly fortunate result of the recently expired copyright in Sullivan's music. The intoxicating tunes have been brilliantly arranged and scored by Charles Mackerras (who also conducts): even the faithful should recognise his fine taste and abstain from pedantic reproach.'

His name was now before the public. But that, as he said, was 'on the light side'. On the serious side, he was able to follow it up by persuading the director of Sadler's Wells Opera, Norman Tucker, to stage Janacek's opera, *Katya Kabanova*. He made a tape of it at the BBC, played it to him and convinced him. He was to be assistant conductor at rehearsals. Then, as so often happens with the performing arts, whether it's a Shirley

MacLaine or a Charles Mackerras, chance precipitated him into the major role. The conductor, Michael Mudie, became ill and Charles had to take over the opera and conduct it. This really launched him on his career, for it was the first time a Janacek opera had been staged in England. "It was a *succés d'estime*," he said, "it brought me to the attention of many musicians, opera people and critics who had not noticed me before — or not much."

They moved to their first house at Finchley and his determination now, as he slogged away widening his knowledge of the operatic repertoire at Sadler's Wells, was eventually to put before the British public the whole of Janacek's works, and at the same time to make a detailed study of Handel and Mozart scores, for baroque music was his other great love and he was looking for insights on ornamentation as the composers themselves would have expected it. So he began what was to become intensive research on the subject and over the years became well-known for his work as a musicologist. "In regard to baroque music," he said, "you are either a Bach and Haydn man or a Handel and Mozart — it seems to be impossible to be both."

The Sydney press, meanwhile, reported such diverse things as his standing in at a concert at the Albert Hall for the Japanese conductor Takashi Assahina, and his attendance, together with Melbourne painter, William Dargie, Sydney pianist, Dorothy Roberts and the Australian High Commissioner, Sir Thomas White, at a farewell for Sir Eugene Goossens, who was returning to Sydney. This party was held, they reported, 'in the huge reception room of the Dowager Lady Swaythling's Kensington home' — a phrase which sounds like vintage Noel Coward, who was indeed writing his witty commentaries on society at the time and had just launched his new comedy, *Relative Values*, in the West End.

Alastair, who had graduated from Cambridge and was teaching at a school in Sussex, went up to London for operas and concerts whenever he could and the two brothers saw something of each other, a pattern which was to develop as the Mackerras clan began criss-crossing the world with increasing frequency for the furtherance of their careers and with the same appetite and zest as their mother.

In 1953 Charles and John Cranko combined their talents once more and this time, it was their music room at Finchley which resounded to the creation of ballet. Here they produced *The Lady and the Fool* and Charles arranged music from the lesser-known works of Verdi. The ballet was tried out in the counties early in 1954 and was staged in London in the spring, with Kenneth MacMillan as one of the principal dancers, and received very favourable notices. The most interesting of these, written by the distinguished critic, Desmond Shawe-Taylor, appeared in the journal *Gramophone* and read in part: 'The story is unsubstantial but attractive . . . the score . . . lively, melodious, rhythmical, brilliant . . . none of the tunes is familiar though several jog the musical memory . . . some of the music he sets simply, some he embellishes with a *cantabile* counter subject; sometimes he orchestrates that which is patently early Verdi in the manner of *Otello* or *Ballo*; and sometimes he throws all to the winds and slaps on orchestral colour more appropriate to Richard Strauss. Climaxes are too many for the dimensions and content of the ballet . . . but the score is fundamentally apt for dancing, with tunes that delight the senses without distracting them from attention to the ballet.'

A mini-migration of Mackerrases from Sydney to London was occurring at this point, for on Alastair's return, Catherine set sail with Joan and Elizabeth, the former for advanced violin study, the latter to study ballet. The three, having disembarked at Naples, had a few weeks in Italy, and now arrived in London. They were all delighted at the reunion and the house at Finchley flat rang with resonant Mackerras voices, as it had resounded during the creation of the recent ballet, which they were able to see in its first London production.

There was now a change of direction in Charles' career; he left Sadler's Wells and was appointed conductor of the newly formed BBC Concert Orchestra. Before taking up the appointment, which he had sought in order to widen his repertoire as a conductor, he and Judy had their small daughters minded and went for a holiday to Austria with Catherine and Joan. In between driving about the beautiful alpine country, attending the Salzburg Festival and generally enjoying it all, Charles was able to spend some time in Vienna on his research into 18th century music as exemplified in the works of Mozart. He wanted to build up his chamber music repertoire, but also to begin the study of early performing editions of their scores in regard to vocal ornamentation, particularly in the Mozart operas and Handel oratorios.

It is a controversial matter as to whether or not the music of this period should be played today as it would have been then, that is, with the ornaments, such as appoggiaturas and trills, taken for granted and expected to be heard by the composers, but not indicated in their scores. Since Charles was to become a leading exponent of playing in the baroque style, we must pause to examine the subject.

In the 18th century celebrated singers occupied a position somewhat similar to that of the modern pop idol. Musicologist, Fritz Spiegl, notes that 'they were adored by their public and pandered to not only by the opera directors and leader-conductors but also by the composers.' He said, for instance, that Handel's *Largo* (from *Xerxes*) became celebrated not because it is such a beautiful melody but because it was a wonderful vehicle for carrying the singer's interpretation of it. The singer was expected to be enough of a musician to compose his own embellishments and the merits of his vocal technique were often judged by this. The practice was open to abuse, as some singers began to overdecorate, and by the end of the 18th century the practice was abandoned and composers began to write their vocal music exactly as they wanted it.

"Mozart was on the borderline," said Charles, "but I believe that he expected his music to be performed following the accepted convention of his time and that, for instance, he only wrote out appoggiaturas on specific occasions when the interpretation might be in doubt."

It is known from Mozart's letters that his music was not exempt from 'the flexible gullets' (his own phrase) of singers who added embellishments to suit themselves, that he had no very strong views about it and showed no disapproval of the practice. Famous European singing teachers of the day, such as Corri, Urbani and Mancini, who also wrote on the subject, all agree on the necessity for singers to use appoggiaturas at the end of phrases, though the composer as a rule simply wrote two quavers on the same note. Charles cites many examples from the *Figaro* score, and used Corri's arrangement of it as an illustration in a heated exchange he had with an anti-appoggiatura musicologist in *Records and Recording*.

Then there are other disputed matters, such as the problem of playing trills in the style of the period, since they were played upside down as compared with the way they are played now, that is, a baroque musician played the upper note first, while a modern musician has to be specially requested to do so. Another complex problem Charles found in his search for authenticity was that of *notes inégales*, that is, a row of notes written as if they should be played evenly but which were, in fact, played unevenly, almost as if dotted. "This problem," he said, "is particularly acute in Handel who composed so fast that he wrote some notes dotted and others undotted, seemingly carelessly. Trying to guess his wishes is very, very hard." He endeavours always, when conducting both Handel and Mozart, to interpret those wishes as nearly as possible and marks the orchestra's scores accordingly but he agrees with Spiegl that there is no point in trying to put the clock back with the use of early instruments. He is able to get his baroque effects with modern musicians playing modern instruments.

This study took place over a long period. In the meantime, back in 1954, he conducted the ANZAC concert, with sixteen Australian and New Zealand artists, in the Festival Hall in the presence of the young Queen and received some high praise from Vaughan Williams (whose *Serenade to Strings* they performed) and the music critic, Neville Cardus. He then took up his appointment with the BBC Concert Orchestra and found that they required mainly light classical music. He got through a huge repertoire and in the process developed further flexibility and mental agility, for radio work meant that there were often last-minute adjustments and he was sometimes required to conduct a score that had just that moment been thrust at him. "It all stood him in good stead in later years," Judy commented, "but it wasn't really the right job for him — it was a little bit like a music machine."

He stayed, doing five broadcasts a week and some telecasts, for television was now in general use. His smoking, which had been mild, increased with the pressure of work and began to affect his health. Now, with the all-seeing visual medium to contend with, he also had another problem, which was a habit, acquired from Catherine, of chewing his tongue in moments of deepest concentration. Always pragmatic, he went to a hypnotist with the intention of conquering both. He succeeded as far as smoking was concerned but nothing has ever been able to cure the tongue chewing habit, to which, in fact, all the family are occasionally prone.

During this time, he had the opportunity to make a number of recordings, a notable one of which was with the Australian, Peter Dawson, of the glorious baritone voice which echoes in the memories of thousands. There can scarcely be an Australian, over forty, alive today who can not recall its rich reverberations, particularly in the song which came to be identified with him —

> There was the band with the curious tone
> Of the cornet, clarinet and big trombone,
> Fiddle, cello, big bass drum,

Flute, bassoon, euphonium,
Each one making the most of his chance
Altogether in the floral dance . . .

The recording Dawson made in April 1955, with Mackerras conducting the London Symphony Orchestra, was stereo, and was the great singer's first and last hi-fi recording. The making of it was a memorable event for the rising young conductor and evidence of this and other historic records are today to be found in the display case in the Australian Music Centre, tucked away in a building at *The Rocks*, one of the oldest quarters of Sydney's waterfront.

In 1956, Charles saw his father again, for the first time in nine years. Alan had gone over for a very specific reason, and the trip proved eventful in many ways, not least of which was in his relationship with his eldest son. "I had almost despised my father," Charles admitted frankly, "but now suddenly I began to really admire him." The truth was that it was the first time he had really seen Alan as a personality in his own right. He was full of interesting and amusing things to say and a charming host. He took Charles and Judy to lunch at his club, reciprocal with the Royal Sydney Yacht Squadron, in London, chose the wine, and generally behaved in a manner which was a revelation to his son.

"When I saw him alone, away from the family," said Charles, "I found such a different, outgoing, interesting person — even prepared to share a bottle of wine! I felt I'd been unfair to him — as I think we all did." And they had, indeed.

Judy found a great deal in common with him; they spoke of the Swiss Alps, which he had just visited, and of the silent grandeur of the snow country. He understood her urge, which she was to fulfil several times, to go on a Himalayan trek. "I rather enjoy living with nothing but a small ruck-sack on my back and throwing away all the trimmings of life," said this wife who fills an indispensable role sorting out her husband's hectic itinerary in the various capitals of the world, "and Alan was a very simple person in that way. He needed very little in life to make him happy." In London, they found that he was happiest going off for the day with a packet of sandwiches and doing such things as looking at the boats at Marlow-on-the-Thames. He had not changed, as the frugal sandwiches indicate, but Charles now saw him also in the light in which his engineering colleagues and sailing friends had always done.

Charles resigned from the BBC soon after this, having established a reputation for both his conducting and arrangements, and set out as a freelance conductor. He did not lack engagements. Some of the most notable were two successive Edinburgh Festival appearances, and others in London with the Goldsbrough Orchestra (which later became the English Chamber Orchestra) and the English Opera Group. The latter was directed by Benjamin Britten, for whom he conducted the world premiere of his new work, *Noye's Fludde*. "He was the greatest musician I had really got to know," he commented. "He knew, in his own music, how every little phrase must sound. And in Mozart, for instance, he was always finding tiny significant contrasts in phrases that appear to be the same but really are not."

Charles Mackerras conducting in London about 1956.

He was now invited on a tour, during the course of which he conducted a number of German orchestras and the Vienna Philharmonic, with critical approval. "Everything started to develop so much," said Judy. "He was asked to conduct all over the world. He went with the English Opera Group to Canada in 1957, things were coming up all over Europe, and in 1958 he did a season in South Africa." The latter was for three months with the Cape Town Municipal Orchestra and it was decided that Judy would stay in London with their two small daughters. In Sydney, with half the family away on university vacation, Catherine made an impulsive decision to join her eldest son, and informing the rest of the clan that it was, 'after all, only halfway', she flew across to Cape Town.

"It was exciting seeing my mother there," Charles recalled, "we hadn't met for four years!" Catherine herself was exuberant and told a Cape journalist how wonderful it all was; the city had been a port of call for her in 1917 and 1925, but now she was really getting to know it with her son. "Cape Town is such a dignified and leisurely city compared to Sydney, which is large and noisy and frenzied," she commented. "I particularly like the 18th century Cape Dutch architecture and I am enjoying staying at Prince Alfred House in the delightful artists' quarter at Waterloo Green, Wynberg . . . " (Charles was staying in a thatched cottage in the same cobbled street). She then elaborated on the interesting connection between Prince Alfred House at the Cape and Prince Alfred Hospital, Sydney, and the fact that her great-grandfather, Dr Charles Nathan, had attended the Prince when on this same journey in 1868, soon after his arrival in Sydney, an Irish fanatic attempted to assassinate him. Revelling in providing footnotes to history — correctly foreseeing an article for herself later — and rejoicing at being with Charles and attending his concerts, she enlivened that South African end of summer for him in her own very typical fashion. One of the concerts which stayed in the memory was with the blind pianist, Georges Themeli, as soloist, playing Grieg and Liszt, following a Brahms overture and preceding Beethoven's Seventh, all to a 'thunderously applauding audience and the orchestra at the top of its form'.

Later that year, in London, Charles' work was noticed by the recording producer for Columbia Records, Walter Legge, regarded as being as fine in his own field as is his wife, the exquisite soprano, Elisabeth Schwarzkopf, in hers. "This meant," said Charles, with his customary directness, "that I was taken up by him for awhile and made some records and did a couple of concerts with her."

One of these concerts, at the Festival Hall, with the Goldsbrough Orchestra and its distinguished leader, Emanuel Hurwitz (very much a baroque man), was particularly memorable and included the highly dramatic *Scena di Berenice* of Haydn and the famous aria *Voi che sapete* from *Figaro*, together with the Rondo, *Al desio, di chi t'adora*, and a special cadenza which Mozart wrote for his wife. The whole performance was given with 18th century ornamentation, and fascinating, musically annotated programme notes were provided. The most memorable recording they made was the beautiful *Elisabeth Schwarzkopf Christmas Album*, with Orchestra, Organ and Mackerras's own arrangements of traditional carols; it has become noted for its lyric quality and the inclusion of such items as the ancient *In dulci Jubilo* and the 17th century German hymn, *Easter Alleluia* which Charles regards as 'one of the noblest melodies in existence'.

An exciting event was now impending. It was the Handel bi-centenary year of 1959 and Charles was becoming known as a Handel specialist, with his distinctive interpretations of the composer's works and his belief that 'the difference between Handel and his contemporaries was his incredible gift for melody, within the framework of a contrapuntal style'. For the celebrations, he was appointed to conduct the *Royal Fireworks Music* as originaly orchestrated by the composer, and with the combination of the original orchestral instruments. "These were," he said, "24 oboes, 12 bassoons, several contra bassoons, 9 horns, 9 trumpets, 3 timpanists, a serpent and several drummers."

This, with the Pro Arte Orchestra, is now a collector's piece. The *Gramophone's* critic observed — 'One of the most breathtaking (sounds) of the year has been the tumult of 57 wind and percussion players giving full expression to all the beauty, dignity and power of Handel's *Fireworks Music* in its original open-air scoring . . . ;' while Desmond Shawe-Taylor of the *Sunday Times* described it as "magnificent", and his colleague, Felix Aprahamian, commented, "A more imaginative, worthy or widely enjoyable bi-centenary tribute to the composer would be hard to envisage . . . an assembly of London's orchestral talent that would have

Charles, about the time of the Handel bi-centenary, 1959.

rejoiced Handel's ear and heart seems to have been infected by the always youthful musical enthusiasm of Mr Mackerras . . . a very remarkable record of some of the simplest and sanest music ever composed in our tonal system . . . '' A memorable occasion altogether for Charles.

Now that he was established in this way, with more work than he could handle, and royalties from *Pineapple Poll* alone providing what would once have represented their entire income, they moved to a big, comfortable home at Southgate in north London. The year also held further joys, for he managed to persuade Sadler's Wells Opera Company that the time was ripe for a revival of the Janacek opera, *Katya Kabanova*. This music he now had in his bones and the critics were quick to observe the added strength and certainty with which he conducted, giving an 'immeasurably superior performance' to that of 1951 and making 'the thrilling music live and move with irresistible purpose'. The result was an opportunity to make another splendid recording with excerpts from the opera and other works of Janacek, including *Jenufa* and the *Sinfonietta* and so to advance his objective of bringing all this modern master's unique music before the British public.

The Australian Broadcasting Commission approached him at this point, asking him to tour Australia in 1960, and so after 13 years he returned home, accompanied by his wife and daughters, Fiona and Catherine. Judy insisted on a sea trip, for she often feared the strains imposed by his unremitting itineraries. She herself relieved him of practical matters, such as the interminable packing of suitcases with dress shirts and clothes for all occasions. "For long performances, like Wagner operas," he remarked, "you need two or three shirts, one for each act. One sweats like a pig." Such things, he knew very surely, would always be on hand when needed. He was fortunate indeed that his wife transferred her musical ambitions to the furtherance of his career. In regard to her own, she was content to keep her hand in by playing in a group with other former orchestral players who found themselves with family commitments; they rehearsed regularly and performed every so often as a *Wind Quintet* at various clubs in London.

After his usual strenuous round, the sea trip seemed interminable and by the time they berthed at Adelaide he had had enough and was very impatient to see his family. They flew the last lap. "I suppose you must be Malcolm!" he said, sorting out the twins at the airport, for they had, after all, been seven-year-olds when he left and were now twenty and at the university. Charles and his wife have strong memories of that first evening with everyone crowded round the big round table at Turramurra. "Our daughters were only nine and ten then," said Judy, "and the noise was incredible. They were all talking at once — except Alan. Suddenly, Fiona just burst into tears . . . " It was, of course, all too much, and the family at once realised how frightening they must have seemed. But nothing could hold the excitement for long. Here they all were, as tumultuous and articulate as ever, *Harpenden* even more leafy and welcoming, and he was home.

Fortunately, there was some breathing space before his tight schedule began; they gave a party to ensure seeing all his old friends and the welkin rang. Then, as the settling in process began, he noticed how pervasive his mother's single-mindedness in regard to religion had become and began arguing with her on the subject. Colin's friend, John Sheldon, born and bred a Catholic, also a keen music lover and often at the house at this time, comments, "The religious arguments went on and on between Charles and his mother, yet it never got to the stage where any personal feeling crept in — in other families someone would have got up and slammed the door. It was very consistent and very hard hitting, but the Mackerrases never let emotion take over in argument and that's why it can go on."

Nevertheless, Catherine seems to have been more wary with her eldest son from now on. Colin observed, "Mother looked up to Charles in almost a strange sort of way — he could dominate her, one of the few people who

Charles and Judy, and daughters Fiona and Catherine in the garden at, Harpenden, on his first visit home, 1960.

could. She deeply disagreed with his attitudes to religion — he was very anti-religious — and after this, she avoided arguing with him any more than she absolutely had to. For instance, although she didn't hesitate to put forth ideas about music in other circumstances, she rarely did with him because she feared that he would disagree with her." The answer to this almost certainly lies in her comment, many years later, in a de Berg interview for the National Library, "Charlie is the one with a touch of what I would call almost genius, near genius . . . "

Press comment on his return was summed up by the *Australasian Post* which commented on the fact that he was 'the youngest conductor in this country's musical history to travel abroad and face the world's finest symphony orchestras'. They were interested to find that he had once arranged music for the radio celebrity Jack Davey, who had only recently died, and quoted his tribute to him, "It would be impossible for me to ever forget the endlessly buoyant Davey's personality."

He also retraced the past with Judy and visited the elderly nun, Sister Mary Lawrence, who had given him his first piano lessons at the convent at Pymble. She was old, frail and delighted to see him. They talked of his experiences. "And what do you actually do for a job, Charles?" she then asked. Very little had changed he saw and when, with their children, they went sailing with Alan aboard *Antares*, there was the same realisation. The younger child, Catherine, began trailing a string in the water, as children love to do, and Alan said, "Don't do that Catherine, bring it in, it doesn't look shipshape at all".

The reprimand remains in Judy's memory. "I suddenly saw why he had turned off his own children," she said. "It was altogether too strict,

MACKERRAS FAMILY at 'Harpenden', 1960, together for Charles' visit: — *Front row: L to R: Elizabeth, Charles, Catherine, Alan, Joan. Back row: Colin, Alastair, Neil, Malcolm.*

too soon, and the fun went out of it.'' Somehow, the scene conjures again the Creagh drawing-room and that distant, unforgiving woman, his mother, obsessively embroidering. There would have been no trailing threads there either. However, Charles was now able to accommodate this aspect of his father within the overall personality which he had seen and understood in London, while Judy on this and subsequent visits, formed a close and fond relationship with Alan, for, like cousin Nancy, she understood his complex nature.

Charles was now catapulted into a strenuous series of concerts with the Sydney Symphony Orchestra, both in the capital and in major provincial centres throughout New South Wales. He noted that the SSO's flautists — his old friend, Neville Amadio, and others — were exceptionally good and demonstrated his own versatility with programmes ranging from a Festival of 20th Century Music to Bach's *St Matthew Passion*. In the midst of this, there was a specially arranged concert at Sydney University, whose turrets and towers had seen members of the family pass through for generations and where his father was now lecturing. There, amidst the carved oak, high leadlights and heraldry of the Great Hall, Charles conducted a string ensemble led by that fine Sydney musician, Donald Hazelwood. It was a memorable and satisfying evening for everyone concerned.

An amusing sidelight of this first trip back was the abstemious Alan's reaction to the habit his son had acquired of fortifying himself, not only with glucose tablets, but about half a bottle of champagne before a major concert and of ensuring that a glass was on hand at interval. His astonishment was compounded when he discovered that only *French* champagne would do. Charles was truly not his father's son in this respect.

Next in his itinerary were concerts with the Queensland Symphony Orchestra in Brisbane where he met again that gifted, resolute Czech, Rudolf Pekarek (the resident conductor), whom he had known in Prague in 1947, and who, in 1934, had founded the Prague Symphony Orchestra (FOK), regarded there as second only to the Czech Philharmonic. Catherine, who had decided to accompany Charles and Judy, shared in the excitement of reunions in Brisbane, not only with friends, but with the Ian Mackerras family.

Ian was then Director of the Queensland Institute of Medical Research, his wife, a Research Fellow, and their son David, Charles' exact contemporary, in the throes of his career in the Department of Electrical Engineering, University of Queensland. The cousins had much to talk about, each moving towards eminence in his own very different field, Charles in the public eye, but with a taste for scholarship, David, in quiet academic pursuits, but on his way to becoming known as a world authority on lightning and in demand at conferences around the globe. Again, Judy forged a friendship which was to endure with this branch of the family. There was a directness, spiked with humour, about this young Englishwoman to which the Mackerrases, noted for their outspokenness, responded; they also found, when the occasion arose, a warmth which they appreciated.

There is an interesting facet of her husband's character, of which he himself is aware, and that is a certain resistance in his first contact with others. "It has happened all my life," he says, "I find I start by being negative about people and I am almost always wrong, because I end up by liking or admiring them." It seems probable that some of his father's reserve, and the remoteness which characterized his parents' relationship, is responsible for this initial aloofness. Colleagues, such as Dame Janet Baker, have commented that while he invariably communicates a contagious enthusiasm for the music they are performing, he is not an easy man to get to know personally. But once that hurdle is over, there emerges, Dame Janet found, a 'terrifically loveable human being.' He has, in fact, a natural exuberance that is never far from the surface and is a man who has inspired a great deal of affection.

After concerts in Melbourne and Adelaide, where he met his friend, the oboist Jiri Tancibudek, it was back to Europe, but with the promise to return for the Australian Opera Season in 1963. It is impossible to follow all the highlights of his musical globe-trotting — which began this time with Hungary, Czechoslovakia, and Holland. Then it was back to his base in London and numerous appearances with such orchestras as the Royal Philharmonic, the New Philharmonia and the London Symphony, also the special joys of the Henry Wood Promenade Concerts at the Albert Hall and the enthusiasm of youthful audiences which he described in one word, "Marvellous."

A highly unusual experience during his return season in Australia, when he visited all mainland capital cities for the ABC, was his participation in one of the Queensland Symphony Orhcestra's celebrated Northern Tours. This involves living on a train for two weeks between Brisbane and Cairns, a journey of around 2000 kilometres, giving concerts at coastal centres *en route* and sleeping aboard while travelling on to the next town for the following night's performance. It was a rugged adventure and Charles, with memories of the family's early obsession with trains, took Judy along to inspect the driver's cabin and coal tender; a moment captured by the QSO's first oboe, Douglas Lockwood, who had known Charles at Sydney Conservatorium and himself studied under Charles' Czech friend, Jiri Tancibudek. The photograph was reproduced some years later in a profile on Charles in the London journal *Opera*. The train was of the antiquated wooden variety with the orchestra's compartments coupled behind carriages carrying livestock. It had no restaurant or refrigeration. A veteran of the Northern Tours, the principal trombone of the QSO, Ron Stevens, a big, solid, immaculately dressed man, commented "Charles and his wife, also the singer, Rosalind Keene and the managers, did have a special carriage with a few comforts, and we all had our own ice-boxes, but there was no air-conditioning and we were often clanging along behind pig and cattle trucks. It wasn't conducive to sleeping well, yet we had to front up every night in a new town and appear to be fresh as daisies . . . "

The visit of the QSO to cities like Rockhampton, Mackay, Townsville and the smaller centres is eagerly awaited each year and people drive in from outlying districts for the occasion, finding the train pulled in, with huge white lettering emblazoned on the sides — QUEENSLAND SYMPHONY ORCHESTRA — a cheerful and satisfying sight. In 1963, the QSO went on tour with a small orchestra of about 46, they played such things as Charles' ubiquitous *Pineapple Poll* at the small towns and at the larger centres, Beethoven's *Pastoral Symphony*. Stevens, who has played with the Royal Philharmonic, London, and also the Melbourne Symphony Orchestra, said, "It's very difficult to do large works with a small orchestra, but Charles didn't throw it away as some conductors have done, nor did he put on an act as some others do — though he might have started off to be a bit smart or sarcastic, he soon remembered you can't do that with Australian musicians, they'll give it back to you. He was genuine in his love of music and he handled it extremely well. I enjoyed working under him."

The orchestra did not fail to observe how beautifuly dressed the singer, Rosalind Keene, and Judy managed to emerge from the sooty train for performances and that Charles was impeccable in tails, as in the capital cities. "At the reception after the performance at places like Rockhampton," Stevens remarked, "he always made a superb, witty speech. His own Australian twang had gone completely but he used to tell them all he was an Australian living overseas — and he'd been born in America and not to hold that against him." Judy, he noticed, was fascinated by the 'Aussie-Ocker' accents and herself somewhat amazed the orchestra by casually dropping the occasional swear word, as did her husband, an accepted practice in London and elsewhere in mixed company in such circles, but not amongst the conservative and often much-maligned Australians.

The orchestra were pleased to find that Charles 'fancied a convivial glass among his colleagues'. Stevens had a friend, Peter Andre, in the recording business in London, about whom Charles was interested to hear, and he was often invited along to the Mackerras carriage for drinks and talk. Like many before and since, Ron Stevens found Charles very good company and a wonderful spinner of tales. "But," said the Queenslander, "I think we provided him with the best. It gets very tiring on these tours and one night when we were doing the *Beethoven Pastoral* — in which the brass section doesn't come in until about the third movement — he looked down as he was conducting and found the whole of the brass section were nodding off — almost fast asleep. He thought, 'My God, what's going to happen when they have to come in? What can I do?' But he needn't have worried, because professionalism is somehow built in to people and as soon as the right chords came, the brass section woke up and played perfectly for him!"

This story of the tropics was, of course, told with great gusto when he returned to England. It went down particularly well at a party of Australian artists held in London at a private home soon after he and Judy returned. It was attended by old friends such as Doug McLean, European Representative for the ABC and previously their Music Supervisor in Victoria, his wife, Pam, the pianist Doug Gameley, flautist Doug Whittaker, Peter Andre, of whom Ron Stevens had spoken, and a number of young singers. A photograph, taken by Whittaker on the occasion, captures the confident high spirits of the many Australian artists who have succeeded in making their presence felt in London over the years.

The mid-sixties saw Charles conducting a great deal at Sadler's Wells, and the productions which showed his particular strengths, thereby gathering plaudits from the critics, were a memorable *Marriage of Figaro*,

108 *Scholars and Gentlemen*

Australian musicians in London at the home of Peter Andre, EMI Executive, Classical Recordings, (back row, 4th left), among them, Charles (2nd row, 2nd right), Judy (1st row, 2nd right), Doug Whittaker (back row, 1st left), pianist Doug Gamley (back row, 2nd right) and the ABC's European Representative Doug McLean and his wife Pam (centre, 2nd row), about 1963.

Britten's *Peter Grimes*, and Janacek's *From the House of the Dead*. Each of these was indicative of his special interests. The Mozart was done with grace notes and ornamentation in the 18th century style of which he was an exponent, and the critics found in it 'a marriage of warmth and wit, shaped with outstanding authority and imagination'. Britten's opera was a revival of a demanding work which had not been performed for some time, the sort of challenge which always appealed to him, and he managed to achieve a gripping production with which he was invited to tour Europe; while the presentation of the Janacek work, the weird drama of convict life in Siberia, drawn from Dostoievsky's book, was something very close to his heart.

Interestingly, the eminent Sunday Times critic, Desmond Shawe-Taylor, remarked on the difficulty of establishing balance in Janacek's music. Charles had always been aware of this himself and once remarked, 'A typical Janacek sound is violins screaming up at the top of their register and trombones growling away in the depths, with nothing in between. Exciting as all this is, singing through it is extremely difficult.' Shawe-Taylor felt that Mackerras welded the music together in this production in a way in which 'the fantastic world of the prison — the brutality, hysterical gaiety, quarrels and boasting — is perfectly expressed with this musical idiom . . . every so often, the prevailing harshness yields suddenly to one of those compassionate Janacek melodies — by contrast, rightly scored — which pierce the heart . . . one such falls like a benediction, first on solo violin, then clarinet, then flute at the moment when dark and sleep and quiet, for a brief moment, descend on the troubled ward . . . Charles Mackerras is a superb Janacek conductor and brought out all the force and tenderness of the score. How sad, and how disgraceful, that London should have lost him to Hamburg!'

This indeed, was a *fait accompli*. After hearing him conduct *Peter Grimes*, Rolf Liebermann, the director of the Hamburg State Opera asked him to become Principal Conductor, He would have 'preferred guesting' but since that was not acceptable and the opportunity too good to miss, he took it on. Judy, as well as the London critics, initially felt rather sad about this. "We let our big house in London to a diplomat and moved lock, stock and barrel," she commented. "It was a very interesting three years, but that move to Germany was rather the end of my playing the clarinet. I couldn't start anything like my Wind Quintet over there and when we came back it was too late to revive it . . ."

Charles found the experience valuable because of the vastness of repertoire he conducted with little rehearsal. As a preliminary test, he had been asked to conduct *Il Trovatore* in German, with one piano rehearsal with the principal singers the day before the performance! The repertory system used in Hamburg means that as many as 60 operas are presented in one year, which also means that they are sometimes done without rehearsal at all. He would have liked to see an admixture of the London and Hamburg systems, with more operas in the former, including a subscription system which ensured support of a new or unfamiliar work, and fewer in the latter, with the season divided and more time for rehearsal. However, it was extremely challenging and he made his American debut with the orchestra in New York in 1967.

At the same time he had the satisfaction of converting them to his 18th century ornamented style of presenting baroque works. This was already accepted in England, as was evident in a production of *The Messiah* which he went across to conduct and record with the English Chamber Orchestra in '67. He also prepared and conducted a new version of Mozart's *Cosi fan tutte* for the Aix-en-Provence Festival and the English National Opera.

About this time, with the pressure of his mounting commitments, he and Judy began looking for somewhere, preferably on the Mediterranean, where they could retreat occasionally. While in Italy, someone suggested the island of Elba, which they had not previously considered, probably because, like most people, they inherited from the schoolroom a vision of gloom and the banished Napoleon casting his pre-Waterloo and St Helena shadow. In fact, they found the island, with its high blue vista'd promontories, vineyards and olive groves, a place of great beauty. They promptly bought some land, close to the charming hilltown of Capoliveri and built there.

The Mackerras villa at Elba.

Since this was to be a home away from home, they did not spare expense, imported some marble for flooring in the main room, and soon the enchanting stone villa, with wisteria covered terraces, which resulted from their planning, became just such a haven to them as had San Michele to the writer Axel Munthe at Anacapri, while Elba had the advantage of being more secluded. Catherine joined them there on one occasion, as have most of the family at one time or another, as well as London colleagues such as the Earl of Harewood and his wife, formerly Sydney musician, Patricia Tuckwell. They are also generous with their invitations to old friends to make use of the villa when travelling — Doug and Pam McLean and others, have memories of idyllic weeks there and of the interesting collection of 'Napoleonic' literature which Charles and Judy have assembled. This makes it clear that the former Emperor was happy at Elba, which he regarded as his own small kingdom. It was only his father-in-law, Austrian Emperor, Franz Josef's stubborn refusal to allow his daughter, Napoleon's wife Maria Louisa and their young son, to join him there, that prompted Napoleon to escape from the island. gather his old armies about him, and challenge the English and Prussian armies once again. Charles and his friends have observed that on a clear day it is possible to see from the villa, not only the little island of Monte Cristo, but also Corsica where Bonaparte himself was born. A place, indeed, to conjure history.

Late in 1968, the advantage of Elba's relative seclusion was offset in a most dramatic way. Holidaying there, Charles was stricken with acute appendicitis. This was just before rehearsals were to begin in London for an early edition of *Don Giovanni* on which he was to work closely with the producer, Sir John Gielgud. It was a nightmarish twenty-four hours, for he had to be taken by ferry to the mainland and then face a lengthy drive before he was within reach of a hospital and surgeon. In Australia, this was announced dramatically on the 6 a.m. ABC News. Catherine happened to hear it. There was no follow up announcement and the family were left in a state of great anxiety, for there was no way in which they could get in touch. Fortunately, his resilience stood him in good stead and Judy phoned to say that he was making a good recovery but would require 6 weeks convalescence. It was a severe disappointment to miss the *Don Giovanni*, and it was some years before he had a similar opportunity.

After an extended term in Hamburg, it was London again and then engagements in America where he began building up an assocation with, and a deep respect for, orchestras throughout the United States, such as Cincinatti, Dallas and Chicago. He describes the Chicago Symphony Orchestra as 'one of my favourites in that country, a great, great orchestra'; while a memorable experience about this time was conducting Gluck's *Orfeo* at the Metropolitan Opera, New York, with the powerful voiced mezzo-soprano, Marilyn Horne, in the title role; and later, Meyerbeer's *Le Prophète* with the same singer.

Now came the most exciting development in his career. The critical success of his Mozart productions for Sadler's Wells — *The Times* critic declared his *Cosi fan tutte* the best he had ever heard — led to his being asked, in the latter half of 1969, to become Music Director of Sadler's Wells Opera in 1970. A London journalist, Ralph Mace, interviewing

Charles Mackerras examines a score about the time of his appointment as Music Director, Sadler's Wells Opera, 1970. (By courtesy, The Times, London)

him for an article that was published in the Australian paper, *The National Times,* commented 'the appointment confirms Mackerras's reputation as one of the finest operatic conductors and foremost Australian musicians of today'.

Sadler's Wells continued to work with two companies, one in repertoire in London at the Coliseum, the other on tour in British cities, alternating the roles every two months; the overall standard was regarded as second to none and the practice was to perform the entire repertoire in English. This last point Charles considered a definite advantage. "It means that the audience always knows what is going on," he told Mace. "I so often get the impression when I go to Covent Garden and Glyndebourne that the audience doesn't catch half of what's going on — even if they are fluent in German or Italian. Opera in English does help the audience's appreciation and it's so nice to hear them laugh at the jokes in the Mozart operas . . ."

The ensuing eight years were a major fulfilment. He gave another interview, brimming over with plans for the company, to *The Times* music critic, Alan Blyth, explaining his choice of Beethoven's *Leonora* (the original version of *Fidelio*) as his first production, and his ideas on expanding the repertoire available to London opera-goers. Blyth reported, 'Mackerras, who sprouts fresh ideas with equal measures of enthusiasm and indiscretion, then turned to the character of his company — "Of course, I'm keen about ensemble opera but don't let's get puritanicial about it.

Singers draw the public. People never come to see or hear producers, and not very often to hear a conductor; they want singers . . . if you don't make a fuss of your singers you lose something of the excitement and tension in the house. I hope to be able to wean a few of our British stars off the international circuit and back to the Wells as guest artists . . . ''
So saying, he took over, and it has been said that 'the eight monumental years of his Directorship saw the merging of the touring company with the London-based one, the changing of its name to English National Opera, and a spectacular rise in the standards of its productions and in attendance figures.' [2]

His own comment was, "A marvellous experience . . . both it and I improved together".

During this time, Lord Harewood became managing director of the ENO and had the same flair for, and interest in, presenting unusual and adventurous programmes, so that as well as the standard repertoire, they did most of the Janacek operas, Handel's *Semele*, rare works of Martinu and Bartok, and Donizetti's *Mary Stuart* with Dame Janet Baker in the title role.

Charles developed a special relationship with Dame Janet over the years and she sang the leading roles in a number of his productions including *The Damnation of Faust* (Berlioz), *Dido and Aeneas* (Purcell) and the title role in Handel's *Julius Caesar*. "Some soloists are inclined to bring fixed ideas of how they want the performance," says Charles. "With Dame Janet, there is marvellous co-operation. She is one of my favourite artists, one of the very best people to work with. She produces plenty of ideas, I have my own, and we work together so that the whole thing develops. It is an ideal working relationship. Apart from which she is extremely versatile. A great interpreter of Bach, Handel, Donizetti, Elgar, Britten, Mahler. Her interpretation of Mahler's *Song of the Earth* is magnificent." The feeling of having established an ideal professional relationship during those years, together with friendship and affection, is reciprocated by Dame Janet. She has commented also on the special qualities she finds in him as an operatic conductor, such as his ability to give as many cues to the singers on stage as he does to the orchestra in the pit. This, she says, establishes a feeling of security and *rapport*, so that, together with his 'amazing preparation and grasp of the score, suddenly, you can fly!' [3]

He had constant administrative worries at Sadler's Wells, since the government subsidy did not cover rising costs. This was one of the many points made in an excellent article about this time in the *Manchester Guardian* with the amusing title: *The Covent Garden conjuror rushes on*, a phrase which was taken from an anecdote of Judy's. She had frequently the task of collecting Charles' tails from the dry-cleaners and one day the proprietor asked her, "What is your husband then, a conjuror?" About to say no, she reconsidered and answered that, in a way, he was. "Conductors do have something in common with conjurors," she told him, "the wand,

---

2. Maestro, Encounters with Conductors of Today, Helena Matheopoulos
3. Maestro, Encounters with Conductors of Today, Helena Matheopoulos

the creation of an illusion, the imposition of personality, the importance of timing. Above all, the blend of art and technique that results in a kind of magic.''

Charles himself has said many times, in one way or another, that the art of the conductor lies in interpretation, expressed through an emanation which welds together musicians of differing temperament and attitudes so that they play as one man in the style he wants. This emanation is a mysterious thing. He feels that his particular gifts probably lie in making the right *motif* and melody come through, 'in making orchestral colour sound interesting and in clarity of parts'. The conductor's art also has something to do with pulse and tempo and results are often achieved through a special feeling for a composer. "What makes me perhaps a good Handel conductor," he has said, "is that I have a more unerring feeling for the right tempo in Handel, than I do, for instance, in Bach." [4]

Charles and Judy

---

4. Conductors on Conducting, Bernard Jacobson.

There were two seasons in Australia during the first part of his ENO directorship. In 1971 he visited all the capital cities. Judy, with her feeling for remote places, whether the Himalayas or the deserts of the Australian interior, declined to fly with him from Adelaide to Perth. Instead, she asked his brother Neil and his wife to accompany her, and crossed the immense Nullarbor Plain by train, thus gathering into her consciousness something of the silences and vastness of the country.

The other occasion was in 1973. They had been saddened a few weeks before leaving London to learn that Alan, after a long illness, had died; he was in his 74th year. Charles had hoped to see his father once more. Alan had, however, known that his eldest son was to play a major role in the exciting three-month opening season of the Sydney Opera House and that was some satisfaction.

"This time," said Judy, "Charles treated our two daughters, who'd just finished their degrees, to a world trip and they came out ahead of us to see Bangkok and Bali also." Charles was asked at Sydney Airport whether the Opera House would now entice him to work permanently in Australia. He replied that although he was honoured as an Australian to be invited to do the opening concert and felt sure that the Opera House would bring fame to Australian music and make cultural things more important to people, he could not give up a career in other parts of the world 'because there is now a superb concert hall here'. Nevertheless, from this time, he does seem to have felt that he was 'being pulled in all directions'. He settled in with Alastair, began rehearsals, and visited Catherine at *Balvaig*, driving constantly past all the pleasantly familiar landmarks, and had the same feeling of coming home as he did when returning to London from Europe or America.

The opening concert at the Opera House, on the 29th September, was an all-Wagner programme with the Sydney Symphony Orchestra and the Swedish singer, Birgit Nilsson, the world's greatest Wagnerian soprano. It was a glittering, dressed occasion, and for the entire Mackerras family, who knew their Wagner as few did, a proud one. Catherine, resplendent in lace, must certainly have thought, as Charles raised his baton that night in the soaring, beautiful building, embracing the harbour that generations of MacLaurins and Creaghs had loved, of the five year old boy reaching for the handle of the wind-up gramophone at *Balvaig*, putting on a record from his grandfather's collection and 'getting to know his Wagner . . . '

There were three youth concerts to come and he also conducted *The Magic Flute* for the Australian Opera Company in the presence of the Queen; this was also very memorable for him, but he found himself critical, and remains so, of the size of the orchestra pit, which he considers inadequate.

He was soon back at the helm of the English National Opera, and in 1974, he was awarded the CBE for his dedicated work. In the same year, the Sydney Symphony Orchestra undertook a European tour with its Chief Conductor, the brilliant Dutchman, Willem van Otterloo, with great success. At the Edinburgh Festival, critics actually preferred them, on the occasion, to the Vienna Philharmonic, and Charles, in the role of alternate conductor, did several of the concerts. He was delighted with their performance. The string section, with leader Donald Hazelwood, received special praise, both under van Otterloo and with Charles in a programme in which Dvorak's music was featured. His longtime friend and colleague, Charles Buttrose, then publicity manager for the ABC, has written interestingly of this tour [5] and the *Sydney Morning Herald* music critic, Roger Covell, who travelled with the orchestra, was able to report back, on the whole, very favourably. Australian music had indeed come a long way. It is one thing for individual singers, from Melba to Sutherland, to be lauded in Europe, but quite another for an Australian orchestra of 96 players — though many of them admittedly are drawn from that fecund source — to hold its own so well.

In 1975, Charles saw Catherine for the last time when she made a brief visit to London and was able to see him conduct the centenary performance of *The Mikado* at the Savoy Theatre — and no doubt recall his lifelong facility with G & S opera, not least of which, his 12 year old performance as Ko-Ko. It could hardly have been a more fitting farewell for mother and son.

Charles' extraordinary physical stamina, which enables him to undertake performances in, say, Prague, Vienna, Milan, London and Edinburgh, with a flight across the Atlantic to appear with an American orchestra, all in a matter of weeks, made it possible for him to keep his name before a vast music-going public. This, of course, is necessary in the international field, but at this time he had also to keep firm direction of the English National Opera. Perhaps the pace at which he worked was partially responsible for some complaints amongst the chorus at the ENO. He seemed particularly prone to single out some member of the chorus for criticism early in rehearsal, sometimes they felt, 'unjustly', though at later rehearsals a conciliatory remark might be made. A leading Australian singer, commenting on this, feels that it would have had little to do with fatigue and everything to do with his hyper-sensitive ear. She remarked, 'All the maestros do this — and it happens with principals as well as members of the chorus. Their ears are so very, very finely tuned that if anyone, on any particular day, sings a note just minimally abrasive to that fine tuning, they hear it at once — and complain. Principals sometimes defend themselves but they will automatically try to adjust.' It seems that members of chorus, while not able to speak out, would also 'automatically try to adjust' — hence one gathers, the conciliatroy remark later from the podium.

In any case, apart from these normal pressures, by 1979 he began to find that the administrative work with the English National Opera, such as negotiations with soloists, was beginning to encroach on the time he wished to spend as a musicologist. He had much yet to do, particularly on the varying editions of Janacek; and if he were to become a freelance, he could ensure that he had time for it. Accordingly, he resigned as music director. It had been a very rewarding eight years in every way, and he was knighted in the New Year Honours List for his services.

---

5. Playing for Australia, About ABC Orchestras & Music in Australia, Charles Buttrose.

So it was as Sir Charles and Lady Mackerras that the pair took a well-earned rest at their delightful villa at Elba. All his life he had enjoyed swimming, and now, as he said, "I suddenly took to sailing again." He bought a small sailing boat, which he has continued to enjoy, and regrets quite strongly that he did not make the move in his father's lifetime. After Elba, it was London and preparation for an Australian tour. In Sydney, a surprise of a quite unusual nature awaited him.

Judy had been in the centre of a conspiracy with Roger Climpson of Australian television Channel 7's *This is your Life* series. Climpson had felt that it was a most opportune time to do a programme on the country's first international conductor, and had made a dozen preliminary phone calls to Judy in London making arrangements. They managed to get the new knight into EMI studios in Sydney, on some legitimate pretence, soon after his arrival and so it all began. Family and friends from everywhere began materialising one after another to his delight during the half-hour telecast. Colin (now Professor) came from Brisbane, Malcolm and Uncle Ian Mackerras from Canberra, Joan from Suffolk, Mrs Kadainkova from Prague, and from Sydney itself that early saviour of his, Neville Amadio, and many others. It was his life lived over. There was a wonderful party afterwards and of course a family photograph, with Uncle Ian, the last of the older generation, fond, frail and distinguished (he died only a few months later) in their midst.

Fortunately, there was a day or two before Charles' tight schedule commenced and they gave a party themselves at *Balvaig* to ensure that

Mackerras family, Sydney, 1979:— *Back row, Neil, Malcolm, Colin, Alastair, Elizabeth. Seated, Joan, Judy, Uncle Ian and Charles*

they really saw something of their old friends. John Parkinson has a pleasant recollection of the evening and recalls with a smile that Charles spent the greater part of it 'sitting on a sofa with the beautiful New Zealand singer, Kiri te Kanawa, talking with the closest attention'. "Oh, it was a very important matter of business!" said the homecomer. As ever, Charles and music were inseparable and his world of concerts, operas and musicians obsessed him — on this occasion, to the male eye, somewhat enviably.

In 1980, he was able to spend considerable time in Vienna, with the skilled engineers of the Decca studio, recording the works of Janacek, in the original language, with the Vienna Philharmonic Orchestra. It is interesting to look at him there through the eyes of a young Australian conductor, Brian Stacey, who went over to study with him.

"Charles Mackerras was the natural one to approach when I needed experience overseas," said Stacey, a New South Welshman with an outgoing personality who had been conducting for various Australian performing companies, such as Queensland's Lyric Opera. "Not only was he Australian, but I admired his tremendous versatility and the diversity of the work he tackled."

Their first meeting in Vienna was fraught with setbacks — for Stacey. He had been told to phone on arrival and did so, from his *pension*, to Sir Charles at the Hilton. He phoned all afternoon and into the night with no result. He tried next morning at 8.30, got through, and said to the stringent voice that answered "I'm your student, Brian Stacey." The maestro told him to ring again at 10.30 and hung up. Stacey, on his first trip out of Australia, wondered what sort of disastrous course lay ahead of him. At the appointed hour, he went to the Hilton. Charles came down and with the quick smile which is his chief charm, greeted him warmly in the Australian vernacular. It was a *volte face* which Stacey accepted with the greatest relief. In five years of what was to become a very close association, he found his tutor — "An amazing man — but *not* in the early morning."

His first afternoon in Vienna was spent at the Decca studio listening to Charles make the recording of Janacek's *The Cunning Little Vixen* and was equally unforgettable. Charles himself has spoken of 'the absolutely gorgeous string quality of the Vienna Philharmonic', and Stacey was now to experience it in exceptional circumstances. He says — "The first thing that hit me was this exquisite sound. I was spellbound, actually in tears some of the time, because of the things that were happening in that place. This exquisite string sound, the like of which I'd never heard before, such as you never hear on the recording. And the next thing was this extraordinary man standing up in front of this orchestra with all the command in the world — and the wonderful technique he has with an orchestra, speaking to them in German, and the singers in Czech, and somebody else in Italian. He spoke fluently in four different languages that afternoon. And then his prodigious knowledge and understanding of Janacek — it's legendary now, of course. But I still consider that particular recording is one of the best that has ever been made of this work."

Charles makes little fuss of his own gifts; he says that musical ability is innate but admits that 'one has to work hard at it', while his skill as a linguist is something which he takes entirely for granted, as do European conductors generally. He speaks a little Hungarian and Russian as well as those in which he is fluent, and insists that it is simply 'a matter of picking them up'. It is, nevertheless, a very useful gift and adds another dimension to his *rapport* with musicians, of which many have spoken. "It's a combination of this personality — an attitude that gets the best out of people by making them feel comfortable rather than bullying them — and a very profound musicianship," said Stacey. "He turns out a masterful musical rendition of practically everything that he does, but without tremendous showmanship and the sort of things one associates with more fiery conductors. That's not what he's about."

Stacey returned to Vienna the following year for further studies, and found Charles, who was about to do *Jenufa* with the Vienna State Opera, already working on the score, as he so often does, trying to get back to Janacek's original ideas through the maze of alterations made by various Serbian conductors. "They had felt that Janacek's orchestral naivety was actually wrong," said Stacey. "We spent a week getting the parts into order, then sitting there with our blue pencils rewriting parts. And then Charles went into the performance with the Vienna State Opera — with no provision made for orchestral rehearsal whatsoever. Just a bit of work with the singers and one dress rehearsal. It is far from ideal, but the fact that he is able to do it, has the resources to do it, is amazing."

He later stayed with the Mackerrases in London, at their new home at Hamilton Terrace, and sat in on Charles' rehearsals at Covent Garden and with the English Chamber Orchestra. He also travelled with him to Wales, and then back to Vienna, when Charles was asked to do a Master Course there on the operas of Mozart. "It was very exciting for him," said Stacey, who enrolled in the course himself. "He was the first non-Viennese conductor to be asked to do this and it meant recognition for him as an authority on Mozart."

Charles asked the young Australian to act as his assistant, which he did, and he was regarded by the Mackerrases, whose two daughters had married, as part of the family, getting to know the relaxed man with his idiosyncrasies and fund of humour as well as the dedicated musician. He heard about the trials of writing a cadenza for Callas in *Lucia di Lammermoor*; of conducting *Turandot* with Franco Corelli who invariably bashed the stage gong so hard at the end of Act 1 he tore holes in the curtain; of doing scenes from *Otello* with del Monaco on television and the singer's avid cries of *Un bacio, un bacio ancora, un altro bacio*! as he fell upon the beautiful model playing the lifeless Desdemona, covering her with kisses, while his wife sat 'very much cast back' in the audience with Judy! He shared some of the two pints of fresh yoghurt Judy provided daily for her spouse, and understood his occasional abstractedness which might appear as rudeness. He aided and abetted Judy in her efforts to save him from himself in his costly love for electronic gadgetry and audio equipment, which he is continually renewing, at the same time sending off the 'old' equipment to the London Institute for the Blind. He discussed with Judy her passionate concern about nuclear power, her anti-nuclear stance, and Charles' increasing involvement in this crucial issue, which they believe has already affected the welfare of their small grandchildren.

So it was behind the scenes with the man and his family as well as the musician and musicologist. He developed a strong affection for both and the results of his studies are apparent. Brian Stacey subsequently became Music Director of the Australian Ballet (Melbourne) and is currently working with the Victorian State Opera for whom he recently conducted *The Barber of Seville* which was televised by the ABC.

For Charles, the wheel has turned full circle. The oboist with the Sydney Symphony Orchestra in 1945, returned in 1982 as a conductor of international standing, to become that orchestra's Chief Conductor for a four year period and the first Australian to hold that position. It means three months of the year in Sydney where he stays at his 'quarters' at *Balvaig*, sometimes accompanied by his wife, sometimes not, when the call of their English grandchildren is too great. Personally, it has meant closer ties with his brother Alastair and sister Elizabeth who are also at *Balvaig*, which remains, after three generations, the family centre in a city which, even as an inveterate cosmopolitan, Charles still finds exciting.

Donald Hazelwood, concertmaster of the SSO since 1965, the tall, softly-spoken man of quiet distinction so well-known to Sydney concert-goers, who has played under Goossens, van Otterloo, Fremaux — all of whom he admired — and others of differing quality, has interesting comments to make about the Mackerras style of conducting — "Sir Charles is a very active man on the rostrum, he gives a great number of cues, and very accurate cues, to the instruments. Also, he has the sort of voice which penetrates and he never has to ask the orchestra to be quiet at any stage. This, "he adds, with a smile," can be fairly overpowering

Brian Stacey, (By courtesy, The Courier-Mail, Brisbane)

Donald Hazelwood, Concertmaster of the Sydney Symphony Orchestra.

Sir Charles Mackerras with his cousin, Dr David Mackerras (Brisbane), 1983.

at the end of a day's rehearsal if you're sitting close, but it is an advantage for a conductor. With many of them, players at the back miss out on valuable instructions." An unexpected by-product of early practice with other resonant Mackerras voices round the Turramurra table, he agreed, and went on to say that he felt he was very much one of the breed — "The Mackerrases strive from the word go, and I've noticed over the years, gradually, he's the sort of person who goes from strength to strength. Of course, the look of each conductor is totally different, I mean in the use of the baton. some conductors can look marvellous and be quite awful. They're spending their whole time trying to look beautiful for the audience and actually doing nothing about what's happening in the music side of it. Sir Charles is concerned with the music and the orchestra. He covers a tremendous range of works. Even in short periods with us, he's done everything from Haydn and Mozart through the whole gamut to Wagner and modern Australian." He found memorable the 'seven splendid concerts' they did with him in 1984, presenting the Berlioz opera, *The Trojans*, in concert version, with Margreta Elkins as Cassandra and Lauris Elms as Dido, while Sydney music critic, Roger Covell, commented in the *Sydney Morning Herald* after Part I of the series, 'Sir Charles thrives on the deployment of vigorous and contrasted musical multitudes,' and spoke of 'his supremely confident supervision of the agile rhythms and smouldering rhetoric of Berlioz's music'.

The SSO's Benevolent Fund Gala Concert that year, for which they sold standing room, and for which he conducted a programme of Gilbert & Sullivan, was a gala one indeed. An extended ABC radio audience was reminded, after the ovation which followed *Pineapple Poll* at the Opera House, that this was the man, who as a four-year-old, had delighted his mother at St Michael's Church, Vaucluse, by discerning a resemblance to *The Gondoliers* in the hymn *Onward Christian Soldiers* — for which Sir Arthur Sullivan had indeed written the music. Even through the air-waves, the excitement and pleasure of that Sydney audience could be felt.

Hazelwood, who is amusing on the necessity for remembering to tuck his fiddle under his arm to be free for handshakes on these occasions, summed up, "I consider that the orchestra has maintained a very high standard indeed during his work with us. Of course, comparisons will always be made and many different opinions will be forthcoming, but by and large it has been a productive time for both Sir Charles and the orchestra." Inevitably, there are differences of opinion among long-term subscribers who remember the sparkle of the orchestra under Goossens. A former European of the more romantic school, for instance, is one of the dissidents, while the University of Sydney's Professor Simon Prokhovnik and his wife are amongst those who have enjoyed the lively attack of the orchestra under the Mackerras baton.

In 1984, one of his most satisfying experiences was conducting that most prestigious of orchestras in Czechoslovakia, the Czech Philharmonic, and also the Czech Philharmonic Choir, in their own music, Smetana and Janacek, and recording the latter's *Glagolithic Mass* with them.

The tri-centenary of Handel's birth made 1985 another great Handel year for him, but mid-stream misfortune befell him. After conducting in Paris, he flew to Australia in late June to fulfil the fourth and final year of his contract as Chief Conductor of the Sydney Symphony Orchestra and was looking forward to a strenuous programme which included Berlioz's *The Damnation of Faust*. He conducted his first three concerts, as scheduled, and was then laid low at *Balvaig* with what appeared to be the prevalent influenza. It proved instead to be hepatitis and he was forced to cancel all engagements. It was a bitter disappointment as he had particularly looked forward to his concluding season with the SSO. For Judy, who flew from London earlier than intended to look after him and supervise the rigorous diet necessary, the cancellation of his concert at the new Performing Arts Complex in Brisbane also was a major disappointment, as she has more friends in Queensland than anywhere else in Australia and it is the home city of Charles's brother Colin and cousin David, of whom they are both fond. One is reminded of the comment of the Mackerras's grandfather, Dr Charles McLaurin, when writing on the nature of war and combat — 'Man's natural enemies are germs . . . not his fellow-man.'

Sir Charles Mackerras, conducting at the Sydney Opera House in the mid-1980s. (By courtesy, Sydney Opera House Trust)

Charles, fortunately, is resilient and combated this random invasion well. By August he was able to fulfil an engagement in San Francisco to conduct the Handel opera, *Orlando*, with Marilyn Horne, and undertake further concerts in the United States before returning to the U.K. and his multitude of engagements there and in Europe. There are many exciting prospects ahead. In January 1987 he will take up an appointment as Musical Director of the Welsh National Opera at Cardiff, and the same year has been invited to do a Gluck opera for the Gluck bicentennial celebrations in Vienna. Both he and Judy look forward greatly to returning to Australia in the bicentennial year, 1988, for a major production with the Australian Opera Company and several concerts, while engagements in Europe and America extend into 1989.

Moving about the world in this way, does he still feel that any particular place is home? Judy says, "It's very difficult for him to know where his roots are. He's actually spent far more time based in England and Europe than he has in Australia, so that he feels very much pulled in all directions. It's quite a problem for both of us really. As he married me, and created English children and English grandchildren — we have just had twin grandsons presented to us, one of them named for Charles — we belong much more over there — or certainly I do. I love coming out here, of course, but it's a very long way and it does cut me off from everything else.''

He himself, at *Balvaig*, working at the familiar round table at which the family used to gather, his eye passing from its dark curve to the audio equipment where the old wind-up gramophone once stood, said, ''It's true that I don't have a strong feeling of belonging anywhere, but I have a much stronger feeling of belonging here than I do anywhere else.''

He was soon to fly once again to the other side of the world, becoming, for us, an Australian abroad, but more importantly, recognised by his colleagues, whether in London, Vienna, Prague, Cardiff, Chicago or Sydney for what he is — a musician's musician.

Chapter 5

Alastair

It was October, 1950, during a spell of particularly dismal weather, that Alastair arrived in Cambridge to take up residence at St John's College and further his studies in mathematics and classics. He was twenty-one, had been happily teaching at Trinity Grammar School, Sydney, and had gone to Cambridge only on Catherine's insistence.

He had come over by ship in July and after three weeks in Europe, discovering the joys of such cities as Lucerne and Paris and attending the Oberammergau Passion Play, he had spent a fortnight with Charles and Judy in London. He liked Judy very much, made the acqaintance of his infant niece (whose sister was soon to be born), and of MacLaurin relatives and family friends with whom he went off to the Albert Hall and Covent Garden, and thoroughly enjoyed himself. The contrast now was rather stark, a fact which was somehow symbolised by the empty river.

He had been told about the beautiful Cam but it was suffering its annual cleaning process. "They do this by means of their locks, so that tins and such debris can be taken out," he said. "It was absolutely empty when I arrived — nothing but a dirty ditch!" Also, he noticed that English and European buildings generally were very shabby, showing the effects of the six years of war and the five year post-war period, during which all efforts had to be concentrated on the gradual return to normal living and no cleaning or restorative work could be contemplated. He was not at all happy at Cambridge for some months.

"It was cold and foggy and I was lonely and didn't know many people there," he said, his feelings exactly those of his grandfather, Charles MacLaurin, when sent forth from Sydney to Edingburgh University in the 1890s. Even the fact that Charles and Judy were in London did not really lessen the feeling.

The winter months only worsened matters for him. He wrote long letters home. "Now," his sister Joan recalled, "it wasn't so much Charlie's letters that were being read aloud at the dinner table as Alastair's. We used to love sitting and listening to them, all very quiet, we enjoyed them so much. He used to write a lot of detail, thick letters, air mail paper all covered in his beautiful handwriting."

Deprived suddenly of that warm circle of interested, noisy brothers and sisters, for whom, on Catherine's frequent trips abroad, he had acted *in loco parentis*, he made up for it with his letters. He told them about his visit to Rome at Christmas for the ordination of his Australian friend, Ian (now Monsignor) Burns. He described for them the positive side of life beside the Cam — the ceremony of St John's Dining Hall and the historic portraits with which the walls were hung, the gowned figures crossing the Bridge of Sighs, the mediaeval architecture, the quadrangles, the heraldry, the glories of the stained glass, the fan-vaulted ceilings, the chapels, the music and the choirs. He described his Tutor, Mr Howland, who was very friendly and affable; he told them of a remarkable Australian, Sir Harold Bailey, who was Professor of Sanskrit there and considered by some to be the most distinguished Scholar of Queen's College since Erasmus. He described the Catholic Chaplain, Monsignor Gilbey (of the Gilbey Gin family) with his rich, beautiful voice, as being 'one of the most amusing, charming and intelligent men I am ever likely to meet'. He described his rooms — bedroom, sitting room and kitchen to himself. He told about the 'Bedder' who tidied up and had eight sets of rooms, otherwise know as a staircase, of 'young gentlemen to do for'. He told how you had to wear your gown when you visited your Tutor and even round town at night. The Proctor, accompanied by two bulldogs — men, not real bulldogs, he explained — patrolled the streets and fined you 6/8d if you were not wearing your gown! They hung upon it all.

Suddenly, in spite of his best endeavours to cheer himself up, he felt he could no longer stand the cold, the fog and the loneliness and wrote to say that he had decided to return home and not to finish his degree. "My poor mother got into a terrible state," recalled Joan. "She bombarded him with cables and letters and said, 'Oh please, please don't leave Cambridge!' and 'Do, do finish your degree, it would be dreadful if you left!'" The family had to dissuade her from getting on a plane and going over to reinforce her pleas with her presence.

Fortunately, Alastair managed to settle down without more ado. Apart from anything else, he saw, as Catherine clearly did, that it would have a bad effect on his career if he did not stay. Furthermore, he had been in touch with old Sydney friends — Tony Melville, who had started at King's College at the same time as he had at St John's and with whom he had been to Sydney University; Peter Young, with whom he had taught at Trinity Grammar, who was now reading history at Oxford; and John Parkinson, friend from infancy, who was teaching at a Prep school in Sussex. He had also made several friends at Cambridge who shared his interest in music, one of whom, Brian Harrap, from Melbourne, enjoyed making occasional dashes with him to London for concerts or operas, and he recalls a particularly fine performance of Wagner's *Siegfried* they saw together at Covent Garden on one of these sorties.

He now decided it was time to try some sport. "We were all very unsporty when we were young," he commented, "notably unsporty, the whole lot of us. But I thought I'd better do something — handy for a schoolmaster — so I took up rowing, that being the one thing you can take up at a later age." He began rowing by the hanging willows and the richly grassed banks of the Cam, now in full flow, and found the whole place and the mellowness of autumn quite lovely, though he maintains that he was 'never much good at the sport, being far too physically lazy'.

Alastair, aged 22, 1950.

He compensated for this by working extremely hard reading Latin and Greek.

During this time, he took instruction from Monsignor Gilbey and became a member of the Roman Catholic Church. He had long since decided on this course, but had refrained from going through with it at home out of consideration for his father. He liked the theological concept of authority and obedience held by the Roman Church, as did Catherine, and having made 'the big leap to faith', this was the church in which he wished to practise it. There seems no doubt that he was influenced by his mother's depth of feeling and the potency of her arguments on the subject, but it also fulfilled a need within his own nature. He seems always to have been the quintessential schoolmaster, combining a love for the young and for teaching with a certain austerity, asexuality and self-sufficiency. He has always reached for the realm of the spirit, and be found the most satisfying expression of the metaphysical in the rituals of the church and in the music inspired by it. He also seems never to have obtruded or pressed his beliefs on others, as Catherine was inclined to do, and he is a man for whom tolerance of attitude and behaviour has invariably been a goal.

Catherine used to say that Alastair was 'born middle-aged'; one of her striking remarks which, while overstated, had some truth in it. Certainly, his early acceptance of responsibility bore it out, and whatever feelings of insecurity and loneliness he suffered initially at Cambridge were not apparent to others. Squarely built, with a straight-backed step, an improbably round face and a direct, bespectacled gaze he had an aplomb and presence beyond his years; this was directly attributable, of course, to the confident articulateness which had long reigned in the Mackerras household. His friend, Tony Melville, had a similar quality. In the summer of '51, the pair acquired an old London Taxi which they dubbed 'Desdemona', and with another friend, John Miller, now Professor of Mathematics at Monash University, toured England and Scotland. The hills and valleys resounded with their comments. Their visit to Edinburgh was particularly satisfying to Alastair, for it held so many MacLaurin associations of interest to him as a scholar. There was not only his great-great grandfather, James MacLaurin, the St Andrew's Headmaster, but an early 18th century collateral ancestor, Colin MacLaurin, who had been a young professor at Edinburgh University and after whom the MacLaurin Theorem (*'really a very nice theorem'*) is named.

Back at Cambridge, he finished his course, graduated 'quite well' in classics and a few years later went through the process of converting his degree to M.A. (Cantab). "You see, a B.A.'s the same as M.A. in Cambridge. Also in Oxford," he commented. "An M.A., you buy. It was around ten pounds then. It is only a question of status — it means you can vote for the Senate and that sort of thing. It doesn't indicate any more in the way of academic things at all." An interesting fact which is probably not widely known in Australia, since not many academics would think to disclose it. There is currently, he says, pressure at both universities to change this to a more normal system.

In 1952, he received an appointment as a junior assistant Master at one of the famous English Public Schools, Christ's Hospital, Horsham, in Sussex, the school at which the distinguished Headmaster of Sydney Grammar at the time, Colin Healey, had spent the greater part of his career. Alastair taught for a year at Christ's Hospital, which is markedly different from other English Public Schools in a number of ways. To begin with, its uniform, at that time, dated back to the 17th century and involved the wearing of yellow stockings, frilled shirt and blue coat by students. It is also a school which has a very high scholastic standard, maintained partly by the awarding of scholarships, which also enables the less affluent in the community to find a place there. This emphasis on both tradition and scholarship, particularly the latter, undoubtedly had an effect on Alastair. He saw that the top students reached a higher academic standard than their Australian counterparts and that more provision was made for them in most of the arts, though perhaps less in sports, cadets, and interestingly, debating. Apart from the anachronistic uniform, he found a very much more formal atmosphere than at Sydney schools, discipline much the same, but boys generally not as easy to get to know or to manage.

As a Master in a boarding school, he found it impossible to get up to London for concerts and operas and had to be satisfied with his records, making up for this with vacations in Europe. In the summer of '52, he toured Italy, Switzerland and part of Germany with Peter Young and

Tony Melville and in the following winter went with John Parkinson on a 'monastery tour'.

John has many memories of those interesting weeks and noticed that the combination of erudition and confident expression in such a young man as Alastair did not always bring out the best in people. "We stayed at monasteries most of the time," he recalled, "and I remember being rather shocked at an English schoolmaster who had just met Alastair and said scathingly, 'The whole room is filled with Alastair Mackerras'." It was a criticism often sustained by Catherine. "I think that man was probably very envious of the Mackerras intelligence and drive," John added in his quiet, distinctive voice and the smile that goes with his aesthetic features and long, slender frame. He shared the opprobrium of the next sharp comment from this critic, whose brother was a Benedictine monk, 'Of course, staying at monasteries is a cheap way of living'. The travellers, both with strong religious convictions, which Alastair has maintained throughout his life, went on their way, very much more perturbed by the appalling evidence of wartime destruction in Germany, than any such criticism. In fact, these European journeys undertaken by Alastair were to provide him with a fund of illustrative material about

Dr John Parkinson, lifelong friend of Alastair and the Mackerras family, in his Cambridge days.

people, places and historical highways and byways with which he is well-known for enriching even his mathematics classes.

Meanwhile, he had been in touch with Sydney Grammar School Headmaster (Colin Healey), who now offered him an appointment as a junior assistant Master. He returned home in January 1954 and found his mother, Joan and Elizabeth at Turramurra poised and ready to leave for Europe themselves. Neil was working and studying Law part-time, also engaged to be married and it was the girls' turn, said Catherine, 'to further their careers abroad'. She had timed their departure for his return, since Alan, Neil and the fourteen-year-old twins, together with whatever domestic help was available, would need him on hand to see to the smooth running of things.

So it was not only to teaching, tutoring and mathematics that he returned, but to the world of young brothers, the sound of practice (Colin was assiduous at the piano at the time), the cutting of the big, awkward, chunky school lunches for which the Mackerrases were known, and to the preparation of family meals at *Harpenden* where they knew they could expect from him, as Neil had once remarked, 'steady form, though not a big repertoire'. At weekends, following Catherine's instructions, each fended for himself and they became dab hands at the making of omelettes, though Colin has a memory of one of his dramaticallly catching fire, of his discovery that water simply fuelled it, and of a leap to the garden to hurl flaming curtains to the ground. There was something to be said, after all, for their brother's dependable week-day offerings.

Alastair was aware of the wrench it had been to his father parting with Elizabeth who, at sixteen, had waved ecstatically with her mother and Joan from a maze of streamers as their Italian liner pulled out. On the other hand, he also knew the pleasure his father felt in his appointment as a Mathematics Master at Grammar, for, as their friend John Goldrick observed, 'Sydney Grammar seemed almost to be a substitute for religion for Alan'. The months should pass quickly enough. Even so, it was an inspired thought of Alan's to end the summer holidays by taking them to the Snowy Mountains, where the first stages of the great hydro-electric scheme were under way. At the Snowy, he was a mine of interesting information and especially captured the imagination of young Malcolm who, with a naturally curious bent, had always shown much more interest than the others in the generation of electricity. It was a promising start to their all-male year at *Harpenden*.

Alastair had been appointed Form Master of IA and also teacher for Honours Maths. When term began he drove off, with the twins aboard, in Catherine's trusty Hillman. Turning into College Street again, he felt a second homecoming. There, on one side, were the plane trees, palms and fountains of Hyde Park; on the other, the satisfyingly classic contours of the Blacket wings of the School flanking the famous 1832 Hallen central building, with the black and gold flag flying above the sandstone, the whole set in two precious acres in the heart of the city and enclosed by the low, finely proportioned stone and cast-iron fence.

They were the fourth generation of their family to know and appreciate the great tradition of the old School, established by Act of Parliament in 1857, and that outstanding surgeon and citizen of Sydney, their great-

great-grandfather, Dr Charles Nathan, had been one of the signatories to the petition which resulted in its establishment. Sir Normand MacLaurin, of course, married Dr Nathan's daughter, while her brother, Ted Nathan, had been an early long-term Master. Sir Normand himself, when Chancellor of the University, was *ex officio* a member of the School's Board of Trustees, and it had been kept in the educational forefront by a series of fine Headmasters, including the current one, Colin Healey, who was then, as his new appointee later remarked, in the process of 'bringing the School into the modern world'.

As a junior Master he found himself particularly fortunate. The Master of the Lower School was a man who had a profound and positive effect on him — the elderly 'Bill' Ritchie, of whom he said, "He was, in my opinion, the perfect Schoolmaster. He had a marvellous blend of firmness and gentleness, of aloofness and kindness, of seriousness and humour, and he was immensely good to junior Masters." As well, in his own field, he found a guiding light in a fine man and mathematician, Kevin Hardie, soon to become Senior Mathematics Master and to hold the position for fifteen years. "I was a junior member of the department and later his Second Master," he said, "and he took very great care of us — and also, you see, set us an example."

This was not all, for he formed a close friendship with an older scholar and bookman, Alan Swan, a colleague for many years, who taught Latin and English in the Lower School. Both men particularly enjoyed teaching boys at the beginning of their secondary school education, and Alastair recalls that on the several occasions during the years when Alan Swan was offered promotion, he refused it, saying, "I don't believe in exchanging the substance for the shadow". He understood this attitude, for these years of teaching were amongst his happiest.

He was now to be found again, as John Parkinson remembered him in their days as senior students, walking through the playgrounds at Grammar in the midst of a cluster of boys, all full of talk, questions and requests, "He's a very, very charismatic fellow from the point of view of boys," said Sydney lawyer, Malcolm Turnbull, one of his young pupils a decade on from this but speaking also for these earlier ones, "he's very affectionate, just has a way with them. He's also firm but fair. All these things characterise him. A very lenient man but with a stern sort of attitude about him."

At home, postcards from Europe telling of the adventures of Catherine and the girls arrived regularly. Nothing changed very much at the dinner table where Alastair served his 'reliable repertoire' of roasts and grills, the twins stepped up their exuberant flow of talk, and Alan found as little breathing space in which to make a contribution as with the whole family gathered. Catherine had indeed set the pattern. Nevertheless, a quiet companionship developed further with Alastair and his father, in whose estimation he had always been second only to Elizabeth. They had their common interest in mathematics, but Alastair also realised that, within the family circle, it had become necessary to take the initiative with his father and seek him out for talk and discussion. This he did and during his years at Sydney University he often spoke with him about religion. He found him to be 'an old-fashioned rationalist' and quite immovable, but the discussions in themselves formed a meeting ground which clearly meant something to Alan.

Now, quite often on Sunday afternoons, with the weekends' sailing activities over and *Antares* safely at her mooring, he liked to go for walks round the leafy and comparatively unbuilt up areas which still remained around Turramurra and Alastair, if he was at home, accompanied him. They talked about such things as education and universities, on which they were 'in substantial agreement', while Alastair, having become a Catholic, left that subject alone, and ranged instead on to the general state of society in Australia as compared with England and Europe. "My mother always used to take the view that things in Australia were pretty dreadful," said Alastair, "but father took the opposite view — things were always pretty good here. Then, or course, we talked about mathematics. But, also, you weren't required to talk all the time, it was quite possible just to walk in silence." The pair, strolling together in this companionable way, form a pleasant contrast to the general tenor of Alan's experiences within the family, and must stand beside that other of Elizabeth, fair and slight, reading aloud to him in his study of an evening during her anti-school adolescence.

Alastair was always conservative in dress, wearing a dark suit both summer and winter at school and invariably a gown, but he did have, at this point, a rather distinctive green sports coat. Due to obvious limitations in space at College Street for playing fields, Grammar had acquired, as a major mark of its Jubilee in 1907, sports grounds at Ruchcutters Bay. These, about three hectares of low-lying ground reclaimed from Chinamen's Gardens and seagulls, with a flooding and drainage problem which had to be overcome, were named the Weigall Grounds, for the Headmaster, Albert Weigall, the bearded, venerated *Old Chief*, then coming towards the end of his forty-five year reign. Every so often Alastair made a dutiful appearance at Weigall in his sports coat to watch Grammar matches played there against Kings School, Newington College, Shore and other members of the GPS. The combination of the green coat, his substantial build and round face, prompted one of the boys to nickname him *Mango*. This stayed with him for some years and later, when a journalist asked boys at the School who knew nothing about the sports coat, how he had acquired the nickname, they conferred amongst themselves and decided that a Latin dictionary might provide the answer. They found that the word meant *a dealer in slaves*. This they thought extremely suitable and promptly gave it as the source, a myth which has been perpetuated. "Not very nice, is it?" said Alastair, his face belying the words and clearly approving their enterprise.

He now instituted two of his most famous customs: the taking of groups of boys during the summer vacation to Kiama on the coast south of Sydney, where he rented a house by the sea, and the dispensing of chocolate frogs at School for various reasons. The first was a direct follow-on from earlier group holidays when he had taken the children of family friends to Alan's cottage at Leura in his university days, also the Kangaroo Valley holiday of special memory for Colin, which he had organised with Tony Melville. "I think I must always have been directed very much towards children," he commented, "probably because of the twins and being virtually a parent to them for awhile." It was true and we shall look again at the Kiama holidays and their effects, through the eyes of the students. The other custom became a daily affair and was a result of his own adolescent years.

The Master of the Lower School when he was a student at the Grammar School was Keith Lumsdaine, who had also taught Latin and had a considerable influence on him. "He was an excellent Schoolmaster," said Alastair, "and if we got good marks in Latin he used to give us chocolate frogs. When I came back as a Master, right from the start, I used to give them to the boys in my form on their birthdays. It just gradually grew from there." It is hardly surprising that Alastair, with his strongly held belief that the young deserve kindness and affection in the throes of their disciplined study, should have taken up the chocolate frog as one small means of expressing this — his own sweet tooth undoubtedly held grateful memories. The chocolate frogs are now legendary and frequently used as a test of his own memory. He makes a habit of trying to know all the boys' names by Easter each year. "Oh, but he *has* to know your name," said a present pupil, grinning, "otherwise — chocolate frog!" Just how 'Old Sydneians' among the dental fraternity look back on the practice remains to be seen, but it is an eccentricity which has the unqualified approval of several generations of schoolboys.

In 1955, with Catherine home again, and more time for his own interests, he renewed his diversion as a train buff and was often accompanied by another young colleague and friend, Rodney Knock, who enjoyed the whole family, made the apposite remark about Catherine 'wringing ideas by the neck', and admired Alan as an ' international libertarian'. Rodney was catapulted into being football coach when he joined Grammar's staff to teach History. "I didn't know half-back from five-eighth," he said, "and I had to handle five junior teams. Colin was one my conscripts."

Alastair, meanwhile, undertook to be Master of the Chess Club of which his young brother was a keen member, and somewhat to their surprise, Colin subsequently became runner-up in the New South Wales junior championship. It is an instance of the bonds within this 'community of brothers', for it was Charles who, having acquired the rudiments of the game from their father, had set the pace for the family interest in chess. Alastair also had the satisfaction of seeing Colin win the Captain of the School award (at Grammar this means first in literary subjects) in '55, and the following year, when he taught him Honours Maths, the prestigious Senior Knox prize. He did not teach Malcolm, now in the same year as his twin and in the throes of his 'late developing', but observed his consistent interest in the dramatic political scene. At this particular juncture, Prime Minister Menzies, who was locked in battle with Opposition Leader, Dr Evatt, in the aftermath of the Petrov Affair, was his hero. Whenever he got the chance he put in his spoke at the dinner table — restored to its full debating vigour with the return of Catherine.

The Grammar School centenary, 1957, was now on hand and their magazine, *The Sydneian*, was a special issue with a history of the School written by Alastair's friend, young staff member and Old Sydneian, Rodney Knock, with the distinguished editorial assistance of that

134 *Scholars and Gentlemen*

THE STAFF
Back Row: R. W. MACLAY, D. C. S. SMITH, E. G. BLA
M. G. GREENING, F. C. EARLE, R. C. KNOCK, SE
A. R. FRASER, R. J. HOLLAND, H. A. MACDONALD
COWDERY. Second Row: A. M. MACKERRAS, A. L.
C. D. TAYLOR, R. M. GLENVALE, A. P. SCOTT, W. E.
A. J. HILL, A. T. KEEBLE, H. A. RITCHIE, C. O. HEAL
F.

Sydney Grammar School Staff, 1956.

STREET, 1956
)RAN, D. E. LLOYD, B. W. ROOS, R. J. STEVENSON,
A. WELLS. *Third Row:* J. M. HIGGINS, R. H. PARR,
L. O. SCOTT, P. M. TRIMBLE, P. G. YOUNG, G. F. R.
W. WEBSTER, A. W. AUSTIN, M. W. ROBERTSON,
A. K. SWAN. *Front Row:* K. P. HARDIE, I. M. EDWARDS,
SON-NORMAN, A. S. SAMS, D. A. CARR, R. L. ROFE,
LL.

Sydney Grammar School, College Street, 1956, from a drawing by Douglas Pratt.

competitor for university History Honours with Catherine, Major-General Victor (later Sir Victor) Windeyer. Sir Victor was then Vice-Chairman of the School's Board of Trustees, of which he had been a member since 1943, and a year away from his appointment to the High Court. The history was not only well written but also finely illustrated. Text and photography together brought to life former personalities and sporting teams, highlighted such things as the very great importance of the Cadet Corps in earlier days, gave the background of the main School buildings, the outstanding War Memorial Library, School House at Randwick and the two new preparatory schools at St Ives (Headmaster, E.R. Dent) and Edgecliff (Headmaster, R.W. Billing). A photograph of the staff at College Street in 1956, with Headmaster Colin Healey, includes a youthful Alastair, standing to one side with the air of one who has been about more central matters and will return to them again as soon as possible, which is very characteristic of him.

Several items in the history are of considerable interest in our context; the site of the School where Alastair has now spent much more than half his life, how it came into being, and its objectives, which still apply and to which he has dedicated himself.

The site, which was chosen in 1830 for the initial Sydney College, for which the street was named, was described as — 'a fine open spot . . . in the vicinity of the Government Domain; a spot the most airy and healthy in the town of Sydney'. When Sydney College, designed by the architect Hallen and the oldest building in the present School, was forced to close its doors due to the severe financial climate in 1850, the proprietors, with the formidable backing of William Wentworth, managed to convince the Legislative Council that the time was ripe to convert their School to a University. A University Incorporation Act was passed, and in October 1852, Sydney University came into being in an impressive ceremony in what is now known as the *Big Schoolroom* at Grammar.

It soon became clear, however, as statesman Henry Parkes saw and pointed out, that New South Wales was trying to run before it could walk, and that the new University was impeded by the lack of a Grammar School, for the principal, Professor of Classics, Dr Woolley, was forced to waste valuable time 'drumming declensions and conjugations into the heads of his students'. Accordingly, in 1854, Parkes presented a petition with several hundred signatories, amongst whom were such well-known men of the colony as John Fairfax, George Wigram Allen, Edward Cox and Dr Charles Nathan, who submitted that 'by erection of a Grammar or High School, and by the encouragement of first-rate masters, with a partial endowment, supplemented by liberal fees to be contributed by parents, the youth of Sydney might be at once raised to an equality . . with those of English cities . . (and) a nursery provided for our University'.

This was handled by the parliament's Committee on Education, Chairman of which was Sir Charles Cowper, a name which was to become synoymous with Sydney Grammar School, for, as well, his great-grandson, Sir Norman Cowper, 100 years later, became chairman of the Board of Trustees, holding the office for 22 years. In 1854, Sydney Grammar School was thus created by Act of Parliament and provided for twelve Trustees of whom the Crown would provide three, the University three and six would be prominent laymen. The speaker, Sir Charles Nicholson, also Chancellor of the University (which had moved to its permanent premises), was the most prominent of the first Trustees. He had testified that 'the trade of teaching appears to be the resource for every broken down invalid who has failed in any other profession', and he now went to England and there recruited first-rate staff from eighty applicants.

The Preamble to the Act setting up the School has been its guide for one hundred and thirty years and declares its purpose to be — ' . . . for the better advancement of religion and morality and the promotion of useful knowledge . . . conferring on all classes and denominations . . . resident in the Colony of New South Wales without any distinction whatsoever the advantage of a regular and liberal course of education'.

This, as the authors of the history observed, 'expresses a fundamental idea. Subject to payment of the fees, and to there being room in the School, and to their comporting themselves as the School requires, all boys have been welcome.' The Act itself provided that parents or guardians would 'secure that religious observances be carried out' as approved by them. So it has remained, becoming broader with the times and the changing character of the community; and at Assembly once a week general prayers are read.

"We are a polyglot lot," Alastair observed recently, looking in a pleased fashion at the boys as they trooped out the gate after school. "It's because we're non-denominational, you see. And also because of the selective entry. They all come here. The place is full of Jews, Greeks, Lebanese, Chinese, Arabs. They're nice boys. There's an Anglo-Saxon one there. A Protestant Anglo-Saxon one there." The great majority of the School is, in fact, Protestant and Anglo-Saxon, but the religious and ethnic admixture of students is certainly an excellent thing.

As long ago as 1888 the School was accused of 'catering only for clever boys', a charge which Alastair hears very frequently close on a century later, but the fact remains that this particular School was founded to form a 'nursery for the University' and this it has done. As Alastair has often remarked, one way or another, there is ample choice of fine schools for those whose abilities and ambitions do not incline to the academic. Many of Grammar's students have later become prominent in the professions. Apart from some of the great names to be found amongst them — Sir Edmund Barton, Australia's first Prime Minister, Sir Kenneth Street, Chief Justice of New South Wales fifty years later, and writers ranging in time from A.B. (Banjo) Paterson to R.D. Fitzgerald — there has been a solid core of eminent legal men, scientists of the calibre of Ian Mackerras, theologians, professors and medical men such as Dr Charles MacLaurin, to say nothing of such delightful personalities as that man of words and cricket, Alan McGilvray. They all knew Grammar's *Big Schoolroom*, where Sydney University's first ceremonies were held, and subsequently all major School occasions. As the 1957 history observes — 'when, after 1918, the great carved memorial was placed at its northern end, the *Big Schoolroom* was more than ever full of hallowed memories . . it is both the visible dwelling place of the School's spirit and the centre of its active life. It is an honoured hall rather than a chapel . . used on occasions both solemn and gay, for remembrance ceremonies, for Speech Days, for School dances, for concerts and for plays.'

New buildings in the 1980's are changing old customs, but the *Big Schoolroom* undoubtedly contains the essence of what the School and its traditions mean to Alastair and generations of Old Sydneians.

During the following few years very little happened to disturb the even tenor of his ways. He wrote and had published two text-books on mathematics — *Progressive Mathematics I & II* — with which he felt quite pleased at the time but later found that he 'didn't like teaching from them, pretty rotten really', and was not surprised when they went out of print. He found the summer weeks at Kiama a success and decided to build a holiday house there.

"He chose the block at Kiama with very great care," remarked Peter Young, who stayed with him at the Brighton Hotel while he looked about. "He'd compare the various blocks and stand up on something to see what the view was like a few feet higher." So, *like stout Cortez, with eagle eyes,* he *stared at the Pacific*, and with a pleasant sense of new undertaking, judged the amount of ocean his young charges could take pleasure in if he chose well. This done, he called on his architect brother-in-law, Andrew Briger, Elizabeth's husband, to design a casual dormitory-style house into which eight boys and several Masters might be reasonably fitted. So, with some initial financial assistance from Catherine, the house which was to provide so much pleasure for so many boys over a long period of years, came into being. Colin and his university friend, John Sheldon, were enthusiastic members of these house parties and those that Alastair organised in the Blue Mountains during the winter vacations.

In 1960, a young Prep Master, Peter Harwin, whom he had met with Alan Swan and Edgecliff Headmaster, Reg Billing, joined the group and became one of the house party devotees. Harwin was also a train buff, and often accompanied Alastair on his expeditions. "We were steam train fanatics," Harwin recalled. "We used to ride on the engine cabs. There was a marvellous occasion once when we lost a train. We'd taken the boys for a trip on a semi-goods train from Kiama to Nowra and were coming back. Suddenly, we came unhooked and lost the train in a puff of smoke! The boys were very amused, but Alastair was worried that the lamb he had back in the oven at Kiama might get burnt . . ." He was aware, no doubt, what the boys' priorities would be when they eventually did arrive.

Peter Harwin met the Mackerras family and formed a strong attachment to them, particularly Catherine. He saw that Alastair was very like her in his love for young people, as well as in his approach to theology and in his beliefs, which Peter himself came to share. His impression of Alan was of 'a learned gentleman' whose 'quiet manner had a stabilising effect on Catherine who was very bouncy and explosive and might otherwise have been overwhelming'. The last adjective seems to have summed up for many Catherine's larger than life qualities. Peter met her frequently with Joan at Kiama, where they covered a great range of topics and Catherine was delighted to find that Sydney University students still studied Dickens. They grew very close and he also found himself for a time in love with Joan. The Mackerras mystique is certainly something with which he is well acquainted.

The next happening was a crucial one in Alastair's career. At Sydney Grammar, the office of Master of the Lower School has always been an important one and at that time it carried with it the position of Deputy Headmaster and was held by Mr Aubrey Hanson-Norman, a very senior man, as was usual. He had seemed in good health, but in June 1961, he suffered a stroke and died within a few weeks. Alastair had filled the acting role during the weeks of his illness, and now, at the age of 33, was appointed Master of the Lower School. Since the position was usually given to a man in his fifties, this was very unexpected indeed, and it would seem that the Headmaster, Colin Healey, observing his capacity and inherent suitability, had recommended him to the Board of Trustees, who, in turn, had swept custom aside.

Their confidence was justified, for it was clear from the beginning that, in addition to teaching, administrative work suited him. Although he frequently proclaims that he is physically lazy and frankly admits that he avoided cadets and sport when at school himself, he is in all other matters, as Peter Young has often noted, 'quick, clever and efficient'. He has a horror of allowing work to bank up and, in fact, never does. In his new position, he began to display an ability to make things run smoothly at staff meetings and to dispel any ill-will that might be brewing with some unusual remark or quip. This, together with a wizardry in drawing up timetables and the fraternity he maintained with the boys without sacrificing discipline, soon became his hallmark, and perhaps also, a pointer to the future.

The use of the cane at this stage was something universally accepted in both GPS and State High Schools throughout the country. 'Six of the best' was the way the boys put it at the time and most seemed able to accept this form of punishment, without nursing grievance, when they realised that their behaviour warranted it. Alastair's comment to a couple enrolling their son at the Lower School in the mid-sixties was, "It saves a lot of talk and works miracles." He added cheerfully, in his usual down to earth fashion as he pointed out his own, "I buy them in the basket department of Mark Foys." This must have sounded somewhat alarming, but they were actually used only when a pupil stepped right out of line and he has long since discarded them altogether.

In 1963, the Headmaster was worried by the pressing need for more space and the President of the Old Sydneians' Union, Lyle Moore, who was also the President of the Liberal Party of New South Wales, managed to persuade Prime Minister Menzies to allow Grammar to take over the old Palladium building which was then being used as part of the P.M.G. and bordered the School at the back. The building itself was something of an eyesore, but it had been part of the life of the city since 1915 when it was built as a dance hall and given the unlikely name of *Imperial Salon de Luxe*. "It was a roller skating rink when I was a boy in the school," said Alastair, "and I am told that Wirth's Circus used to perform there." However, its acquisition created valuable space; a gymnasium, for one thing, was provided there and Alastair was able to use a school flat in one of the small adjacent buildings and thereby saved much daily travelling time from Turramurra.

He observed Mr Healey's achievements and methods as Headmaster and was very much impressed. Years later, when Colin Healey was Guest of Honour at Speech Day, he was to say of him and of Sir Norman Cowper, then Chairman of the Trustees, "These two men, in my opinion, have done more for the Sydney Grammar School than any other people in recent times . . . .it is not too much to say that they put it on its feet again after the war and brought it into the modern world. They founded the St Ives Preparatory School and bought Edgecliff, they built the War Memorial Block and the Science Building." On a personal level, he noticed that the Headmaster, a man of great understanding, combined very high standards with a practical approach. The daily comfort of his pupils was something he took into account, and he dispensed with long-standing convention and allowed the boys to remove their ties at school in summer. He implemented the Wyndham Scheme, installed Grammar's effective Tutor system and 'never allowed himself to be carried away by theories of education'. Not everyone saw or understood his essential kindness but, importantly, if a Master or a boy found himself in some sort of trouble or difficulty, he was 'at his best'. This was a model Alastair took to heart in the position he held himself. Most of the staff and pupils were sorry when the Headmaster, in 1965, accepted an invitation to become Principal of Scots College, Melbourne.

The new appointee was an Englishman, Mr Peter Houldsworth, who had been teaching at Harrow School. He came to Australia at a difficult time, a time of flux in the community generally, with an affluent society and a younger generation beginning to question the establishment and look to alternative lifestyles. There was a restlessness among students; many wanted a more flexible system in schools, allowing more personal choice. Furthermore, in public life, the practice of appointing Englishmen to positions of importance in the community was beginning to be frowned upon.

As John Sheldon put it, "People were starting to revolt against having an English Archbishop in Sydney and an English Headmaster. They wanted an Australian. And it's no good pretending that a school like Sydney Grammar is the same as a school like Harrow or Westminster or even a British Grammar School — it's a school with its own quality, a special Australian quality which is felt very strongly. Apart from that, there is a certain type of English Public Schoolmaster who really should stay within the system. I had met Mr Houldsworth when I was teaching in England and found him a very charming man. But when I came back here to take up my appointment I found the place in some turmoil. He just did not fit in here. He did all sorts of good things but they just seemed to be misinterpreted. And there was a lack of *rapport* with staff."

Alastair also saw the situation. The good things were very apparent, such as the moving forward of the Christmas holidays by a week to save the waste of schooling after Public Examinations; and on another plane, the planting of extra trees in the grounds. It was the manner in which the Headmaster went about things that was unfortunate. This was illustrated forcibly in the Music Department which had been set up by Healey and was headed by an Australian musician, Graeme Hall. Joan Mackerras, who was now highly qualified, was violin teacher. The Department was running very smoothly, but the Headmaster ignored this fact and brought out from England another Australian musician, Peter Seymour, who had impressed him in the U.K., and placed him over Hall. Disruptive moves of this sort antagonised staff. The dynamic, innovative Seymour proved to be excellent but the appointment created division at the time. And as far as the pupils were concerned, if some had found Mr Healey a little aloof, almost the entire student body now found the new Headmaster infinitely more so. Alastair felt some foreboding, but perhaps the visible signs of unrest would bring a change of attitude on Houldsworth's part.

At home, the family had become depleted, and Alastair, who remained at his flat at the School, assisted his parents to move from *Harpenden* back to Rose Bay, where *Balvaig* had been turned into two flats, one of which was occupied by Elizabeth and her husband. Alan was reluctant to leave the relevant quiet of Turramurra but Catherine took the move in her stride. Alastair recalls, during part of the moving procedure — when instructions weren't being given as to where things should be placed — the usual avalanche of talk and opinion. Catherine was particularly emphatic at the time on the matter of Australian troops being sent to Vietnam. "We shouldn't be in there," she said, and when he upheld the principle for which they were being sent, she replied, "But it is not our business." She was much in advance of general informed thinking and it seems to have been another instance of her strong historical sense.

Several incidents occurred around 1967 which reveal some of the difficulties inherent in positions of authority within any school, and of Alastair's method of dealing with them in particular. Malcolm Turnbull, who was later to distinguish himself scholastically (he is one of the several Rhodes Scholars over the last decade the School is proud to claim), ran into trouble when he was in the Lower School and also a boarder. "I was a very precocious, bumptious sort of youth," he said, "and they had a very elaborate fagging system at the small boarding house. You cleaned all the prefects rooms, made their beds and performed sundry other menial tasks for them. These 'duties' were imposed for various crimes committed, and if they didn't like you, you never stopped committing crimes. I, being very bumptious, told various prefects that I wasn't going to submit to this sort of rubbish. I was then assaulted by four of these fellows who were big eighteen year old men. They belted me up and kicked me. It was really quite a serious bashing. I mean, if it happened to you in the street all the people involved would go to jail." Although this had happend at Randwick School House and not the School grounds, he felt instinctively that Alastair was the one who would see the realities of the situation and that the whole system needed to be looked at. He accordingly went and saw him. "He spoke to the Headmaster at once," said Turnbull. "Everything was sorted out, and these so-called prefects were pulled into gear. Alastair is very swift in his retribution to people who are really doing the wrong thing." It is a strength for which he has also been criticised over the years, particularly by those not in prossession of the full facts of a case.

Similarly, another incident which occurred about this time, is indicative of his straight-speaking with the young. "I was in Second Form," Turnbull recalls, "and a boy was accosted by a Master on the grounds of selling French letters. The Master, in great fury, dragged this unfortunate youth up to Mackerras, doubtless for the purpose of beating him, and Alastair was in great strife because he really wasn't aware of what this terrible thing was for. He had a sense of humour. He stood up in the Lower School Assembly and held this French letter up, still in its packet, and said that this sort of thing was not to be peddled round the School — and added that he'd never seen one of them before that morning. The kids respected him for that." Alastair also discovered that the main sin his pupils had committed was, as Turnbull said, 'filling the things with large quantities of water and dropping them out of windows on passers by . . . '

An eccentricity of Alastair which he shares with other members of the family, noticeably Colin, is his practice of humming or singing passages from operas or concertos, or whatever happens to come to mind, as he goes about his daily activities. He has been told that he even sings in the classroom but is not inclined to believe it. Certainly, music is so much a part of the Mackerrases, it is never far from them and in moments of relaxation invariably with them, if not on record, or in the opera house, or concert hall, then on their air waves or on their lips. "Alastair must be the only person known to mankind who can whistle the whole of *Parsifal* from beginning to end!" said their friend, Tim Yates, while former pupils of Alastair vouch for Wagnerian themes wafting with sea breezes and along bush tracks at Kiama or simply sounding above the sizzling of sausages and steak as he prepared barbecued meals for them.

"It was the most wonderfully relaxed atmosphere," said John Sheldon, who had taken a further degree at Cambridge and was now teaching Latin and Greek at the Grammar School, "just like a family holiday. Alastair has this real interest in getting to know the boys as people, which is what you could do in that atmosphere." He used to endeavour to take virtually all the pupils from his form and some others, over the six weeks' holiday, eight at a time and a week at a time, which meant forty-eight students in all. It was, Malcolm Turnbull recalled, 'a much prized sort of thing, a treat, for which parents just contributed basic food expenses'.

"It was a marvellous period," said David Gonski, also from the legal world and one of three brothers who went to the School, "rather like an Outward Bound camp. It was a time for teaching us the finer things of life which many of us did not know. He took us swimming and talked about the history of the area and organised bush walking and expeditions. He led us out of the more straight type of reading into the more exciting. And the teachers who came were versed in Latin which we hadn't touched on. It was very exciting. And also it made you close to your school mates."

In fact, Alastair, together with John Sheldon, Peter Harwin and other Masters who went over the years, used to cap the days by reading to the boys each night. Stephen Leacock's humour as a writer appealed to Alastair — '*The harder you push a bike, the faster it goes; this is because of natural science*' ("Must be natural science," he says when his car does inexplicable things) — and Leacock was usually among the authors chosen. Peter Harwin commented, "We'd sit on the bed and they'd have their lights out and we'd read them stories from Leacock, Saki, Sherlock Holmes, Wodehouse and Buchan". A pleasant image to conjure, in an age when we are so constantly being presented with depressing ones, are those First Formers, drowsy from sun and sea and bush, replete with food and talk and companionship, drifting off to sleep to such narrative fare and affection.

The problem, of course, was that it was hard enough to get round all the boys in the A Maths class Alastair taught, let alone those in B — F grades who no doubt felt somewhat left out. Though perhaps, not having been taught by him, they didn't realise just what they were missing. "We used to look forward to his maths lessons on Friday afternoons," said David Gonski, "not because you learnt so much about maths, but because it was his and he told you all the juicy things that were happening in the School and outside the School — it was a liberal education!"

About this time, one of his pupils father, Dr Tony Edwards, a young man of thirty-five and an academic physiologist, whom he had known as a boy at Turramurra, died of cancer. The pupil, Stephen Edwards, was the eldest of a family of two boys and two girls and their parents had been ideally happy. "It was very sad," Gonski recalled, "and I remember when Stephen wasn't at School, Alastair explaining it to us with great compassion. In fact, over the six years I was there, I actually remember him explaining a lot of deaths to us. He's a very compassionate man."

Alastair took a particular interest in Stephen, and his brother Peter when he came to the School the following year. They were clever boys, keen students, and responsive. He came to know their mother, Sue Edwards, and their two young sisters, Frances and Margot, found them altogether a delightful family and a friendship developed.

By final term in 1968, the situation at Grammar was a very unhappy one. The senior boys had become restive. Some, very much a product of the questioning 60's, were resentful of compulsory cadets, compulsory football and such things as having to keep hair length above the collar. They had been feeling discontented for some time. One of them, Alistair Bell, who had come through the Edgecliff Prep School, often availed himself of Alastair's open door policy as Master of the Lower School and spoke to him on the subject. "The problem at Grammar," he recalled, "was that if you didn't fit into the mould, they blamed you for it. The School didn't have any capacity for seeing its own shortcomings. It's essentially controlled by its history. By the Old Boys. And I don't think that's right. I think it's really up to the parents, teachers and students to decide how the education programme should be run. There was no flexibility. They paid 90% of attention to what you did wrong and not really any attention to the things that you did want to do or might be good at. It was bad for confidence. And from my observations, the effect of caning people and putting people in detention — the detention Master loved every minute of it — was very much like the effect we see of people being put in Long Bay. They come out more disenchanted with the system than ever and less likely to do the right thing. Then, there was the very rigid attitude to military training, cadets and football. Alastair Mackerras was very sympathetic but he didn't seem to be able to do anything about it." It was a question of hastening slowly, as will be seen, for change could only be brought about when presented by a Headmaster within the framework of the School's constitution.

These rigid policies were not only accepted by, but greatly exacerbated by, the aloof attitude of the Headmaster. "He was very cold and very arrogant," said Malcolm Turnbull. "He just had no comprehension of how to deal with Australian boys. I remember when I was in Second Form, I wanted to start a History Club and I had to make an appointment two weeks in advance to see the Headmaster. Well, that's bizarre, quite bizarre. He just couldn't have been that busy." Alistair Bell used the phrase 'quite bizarre' about the militaristic manner in which P.T. classes were held. So, whether it was a pupil who was highly suited to the School or one who wished someone had suggested to him that he go to another, right through the whole mainstream of students there was a feeling of disaffection. There was also much dissension amongst the staff.

Finally, when an obscene remark about the Headmaster was painted on the wall, also the phrase 'SPTH is a four letter word' on the banner above the School, both in mid-October when the Sixth Form leave for 'Stu-vac' before the H.S.C. examination, it was clear that something had to be done. Alastair spoke to the Headmaster and tried to persuade him to resign. He would not consider it, so Alastair asked him to arrange an appointment for him with Sir Norman Cowper, Chairman of the Board of Trustees on the matter. He also spoke to an old school friend, Graham Crouch, who was now a Trustee and who spoke to the Chairman. Alastair himself then told Sir Norman that the Headmaster had lost the respect and confidence of Masters and boys and that the only real solution was for the Board to suggest to him that resignation was the best course. He told him that in speaking thus he was aware that he was putting his own job on the line, for, if the *status quo* remained in regard to the Headmaster, then he himself would not be able to work under him.

Five or six more difficult weeks of term remained. Alastair did not speak again during this time to Sir Norman or any other members of the Board. Mr Houldsworth had a number of interviews with Sir Norman and the

Alastair finds relaxation as train buff, with young Stephen Edwards and his friend, Ted Marr, in 1969.

full Board on the whole grave matter and was disinclined to resign. Discussion continued.

This period was, of course, extremely unhappy for Alastair. Not only was his career in the balance, but he was temperamentally badly affected by having precipitated the final, inevitable crisis. Since Catherine's early ban on 'fighting' in the Mackerras household, as adults the family were, as Alastair remarked, 'no good at rows'. He now 'felt terrible'. After three weeks, a decision was reached by Mr Houldsworth. He resigned at the end of term, 1968, returned to England, and in due course took up another appointment. The Board, meanwhile, appointed Alastair Acting Headmaster, to commence in 1969, and did not immediately advertise the position.

Alastair's old friend, John Parkinson, called to see him that Christmas of '68 at Kiama and they discussed the subject. "After the part I've taken, I will not apply for the position," Alastair told him. "If they were to invite me, if they were to call upon me, then, in that case only, could I accept."

The Edwards boys were amongst those at Kiama that worrying vacation and he continued to see a great deal of the whole family. Sue Edwards — formerly McCubbin, a granddaughter of the painter, Frederick McCubbin — was feeling as much in need of cheering company as was Alastair himself. "I was very depressed," he said, "and so was she. She had been very much in love with her first husband. We seemed to do each other some good. And the children were lovely." It is no wonder they reciprocated his affection. It was as though ordained that he, so ordered and caring, should come into their disrupted young lives. As far as he and Sue were concerned, it seems to have been a classic case of the attraction of opposites. She was in no way a disciplined person, but intelligent, warm, effervescent and very pretty indeed; her interests lay in the world of artists. She had found it extremely hard to cope with the tragedy that had beset her. Now, the breadth of the companionship she had with Alastair must have seemed like coming into harbour.

He took up his temporary responsibilities at the beginning of the new school year and expected a difficult time ahead. In the event, he found a great deal of co-operation and support from everyone concerned, including, with very few exceptions, the boys themselves. He was so delighted at the manner in which they co-operated that when this spirit was exhibited by the not very strong 1st XV, taking out an unexpected victory over Scots that season, he behaved in a most uncharacteristic fashion and ran onto the field at the end of play!

After some months, the Chairman of the Trustees told him that the Trustees were going to advertise world-wide to fill the position of Headmaster and asked him personally to apply. With some hesitation, he did so. In August, 1969, the Board came to their decision. John Sheldon commented, "They were clearly looking round for someone who could put heart back into the School again. They needed someone who knew it well and was absolutely dedicated to its well-being — and had proved himself in a position of importance and responsibility as Alastair had done as Master of the Lower School. He had been very popular and they knew he would make a good Headmaster — unusual, no doubt, but still a man of tremendous ability and great heart."

The Chairman, Sir Norman Cowper, addressed the staff in the Common Room and announced Alastair's appointment. He commented, as Sheldon foresaw, that Alastair would probably not be a conventional Headmaster and 'a lot of people may think that he may be a little bit way out', and then came to the crux of the matter, concluding, "He somehow seems to have the knack of winning the respect and the affectionate obedience of the boys". So they put their trust in him. At the same time, Sir Norman announced the appointment of John Sheldon as Master of the Lower School. Alastair did not learn until several years later that the Board had deliberately waited some time to advertise so that they could 'see how he went as Acting Headmaster'.

"For Alastair," remarked John Parkinson, "the achievement was that as both a Roman Catholic and a bachelor, he was appointed to the Headmastership of a School which, although a non-sectarian School, is almost entirely non-Catholic in its Board, boys and Old Boys. So it was a great tribute to his personal worth, that with those two handicaps, they were brave enough to appoint him Headmaster."

In the August holidays following his appointment, he spoke to Sue about their relationship and discussed marriage with her. She accused him laughingly of wanting to marry her for the children, and he certainly did find them a great joy, but they both also found pleasure and happiness in each other's company and decided to marry. Peter Harwin, who had just returned from several years teaching in Portugal, gave them a memorable engagement party. Her young family were delighted, as was Alan, who already enjoyed taking the two girls sailing. Sue was well able to hold her own in the conversational stakes with Catherine, with whom she had swiftly formed a bond. Nevertheless, Catherine had some misgivings about the forthcoming marriage. She saw how deep was their divergence in temperament and in emotional needs, and was conscious of the pitfalls that might lie ahead. Never intrusive in the lives of her family, she said nothing. Another who had similar reservations was Kate Wilson, Catherine's friend from Turramurra days, who was also an aunt of the Edwards family and extremely fond of both Sue and Alastair. She was in London at this time but feels certain that if she had been in Sydney she would have voiced her thoughts. It is doubtful, however, if either was in any mood to heed advice.

"Sue had a lot of the McCubbin in her," said Peter Harwin who was charmed by her. "Her twin brother, Charles, is a painter in Melbourne and we often talked of the family and compared the McCubbins and Boyds — Martin Boyd being my favourite Australian writer. She had a great gift for friendship. She was lovely. A very sensitive person. But she was very different from Alastair and it was clear from the outset that there would be difficulties." He recalled that they made what they called 'a non-aggression pact', declaring that they would not try to change each other. It seemed to him a very intelligent attitude towards their inherent differences.

Alastair's immediate concern from his new perspective as Headmaster, was the trend he found of boys having so much extra-curricular activity, whether music, art, woodwork, cadets, or sports of every kind, that they were run off they feet. He saw that one of the laudable objects of the Wyndham system — 'to educate for leisure' — would actually defeat itself if, in the process of doing this, they found themselves with no leisure at all. He commented on this in his first Speech Day address, recalling that in his youth at the School there were 'large satisfactory blocks of time' when he was free to do as he liked. "I can remember how I used to look forward to them and to enjoy them," he said, "I could work or read or play or idle or dream just as I pleased. No one fussed us. *What is this life, if full of care, we have no time to stand and stare?*" This was clearly a foreshadowing of the freeing of boys from too many compulsory activities, which was one of his aims.

One summer day, late in December 1969, with hopes high for the future, Alastair and Sue were married at St Mary's Cathedral, the great church into whose cool depths Catherine had stolen as a schoolgirl, whose white marble altar and kneeling figures had made such an impression on her and whose joyful clash of bells had drifted across the city to 155 Macquarie Street to entrance her as a child. The family, together with a small group of friends, watched the pair exchange their vows, and any constraint that Alan might have felt at the setting would certainly have been counteracted by his pride in Alastair, the School close by, and the happiness on the faces of the four step-grandchildren he was about to acquire.

They went in the New Year, 1970, to live at Grammar's spacious, rambling 'Headmaster's house' at Mosman. Sue introduced Alastair to artists and her world of art, which, his friends noted, broadened his horizons and did him no harm at all. She, in turn, found weekends at Kiama walking on Seven Mile Beach with the family, going on picnics

148   *Scholars and Gentlemen*

and exploring the coutryside, a joy. They were very happy and differences seemed minimal indeed.

It was an exceedingly busy school year. Meetings with the Trustees involved detailed planning of a $3.6m redevelopment of the School's buildings, in which a four storey complex with modern educational aids was to be built on the site. It provided for a bigger language laboratory, closed circuit television, audio visual aids, a debating chamber, a senior students' common room, a new library (Grammar's was by then the largest school library collection in Australia), lecture theatre, gymnasium, covered playing area and a car park. Sir Norman Cowper was the driving force in this big enterprise. He launched an appeal for $1m to help pay for it, quickly raised $300,000 and then organised a dinner, attended by about eight hundred and with Sir Robert Menzies as guest speaker, to act as a

Alastair's wife, Sue, at Kangaroo Valley, 1971 (Alastair was the photographer).

further spur. He himself outlined the plans, assured everyone that the main historic sandstone buildings would be left untouched and generally fired enthusiasm. Alastair saw that the targets set, both financially and in the expected four year building period, would be achieved. He was exceedingly thankful for the force of Sir Norman's vision and for his dedication.

On day to day matters, he wrestled with many problems. He always felt it important, as do the majority of educators, for pupils to look neat. Here he was in conflict with the trend for long hair which seems to have been a symbol of self-assertion amongst many of the non-conforming young of the 60's, since it could clearly not have been for comfort in Australia's climate. He therefore appointed a Master to superintend 'hairstyles' and asked for the co-operation of parents, persisting with the matter until he saw that the students' hair at least cleared their collars. Young Alistair Bell found the requirement an infringement of personal liberty, the last straw in 'a very rigid system'. On Speech Day, 1969, a prefect, with whom he had been through Edgecliff Prep, insisted, with the backing of Alastair as Headmaster, that Bell have a haircut and shave (the latter he has never done since, so strong is his preference in the matter). It does seem unlikely that the assembled dignitaries that day would have noticed a dissenter in the midst of the general body of students; certainly this severe treatment made a deep mark on Alistair Bell who did not return the following year. He completed his studies at the Australian Independent School where his brand of non-conformism was acceptable and where he was very much happier. Intelligent and sensitive, as well as self-willed — he probably inherited his stubbornly determined attitudes from two pioneer grazing families — he did find pleasure in English, art, music and several sports at Grammar; he also appreciated efforts made by Rodney Knock, as Form Master, to ease his path a little. Today, however, as a professional musician, with experience in fields as wide apart as wheat testing and instructing in sailing, he still retains bitter feelings towards Sydney Grammar.

Rodney Knock commented, "Alastair Mackerras believes that only one or two things in life are important — moral behaviour and education of the mind, learning. He will *not* get het up over minor things." Why then, insistence upon such matters as length of hair? Because, perhaps, these things are part of larger issues. He believes strongly in the principle of 'living under authority', in the acceptance of authority, a concept which had been imbued in him at an early age and which he invariably upholds in matters both far-reaching and small.

He had yet some mellowing to do and it was unfortunate that a young relative, who seemed to have a propensity for getting himself into trouble, did not cross his path a little later when the Mark Foys canes had been discarded. Piers Laverty, who recently won a coveted scholarship to the prestigious Pottery School at Wollongong, and is related to the Mackerrases on the Nathan side, also had a very unhappy time at Grammar. He was wrongly blamed by students for reporting to Alastair some unpleasant fruit-throwing episodes by a group of Grammar boys — the foreman of a gang of workmen on the Bridge who were thus harrassed actually reported the matter and Piers was simply a spectator. A pupil was expelled as a result and the boys thereafter made Piers' life miserable. Alastair did what he could to rectify the situation but Piers seemed unable to keep out of trouble and on one occasion he found it necessary to cane him. English Master, Jeremy Nelson, who regards Alastair as an exceptionally fine Headmaster, and is married to Piers' aunt, Venetia, commented, "It's a School that isn't digestible for some boys. Piers tended to centre all his disapproval and disappointment and suffering at Grammar on that caning, with Alastair at the centre of it, and it is a burden which he must now walk away from and cease to carry. I'm glad to say that although caning was a custom for a very long time at the School it no longer is, for it does produce rancour of this kind." Particularly, no doubt, if a boy is basically unhappy. Piers could be described at this time as a disaffected pupil, one who had no desire whatsoever to study or profit by the calibre of teaching available to him, and admits that he should never have been sent to Grammar, for he found all his years there 'a waste of time'.

Complexities and difficulties of this kind seem inseparable from the running of a big school and have for that reason been analysed in some detail. Alastair also noticed that there was still an overall restlessness among many of the young who, he observed, 'respected nothing and nobody' and therefore had 'a sort of moral formlessness' which he considered much more dangerous in its effect than the severe disciplines under which other generations had laboured, for the latter had at least had 'a pattern to grow to'. He was aware that part of the malaise lay with his own generation, with parents and teachers who seemed to have lost confidence in, and partly abdicated from, their task of training the young people.

He was especially glad that first year of the support of the staff, in particular, John Sheldon and the Senior Master, Bob Ross, whose 'witty sallies' and practical help lightened much administrative work. An essential factor also was his relationship with the Chairman of the Board of Trustees, Sir Norman Cowper, who extended warm friendship as well as sound advice and was generally 'a tower of strength'. It is interesting that both men, the older and the younger, went back, one way or another, to the inception of the School, and Alastair must also have thought of that august forebear, Sir Normand MacLaurin, sitting in that very boardroom on his busy round in the 1890s.

He now set about trying to instil a more positive attitude generally. He noticed that most senior boys who were 'centres of disaffection' were those who were not really interested in further study; their parents had simply sent them back to school in the hope that they would mature there. He urged them to leave, take a job and see a little of the world. That way, he told them, they would be likely to mature much more satisfactorily. Those who were destined for tertiary education, who formed the big majority at the School, he urged to choose their Faculty in advance, and their subjects accordingly and not to try to cover too many options. Whilst acknowledging the importance of sport — he was known to have attended as many as twenty sporting events in one weekend to indicate his support — he began the process of allowing more flexibility in extra-curricular activities, so that music, debating and drama groups became legitimate alternatives. He urged all students to take part voluntarily in one or other of all these activities, for without them no real school spirit could be achieved. He was very much aware of the *esprit de corps* built up by the cadets during the School's long history. Membership for senior boys had always been voluntary but a condition of enrolment was that boys in Third and Fourth Form be members of one of the three Cadet Corps. He saw no reason as yet to alter this requirement. The business of life, he told them, was to learn to *want* to do what you ought or must do. Cadet camps were something not at all difficult to fit into that category.

Since the State's educational system now required a wider range of subjects to be undertaken by pupils, with internal tests supplementing public examinations, he appointed a Committee of Masters, headed by Peter Young (Assistant to the Headmaster), to enquire into the best use of school time. The outcome of this was the conclusion that morale was likely to depend increasingly on boys tasting some success in their work and in their confidence and ability to undertake it. The School's first duty then, it was agreed, was, more than ever, the provision of good teaching. Meanwhile, he himself worked strenuously to provide the new timetables necessary.

David Gonski, who was one of those delighted to have debating as an extra-curricular activity and to be regarded as not a lesser person for that preference, gives a vivid glimpse of Alastair about this time. "Not only was his door wide open as Headmaster but he was still swamped in the playground by boys running around wanting to talk. He seems to know what they want. And when the School was required to increase the number of options available, he showed his genius for administration. He found he couldn't fit all the 40 minute periods into a week, so he thought of a scheme he had seen at a school in England and said, *I think if we had a six day week it would work much better.* It seemed impossible with School only open five days, but he worked out a six day timetable. So at Sydney Grammar the timetable runs on a cycle of six days. Whereas before, when you got your timetable, it said Monday to Friday, it now said A, B, C, D, E, F and Monday could be any of those days. The Sergeant-at-Arms pinned up the name of the day — A or whatever — on the big board in the playground. The only thing that was fixed was cadets and sport. It was a brilliant idea, very confusing but brilliant. And it worked . . . " Alastair has since facilitated its use by several other schools.

He also succeeded in introducing flexibility into the prefect system, which had been based almost exclusively on sport, so that more often than not the members of the 1st XV were all prefects. The choice is now made by the Headmaster on all-round abilities and he has also instituted a student election. The result of the student election is not binding, nor is it made known, but it is taken into consideration, together with other information, when his choice is made; the Headmaster also names the Senior Prefect. Malcolm Turnbull found himself in this role in 1972, and was also, at the end of the year, Captain of the School. "I was amazed at Alastair's patience with difficult pupils and their parents," he said. "He's so tolerant. There was one boy, I remember, I'd have *had* to boot out! He just puts up with it all."

None of the changes he implemented happened easily or quickly. "I was badly in need of an opportunity to take some stock," he said himself, "and to try to clarify my sometimes conflicting thoughts." The Trustees suggested that he and his wife take a trip to Europe and the United States and look at developments in the educational field. It was also suggested that they take note of modern school buildings, for at this point it was the intention of the Trustees to move the School from College Street to Edgecliff.

"It was a wonderful experienece for both of us," he said. "We inspected about forty schools of very different kinds — traditional schools, boarding and day schools, selective, comprehensive, vocational and technical . . . and non-graded schools." They talked to Headmasters and administrators and saw the schools in operation. As before, he was impressed with the English Public Schools but felt they had little relevance in the Australian context. On the other hand, he gained insights from visits to several large day schools — "They were very like Grammar. I recognised the atmosphere the moment I went inside them. To me there is much sound common sense and wisdom in these schools."

While in England, he and Sue stayed with Charles and Judy, which was a great pleasure all round, added to by the unexpected appearance of their cousin David Mackerras, in London for a conference. Then it was on to the United States where they deliberately sought out some of the more modern schools to inspect. It was Alastair's first visit to America and while extremely grateful for the warmth and hospitality extended to them everywhere and for the amount of time heads of schools and colleges spent with them in discussion, he remained unconvinced by 'the continual emphasis on new practices' in education. He saw little virtue in Open Schools, modular scheduling (which he described as only 'tinkering with the timetable'), or very lavish audio visual equipment. He was more impressed with two Directors of Educational Research whose job it was to evaluate trends and who found that new syllabuses in nearly all subjects were proving no better than the old. He saw that the system in the United States of admission of students to universities from schools on their school record had the merit of giving broader scope for teaching, but he was concerned at the talk by many teachers of the 'student being responsible for his own progress' and of 'self-paced learning'. After 'much meditation and a great deal of reading on the subject', he decided that this attitude had come about not so much through 'a revolt of youth', but through a large scale loss of confidence by teachers in their mission to teach and also as a result of the collapse of parental authority, phenomena which he had previously observed in Australia. He felt sympathy for the young who had 'a good deal more sense and justice on their side than we care to admit'.

Back in harness and grateful for the fine leadership displayed by his Deputy, Bob Ross, during his absence, he set about the process of consolidating the direction in which his Headmastership had already taken the School. He was convinced now that his educational beliefs, though they might be disputed by many, were based on a solid foundation. He was strongly of the opinion that the School's reason for existence lay in its being an independent one, with an independent board, and that it should pursue its own policies. He spoke of the need to create 'new myths' while never departing from certain 'ineluctable truths and ideals'. One must 'change to stop things changing'. The structure of compulsory Cadets had long served the cause of School spirit, but now appeared to work against it. The newly elected Whitlam Labor Government had, in fact, refused to provide funds for compulsory Corps. Membership of the Cadet Corps would therefore become voluntary; it seemed, he said, 'that the spirit of the times decreed it'. A voluntary Corps would probably work better in future and that was 'saying a great deal'.

He indicated that the existing policy of giving a wider choice of sports and activities — such diverse things as soccer and 'helping the Smith Family' — would be extended, which would probably mean accepting less success in some of the traditional Great Public Schools sports. He pointed out that things were 'not going to the dogs' as far as all these matters were concerned, in fact, Grammar had won two GPS Premierships in 1973 and he urged the disgruntled to put matters in perspective. He saw much about him for which everyone should be very thankful, whether it was the School Orchestra — second to none in Sydney — or the Women's Association, whose work, he said, in his typical way, 'filled him with wonder and very great gratitude'. He also felt that the decision made by the Trustees to phase out by 1976 the boarding section of Grammar, School House, at Randwick, was a correct one.

He stressed his belief in the primary importance of good communication between staff and boys, particularly senior boys, in keeping morale high, He dealt explicitly with the Karmel Report, as he was to deal with others during the following decade, saying he found it 'materialistic and anti-intellectual in character', and declared that, for him, schools were 'places of Scholarship'. He admitted that it was an 'elitist philosophy of a kind', but gave warning that he would continue to promote it. The School was set firmly on its course.

It was in this year, 1973, that Alan Mackerras suffered his fatal illness, and we shall look later at his and Catherine's last years and Alastair's closeness to his parents. His own personal life at this time held both excitement and unexpected anxiety. The excitement was provided by the wonderful Opening Season of the Sydney Opera House, with gala nights, Charles conducting on a number of occasions and family and friends in attendance. The anxiety was to see his wife, Sue, drift into a state of depression.

"She was a great little girl, but she found it extremely hard to cope with what happened to her," said Kate Wilson, the Edwards family aunt and Mackerras friend, speaking of Tony Edwards' death. "I feel that Alastair was meant to come in there, he was just so sane. And those children loved him — and still do. And then, you see, you couldn't help loving Susie, she was so gay and full of fun. But, of course, she was looking for another Tony." It does seem that she was seeking the kind of emotional fulfilment she had experienced with her first young husband, and this, with Alastair's temperament, was not to be.

Looking back, Alastair blames himself in many ways. "We were incompatible," he said. "I think now, although of course I didn't at the time, that I probably wasn't prepared to change my bachelor ways." This, it seems, Catherine had foreseen. He is certainly very self-sufficient and as his brother Colin observed, 'he doesn't need anyone to look after him the way most men do'. Alastair remembers Sue commenting several times to him, "I've never known anyone as independent as you in my whole life. You don't need anybody. You don't need anything." This *cri de coeur* was naturally exaggerated, for, to begin with, he very clearly needs to have the young about him, but there is an element of truth in it. He can seem discomfitingly remote. One friend describes this as 'a sometimes daunting abstractedness that one needs to know how to walk through, for the warmth is there,' and another as 'a certain brusqueness and abruptness which you learn not to be offended by because you know you have his friendship'. It is a characteristic which is seldom, if ever, demonstrated with the young with whom he is very warm and open. It seems probable that Sue, who had obviously learnt how to reach him, found herself, as her depression grew and therefore her need, floundering against this rather formidable aspect of him, or perhaps she simply lost her understanding of it, so that she was unable to absorb his much needed strengths as she had initially done.

In 1975, Catherine, who had lost much of her drive and vitality, and whose health was now indifferent, felt she wanted to travel once more to England to see her daughter Joan, and Sue offered to accompany her. The pair set off and had several very satisfactory, if not entirely worry free, weeks away together. After some time with Joan, who was immensely sad to see her mother's deterioration in health, Charles and Judy arranged accommodation nearby for them in London, as the stairs at 10 Hamilton Terrace were now out of the question. "Sue was wonderful to Catherine," said Judy. "She was very grateful to her and so were we, because we never saw Catherine again." At home the two Edwards boys were at university, the girls at school, and the four were happy to be with Alastair at Mosman. Altogether, there were reciprocal needs and much affection.

A vital decision was taken by Grammar School Trustees that year. They had been investigating for some time the feasibility of moving the whole School to Edgecliff where more space for rebuilding was available. Instead, it was decided to demolish the old Palladium building, rebuild there, and remain at College Street. The wisdom of that decision is apparent, and it was the last important one made under the chairmanship of Sir Norman Cowper. He retired at the end of the year and Alastair commented at Speech Day, "I doubt if it will ever be known what Sir Norman Cowper has done for the School over the years; he has been on the Old Sydneians Committee for over half a century, a Trustee for 42 years and Chairman for 23 years. He has been a tower of strength to successive Headmasters with his wisdom, humour and warmth; I never knew a man who could settle a row with such skill. I never knew a more generous-minded man. I doubt if a petty thought has ever crossed his mind." The following year, when Sir Norman attended Speech Day as guest of honour, Alastair felt there was something 'vaguely unnatural' about welcoming someone to an occasion over which he had presided for so many years. It was the end of an era of truly remarkable service and dedication. Another old Sydneian, Graham (G.J.) Crouch, a Trustee of some years standing, with a long association with the School, and as Alastair observed, 'a firm grasp of its affairs', stepped into his distinguished shoes.

Graham Crouch and Alastair were well-known to each other from their own student days at the School. Also the former's sons were at Grammar throughout most of their school life, and he has vivid recollections of calling to see Alastair in the early morning when he was Master of the Lower School and finding him in his study inundated with small boys all talking at once, enjoying themselves hugely and 'not wanting to be shooed out of the room'. He has memories of dropping his sons off for a week at Kiama and finding Alastair 'cooking the barbecue or making the milkshakes with boys and parents all about'. He was well acquainted then with this central aspect of Alastair. He was also aware of his administrative ability which had been apparent to him in the incisiveness of the memoranda and recommendations he had presented to the Trustees over the years. For both, it was an excellent foundation on which to build.

This was an extremely difficult time for those administering secondary education in New South Wales, for various aspects of the system were being dismantled. For instance, external examination for the School Certificate was replaced by assessment within the schools and Alastair worried that 'eventually the standard of the Higher School Certificate would be undermined'. Since it formed the basis of determining much sought after university places, he hoped that a similar fate would not overtake it, for he felt it to be the most equitable system. He pointed out that Public Examinations were invented to give the non-privileged a chance of competing with the privileged, adding, "There is irony in the fact that many people want to abolish Public Examinations because schools such as ours do so well at them." He pronounced himself an old-fashioned educationalist and therefore proud of the fact that Grammar students were doing increasingly well in both the High School Certificate and the University of New South Wales Mathematics Competition.

Music at the School, under Peter Seymour's direction, had now reached a level where the Choir was good enough to be invited to take part in ABC and Philharmonia Concerts and in Australian Opera productions, and about a quarter of the School was actively involved in either the choir or instrumental groups. There were complaints from many that football had suffered commensurately with this change in emphasis, and also because of Alastair's dislike of the sport, on the other hand, the School was doing very well in other sports and had won several more Premierships, while the new gymnasium, equipped with squash courts, was in tremendous demand. Alastair was amused by a parent's description of a typical Grammar School boy passing through the Town Hall station — "Left hand dragging a Grammar bag, right hand holding a violin case, an airways bag with sports gear slung over his shoulder, a squash racquet under his arm and his train pass in his teeth!"

His aim to produce, above all, a happy and balanced School community seemed to be coming to fruition. Sadly, at home a major crisis was impending. Sue had declined into a deep depression and had come to regard herself as being quite without solace. It was clear that the situation could not continue as it was. In 1977 her psychiatrist advised her that it would be better to separate; she and Alastair agreed to this. It was also the year of Catherine's death. Her father's estate had then been duly divided amongst the family, Charles and Elizabeth combining to buy the

Balvaig property, with Elizabeth remaining in the upper floor unit and Charles possessing the lower floor unit, which would be useful for his visits to Australia. Alastair now went to live in the latter and the Grammar School Trustees came to an agreement with Charles; they paid rental for it as the Headmaster's Residence, with part of that rental, at Charles' suggestion, forming Music Scholarships to enable boys with ability, who may not otherwise have had the opportunity to attend Sydney Grammar, to do so. Alastair still visited Sue and his stepsons and daughters constantly and managed to persuade Sue to join in the barbecues which he provided for the young people at their home at Mosman.

The pressure of work for all Headmasters in third term, with so much evaluation to be done, is very great and he has always been the despair of his secretary, who, in an endeavour to protect him from callers, firmly closes the big cedar door between his study and the ante-room where people wanting to see him first appear. He promptly opens his other door so that, should there be an anxiously hovering pupil, he will see him. Peter Harwin commented, "Boys come to him with all sorts of personal and emotional problems and he listens to them all and is very sympathetic. He's had to deal with so many of them, some with certain raffish habits and that sort of thing, that he would never have known anything about, and he advises and helps them. It's astonishing really, because he had such a sheltered life as a young man. But he's seen more or less 360° of the human arrangement now. And he's learning all the time himself. He never stops

Peter Harwin, Headmaster, Sydney Grammar Preparatory School, Edgecliff and family friend.

John Sheldon, Master of the Lower School, SGS, and family friend, on holiday at Berry.

learning and he passes on his knowledge when we ask for advice with our pupils."

In August 1977, during the European summer, Alastair went for a brief period to England and then had a few weeks in Europe. He heard Charles conducting in the South of France, was amused to be mistaken for him in the street the next day, and generally found the time a very necessary unwinding from many stresses. Peter Harwin was in Portugal on long service leave and keen to show him something of the country which he knew well and which Alastair had not previously visited. They met and toured about for a week. Alastair was greatly taken with 'the uncorrupted peasant people' and the old history of the region. "But I got terribly frustrated with him there," said Peter. "He's a great connoisseur of ice cream, you know, and he wanted to taste all the different varieties. We'd be in a little village somewhere and I'd be pointing out some wonderful painting and he'd say, 'Look, there's an ice cream. Quick, let's get that fellow.' My Portuguese isn't very good and I got very cranky!"

Back with the reins at Grammar, he found one of his concerns to be the choice of careers for the boys and therefore built up the Careers Department. He had become aware of the unhappy results of uninformed and poor choices and wanted to ensure that each set off on a career that would be, to a reasonable extent, satisfying or fulfilling. "Unless it is in harmony with the basic personality of the boy", he said, "and within his intellectual capacity, then it is a poor choice." He hoped none would turn out 'a square peg that has to fit into a round hole'.

That year, 1978, was his tenth as Headmaster and he received a letter from the staff which touched him deeply. It contained the sentence, "We feel that Sydney Grammar School is a very happy place to teach at. The combination of good discipline, high academic achievement and an appreciative student body has created a climate of goodwill and high staff morale." He was grateful, he told them, for their 'constant help, support, advice and at times comfort' and also of the 'very obvious support and goodwill of nearly all the boys'. It was a fulfilling School year capped by victory for both their Eights in the Head of the River, both boats presented by the Parents and Friends, and one named for him. He was delighted to see that the *Alastair Mackerras* was more buoyant than he had ever been! The following year there were also successes in cricket, tennis and athletics — the latter the first for twenty-five years — so for the time being even the rumbling of dissatisfaction over football ceased. He also observed how smoothly things were going with John Sheldon as Master of the Lower School. He was not only undertaking all the usual responsibilities of that job, but was also dealing extremely efficiently with the complex problems of the Entrance Examination.

These very positive things were the reverse of the situation in his personal life. Since his separation from Sue eighteen months before, on the advice of her doctor, there had been much quiet agonising on his part. He felt the decision had been the only one, but worried deeply that if they had managed to stay together it may possibly have had some beneficial effect on her. Her family thought not, and he saw them constantly. In 1979, when Sue was really very debilitated, she was beset by a gynaecological problem. Her early death was an infinite sadness. Their good friend, Peter Harwin, speaking of their first years of marriage, said, "Sue and he loved each other. They both gave each other something that, had they not married, they wouldn't have gained, I'm quite sure of it. No matter how much water is under the bridge, they left their mark on each other — and it was a better mark."

He was fortunate, during those difficult years of separation from Sue, to be close to Elizabeth and her family at *Balvaig*. It was also a comfort and help to him that Elizabeth was very fond of his stepdaughters, Frances and Margot, who frequently visited. In this area of the old MacLaurin home, was the drawing room where he and Charles as small boys had played their grandfather's wind-up gramophone, and there now were several of Catherine's exquisite Persian rugs and the memorable Mackerras 'round table', restored to its original position at *Balvaig*. It was a quiet refuge where he could listen, when time permitted, to his Bach or whatever he felt the need to play from his long-gathered, extensive collection, while his church, St Mary Magdalene, Rose Bay, was close by.

The nine years since his marriage to Sue had taken Alastair through many emotions, from the happiness of the first two years, to the anxiety and worry of their increasing incompatibility in 1975 and 1976, to the misery and doubt of the rightness of separation as a resolution of their problems, to the final tragedy of her death. It left him with an inner sadness and a much closer understanding of the sometimes desperate difficulties of human relationships, and of his own and others' frailties and complexities.

At School now, he found himself having to deal with charges of elitism. Grammar was experiencing astonishing success with Higher School Certificate results and they now reached a peak. There was much comment and Alastair was at pains to defend the School from being over-selective, pointing out that apart from the fifty students who were in the top 5% of the State, the results *at all levels of ability* were better than might have been expected. The success of the best candidates was due 'partly to their native intelligence', but the overall success of their students to 'sound teaching by a devoted staff'. He refuted the often held claim that the School concentrated on the very intelligent to the exclusion of others.

The Sydney painter, Graeme Inson, who was commissioned about this time by the Trustees to do a portrait of Alastair for the *Big Schoolroom* (he had previously done a fine portrait of Ian Mackerras for the Queensland Institute of Medical Research and feels that the Mackerrasses as a family, 'fit like bookends'!), commented on this vexed question of entry to the School. "It's easier to enter heaven than Grammar — they want the *crème de la crème*." Since this sums up the prevailing impression and is often aimed at Alastair, it is important to look at the matter.

Mr Justice Lockhart of the Federal Court of Australia, an Old Sydneian and a member of the Board of Trustees of Sydney Grammar, feels that the situation is not properly understood. Entrance to the School is one-third each from three sources, the two Preparatory Schools, Edgecliff, (about 300 boys) in the Eastern Suburbs, St Ives (about 400 boys) on the North Shore, and from outside the Schools. All of them sit for the entrance examination which therefore necessarily covers a wide spectrum.

"Boys from the two Prep Schools," he said, "are accepted into Big School, whatever the outcome of the examination, *provided the Headmaster thinks they can cope.* Very few boys are not accepted. The criterion is always, *Is this boy going to be happy at Big School?* If he's a boy who is quite incapable of handling a load, then it's not fair to him to send him on. But the situation is examined very closely. As it is, a lot of boys come into Sydney Grammar School who, quite frankly, on any intellectual elitism system wouldn't have a hope of getting in. So it's wrong for people to think that Grammar operates only on the basis of a boy's academic excellence — it doesn't. On the other hand, the trend thus far, for the third of the School who come from outside, is that we have far more boys sitting for the entrance examinations than can possibly be admitted and the result is that you tend to find the intellectual cream survive the test.' You get some very bright boys indeed from the Prep Schools, so this mix of boys, primarily from the Northern, Eastern and Southern suburbs, plus the boys from outside, is what keeps the intellectual attainment of Grammar high. The School's always been rather proud of its intellectual tradition. And there it is, in the centre of a very large, sprawling city — with its sporting facilities quite disparate, and barely adequate, over at Weigall. You have to look at Sydney Grammar, past, present and future, and ask what has it got to offer? Look at Kings, with its magnificent playing fields and boarding system. Look at Riverview. Look at many of them. They all have wonderful facilities. So, Grammar must offer something, to survive, if you like. So what it offers, in a sense, is a sort of antipodean Winchester." He laughed and added, "What's wrong with producing bright boys? And they're well-balanced boys. Alastair Mackerras is a remarkable Headmaster in that he tries to strike this balance between Grammar producing the goods intellectually, and yet not just being a school of elitists. If anything's been lacking, it's the public relations side of this. A lot of people have formed the wrong impression. Alastair's a true Mackerras, he'd say, 'There's my policy. And that's that. Take it or leave it.'"

This assessment is reinforced by Alastair's response to attacks made by the Sydney press and even by some Old Sydneians in the early 1980s on his so-called 'elitist' educational philosophy. He asked everyone, in the interests of rational debate, to use the word 'academic' or 'intellectual' rather than the pejorative one and summed up his attitude in his 1982 Speech Day address — "I believe that it is only possible for some things which I value in education, such as high intellectal standards, the study of foreign languages or a high standard in artistic matters, to flourish in a situation such as we have at Grammar. I agree with F.R. Leavis who wrote 'It is impossible to question the clear fact that only a minority is capable of advanced intellectual culture. It is disastrous to let a country's educational arrangements be determined, or even affected by, the assumption that a high intellectual standard can be attained by more than a small minority.' Hence Dr Leavis and I could reasonably be described as 'elitists'." He thus uncompromisingly underlined the very matter of contention. Inevitably, the press reported the Leavis quote and not the preceding sentence.

He did not mention. at that time, his equally strongly held belief, which is undoubtedly the factor that enables him to achieve balance within the school, that pupils need 'a measure of warmth', that 'caring for the young is the most effective way of teaching them'. He has been known, on catching sight in the School grounds of one who comes into the 'battler' category and whose work has improved, to stop, shake him by the hand and tell him so. This attitude is an important ingredient of his educational philosophy.

The antipodean-Winchester phrase, nevertheless, seems particularly apt in regard to Grammar. Old Sydneians, David Gonski and Malcolm Turnbull, whose views have been discussed and who were both taught by Alastair, each have a small son booked into the School. "Grammar always has been an academic School," Gonski pointed out, "and I think it's good that it is so. I'm delighted that there is that option, a choice for an academic life for my son if he is good enough. If not, he can be sent to any other number of schools that are sports oriented." Turnbull agreed, adding, "I'm very grateful to the School and very positive about it, so, of course, I hope to send my son there but I would not be inclined to send him if I thought he might have difficulty keeping up." This sort of objectivity, perhaps not always easy to arrive at, does appear to be necessary.

Alastair spent a few brief weeks abroad in December 1982 and while in England met, after fourteen years, Peter Houldsworth, whom he had succeeded in such unusual circumstances as Headmaster. He was pleased

Alastair relaxes with Peter Harwin (left), an Indian Headmaster, Mukherjee and John Sheldon at Berry, 1983.

to find that Mr Houldsworth was philosophical about the past and bore him 'no ill-will'.

About this time, his capacity to make severe, unpalatable decisions was called upon when he found it necessary to expel a member of the Sixth Form for very poor behaviour on his last day; the staff were supportive and as in any such serious matter he himself spoke personally to the age group involved. It seemed, indeed, to be a season for dealing with difficulties, for dissatisfaction with Grammar's rather poor showing in some competitive sport, had become widespread.

Jeremy Nelson, English Master, and former football coach, comments, "Grammar is not running the kind of School that allows the boys to cope with GPS competition under pressure. It can only create disappointment and a sense of belittlement to lose all the time. What they need are friendly matches, outside GPS, just to enjoy the game." The clear-eyed young Senior Prefect of 1983, also a member of the 2nd XV, Robert Bryant, fresh from delivering a speech at assembly in which he had suggested a light-hearted competition 'to break up the rigours of second term', remarked, "It wouldn't be keeping up with the times to think that Rugby is the be-all and end-all. Everyone's realising this and if a boy wants to do music rather than Rugby then he should." He went on to describe a GPS football match they had had the previous week with Sydney High. "A couple of the boys said how much they enjoyed playing Grammar because they felt that Grammar was the only GPS School that got on with them and understood them." Both teams clearly accepted the match in the same spirit and both, Bryant added, often felt that the other GPS schools regarded them as 'outsiders'.

Parents of Grammar boys are very used to seeing them do well scholastically, in debating, in music, in most of the things they undertake. It is therefore difficult for them, and often for the boys themselves, to find the School consistently on the losing side in GPS matches. Rodney Knock, referring to Rugby, put it bluntly, "The fact is, the School cannot field the quality of teams, and GPS is a great incubus that hangs over us. We can't really compete, yet must." The reasons for this are clear enough. The playing fields are a kilometre from the School, making practice difficult; the School, being academic in emphasis, does not attract those looking for a distinct sporting image; there are few repeat sixth formers and virtually no country boys; many are of light build and there are a bigger proportion of pupils of non-British background than at most GPS schools and these boys are inclined to choose soccer. Despite these well-known facts, parental dissatisfaction was strong and in August, 1983, Alastair felt the time had come to confront the issue and did so in an address to Grammar's Women's Association.

He stated his own unchanging priorities, reminded them of the practical difficulties detailed above, and then declared his support for team games. "Most boys enjoy them, they encourage physical well-being and both of these aspects," he said, "contribute to intellectual well-being . . . (but) I do not believe that team games are peculiarly fitted to build character. They can build or spoil character in the same way that any experience in life (can) . . . I do not accept that team-work and leadership are better learned in team games than elsewhere . . (such as) in an orchestra, in debating, or the Endeavour Club . . . and I absolutely reject the frequently stated proposition that boys involved in sport have more school spirit than others . . . let me make it clear that I will not make Rugby compulsory in any part of the School . . . I will not make attendance at 1st XV games compulsory . . . people talk loosely about the dreadful state of sport at Grammar. In fact we had a good deal of success in most sports from 1975 to about 1981, according to the sports historians more than at any time since the late 20s; and we continue to do well in certain sports such as tennis and soccer . . . I see an essential conflict between the way I try to treat boys in the School and Rugby. I try to treat boys gently and encourage them to treat each other in a civilised way whereas I see Rugby as rough and brutalising . . . I am at pains not to do anything which would encourage a revival of that sort of single-minded mania which used to be associated with Rugby at Grammar and which still exists at other GPS and Associated Schools. Such an atmosphere makes it all but impossible for any alternative to exist except as a 'fringe activity for mutants'. . . . being an Independent School we will play and conduct the game, if we play it at all, our way and not as some other schools do . . . serious attempts are being made by Headmasters to reduce the Rugby and Rowing frenzy, recently described by Bob Outterside, Headmaster of Sydney High School and himself a former international Rugby player, as a 'kind of madness' . . . GPS Headmasters are more sympathetic and understanding of the reasons for our plight than some of the Grammar community are . . . so I ask that you try to understand the situation of coaches and not just assume that they are incompetent or don't care . . . However, I will encourage a reappraisal of our coaching methods and more emphasis on basic skills in the preparatory schools and here." It is interesting that in a recent article, *The Bulletin* feature writer, David McNicoll, supported his anti-football stance, deploring the number of serious injuries that occur in schoolboy Rugby.

In any case, he spelt it all out very clearly to parents. But it is another of those problems that will not go away. If Grammar remains within the GPS system, and many parents clearly want it to do so — probably more for the status of the School in Sydney than anything else — then it would seem that all concerned will have to reconcile themselves to Grammar competing and not winning, in Rugby specifically, and adopt as cheerful an attitude as do most of the boys.

Meanwhile, even on cold, dank, wet, miserable mid-winter mornings, Alastair turns up, raincoat to the fore, at Weigall to watch the football. Slung over the raincoat is a cassette player. His friend Tim Yates, arriving one such morning with his son — representing Kings — for a match, heard Verdi issuing forth and recognised *Falstaff*. "This is my detention for the boys," explained Alastair. "I make them record operas for me so that I can listen while I watch this jolly football . . . "

At *Balvaig*, Alastair found the companionship of Charles very congenial once again. For several months each year, since his four year appointment as Chief Conductor of the Sydney Symphony Orchestra, Sir Charles has been in residence at his 'quarters' there and the two share much in common, including the extensive audio equipment and record collection in that much used wing of the family drawing room. Alastair enjoys hearing pre-rehearsal recordings and discussion, while Charles sees some of the lighter-hearted aspects of his brother in his Headmaster role. Working on his musical scores at night, he finds it highly amusing to listen to Alastair's handling of problems, such as telephone complaints from the Railways Department on the behaviour of his pupils. 'Well, now,' says Alastair, 'I've checked that out, and I'm afraid you turn out to be right on the matter. The boys *were* beating each other up between St Leonards and Artarmon stations, but I just want to check with you about the reported incident between Lindfield and Roseville. The boys admitted to it between Chatswood and Roseville but not between Lindfield and Roseville — I'd like your comment on that?' "It's really very funny," says his brother, "He's so terribly polite, he must defeat them. I know what I'd say!"

Their nephew, Alex Briger, and a 1983 Sixth former, John Benson, agree that he does a lot of sifting out of misdemeanours on such matters as this — they refer to it, grinning, as 'his detective work' — so that boys don't get wrongly blamed. They were two among the twenty-two players in the School's string orchestra, named the *Alastair Mackerras Chamber Orchestra*, and were giving impressions of a recent overseas trip they made with the orchestra. The *Sydney Morning Herald* had headlined the event with photograph and article — SCHOOL ORCHESTRA HITS HISTORIC NOTE WITH TOUR OF BRITAIN.

It was the first Australian school orchestra to be invited to tour and excitement was high as they set off, with teachers and conductor Joy Lee, to perform at such places as Marlborough College and Coventry School of Music with a repertoire of Vivaldi, Corelli, Holst and Elgar. The boys found the experience 'fantastic' and also had 'a great time' in France where they played at a castle in Villers Bretonneux and enjoyed feeling at ease with the language and the students there. "It was in the north," said John, "just where the front lines were in World Wars I and II. We played the Marsellaise and they all sang and clapped." (This was where Ian Mackerras was gassed during World War I.) It was an unforgettable few weeks for them all and gratifying to Alastair to see them succeed so well. That year the Grammar orchestra also had the remarkable pleasure of playing in the *Big Schoolroom* at a concert conducted by Sir Charles (young Alex had taken the initiative and written to his uncle with the enterprising suggestion). "He took the final two rehearsals as well," said John. "It was very good for the orchestra and we enjoyed it very, very much because all his remarks were so pertinent — everyone took notice!" It was a delightful evening and tickets were at a premium: the concert was 'Farewell to Big School', for the new auditorium was soon to be opened. Alastair, Sir Charles and Peter Seymour spoke of nostalgic earlier days and the gradual rise to the present standard of excellence of music in the School.

A few months later the Official Opening of the Auditorium took place, with Sir Charles performing the ceremony in the presence of the Chief Justice Sir Lawrence Street, the Trustees, members of the Foundation, and many oher distinguished guests. It was, as Alastair remarked in his address, a most memorable occasion and for him a wonderful one. "For," he said, "it represents the crowning point of my planning for the school over 13 years, that is, for the buildings of the School." He spoke of the

Headmaster, Alastair Mackerras, with his sister Elizabeth Briger, her son Alex, and the Alastair Mackerras Chamber Orchestra with conductor, Joy Lee, in the Big Schoolroom at Sydney Grammar just before their overseas tour in 1983.

Chairman, Graham Crouch, saying, "He has great drive and energy and the capacity to persuade more faint-hearted people, such as me, that now is the time to act. This Theatre is probably his greatest triumph as the need for it was not so obvious . . . if you're going to teach Music and Art, you should have proper facilities, but we could have gone on muddling along in the inconvenient way we have done for years without this Theatre . . . the Chairman will have a secure place in the history of this School." He went on to speak of his own 'faith, or vision if you want to use a more grandiose word', in the nurturing of 'the really splendid boys who come into this School year after year', of his feeling for them and his belief in the importance of their academic successes. "Finally," he said, "it has always seemed to me that there is a strong streak of both anti-intellectualism and Philistinism in the Australian community and that is far stronger among the intelligent and educated Middle Classes than is healthy . . . most private schools, certainly boys' schools, have consistently thrown their weight on the wrong side until very recent times. If I thought that I had contributed a little towards improving this state of affairs, then I would believe that I had not lived entirely in vain. That is the reason I support Music and the other Arts so strongly in this School and that is why so much of this splendid building is devoted to them."

His agreement with the Trustees on becoming Headmaster was that he have one term's leave every five years (a normal requirement in most prominent schools in Australia and New Zealand) in order to take stock of things and 'because it is valuable to get right away and see how other people do much the same things'. He had been briefly in England at Christmas, 1982, and had enquired at his old college, St John's, Cambridge, what the prospects were of his being elected to a Schoolmaster Fellowship for a term in 1984. Usually, he learnt, younger men without experience at Cambridge are chosen and preferably residents of the United Kingdom. He thought no more about it but found that he must have had some 'friends at Court' after all, for he was duly elected.

In 1984, after taking a few weeks long service leave which he spent in Italy, he took up residence for a term as a Schoolmaster Fellow at St John's College for a period of study and reassessment he needed very much. He chose to 'revive' some of his Latin and Greek and to do some reading in Ancient History; to improve his German (he found this difficult); to clarify his views on the vexed question of highly competitive games in schools which, he felt, tended to be anti-educational in character, e.g. Rugby football, which by its nature leads most easily to excesses. In this last mentioned objective he was assisted by Professor Hirst, Professor of Education at Cambridge. He is still delving into this matter.

Cambridge itself he found much more beautiful than the period he spent there in his youth. He struck halcyon weather, appreciated all the refurbishing of the old buildings, enjoyed all the 'small out of the way Courts and nooks and crannies', found his room in a new centrally heated building very comfortable, the addition of women undergraduates an improvement, as also a reduction in formality so that the wearing of a gown was now only required when dining in Hall. He made a habit of speaking to as many students, both graduates and undergraduates, as possible and found them 'uniformly pleasant, sensible and serious', but definitely pessimistic, with such problems of the world as nuclear missiles and unemployment looming large. "I was conscious of more than the polite interest in Australia than I used to strike," he said. "Many think of it as some El Dorado, safely distant from such horrors as nuclear missiles!" Interestingly, they were pleased to be spoken to by 'a don', for the dons, so he was told, usually only speak to them on tutorial matters and 'dont't take much interest in them'.

He renewed friendships and also, during this time and for a week or so after his Schoolmaster Fellowship term at St. John's came to an end, he 'systematically visited schools of various kinds to find out the current thinking in England' on vital educational matters. He found, in general, that he admired the adaptability of the English Public Schools, especially their ability to change with England's changing role in the world. He saw for himself what he had read,[5] how they had turned themselves from 'the Public Schools of the 60s, which had the sort of values which most of the GPS still have, into the Public Schools of the 80s, which advocate co-education and the elevation of academic and cultural excellence above athleticism and Philistinism'. He left England with the impression 'that English schools are more in tune with the way things are moving than their counterparts here are'.

On his return, he found the School, which had been in the excellent hands of his very skilled Deputy, Bob Ross, in such good shape that he 'seriously wondered' whether he was needed, and was also 'struck afresh by the quality of the staff'. The warmth of the boys' welcome made him glad indeed to be back, and as he took up his duties again, in the always exceedingly busy third term, he found that he was 'needed after all'.

He was, in fact, confronted by the most serious problem of our times — the use of drugs by the young. He was conscious immediately of a great deal of talk about drugs among staff, parents and boys and knew that Mr Ross had started investigations on the matter at the end of the second term. During his first weeks back, he had to question around 20 boys 'about drug dealing or using'. The trouble was centred amongst a group of boys in the Fifth Form, and he found it necessary to expel four students for smoking marijuana while in the care of the School. This had an unsettling effect amongst the Fifth Form, and five more boys were subsequently expelled for various offences, such as truancy, gross rudeness, or smoking cigarettes after warning. He found, fortunately, that he had the support of the staff and of the rest of the School, and that 'the parents of all of those expelled were very understanding, although, of course, distressed'.

He addressed the School at Assembly after these unhappy events and stated his views on the matter, telling them he abhorred the use of personality-affecting drugs. "We may not think much of our personalities but it is all that we have . . to attempt to change your personality in such a way . . . (is) a most destructive thing to do. My experiences in life have given me an absolute horror of alcohol . . . as for marijuana, neither I

---

5. The Public School Revolution by John Rae, Headmaster, Westminster.

nor anyone else know whether it is as dangerous as alcohol or not, as its long term effects, for instance, on your children, are not known . . . to experiment with it is folly in the extreme." He went on to point out that habits, both good and bad, are addictive, and he wanted them all to know that drug using would not be tolerated or condoned in the School. He found during his investigations that rumour and gossip had exacerbated the situation, for many boys who were thought to be involved were absolutely innocent, but he also found a higher level of deception among them on the matter than was normal. "I think I understand some of the reasons for this," he told them, "but I ask, when you are confronted with a situation in which you are asked to give evidence in this or any other matter, that you tell the truth about your own part in it . . . if I find that a boy has been lying to me, then it is hard for me ever to believe a word he says again — and that is a very serious thing for him and for me also." Thus he dealt with this most pervasive of modern ills. His general *rapport* with the vast majority of students has survived the crisis.

That year saw the retirement of his longtime friend and colleague, Assistant to the Headmaster, Peter Young, to whom he paid tribute in his Speech Day address as one of the best Schoolmasters he has ever known. He commented on his versatility: he had 'run a model Geography Department, been a Tutor, shown himself particularly able in handling students who get into trouble, and had coached the 1st XI to four Cricket Premierships.' There seems no doubt that both School and Headmaster have been extremely fortunate in having men of such calibre. Alastair also commented on that occasion on both his Deputy, Bob Ross, and Master of the Lower School, John Sheldon, and the 'major blessing' it is for Grammar that neither of these men, each of 'great intellectual ability and wide education', has so far shown any inclination to become a Headmaster elsewhere.

So, we bring the School, and Alastair himself, to the mid-1980s. In April, 1985, he crossed swords with the *Sydney Morning Herald* following a largely inaccurate assessment of the School in their magazine section (Good Weekend) entitled SYDNEY GRAMMAR vs THE PHILISTINES, *The last bastion of academic elitism stands firm*, in which, as he said, Grammar was depicted as 'a pretty dreary, unhappy, inhuman place, peopled by shadowy masters and most intelligent boys . . . academic snobs and social outcasts . . . and less than brilliant victims'. He refuted this and also dealt with the particular slant the article had placed on the problem of drugs, as well as Grammar's attitude to sport. There were several supportive Letters to the Editor, and in July, the article on Grammar in the series *Smark's Schools Report* presented a much more balanced view, and at the end of the year, the paper covered Grammar's Speech Day fully and accompanied the article with a photograph of Alastair, in academic regalia, awaiting the official party on the Town Hall steps. Sydney's premier paper seemed to have decided that perhaps they did have rather a remarkable, if controversial, man in their midst.

However more complex and time demanding administrative matters grow, he still keeps his 'open door' policy and his resolve to know all his pupils by name by the end of first term. As Peter Young observed, "It's a formidable thing, a memory like that. It's terribly important to a boy of fourteen who might be having a tough time at home, or is down in the dumps and perhaps getting into trouble at School and really can't stand it much longer, and he meets the Headmaster at quarter past eight in the morning going up the steps and hears, 'And how are you this morning, Tom?' Well, Tom is lifted immensely, and these are the things that matter.''

He still teaches Maths, adding as always, a commentary on political and School events, and an anecdote or two, often about the opera he happened to be humming when he came in. He also dispenses chocolate frogs if he makes a mistake on the blackboard — too infrequent a happening the boys lament. He has bought a holiday house at Berry, since Kiama has become 'rather built up', and has named it *Merilba* after the northern New South Wales property where he spent so many happy holidays in his youth. He has dinner every so often with old friends and colleagues such as Peter Harwin (now Headmaster at Edgecliff) and they talk, philosophise, listen to music or play bridge. You will still meet him on his way through the grounds at Grammar surrounded by boys, questions and talk; you will still meet him at Weigall sportsground at weekends, or of an evening on the staircase at the Opera House, humming an aria, but ceasing mid-tune to return a greeting ('I always assume they're Grammar parents ... '). And he remains as firmly outspoken as ever on his deeply meditated educational philosophy.

John Sheldon, speaking from experience of teaching under five Headmasters and attending many Senior Masters conferences, feels that Alastair has managed to achieve exceptional staff unity. "The whole staff is behind him. It is rare." Jeremy Nelson adds, "Perhaps it is because he asks advice, listens to everybody's point of view and is open, just and wise." Judge Lockhart comments with a smile, "He is also an adroit politician. But where he is unique is in having both the respect and affection of the boys. Those are rare qualities and he has them." The Chairman of the Trustees, Graham Crouch, sums it up for them all, saying, "He has breadth of mind, humaneness and a great ability to communicate at all levels." It is a very positive and convincing body of opinion.

Alastair has also re-emphasized the role of Sydney Grammar as 'a nursery for the University', and his original stamp has been on the value he has placed on cultural activities and achievements of the boys. Perhaps, under his Headmastership, the School may distance itself further from the mainstream of the GPS system; on the other hand, he may seem, with his wholistic view on education, to be a leader in the field.

A final vignette is the late afternoon in his study at College Street, sharing tea and homemade biscuits (provided by thoughtful Grammar mothers), sitting in his solid oak Headmaster's chair and commenting that although it is the original one, installed in 1857, it's more comfortable than the one he has to sit in at Assembly. He glances at the Austrian Castle Clock on the mantelpiece, which was presented by the staff to his ancestor, Scottish dominie, James MacLaurin, whose portrait presides over the black marble fireplace, and declares himself 'terrified' of getting behind in his work. His secretary enters and says that he never does. Senior Master, Bob Ross, comes in and has a brief word with him on an article

Alastair Mackerras, Headmaster, Sydney Grammar School, in his study at College Street.

for the next Newsletter and departs with the quip, "I'll leave that with you to look over during the weekend — sometime when you're not watching the football." There is laughter.

In the corridor, a senior student is hovering and receives a nod which means that he will be looked after shortly. The School bell clangs. There is an exodus of grey-suited figures below and Alastair points out this one and that one. "They're not a bad lot," he says, pausing and gazing benevolently down upon his charges as the sun slants past him to the book-lined walls. So, we leave him, guiding one of our oldest, finest schools, in the heart of the city which, more than any other, reflects the character of this country, one who must rank amongst Australia's great Headmasters.

Chapter 6

Neil

"Neil, you are eccentric," said Catherine, exasperated. This was at the time of his rebellion from the academic life and his dramatic announcement that he wanted to go on the land. For one who had shown signs of exceptional brilliance from early childhood, surprising even his own family when they found that he was able to read and write before he went to school, it did seem a marked sign of eccentricity.

It is a label which, indeed, still fits if his career is to be measured by conventional standards. At the same time, he could just as easily be equated with that famous eccentric of the writing world, Xavier Herbert, who had the same extraordinary flow of words, and importantly, the same feeling for the misfortunes of the Australian Aborigine and the injustices that have arisen from the clash of cultures in this country. Herbert, however, espoused the cause in fictional works. Neil Mackerras has done so in the District Courts and in the magistrates' courts of northern New South Wales. He has dared to rock the boat in the most practical manner. Has he been effective? We shall follow his career from its inception as a member of the establishment in Sydney and at the Bar, to his present position, as solicitor attached to the Armidale office of the Aboriginal Legal Service, and gauge the effects of an impetuously conceived but courageous attempt to put ideals into practice.

In the early 1950's Neil studied Law part-time at Sydney University while working full-time at the MLC. He was the eldest son at *Harpenden* at this time — Charles in London, Alastair at Cambridge — and found himself the focus of Catherine's attention and interest on all matters to do with his career. This seemed to fulfil a deep need in him and undoubtedly had a very beneficial effect. For several years he studied unceasingly, his only recreations the music which was part of their family life and the entertaining of his young twin brothers and their friends which he knew was helpful to Catherine and which he himself enjoyed. One of these was John Sheldon, who commented, "Neil was a very interesting chap, strong on the political side and full of ideas. He was like his mother, the words would absolutely tumble out and he would be a very engaging companion." In fact, he put himself out to amuse them and felt he was finally fulfilling his mother's early request to him and to Alastair 'to help in the bringing up of the twins'.

A frequent visitor at their musical evenings about this time was a quiet, good-looking, clear-eyed girl with a voice whose timbre could match the Mackerras decibels when necessary. This was Elizabeth Connolly, whose mother was a friend of Catherine, introduced to her by that memorable Loreto Convent educationalist, Mother Borgia. In 1953, Elizabeth decided to become a nun and entered the Sacré Coeur Convent at Rose Bay. Neil realised very quickly just how much he had taken her companionship for granted, and towards the end of her year in the novitiate he found his thoughts turning constantly to her. He went and poured his woes into the ears of an elderly priest who had taught him at St Aloysius, mentioning in the course of their talk that Elizabeth suffered from asthma. The priest thought it unlikely in those circumstances that she would stay in the convent, and so it proved. Elizabeth stayed only 15 months, for asthma and the convent did not agree, and soon afterwards they announced their engagement. His boisterous twin brothers told their friends gleefully, "Neil's fished Elizabeth out of the convent!" It hadn't been quite like that, but their separation had certainly brought him to the realisation that he was in love with her.

He had a great deal of study still ahead and Elizabeth went to Europe for six months with her brother, thus enabling him to concentrate exclusively on his textbooks until the following November when they were married. He seems to have had some sensibility still in regard to the convent's loss and his gain, for he decreed that it was to be a wedding entirely without speeches. John Goldrick, who was best man and knew Neil's gifts as a speaker, as well as the generally accomplished flow of talk among the Mackerrases and their friends, was dismayed. "It got me by the throat," he said, "it seemed unnatural." He therefore disobeyed instructions, gave tongue himself, and was glad of it — as were the assembled guests and, no doubt, Neil and Elizabeth as they set off for their honeymoon in Melbourne.

They had bought a small brick cottage in Cudgee Street, Turramurra, which Neil dubbed *Cudgee Castle* and it now had to be made habitable. For some time after their return the sounds of music, which invariably accompany members of the clan, had to compete with the clang of tools as he delved into the mysteries of carpentry and plumbing, and managed, amongst other things, to install a shower for their use. Before settling to the process of becoming a barrister, he took Elizabeth for a brief holiday to the New England district which had captured his heart during summer weeks spent there as a boy at the property, *Merilba*. Then at Cudgee Street, they practised the strictest economies and Elizabeth, formerly from the country, took to making her own bread and rendering down fat to convert into soap, struggling in the process, their friends remember, with 'terrible globules of glub'. It was at *Cudgee Castle* that the first three of their family of nine — three daughters, Helen, Dorothy, and Susan — were born.

Neil graduated *proxime accessit* to Elizabeth Evatt in Equity, which pleased everyone, particularly Catherine, for it reminded her of her own final year at university. She continued to take the keenest interest in his burgeoning career, as John Goldrick recalls. He, himself, had just completed a year as Associate to Mr Justice Maguire (Supreme Court, NSW), and when he went to the Bar, he arranged for Neil to take over

Neil and Elizabeth with best man John Goldrick and Alastair.

from him. "Our Judge, Hugh Maguire," he remarked, "must have had about 17 Associates over the years — Neil was his third. He was very surprised one day, when, coming up to the Central Criminal Court at Darlinghurst to preside over a murder trial, he saw his new Associate and his new Associate's mother, Mrs Mackerras, sitting in the back of the court. Later he was delighted to invite Catherine Mackerras in for morning tea . . ." Catherine, as a personage, seems always to have been welcomed in Sydney — no doubt, on this occasion, to Neil's gratification.

During his years at the MLC, Neil had become well-known to the company's solicitors, Freehill, Hollingdale & Page and when his year as an Associate was completed, he joined their staff as a solicitor's clerk. This was a very formative time. The firm was acting for Toohey's Brewery in a series of tenancy cases and briefing R.M. (later Mr Justice) Hope. Neil found himself very much in accord with Mr Hope and decided to study his book — Hope & Freeman's *Landlord & Tenant Practice & Procedure in NSW* (4th edition). At the same time, he increased his activities as a member of the Liberal Party and became secretary of the Turramurra branch. He also met Eric (later Sir Eric) Willis and sat with him on United Nations organisations such as UNESCO, Freedom from Hunger and Unicef. "He had a strong streak of idealism," said Sir Eric, "and was concerned at that time with organisations relieving hunger and hardship." As well, he was a believer in decentralisation and secretary of the Australian Decentralisation & New States Movement. These threefold interests then, expertise in a particular legal field, participation in politics, and deep involvement in welfare, were indicative of the varying directions his career was to take.

In 1956 he changed course politically. Four years before, on a visit to Melbourne, he had met B.A. Santamaria, the forceful leader of the Catholic Social Studies Movement, otherwise known as *The Movement*, which, with the support of Melbourne's Archbishop Mannix, encouraged political activism amongst Roman Catholics and worked to reduce the Communist influence in Labor and union circles. Neil was already a member of *The Movement*, and of the National Catholic Rural Movement of which Santamaria was also the director, and he now formed a friendship with him. This resulted in 1956 in his abrupt resignation from the Liberal Party and his joining forces with Santamaria in the formation of the new Democratic Labor Party.

The reasons for the emergence of the DLP were in themselves dramatic and it is necessary, in our context, to examine them briefly, for Neil was keenly aware of and concerned with them. The dominant political issue of the 50's — the first years of the Menzies Coalition Government — was Communism. At the outset, a referendum to give the government power to outlaw the Communist Party was very narrowly defeated. Amongst the Australian people generally, there was apprehension at the increasing infiltration by Communists of the unions, particularly the powerful transport and maritime unions, at a time when China's Russian alliance, combined with her expansionist policies in Asia and strong anti-United States stance, posed what seemed to be a real threat to the country. The Labor Party itself was divided on the issue and bitter faction fighting and sectarianism in Victoria in 1954 led to Dr Evatt (Federal Opposition Leader) attacking *The Movement* and the Industrial Groups who dominated both the Victorian and NSW ALP Executives.

In 1955 the famous *Split* occurred — for some time there were two ALP Victorian Executives claiming to be the 'official' one — and the Labor Party proceeded to tear itself apart. The Bolte Liberal Government was elected to office in Victoria, the Cahill Labor Government held in New South Wales but it was a tight situation, and on the Federal scene Dr Evatt was dogged by his role in the Petrov Affair. The disarray was complete when 7 Federal MPs belonging to the Industrial Groups were expelled by the Federal Executive from the ALP; they left Caucus and became known as the 'ALP (Anti-Communist)' group in parliament. Menzies, seizing the opportunity, called an election on the pretext of synchronising House of Representative and Senate Elections. His Coalition Government gained an increased majority and the Anti-Communist Labor members lost their seats. It was at this point that Santamaria saw the need for a new party.

He himself was in the throes of implementing instructions from Rome to sever *The Movement's* connections with the episcopacy, and converting it into an industrial group, the National Civic Council. He decided the time was now ripe for the formation of a new middle of the road party — the Democratic Labor Party.

"I was never on the right of the Liberal Party in any case," said Neil, "but I think it was simply loyalty to Bob Santamaria, as a friend and leader of *The Movement*, which caused Elizabeth and me to attend a private meeting he called at a restaurant at Tom Ugly's Point just outside Sydney, to speak about his plans to form this new political party."

Santamaria told the assembled gathering, in effect (he has since spelt it all out in his writings) — 'The totalitarian threat is no less mordant because it is a Communist rather than a Nazi totalitarianism which we confront . . . the one important issue, is to prevent the weapons of political power from falling into the hands of any Australian party which might ultimately do a deal with Communist China.' He advocated the expansion of trade with non-Communist Asia, particularly Japan, and encouraging Asian migration — a sufficient number of races to dispel forever the myth of racial superiority inherent in the so-called White Australia Policy. The proposed Democratic Labor Party would aim at being 'a small dynamic group, freely organised, not concerned with electoral success and devoting itself to a great social and political idea.' Preferences would go to the Liberal Party, thus helping to keep the Menzies Government in power, while at the same time spreading a new, enlightened message, neither extreme right nor extreme left, and providing an anti-Communist focus. Common sense and justice for the little man would be a major plank and they would 'espouse the strengthening of defences and a vision of Australia as leader of an anti-Communist Pacific Community and as a mirror of Christianity to Asia.' Neil's imagination was fired at once; he had always the making of a crusader in him and thought then of Santamaria as 'the Great Saviour of Australia from the Communist Menace'. When Santamaria asked him to join forces and assist in forming a New South Wales branch of the Democratic Labor Party, he promptly resigned from the Liberal Party and did just that.

He enlisted Catherine's immediate support, for the ideals and objectives of the new party were in accord with her own beliefs. She was, of course, something of a rebel herself and also approved the role of the crusading Christian. Furthermore there was a potential leader on hand. Among those expelled from the ALP NSW State Executive in the recent Labor Party turmoil, was a man named Alan Manning who was keen to find an avenue for his moderate policies. Neil, with Catherine's help, arranged a meeting at Hornsby, with Manning and other interested people, and formed the first Democratic Labor Party branch in Australia.

"We all trooped off to this hall in Hornsby," said John Goldrick, one of those whom personal loyalty brought along, "and there was Catherine

Mackerras, Neil, and this politician who had risen like a prophet from the desert. It was thought that he might just have the charisma to get this middle party going."

This did not come to pass, but it was the beginning of 16 years of close involvement by Neil in DLP affairs. He became secretary of the Hornsby branch, later a member of the NSW State Executive, and stood for parliament on four occasions, the first two — we shall examine the others later — being for the Federal seat of Robertson (Hornsby-Gosford-Wyong area just north of Sydney) in 1958 and 1961. In order to win some marginal support in this seat he had an uphill battle, as did John and others who found themselves at the polling gates on his behalf, pressing pamphlets upon reluctant voters who were clearly already committed to one or other of the major parties. Nevertheless, the Democratic Labor Party managed to establish itself overall, winning nearly 10% of the vote in 1958, while in 1961, a year of economic recession, its preferences were indeed needed by the Menzies Government which narrowly escaped defeat. Over the years, DLP representatives gave valuable service in the parliament, amongst them, Senator George Cole (Tasmania), their first Parliamentary Leader, his successor, the pragmatic former Labor Premier of Queensland, Vince Gair; and Senators Frank McManus (Victoria) and Jack Kane (NSW). Neil came to know them all well, respected their ability and had a particular admiration for Jack Kane both as man and parliamentarian.

Meanwhile, in 1957 he went to the Bar and his practice became centred on Landlord & Tenant cases. In the fifties and sixties the post-war housing shortage had not yet been overcome, owners wanted to get tenants out, and tenancy cases were staple diet for many newly admitted young barristers. "In those early days," said Neil, "we appeared for tenants under the instructions of the Public Solicitor for 5 guineas the case, no matter how long it lasted, or for the Commonwealth Attorney-General's Legal Service Bureau, for 3 guineas a day." He shared a room in the new Wentworth Chambers with John Goldrick, who still recalls the reverberations of the resonant Mackerras voice in that 16 ft by 12 ft space, and since his own is not noted for its pianissimo effects, he wonders how they survived the 10 months they spent there. But survive it they did, with friendship unimpaired.

It was customary at that time to read with a senior barrister when coming to the Bar and Neil approached R.G. (later Mr Justice) Reynolds, who agreed. "I wasn't able to teach him anything really," said the Judge, now retired, "he was rushing from court to court in Landlord & Tenant cases, and I was busy in Common Law — accident cases and all sorts of things." Apart from this, they did not seem 'to jell as master and pupil', for Mr Reynolds found him rather too intense and remembers the sharp, loud raps on his door, whether he happened to be in conference or not, which he knew heralded Neil's approach to ask if he could be of assistance. "A very nice man," he commented, "but we did not seem to be on the same wave-length." This must be said of several other legal colleagues during these years who found him 'very capable', 'very meticulous', in fact, 'a bit of a whip', but commented on the 'extreme detail' into which it was necessary to go when arguing opposite him in court. It is unlikely that Neil himself was aware of this reservation, for even if it had been implied at the time, he would have been far too preoccupied with the cases on hand to notice.

On the way to Chambers one morning early in 1958, Neil met again R.M. (Bob) Hope, with whom he was aware of a considerable *rapport*, and was interested to learn that following extensive amendments to the Landlord & Tenant Act, he had been asked by the Law Book Company to write a new edition of the Hope & Freeman textbook on the subject. He was doubtful if he could find time to do it. Neil at once offered to assist, his offer was accepted, and he was now in the throes of work on the book. It was a task for which he was well equipped, since he was not only exceedingly industrious but endowed with a quite phenomenal memory, very useful in recalling cases. His practice was now almost exclusively Landlord & Tenant work and had grown to such an extent that he frequently found it necessary to go to his Chambers in the early hours of the morning, sometimes as early as 3 or 4 a.m., and use a dictaphone in order to keep abreast of it. There was little in regard to the Landlord & Tenant (Amendment) Act with which he was not conversant.

So he immersed himself in the textbook and the citing of definitive cases on such matters as — *The onus of proving that consent has been unreasonably withheld is on the tenant*; *The landlord is not bound to give any reason for refusing his consent*; *Failure to take care*; *Nuisance or annoyance* (the word 'nuisance' he noted, is used in its legal sense, but 'annoyance' is a wider term and covers anything to which reasonable people object). He found himself challenged by and enjoying this new writing role, as well as the many conferences with Mr Hope (the former co-author, Allan Freeman, was included for historical reasons only). As a comparative fledgling in the legal world, he thought only in terms of acknowledgment in the preface of the completed book and perhaps some minimum payment. In the event, he was surprised to receive a cheque which represented half the senior man's fee and delighted to discover his name in the title — Hope, Mackerras & Freeman.

His characteristic impetuosity was at this time manifested at home. His three small daughters were a joy, but he became so carried away by the intensity of his longing for a son he persuaded Elizabeth to agree to their fostering a boy, a six-year-old, named John, who was a State ward. There was a wave of consternation in the family circle at this, particularly when, some months later, Elizabeth mentioned that she herself was to have another child. She was not physically very strong, having suffered from asthma all her life, a condition which fortunately was less severe during her pregnancies. They moved to a more comfortable home in Gilda Avenue, Wahroonga which Neil, with his pleasantly light touch for the naming of houses, called *Rigoletto*, the opera in which Gilda is the heroine, and the following year the first of their sons, Thomas, was born. Elizabeth now had four infants under five to manage as well as John, and the only sensible course was to make other arrangements for him. This was duly done and he went to the care of a Catholic orphanage. He had been with them for 16 months; it was a difficult step to have to take and of course even harder for the child. However, as with many of Neil's impetuous acts, good ensued, for he remained in touch with the boy and always concerned himself with his welfare. A genuine love for the young was as innate in him as in his brother Alastair, and he frequently took parties of children from the orphanages on picnics and outings.

Work proceeded at what many would have considered an alarming pace, for he sometimes even slept at Chambers. He came more and more to represent the landlord in Landlord & Tenant cases. "Neil was convinced," John Goldrick commented, "that it was unjust that a landlord should not be able to get possession of his or her property, and he fought very hard to achieve that end." This was yet another crusade, and a case in point, close to home, occurred when Catherine found it necessary to engage a colleague of his and undertake a protracted legal case in order to resume possession of *Balvaig* for the use of Joan and Elizabeth. There were protected tenants in the two flats into which the house had been divided after her mother's death, and they were paying something absurd like the equivalent of three dollars a week.

Following the Landlord & Tenant (Amendment) Bill, 1964, Neil attended a legal seminar arranged by the Riverina Law Society of Wagga Wagga in south-western New South Wales and presented an excellent paper on the whole complex matter.

'Of all the anomalies in an anomalous Act,' he said, 'that the "fair rent" is based upon the capital value of the premises at 31st August, 1939 to the exclusion of any other date, has now been held by the High Court not to exist. It is, therefore, of the first importance to preserve the effect of the recent judgment . . . ' He went on to point out that the judgment merely required the Fair Rents Board to have regard to the present day capital value, and left the Board with a very wide discretion which could well be exercised to keep rents down to 1939 levels; to discourage this and to ensure also that tenants 'are not caused serious hardship by universal substantial increases in rent', he suggested a new sub-section which, he felt, 'the Government might possibly be induced to accept'. The paper is technical and deals with numerous sections, sub-sections and grounds which cannot be reproduced even in summary here. But some illustrative points are made in a lively fashion and do give an idea of what he was about, such as —

. . . the proposed new section 21 (IB) is not unwelcome. However, it is still undesirable. It arguably deprives a lessor who has just put a new roof on premises from obtaining any allowance in respect to that roof, because he has not yet renewed a defective down-pipe . . .

Again, he spells out persuasively a complicated case of the disputed tenancy of a two-storeyed shop which is divided into three —

. . . The tenant of the shop, partly to preserve his tenancy, partly to enable himself and his family to live upstairs and partly to enable himself to extend his shop, purchases the premises. Why should he not be entitled to give the tenant of the back of the downstairs Notice to Quit on the ground that he requires the premises to extend his shop?

He is outspoken in regard to 'the re-introduction of the compulsory alternative accommodation provisions' —

. . . The really objectionable feature . . . is that which requires the same alternative accommodation to be available both at the date of expiry of the Notice to Quit and at the hearing of the proceedings. Having regard to the congestion of the court lists and to the technicalities of the legislation, it can often be months, even years

between the date of the expiry of the Notice to Quit and the final determination of the court . . .

He goes on to point out forcefully that —

. . . The High Court judgment has given the Opposition the opportunity to attack the Government (Askin, Liberal) *on this Act. The fact is that the Act has been responsible for hundreds of landlords being virtually compelled to sell their property at low prices to speculators. It has been responsible for thousands of homes being left out of repair, because no landlord could be expected to spend money on repairing them. It has been responsible for the exacerbation of the housing shortage in many directions, but, in particular, by encouraging small families to continue to live in large premises . . .*

He suggests amendments that will improve all these matters and displays a great deal of exact and detailed knowledge. It was hardly surprising then, that when another edition of the Hope, Mackerras & Freeman textbook on *Landlord and Tenant, Practice and Procedure in New South Wales* was required, Mr Hope, then a Q.C., asked him to undertake the major proportion of the work.

"He was a good advocate," Justice Hope commented recently. "His work product was marvellous. He worked very, very hard and was absolutely dedicated to his client's case. They were presented very well and that, of course, was reflected in so many ways in what he did with this publication."

A great deal of re-writing was necessary; he still rose at 4 a.m. but worked on the text in his study at home for three hours before going into his Chambers. This 1966 edition of the textbook (revised with J.R. (John) Dunford in 1971) is still the standard reference on the subject. "Neil revelled in all the technicalities and it is a very technical branch of the law," John Goldrick commented, "but he was also able to stand aside and look with humour at it." He refers to the preface in which Neil quoted from Dickens' *Bleak House* —

"Never can there come fog too thick, never can there come mud and mire too deep, to assort with the groping and floundering condition which this . . . most pestilent of hoary sinners holds this day in the sight of heaven and earth . . .

Tripping one another up on slippery precedents, groping knee-deep in technicalities . . . mountains of costly nonsense . . . "

He was now at the height of his intellectual powers and for the next half dozen years he continued to work at the same fierce pace and to pursue all his varied interests. One cause dear to his heart — the creation of a new State in the New England district, northern New South Wales — was lost. A long-promised referendum was held and returned a NO vote of 54%, a considerably closer result than many had imagined, for it had been apparent that heavy industry in the southern part of the proposed new State feared the move as much as many dairy farmers who were afraid of losing access to the Sydney milk market.

Neil himself became a 'primary producer' at Wahroonga at this point, growing vegetables and keeping a couple of dozen hens. This enabled him to average out his considerable income as well as being of great practical use for his growing brood. Their family now included a daughter, Judith, who was to inherit the Mackerras musical gift, sons Robert and Richard, and within several years was complete with the two youngest, Alison and

John. He decided it would be wise to invest in a Kombi-van and it was, in fact, ideal for transporting his small tribe to school and for weekend outings. This vehicle, with the large handsome man at the wheel and its cargo of noisy, lively children, became quite a feature of the district, causing North Shore citizens to pause in their rose snipping and shrub clipping in some wonderment as it wound through their canopy of green. Often at weekends, the crew of the Kombi-van consisted partly of children from one or other of the orphanages, for the size of his own family did not deter him from this practice, or from doing what he could in their cause.

"He is the Don Quixote of the Mackerras clan," observed John Goldrick, "but then he's Cervantes too — he wrote the book!" He is an extremely unusual mixture, to say the least, with an idealism too often ingenuous, alongside a highly equipped intellect.

Neil had for several years now been a member of the Australian Executive Committee of the International Commission of Jurists, which was chaired by the redoubtable Edward St John, Q.C. When, in 1967, the Law Association for Asia and the Western Pacific was formed, with John (later Sir John) Kerr and Hal (later Mr Justice) Wootten as Foundation President and Secretary-General respectively, he became a member and attended their conference in Kuala Lumpur soon afterwards. It was his first trip out of Australia and the beginning of expanding horizons which, at 38, he richly deserved.

Strangely, or perhaps as a reaction from his work, about this time Neil seems to have carried his devoutness to extremes and in family circles to have become rather pontifical in attitude. Catherine found the latter very baffling. An instance of it occurred, she recalled later, one evening at Alastair's house at Kiama where she and Alan's cousin, Nancy, were spending a week writing, talking, cooking delicious meals and generally enjoying themselves. Neil was on his way back from a case in the area and burst in upon this peaceful scene. He strode up and down in front of the fire and declaimed on the sinfulness, frivolity and inadequacy of humanity at large. Amongst other things, he announced that he had 'forbidden Elizabeth to wear make-up.' He seemed a Victorian presence full of a narrow missionary zeal from which the objectivity and humour of which he was capable had flown. The companionable ease at Kiama vanished also. When his car had roared off into the night, Catherine remained thoughtful. "I'm very fond of Neil," she said at last, "but I don't really understand him. I don't understand how his mind functions." Fortunately, his wife Elizabeth did seem to understand the forces which drove him, for she was entirely supportive and even went along, for the time being, with his stern injunctions.

She clearly realised the conflict of conscience within him. He was very skilled indeed at winning legal battles for landlords and whilst being convinced himself of their rightness, and that, as his friend John commented, 'God was on his side' in these battles, the work was contrary to a deeper need he had — to help instead the little man, the less privileged. It is highly probable that the social upheaval, the student revolts and questionings of the fabric of society in the second half of the 60s also made an impact on him and contributed to his unease. Be that as it may, he was in a cleft stick. His family responsibilities decreed that he continue to develop his flourishing practice exactly as he was doing.

In 1968 the Askin Government in New South Wales made a decision which was a harbinger of things to come. The newspapers carried headlines — *Government Aims To End All Rent Control, Tenant Income Limit Cut*. The Minister of Justice, John Maddison, well-known to Neil from his active Liberal Party days, announced that the Government's policy was based on the internationally held formula that a person should be expected to pay from 20 to 25 per cent of his gross income for rented accommodation, and the State Cabinet's decision in regard to the Landlord and Tenant Act, to lower the gross income limit of 'wealthy tenants' (i.e. those who could afford to pay current value rentals) from $6,000 to $4,000, was in conformity with this. On this basis a tenant of a controlled dwelling could be expected to pay $16 a week in rent and there was evidence that there was ample uncontrolled rented accommodation available for this figure. He added that the Government also intended to eliminate the provision which required a landlord to offer reasonable alternative accommodation to the tenant as a condition of obtaining possession and to place stricter limits on the right of inheritance of tenancies of controlled dwellings. As well, commercial and business premises under rent control would ultimately be decontrolled. All this was precisely what Neil had been working towards for a decade.

As expected, there was a political outcry and the media gave the Labor Party a good hearing with their cries of hardships and dramatic predictions that 'pensioners would be evicted and thrown into the street'. But the protests were hollow, for the Government had made provision for the Housing Commission to have additional funds especially to provide accommodation for pensioner tenants and others whose income was below the $4,000 level. The following year, when it appeared likely that the Government might waver on a controversial section of the last point (those tenants whose income approached but did not reach $4,000 and who had private means of some kind or no responsibilities), Neil wrote to the Minister and urged the Government to stand firm. 'In the new atmosphere,' he said, 'tenants are looking after themselves as never before, moving away from dilapidated and under-occupied houses and flats, to better ones they can nevertheless afford and at the present rate I have not the slightest doubt that rent control as an issue will be completely dead by the next elections . . . My court practice has declined rather than increased but my secretary is busier than every typing documents . . . advancing the trend and helping the parties effect their settlements which I have little doubt are beneficial to all concerned, landlords and tenants alike, the community in general and the Government in particular . . . The best possible evidence of the fact that the tenants can afford to provide alternative accommodation for themselves is the rate at which they are now doing so.' The Minister replied that he was 'in large measure' in agreement with him but commented that 'politics on this issue dies hard in this State.' It was a question of hastening slowly.

Neil himself was standing as DLP candidate for Berowra (Wahroonga-Hornsby district) in the Federal election in 1969. His friend John was by now a magistrate and not at all dismayed that he was no longer available for electioneering, but there was no dearth of helpers. The DLP was in a strong position, its preferences were once again vital, and although Berowra itself was a safe Liberal seat it was necessary to have a DLP presence there. There was some truth in the posters at Wahroonga which, as well as proclaiming Neil's obvious virtues as a family man and one who cared about people, named the DLP as *'The New Political Leader'*, the party 'which cared for Australia's future.' Their four Senators, led by Gair, held the balance of power in the Senate and had done so since the Senate election just before the death of Prime Minister Holt at Portsea in December 1967. The present Gorton Coalition Government was in a shaky position, torn by factions within the party and dissension created by the Prime Minister's authoritarian attitude, so-called cronyism, and a weakening of the long held anti-Communist policy in foreign affairs. On the Opposition benches sat a revitalised Labor Party under the leadership of their rising star, Gough Whitlam. When, a few months before the election in 1969, the Gorton Government's Foreign Minister (Freeth) made a parliamentary statement on possible co-operation with Russian interests in the Indian Ocean, there was alarm in the DLP, the Country Party and amongst a number of Liberals. The DLP took swift action.

The national affairs journal, *News Weekly*, commented, 'After making an agonising reappraisal of the situation, and at the risk of destroying its own electoral base, the DLP threatened to withdraw its preferences from the Government in selected, vital seats if it did not review its foreign policy. The Government did. The policy enunciated by Foreign Minister Freeth was repudiated and the old Menzies line reasserted. The Liberal-Country Party coalition which had been set, full pelt, on the road to electoral defeat was saved . . . ' DLP preferences were crucial to the Gorton Government, which very narrowly retained office, for there was still a dramatic swing against the Government; many had listened to Whitlam's call 'Into the 70s with Labor' and the party gained 18 seats.

Neil was unsettled by these events and restless at the DLP's indirect manner of gaining its political ends. He also had doubts about some aspects of the party's foreign policy, in particular their strong alignment with U.S. President Johnson's Vietnam policy and the continuing conflict there. His brother Colin, by then Resident Scholar in the Department of Far Eastern History at the Australian National University, Canberra, influenced him further and whenever he came to Sydney they had long discussions on the subject and on Colin's reasons for taking the Labor viewpoint. However, Neil remained with the DLP — he was a member of their NSW executive — and was convinced of the soundness of their domestic policies, especially on immigration and decentralisation, and their Senators' useful role in parliamentary debate. Also, the man he most admired, Jack Kane, had recently been elected to the Senate, thus bringing the number of DLP Senators to five.

Neil had by now become a prominent member of the Bar, so that the fees he was able to charge, and his income, grew accordingly. During 1970 he attended the International Bar Association's conference in Tokyo and took his second daughter, Dorothy, with him. In 1971 it was the Commonwealth Law Conference at New Delhi, with his wife and eldest daughter, Helen, accompanying him; on the way home they stopped off

Neil and Elizabeth with their family at Wahroonga

at Hong Kong and he went on alone to attend the Lawasia conference in Manila. That same year they moved house once more, this time to a very beautiful house in Cleveland Street, Wahroonga. He joined a number of organisations to enable him to help causes in which he believed and became a life member of the Australian Conservation Foundation, the National Parks Association and the National Trust (NSW). He had contributed for many years to the Save the Children Fund and now, through the fund, supported a child in Hong Kong, another in a Catholic orphanage in India, and two high school boys in Papua New Guinea, one Catholic and the other Anglican. He read widely on social issues and subscribed to a large number of journals such as *Choice, The Land, The Australian Quarterly, Marriage Guidance* and various conservation, political and religious journals.

In the midst of all this, he felt increasingly tense. More and more, since the pronouncements of Vatican II set up by Pope John of universally beloved memory, since he did so much to banish intolerance and bigotry in the Christian Church, Neil had come to have a feeling for ecumenical objectives. He now rejected, at heart, the crusading aspect of the National Civic Council and the DLP's strongly Catholic bias. Added to this was the conflict he had with his conscience, as a basically idealistic man, in 'consistently representing landlords and evicting little old ladies'. As he said ruefully to Catherine, "What am I to say to my children? *I have made all this money working for developers!*" Yet he felt impelled to continue in the legal field in which he had become expert, and as far as politics was concerned he was deeply committed to the DLP.

In July 1972, spurred by the McMahon Government's budget (William McMahon had now replaced John Gorton as Prime Minister and leader of the Liberal-Country Party coalition), he stood as a DLP candidate for the New South Wales state by-election at Mosman. He was billed as one who served on numerous committees relating to environmental and social welfare, Local Government, and aid for the underprivileged at home and abroad. The electorate was urged to Vote I for Mackerras 'For a better deal for Mosman and its residents.' He polled extremely well, by far the best the DLP had done in that district. But he had become like a top, continually spinning, and had lost the ability to relax and unwind. "He burnt himself out. Worked himself into the ground," said his young brother Malcolm who at that time, with a Federal election of particular interest only months away, had just brought out his useful book on electoral statistics, *Australian Federal Elections*.

Neil decided to undertake a course in hypnotherapy with a specialist in Melbourne, a city he liked and often visited. He benefited greatly from this but wondered later why he was not advised then to leave the DLP and cease taking an active role in politics. His life may certainly have turned out differently. However, there was no such suggestion, and feeling very much restored in health, he accepted nomination and became the endorsed DLP candidate for Bennelong (North Ryde — Hunter Hill area) in the forthcoming Federal election, to be held in December, 1972.

Issues for the DLP were no longer as clear as they had been. Substantial withdrawal of both American and Australian troops from Vietnam was in progress, while U.S. President Nixon's foreign policy — *rapprochement* with the Communist countries — was made clear in his mission to Peking and played down the threat of either Chinese or Russian expansionism. The Australian Labor Party was poised, scenting victory, with a strong leader whose vision on foreign policy was in step with the historical forces at work and who espoused wide-ranging social reforms at home. The Liberals, on the other hand, presented a picture of disunity and Prime Minister McMahon did not seem to be the man to reunite them. Should the DLP continue to throw its considerable forces into endeavouring to maintain the Liberals in office or strike out in a positive campaign of its own? The latter course would almost certainly assist Labor to victory. When Neil discovered, towards the end of October, that the DLP intended to pursue the negative course, he resigned. He found himself firmly caught up in that startling phenomenon of Australian politics, the magical 'It's time!' formula, devised by the revitalised Labor Party after 23 years in the political wilderness.

It was just five weeks to the election, Neil was not only an endorsed candidate, but a founding member of the DLP 16 years previously, a member of the NSW State executive and president of the Hornsby branch. It was a precipitate action by any standards. His colleagues found it indefensible. He posted letters informing them of his decision as he set off for Papua New Guinea to visit his two foster children there, and made his public announcement from Port Moresby. The *Sydney Morning Herald's* correspondent, Ian Hicks, reported the resignation in an article published in Sydney on 27th October and gave details of Neil's formal letter of resignation to the Party's secretary-general, Senator Kane. In this he expressed his deep regret and his feeling that he had "no alternative but to resign from the DLP and every position I hold in it since it has been made apparent from circulars I have been receiving that I (have been) put in the position of having to choose between the DLP and my deep conviction that 'It's time.' However, I am convinced that the DLP has . . . quite magnificently fulfilled the primary objective which we originally set ourselves . . . (which) was to keep the ALP out of Federal office until finally it became fit for Federal office. That objective having been achieved, why continue the DLP . . . (since it) is not in any real sense an independent third party with a long-term chance of survival as such."

The following month, Gough Whitlam, with oratory matching a commanding presence, delivered his policy speech in Canberra at one of the most famous political meetings ever held in Australia. On 2nd December, Labor won the election convincingly and came to office with a comfortable working majority of 9 seats and on a mood of euphoria which had swept the nation and almost certainly every swinging vote in the community.

It is hard not to feel some sympathy for Neil in his precipitate decision, for he was by nature very vulnerable to the feelings of a new Utopia generated by the formidable, confident Whitlam and his team. He was essentially right in his estimate, for the DLP was to become a spent force, but the knife wound he inflicted was about as excusable as the one that provoked the anguished, *Et tu, Brute?* He explained it as best he could in an article, entitled *Supporting the insupportable: the DLP — a retrospect*, which he contributed to the comprehensive book LABOR TO POWER, edited by Professor Henry Mayer, featuring opinion from all sectors and including interesting comment from Malcolm Mackerras on the variability of the swing.

Neil wrote, "As long as I can remember, I have been ashamed of the White Australia policy, and every time it was modified I was delighted . . . I have thought it obvious that Australia's future is multi-racial and multi-coloured and that the first priority of our statesmanship must be to ensure that this both desirable and inevitable future society is harmonious. I thought the plight of the Ugandan Indians presented Australia with a golden opportunity to advance this future harmony and that the situation clearly called for an immediate further modification of the White Australia policy. Mr Whitlam seemed to think so, too, but Mr McMahon evidently did not. Similarly, I have for long been convinced that immigrant Australians and their descendants have very deep obligations both in charity and justice towards the Aborigines and their descendants. I did not admire the manner in which the Aboriginal Embassy was destroyed in July 1972 and I was aghast when it appeared that although the destruction was illegal the government nevertheless intended retrospectively to validate it. These two 'racist' issues were only final straws . . . Most of my reasons for thinking it was 'time' were in accord with what the DLP had long been hammering . . . (It) had quite a creditable record of opposition to racism . . . (and) had as long ago as 1961 jettisoned the White Australia policy." He went on to elaborate his disappointment that after much serious discussion within the DLP, they had decided to conduct a campaign that would be "very largely negative, directed only against Labor, likely to be regarded by the electorate — and by me — as a 'scare campaign' and strong evidence of a wish to die, if necessary, in support of the insupportable. I could not be wholly confident that Labor would win the election despite us, and I came to the conclusion that simple honesty required me to straighten myself out in public. After my resignation I felt as if a great weight had been lifted from my shoulders."

He went on to say that he felt the DLP's "great contribution has been to convert the Senate into a true house of review; a significant constitutional development which I applaud. Its difficulty . . . is that it is an almost explicitly Christian party in a post-Christian nation, a very largely Catholic party incapable of accepting the implications of Vatican II . . . (which was) a conscious attempt by the Catholic Church to adapt itself to the modern world . . . (Vatican II) resisted strong pressure to condemn communism . . . it took pains to find the good in every religion, set dialogue in train with all mankind, acknowledged past faults and embraced the future."

He then commented, with one of his pertinent flashes of humour, on the rigidity of DLP attitudes on moral issues in a changing world — "Most DLP members and supporters feel positively uncomfortable about the more 'progressive' features of Vatican II. In DLP circles the word 'trendy' expresses almost the ultimate in degradation although, curiously enough, the word 'relevant' is quite popular. Mindful of that delightful conjugation, *I am firm, thou art obstinate, he is pig-headed*, I have formulated a new conjugation for today: *I am relevant, you are 'with it', he is trendy*. Perhaps it is all summed up in the phrase 'the solid society', which the DLP recently sought to adopt as a kind of slogan to express its idea of the kind of Australia Australians wish to live in . . . (however) the post-Conciliar Catholic Church is no longer solid and no longer wishes to be."
He wrote a letter voicing similar sentiments to his friend, Bob Santamaria.

It might be thought that having thrown off the yoke of the DLP — for that is clearly what it had become for him — he would devote himself to the many worthwhile organisations to which he belonged, endeavour to diversify his legal practice so that the weight of 'working for developers', as he put it, would also be lifted and then consolidate his already prominent position at the Bar. In fact, his abrupt break away from the DLP seems to have acted as a catalyst. He must soon have realised the deep resentment he had caused amongst his former DLP colleagues and it cannot have been easy to live with, especially for a man with no flintiness whatsoever in his nature. In small every day things he deals always in kindness — he must have kept many stationers happy with the quantities of greeting cards he has bought over the years to send off, with a special stamp from a new issue, to the delighted children of his brothers, sisters and friends on birthdays and other occasions. Yet here he found himself endeavouring to cope with the aftermath of an injudicious and very public blow he had dealt to political colleagues while working, day in and day out, on legal cases which he found not only unfulfilling but, by now, actually repugnant. His discomfiture was compounded by the fact that he also lectured in the law of Landlord and Tenant to the Real Estate Institute of New South Wales. His tension continued to mount and his wife was very much aware of it.

They went to the beautiful Lamington Plateau National Park in southern Queensland for a brief holiday with his brother Malcolm and his wife Lindsay, and Elizabeth expressed her fears to the latter. She was very unhappy for Neil and afraid that his restlessness might lead to another precipitate decision which might, this time, affect the lives of their young family. This proved to be so. But for some months yet he found other outlets, principally, and to everyone's astonishment, taking up the cause of legalised abortion.

This came about through a combination of circumstances. His resignation from the DLP and the expression of his ideas had provoked interest amongst many Catholics, some of whom approved, others asked, 'How can you justify a Labor vote in view of Labor's State aid and abortion policies?' In regard to the later, which Neil then strongly opposed, a priest suggested that he look at the Vatican II Declaration on Religious Freedom. He did so and found a conflict between the declaration that abortion was 'an unspeakable crime' (thereby he noted leaving no room even for therapeutic abortion to save the mother's life) and the decree which stated, in essence, that every individual in his pursuit of truth must have the right to religious freedom and be free of external coercion in the exercise of it.

He delved into the semantics of these deep questions, asking himself, even if freedom of conscience in matters of morality does not fall within the technical meaning of the phrase 'religious freedom', should not Catholics *think* in terms of religious freedom before seeking to impose the pain of the criminal law upon fellow citizens of different consciences? 'Public morality' is a relevant consideration but what if the community, as in Australia, is hopelessly divided on important questions of morality? What if very many citizens, like Aristotle and St Thomas Aquinas, are not persuaded that the life of the embryo can be described as 'human life'? The more he dwelt upon these questions the more convinced he became that abortion, within certain prescribed limits, i.e. involving as well the consciences of doctor and nurse, was a right which came within the Church's definition of religious freedom. His wife Elizabeth, a true small 'l' Liberal, was also — somewhat surprisingly — convinced of the need for law reform in the matter.

Just at this time, the U.S. Supreme Court made several judgments which ensured the universal liberalisation of abortion laws throughout the U.S.A. Neil waited to get copies of these judgments, then wrote a paper — RELIGIOUS FREEDOM, ABORTION and the U.S. SUPREME COURT, *Reflections of a Catholic Lawyer*. He took the matter up with Cardinal Freeman, the Roman Catholic Archbishop of Sydney, sending him his paper and a long explanatory letter; he distributed the paper also to various organisations within Australia and the United States and to friends. The Cardinal wrote a detailed, reasoned reply, debating many contentious points, but concluding, inexorably, "Which is prior: the right of the woman to freedom, or her obligation from the law of nature to bear the child to the time of delivery? To me the 'right' of the child has clear priority over the freedom of the woman in this case. That 'right' should be clear in our legislation."

Neil, though grateful for the dialogue and for the Archbishop's blessing, with which the finely expounded letter concluded, was not deflected in his arguments on behalf of his new cause and tried to persuade his friend, John Goldrick, of its virtues. John and his very lovely wife Margaret, and their family lived then at Clifton Gardens, not such a great distance from Neil, but John was sufficiently disturbed by the matter to sit down and write a long forceful letter against the views which Neil was now putting forth. It should be mentioned that they also extended to approving the many contemporary 'young people (who) jettison traditional Judaeo-Christian sexual morality which they think belonged to an age when mankind was enjoined to be fruitful and multiply and fill the earth and subdue it'! It was a *volte face* indeed, which longtime friends could hardly have been expected to accept. At the same time, a letter arrived from an academic of Catholic persuasion at Fordham University, New York, who found Neil's *Reflections* 'a marvel of solid, objective, dispassionate presentation of a vital topic' and totally agreed with them.

Elizabeth seemed, somehow, to have been able to take all this in her stride, neither did she demur when, in May 1973, he decided to respond to an Australia-wide advertisement by the Victorian Government for an Ombudsman. They both liked Melbourne and it was certainly a position for which his legal qualifications and many-sided interests in welfare qualified him. In his application, however, with the devastating honesty which characterizes the whole family, he mentioned his treatment with the Melbourne specialist. He did not get the job. But it is interesting that in his application he also mentioned, 'If I remain at the Bar I will apply for silk later this year.'

Later that year he did just the reverse. It was September and he was in the northern New South Wales town of Moree representing a city-based landlord in a tenancy case at Moree, a town which has an Aboriginal population of about 2,500. This represents one of the largest concentrations of Aborigines in the State and about one-fifth of that shire's total population. Neil and his legal opponent on that particular day, a friend, Malcolm Ramage (latter a judge in Papua New Guinea) were waiting for the court to announce terms of settlement, when both were struck by the fact that the three Aboriginal youths presently appearing before the magistrate were without representation. They had stolen a car in Sydney and driven to Moree where they had been caught stealing petrol. Two had police records but the third had not, and clearly was about to receive a jail sentence without knowing that he could ask for time to pay a fine. Malcolm Ramage intervened on his behalf and the upshot was that Neil, after consulting an officer of the Department of Social Welfare, acted as security for the youth who was duly released.

"Although according to the book this 18-year-old was being correctly treated," he said, "I felt in my bones that he was not getting a fair deal. And they should all, of course, have had legal representation." He discovered next day that the newly set up Aboriginal Legal Service in Moree was in need of a solicitor and that the job would entail a large amount of 'juvenile work'. He was intensely affected by the situation and already, as he flew back to Sydney, began to envisage the possibility of resigning from the Bar and applying for the job himself. It was a dire community need and he was aware of being in the throes of some sort of Messianic urge which the hardships involved would satisfy. Also, Moree was not so far from Armidale, the educational centre of the New England district with its university and schools, a city he had always liked and where, if he were to make the break, his family could finish their education.

When he reached home, fired by the whole idea, he spoke to Elizabeth about it. It was precisely what she had feared might happen. Her heart sank. Yet she did not seriously oppose him. It is strange that she did not, for she had much strength of purpose and he would surely have paused if she had argued strongly against the proposal. Paramount for her must have been the knowledge of just how deep his dissatisfaction had become and how much he needed her support. She was to regret later that she did not suggest that if he were to go ahead with his plan, she should stay in Sydney with the family until he became established, and also that she did not voice more forcibly her greatest concern, which was the upheaval such a move would be for their children, particularly the older ones who were in their final years at school.

Neil himself seems to have leapt that hurdle and was principally concerned about his ability to handle 'juvenile work', of which he had no experience, if he were to go ahead and make the break. He was a member of the Aboriginal Children's Advancement Society and knew that they had a hostel for Aboriginal boys in Sydney at Sylvania Heights. He drove out there, introduced himself, and 'very quickly decided that there would be no great problem in establishing friendship and trust with Aboriginal boys.' He immediately applied for the position of Moree solicitor with the Aboriginal Legal Service and was appointed by the ALS Council at a meeting at Redfern on the evening of 22nd October. This was a night of particular significance to the entire Mackerras family who were gathered at the Opera House where Charles, in the presence of the Queen, conducted *The Magic Flute* during the opening season of the Sydney Opera House. Neil missed only the first scene of the First Act and then joined them — presumably on his own Cloud Nine as the music soared, and certainly with a feeling of inevitability.

He resigned from the Bar the following week in a blaze of publicity. There were headlines such as — *Lawyer Gives Up $60,000 Rat Race, Top Job Sacrificed for Aboriginals, Drop out Sydney lawyer heads for Moree legal service. .* The last accompanied an article in the *National Times* in which Neil, commented, 'I've charged the developers of Sydney enough for my services over the past 10 years to be able now to afford to do what I really want to do', and explained that 'the main problem for Aborigines on legal or quasi-legal matters is that they don't know their rights and what is available to them.' He was to take a huge drop in income, for the salary he had arranged with the Aboriginal Legal Service, $16,000, although twice the amount they had advertised, was barely a quarter of his previous earnings. However, he set off elated, found a big rambling colonial home with wide verandahs at Moree, arranged for the sale of his 'Sydney mansion', as the press referred to it, and his family joined him six weeks later.

"I was utterly surprised when he left the Bar because he was making such a success of it," said his former co-author, Mr Justice Hope. "He was well on the way to becoming a leading member of the Bar. But he did leave it, and I feel it was because he had a conscience about doing something for the community."

Catherine also realised that Neil was being genuinely idealistic but she was devastated by his move, which followed just a few months after Alan's death. Other members of the family had varying reactions. Alastair was alarmed at Neil's excessive expectations and also at the ramifications of so much publicity. Malcolm felt as Catherine did. "He should have taken silk," he said, "become a Q.C., perhaps have become a judge, and if he wanted to do idealistic things, do them within those confines as other people, like Justice Kirby, have done." He was also appalled at Neil's selling his magnificent home 'at a price he should have been ashamed of.' Colin, on the other hand, wholeheartedly approved of his brother's action, for it was in line with his own beliefs.

The following eighteen months were both exciting and gruelling. He made many enemies amongst the establishment and many friends amongst the Aborigines, particularly the young. From the moment of his arrival in Moree, he decided to get to know the younger children with the object of trying to keep them out of court, or if they did get to court, to be sure of them finding at least one friend there. Moree stands on the Mehi River which winds through the endless plains and it had recently flooded, sweeping away in the process the homes of a large number of Aboriginal people living on Moree Common. They were now living in caravans on the Wirajarai Reserve or 'Mission' and Neil learnt from his friend Malcolm Ramage that a sixteen-year-old from one of these families had that day 'pleaded guilty to a break, enter and steal and had been drunk at the time.' He went to the caravans, made himself known to the family, younger brothers and friends of the boy. "So," he said, "began my friendship with Aboriginal children. Although it hasn't kept them out of court, I think I can say it has been productive."

Four months later a Melbourne journalist, Douglas Aiton from *The Age*, visited him in Moree, drove round the whole district with him and wrote a fine article, entitled *Advocate Extraordinary*, on the extraordinary diversity of his activities, the joyous response of the Aboriginal children to him, but also his inept handling of the hostility of the townspeople by lecturing them on apathy, schooling problems, welfare and housing. A tactful approach to try and enlist the support of the establishment was not within his nature. A direct, caring approach to the Aboriginal people themselves was, and is, his strength.

The early atmosphere was captured well by Aiton — 'His battered car picks its way through the streets and the Aboriginal kids come running from everywhere, screaming "Mister MacKERRas . . . Mister MacKERRas . . . " They climb in and out and all over his car while he drives along and he is busy telling me a short history of each child his eyes fasten on. There's not one whose full name he does not know. He goes into a couple of houses, tells one man of an offer of work . . . tells another about progress made in the conveyancing of a house, gives another two dollars . . . buys an old man a packet of cigarettes . . . and all the time the kids are dancing round, chanting, laughing, slapping the bald patch on the back of his head . . . Later, when there's some peace, I ask him why the kids like him so much. "Aha", he says, "Perhaps it's a bit like Mary had a little lamb, why did it love her so, because, she loved it, you know." And this has continued to be the case.

But the journalist did not see the reverse side of the coin, for the undisciplined joy of the children was expressed in other ways. It did not occur to them that it was a disruptive thing to do to rush wildly through the Mackerras house, noisy and inquisitive, disturbing the studies of the Mackerras children and generally making themselves a nuisance. Two of the Mackerras girls were at boarding school in Sydney, lonely and unhappy and missing their home. The others, who were at the Catholic school in Moree, were not only disturbed by the Aboriginal children's innocent invasion of their house but distressed by the hostility they found at school because their father was the man who was 'stirring things up'. This he was most certainly doing and it was taking its toll on the family. In fact, a certain inhibited Creagh streak within him had never made his relationship with his own children particularly easy, and now it was considerably strained. Elizabeth wondered how long the whole situation could last.

At the same time, Lyall Munro Snr., then the Aboriginal Field Officer in Moree and now the patriarch of the district and Vice-Chairman of the National Aboriginal Conference, speaks of the work he and Neil did together in those days in fervid tones — "Thank God Neil and I worked together, we really changed Moree. We shocked the system and changed

Lyall Munro Snr., Aboriginal Field Officer, Moree

a lot of people. Police didn't realise what we were up against to begin with, and later they did. When we started working together, Aboriginal kids were being convicted — jailed — for silly things like stealing Icy Poles or using a shanghai. We changed that. And when Neil came to Moree we were up against the system, which was for all under-privileged people charged by the police to plead guilty. He started confronting that system. Police used to go to extremes to convict — Neil changed a lot of their attitude. He is a fantastic person. He is absolutely honest — honest above everything. If the political and legal system of the country was flooded with Neil Mackerrases, then there would be fair justice and politics. Of course, Neil is not popular with high society. He upset the system.''

He went on to explain why and gave a specific case in regard to alcoholism, the root of so much trouble amongst his people. "But Aboriginals drink openly," he said, "they don't care if people see. Whereas whites take their flagons and bottles home. The most you ever see are a few drinking a bit in the pubs about half past five. They don't admit they've got a problem. And some of them are wardrobe drinkers. There was one case we subpoena'd — an under-privileged lady was cooking in a household of whites and there had been trouble. It turned out that the white woman of the household was an alcoholic. We had to subpoena witnesses and prove it. People didn't like that. That's the sort of thing that upset the system. Dozens and dozens of cases I could tell you about . . . ''

There was also, fortunately, a lighter side and Lyall Munro recalled with a pleasant, full-throated laugh, a day at Inverell when Neil had driven over to defend some Aboriginal children. "It was quite a big court case," he said "and Neil had forgotten to bring his shoes with his suit. He tried to get into my size sevens and walk into court but couldn't, so we hailed a taxi driver from Moree we knew and borrowed his." The taxi driver waited patiently under a tree for the case to finish. Neil, however, sweeping all before and forgetting shoes, taxi driver and tree, with typical impetuosity decided after the hearing to drive the children over to see the lovely little gold mining town of Tingha . . .

The stories of Neil with children in northern New South Wales are legion. "He was representing some Aboriginal kids at Tamworth," Munro recalled, "and staying at Travelodge. One of the children had a birthday, so he put on a party for them — for all the kids in the place. He was sitting by the swimming pool with them — all nationalities — and he sent round to the Chinese Restaurant for the meal. It was something you never forget. All those nationalities together, Neil in the middle of them — and the Travelodge guests no chance of getting near the big blue pool!" He also recalled flying to Coonabarabran with Neil. "He decided to ask all the children round the place who were interested to come into the court and watch the proceedings — to show them what the justice system was all about. When the judge came in and saw all those faces, *he* wondered what it was all about!" Lyall Munro's pleasant laughter rang out again. Then, on a different note, indicating Neil's absolute dedication to the cause, he continued, "I remember being worried one day about a boy who was in trouble in Guyra. He was on a charge of forgery, he'd become expert at forging cheques and been picked up by the police. It looked serious for him. Neil was on holidays in Sydney. I phoned him at midnight and he drove back in his Kombi-van and was there in the freezing morning at the court before I got there myself. He is absolutely sincere, he will do anything when he feels the case warrants it.''

One incident recalled another, and also other aspects of Neil's work at that time — he was for instance one of those instrumental in the reform of a maximum security institution at Tamworth for youthful offenders — and Lyall Munro remembered, in particular, a European migrant they had both assisted. "Neil helps all those, white or black, who get into trouble through no real fault of their own," he said. "This New Australian at Narrabri had no English. He'd arrived in Sydney 9 months before and since then he'd been in and out of jail the whole time. We both felt the man was a real victim of the system and we spoke for him."

The foregoing account speaks as well for this fine administrator of Aboriginal affairs as it does for Neil. Elizabeth was always glad to see Lyall when he came to visit, and he himself recalls 'many hours spent with Neil and his beautiful wife.'

Yet in spite of all these positive things Neil's problems increased. He was no business manager, he had been prodigal in the Aboriginal cause with his own money, flying up barristers from Sydney for special cases, and his financial resources were running out. In July 1974 he presented a paper at a seminar at Melbourne's Monash University and it was printed a few months later in Monash Law Students Society's magazine *Oracle*. Entitled, *On Serving Aborigines*, it gave a vivid account of the difficulties and read in part: 'As I write this *cri de coeur*, I am just about grounded. Staff and creditors paid late and unpaid, correspondence unanswered, letters unwritten, actions not commenced, defences not prepared, creditors, clients, alike, in embarrassment, avoided. Grossly overworked, hopelessly understaffed. Perhaps worst of all, opportunities missed. And why? Our one great problem . . . How to persuade a fundamentally sympathetic Australian Government to provide us with the resources we need and above all, the money, to do the job.' He goes on to expound on the necessity for first-rate service in the Aboriginal Legal Aid system and why it can be expensive. He gives several pertinent cases, amongst them:

> ' . . . the community which, through its agents, arrests a 13-year-old boy asleep in the back seat of a car outside his cousin's home, at 1.30 a.m., bundles him into a police van, questions him at the police station with no friend present and there charges him with peeping, holds him overnight in the local jail cell euphemistically called the Children's Shelter and obtains from him, the following morning, a written confessional statement, all at a time when his mother, who lives 42 km. out of town, does not even know of his arrest, must expect a considerable sum of money to be spent on his later defence when, in due course, a defender is found. (Suppose he had been the son of a local grazier . . .) And, another community agent having admitted the confessional statements into evidence and convicted the boy (although releasing him on probation), must not that community expect an equally expensive appeal, or conceivably, series of appeals? . . . We have only just begun what we expect will be the long process of challenging, we hope, perhaps the whole of the law of detention pending bail . . . whereby the police State, for its own administrative convenience, fills the jails and distinguishes the rich from the

poor, at the expense of the poor, especially Alfred Doolittle's "undeserving poor".'

He goes on to detail the appalling shortcomings of the system, the need for procedural reform to save costs, the hopelessly inadequate public transport, bad roads and communications in the west which make the attendance of clients and witnesses at court so expensive. He points out that police in Moree are already beginning to adopt a different attitude and 'do their best to inform me or my office whenever an Aboriginal child is arrested'. Even so not enough can be done without adequate funding. His anger, of course, shows through. "Nothing rankles more in the human heart than a brooding sense of injustice", he quotes, " . . . injustice makes us want to pull things down." He points out that the best remedy is to train Aborigines to improve their own conditions. He has found no lack of people with suitable qualifications to fill the desperately needed roles of field officers and secretaries in each and every one of the towns he visits in the huge area, namely, Tamworth, Armidale, Inverell, Narrabri, Coonamble, Coonabarabran, Tingha, Boggabilla, Mungindi and Ashford. There are simply no funds to make the appointments. The whole is a convincing and exceedingly well documented appeal for help. He underlined it by evoking that cornerstone of British justice — *To no man will we deny, to no man will we sell or delay justice or right (Magna Carta)*. He had found many circumstances which made this seem a travesty.

Meanwhile, he had received some rather rough justice himself from the very people he was trying to help. He accepted it philosophically, but his family did not. He very frequently took the side of the Aboriginal children against their parents in argument, and one day as he walked through the Wirajarai Reserve, with a dozen children at his heels, he was personally attacked by the elders. His family found this mortifying, nor did they appreciate it when one of his 'young friends', whom he allowed to drive his car just before being tested for a licence, totally wrecked it. He himself went reasonably happily by train ("I have more time with my papers and briefs" he said) but the journeys to courts in other towns now often meant overnight trips until a replacement car arrived; he was away very often and Elizabeth often found young Aborigines camping on her verandahs. Family dissatisfaction reached crisis point when, in October, after a weekend visit to the older girls at their university college in Armidale, they returned to find their home had been broken into by a group of young Aborigines. Nothing was stolen and no charge was made but Elizabeth now confronted Neil. It was beginning to be a necessity for the family well-being for them to move to Armidale.

"I realised that there would be increasing conflict between my young friends and the family if we didn't move, "Neil admitted," and besides, Armidale was intellectually and culturally a much more suitable place for my particular family to live." He envisaged setting up a practice as a barrister again and establishing an Armidale Bar where he could be of even more service to those whom he wished to serve. He resigned from the Aboriginal Legal Service in November 1974, but remained at their request until Lyall Munro Jnr, chief executive officer of the ALS in Sydney, was able to find a suitable replacement. He stayed on at Moree until April 1975, when, assured that the new appointee, a young solicitor named Phillip Segal, would arrive within weeks, he moved with his family to a farmhouse he managed to find at Kelly's Plains outside Armidale.

Sadly, although Elizabeth and the children were happier, Neil found himself in an even more embattled position. He could find no support in Armidale for establishing a Bar as he had proposed. His attitude in so fiercely and closely espousing the Aboriginal cause, his implicit and sometimes explicit criticism of the establishment, had not endeared him to its members. It was clear that he was *persona non grata* with the professional, academic and grazing community — all of whom, of course, paid lip service to the philosophical ideal of racial equality. He had rocked the boat in far too practical a fashion in the district, it seems, for his background of 16 years at the Sydney Bar to counteract the antipathy he had aroused. However, their two nearest neighbours at Kelly's Plains, Professor Elkins and Max Sewell and their respective families, did not react in this way, were immediately friendly and smoothed Elizabeth's path considerably. Neil, on the surface underterred, went about setting up as a solicitor in the small township of Uralla south of Armidale.

There he continued his work with clients from the Aboriginal community and others in need of Legal Aid. The process of application for Legal Aid is quite lengthy when, as in this instance, the nearest agency was Tamworth and it could take a month for the form-filling processes to be completed and returned. In the meantime, cases had to go ahead and there was no means of knowing whether they were likely to be accepted, or accepted with the proviso that the client contribute $20 or $30, which they very often could not afford. There were many bad debts but this did not worry Neil, nor the several newly graduated solicitors from the University of New South Wales who joined him, all imbued with the same desire to use their talents in the service of the community. Under the name, Neil Mackerras & Co., Solicitors, they continued the uphill struggle for several years with him at Uralla and later opened a small office in Armidale.

During this time Neil felt somewhat estranged from his mother. Catherine, indeed, never did revise her opinion that the giving up of his flourishing Sydney practice had been anything other than a disaster, and it is doubtful if she ever realised just how much he had managed to achieve in his difficult, see-sawing career in the north-west. He was badly affected by her death in 1977 and afterwards visited and spoke with her friend from university days, Louise Hutchinson, who sensed his need for personal solace. It is certainly a pity that Catherine did not at any time meet or talk with the young solicitor, Phillip Segal, who succeeded Neil at Moree and still holds the position. He felt then, as he does now, with the weight of eight years experience behind him, the value of Neil's work and we shall look soon at what he has to say.

In 1978, both the underlying tensions of Neil's position and the enormous amount of work he had undertaken over the past twenty years, seemed finally to catch up with him and he decided he would do something he wanted to do, which was to write about his experiences in juvenile legal work as a contribution to the forthcoming International Year of the Child (1979). He resigned from his practice, which was now down to two, for they had inevitably got into financial straits, and left it in the hands of the remaining highly motivated young solicitor, Peter Clarke, whose wife taught in the district.

In the process of resigning, Neil said publicly that he would not be renewing his licence as a practising solicitor because he felt he could not go on appearing in court, representing the client, mainly the Aborigine, when justice was not being done. His friends, the Goldricks, were distressed at this. "Neil and Elizabeth had dinner with us," said John, "and she was very tense. I felt it was a mere aberration on Neil's part because he had been under so much stress."

This was so, for Neil responded to a request by the Aboriginal Legal Aid administration in Sydney to become a supplementary officer in the Kempsey district in 1979, and appeared quite regularly in Children's Courts at Kempsey, Taree, Coffs Harbour, Newcastle and Maitland, as well as Moree and Armidale and in District Courts on appeals. In May, he was called to Canberra to give his views at the Fraser Government's *Standing Committee on Aboriginal Affairs* and testified that he had noticed a striking lessening of the number of children committed to an institution in towns regularly attended by Aboriginal Legal Service solicitors, and an equally striking improvement in the attitudes of the officers of the Department of Youth & Community Services. He advised that he thought it would be necessary to keep the Aboriginal Legal Aid service in operation until after the turn of the century in spite of greater self-awareness among Aborigines. He said he felt the biggest problem was amongst the 12–15 year olds who grew up fearing unemployment, while only five years previously, 'the same age group had assumed that when they left school they would walk straight into a job. Now they tend to assume that they never will.' He said that he was able to use some of his expertise, gained

Neil and Elizabeth, 1979

through the Aborigines, for the benefit of poor whites. He spoke of the Aborigines' lack of regard for other people's possessions, rising to a certain extent from their own lack of personal possessions. He mentioned overcrowding, saying 'A child without an adequate home is a very sad thing.' He mentioned the tendency of incidents to flare when the young felt some sort of discrimination, and gave an instance of a wild rampage of vandalism by Aboriginal boys in Moree at Easter 1975. He made the strong point that 'in appearing for a juvenile one of the first things to establish is: What is wrong with the home? There is always something wrong with it.' Strengthening the parental home rather than moving the child, was probably best; and prevention rather than cure was the essence of the matter.

Towards the end of that year, as he was beginning to feel the physical strain of covering such a wide area, he announced that he would take no new cases in the furthest towns from his home. He was then asked to appear at Taree Children's Court on behalf of several young Aboriginal boys who were in trouble; he knew them well and they had asked for him. It is not possible here to go into the details of the case, but in the course of it one of the boys (and they were temporarily under Neil's care) took from the motel room the keys of the rented car, which Neil had for the occasion, and drove off. He was subsequently chased by police, arrested and charged with driving in a manner dangerous to the public and without a licence. He was released on bail, but later was charged with being uncontrollable, taken into custody, and Neil was unable to have him released on bail either then, or when he appealed. "So", said Neil, "on the last working day of the International Year of the Child, Taree Children's Court, as its last act, committed this Aboriginal child, though a first offender, to an institution . . . " The upshot was that in the course of the appeal before a District Judge, Neil was exceedingly outspoken; the appeal was allowed but the child was placed on a 2 year bond conditional, inter alia, that he not associate with Neil.

This was an appalling situation, particularly as Neil was to appear the next day before the same judge. He felt extremely angry but nevertheless chased around and managed to get a substitute to appear for his other young client. It seemed now as though his career was really in ruins.

"I feel," said Mr Justice Hope, "that the whole trouble resulted from the pressures which had been building up in him for a considerable time. We appreciated what he was trying to do in his work." It is not known exactly what caused the District Court Judge and the District Officer to change their attitude, but it is possible that the opinion of many leading members of the legal profession in New South Wales was brought to bear. Both men went out of their way to be pleasant when the next case was presented and the crisis was resolved. "Ever since that time," Neil commented, "I have, for my sins, always slept with the keys of my car under my pillow when I have any of my young friends with me. And I have never allowed another Aboriginal boy to drive my car."

He and Elizabeth, with their two youngest children, managed to take a short holiday in England and Europe in the spring of 1980, one of the highlights of which was a few days with his brother Charles and wife Judy, at their delightful island retreat at Elba. Charles was conducting with the

Italian radio in Naples. They met there and went over to the villa. This was something of which Charles and Judy were particularly glad, for if Neil had had to cope with more vicissitudes than any of his brothers, some self-inflicted, others not, he had that year to face, out of the hum-drum and with shocking swiftness, the real tragedy of his life.

Some months after their return, one November morning, Elizabeth was getting ready to take their son John in to Armidale to pick up a microphone from the Physics Department at the university, for use at his school that day, then to drive him to his school, six kilometres in the opposite direction at Kelly's Plains. It was her habit to take prescribed tablets each morning for asthma, and at the same time to give Neil the two tablets prescribed for him for high blood pressure. This morning, she exclaimed to John and to his brother Richard who was there, "Oh, I've taken one of your father's tablets instead of mine!" It was Inderal.

She phoned their doctor to see if she should still take her own asthma prescription; he was not at his surgery at the time and she decided that she would not take it. It seemed to her the safer course and she was not in the least concerned. Neil proceeded to do some work in his office at home, Elizabeth and John set off to Armidale, Richard bicycled to school, Alison had already gone. The older members of the family were by then in the throes of their careers or at university and not at home. The trip to Armidale and back to the school at Kelly's Plains was safely made, but as she was leaving the school she was seized with an extremely severe asthma attack. The school contacted Neil, who gave them the name of their doctor. He was still on his morning round. An ambulance was summoned, and she was rushed back to Armidale and to hospital and medical attention. A school teacher drove Neil to the hospital, also his daughter, Susan, who was then living in Armidale. Neither realised, as they waited together, how serious was this attack, worsened as it was by the events of the morning, more particularly her failure to take her own tablet. At eleven o'clock Elizabeth died.

It was the most shattering blow. Elizabeth had always been there, supportive and loving, and with a strength which had sustained them all through the vicissitudes of the past ten years. The children were brought home from school, the older ones flew from Sydney, Canberra and Dubbo and they all began, as Neil said sadly, to learn to live with the disaster. His brother Alastair and his sister Elizabeth and her family drove to them from Sydney, his brother Colin and cousin David and their wives from Brisbane, Lyall Munro, Phillip Segal and others came from Moree, and 'many people were very good and very kind', — as, fortunately, is the way of things. But he had now to face the yawning, empty gap in his life and, for the sake of the younger children, galvanise himself to work and to return to something closer on hand than the scattered spasmodic Legal Aid cases he had been doing recently.

The firm of solicitors he had founded had shrunk, as we have seen, and the previous year had been taken over from Peter Clarke by another lawyer with strong ideals from Sydney, a tall, bearded, fine-eyed young man, Patrick Dodgson, who, like the other, had felt that he 'didn't want to just stay in the city but get out and do something for people.' Neil pocketed his pride and asked to return to the firm as an employee. This he did and

Neil with Aboriginal children at Armidale, 1985

the firm, Dodgson Mackerras & Co., Solicitors, operated — and Dodgson still does — from Faulkner Street, Armidale. Patrick, fortunately, had one foot firmly on the ground and is a good businessman.

Phillip Segal, the young ALS representative in Moree, equally pleasant and straight-forward but with the enthusiasm of one who has not the worries of self-employment, visited Armidale recently and commented, as friend and colleague of Neil, ''As to whether it's all been worthwhile the answer is yes, because in this community there are very few people who are prepared to speak out against what they see as injustice. And Neil is one man who does so, fearlessly, and he doesn't care who he speaks to or who hears . . . He has great empathy with the children, and because of the social structure of the Aboriginal community, a large number of Aboriginal children find themselves before courts on very minor matters. Neil defends them, speaks out for them and gets them very good results, particularly when the cases go before judges. He commands tremendous respect amongst the bench, many of the judges were barristers when he was a barrister. And Neil's become a specialist in the field of criminal prosecutions against juveniles. He and I are the only ones who specialise in that — it incorporates special rules of evidence and special rules of proofs involving juveniles. Neil is the principle bastion against injustice against juveniles in this town. He sticks his neck out for young people, often at some risk to himself. He always puts his clients head of himself.

He will act for people if they can't get Legal Aid and they haven't got any money. He's not motivated by anything other than his strong sense of justice and he knows no obstacle. If he puts his mind to do anything he just does it. And he's become something of a local legend because of his very distinctive voice — he uses it to good advantage. And it carries!" So, once again, as with Alastair on the school platform or Charles rehearsing an orchestra, the resonant Mackerras voice proves an effective instrument.

Segal agrees with Neil that something needs to be done to get at the social problem which causes so many Aborigines to go before the courts, especially as he feels that magistrates are now very much aware, and take into account any deprivation in background when sentencing. The old maxim, prevention is better than cure, is apposite here. "I am continually reminded", says Neil, "that the most adventurous, the most alert, the most intelligent, the most sensitive, in short, those upon whom our future race relations most depend, are also those most likely to find their way into our Children's Courts, very often, many times."

Until mid-1985 Neil dealt with the majority of Legal Aid cases, and, as has been noted, they present monetary difficulties from the form-filling and bureaucratic angle alone. Patrick Dodgson found his quixotic approach, under the circumstances, somewhat worrying and as a solicitor in private practice saw the need to expand more in other aspects of the law such as conveyancing. But the undeserved factor which faced Patrick — and Neil — was the attitude of the community. The former commented, "One of my commercial clients said to me, 'I hear you're the boong solicitors!' People hate that. The other solicitors, of course, think we're doing a worthy task, but it's also a way of them shunting off their own consciences by giving those sort of clients to us. And they know they're going to be dealt with and they don't feel guilty about the people concerned." He felt understandably restless about the whole situation.

At this point, it did seem that the conflicts with which Neil's attitudes have always complicated his life would continue. Then, quite suddenly, it occurred to the powers that be in governmental circles that the time had come to set up an office in Armidale of the Aboriginal Legal Service and to appoint a Solicitor. Neil had long since lived down his somewhat hasty resignation from Moree, and it must have been abundantly clear that he was the obvious person to whom to offer the appointment. He accepted it immediately and it is a highly satisfactory solution to the problems he was finding in private practice. Meanwhile, until a full scale office is actually set up, he is operating, with Patrick Dodgson's blessing, from Faulkner Street.

Before we leave him, it must be said that the rampant racism, with which Neil himself has long since come to terms, has nevertheless been at the root of his nervous crises over the past decade. Many might feel that he has been on some unconscious 'self-destruct' course in his consistent espousal of the most touchy and complex cause in this country. But Neil himself is sure that no price has ever been too great. He has also learnt to contain his own anger and to put friendship with Aboriginal children in one compartment and legal cases in another, and feels that with this attitude he can be more effective in representing and giving support to the angry and confused young Aborigines who so often find themselves in trouble in the clash of our two cultures. "For those," he says, "I reserve my special love."

In the meantime, he has the interest of his family, not all of whom have quite forgiven him for the traumatic upheaval his initial move to the north caused them, and that of the wider family circle — in particular, a close bond with Colin, whose children in Brisbane regard him as their 'favourite uncle'. He has a longheld interest in genealogy and has traced their ancestry back many generations. He plays some bridge with a friend, Professor Hempel of the University of New England and his two sons, keeps in touch with others, and life goes on.

There seems to have been a gradual change of heart among the establishment in the New England district in regard to this stormy petrel, for there is now no evidence of hostility towards him. It might be thought that the people of an educational centre such as Armidale and the surrounding area, would have welcomed to their midst this man of formidable skills and manifest care and goodwill who had the courage to take practical steps in a cause which they nominally support. Instead, for many years, they turned upon him a very cold shoulder indeed, reflecting, not the graciousness of their city, but the biting winds that blow across the tableland — a sad commentary, not just upon the district, but upon us all.

Chapter 7

Joan and Elizabeth

The lives of the two Mackerras sisters, Joan and Elizabeth, fourth and fifth members of the family, illustrate interestingly the respective influences of Catherine and Alan on their family and the tug and pull of the European as opposed to the Australian scene.

Joan, who has now grown very much like her mother in appearance, and always shared the same propensity for spirited talk and discussion, was strongly influenced by her and accepted her pronouncement that the British and European lifestyles were much superior to the Australian. This was to have a far-reaching effect on the course of her life, as were various decisions made by Catherine in regard to her career, for she was invariably able to persuade this quite forceful daughter that her view was both right and wise — as, in fact it usually was. Elizabeth, not as academically and musically gifted as Joan, but with artistic flair and an extremely independent will, was set on her path by Catherine's determination to allow her children to follow their own bent. Nevertheless, the real turning point of her life came as a result of strong action by Alan, whom it will be remembered, she physically resembled and whose favourite she was. Joan now lives with her Australian husband and their family in Suffolk, England; Elizabeth with her husband, of Russian extraction, and their family, at *Balvaig* in Sydney. We shall take up the differing threads of their lives from the formative years in the 1950s and their joint introduction to Europe by Catherine.

Joan did well scholastically at PLC, Pymble, among interesting contemporaries such as Helen Granowski and Elizabeth Evatt, and continued to take violin lessons at Loreto Convent, Normanhurst, forming a lasting friendship with her teacher, Mother Lua. At the same time, she studied theory and history of music with the distinguished Sydney musician, Dorothy White, who lived close by and a similar longlasting friendship was formed.

After her final school term, she went to Melbourne to stay with the Mackerras family friends, Dr Harold Wilson and his wife Margaret, at their beautiful home at Heidelberg, where, improbably, they also still kept several cows and served rich cream on wholemeal bread and other delicious concoctions which remain gratefully in the Mackerras memory. It was an exciting time, for the major purpose of the visit was to attend, with the

Elizabeth (left) and Joan in garden at Turramurra, 1951

Wilson's flautist daughter Nicky, a music camp being held at Geelong Grammar School. There, to their joy, they found themselves playing in an orchestra under the baton of Sir Bernard Heinze and undertaking such things as a piano concerto with no less a soloist than Hepzibah Menuhin. "Of course," said Joan, "a week of this in that lovely place was just enough to make me realise I couldn't possibly live without music."

On her return, she found to her astonishment, that a career in music was a *fait accompli*. Catherine met her at Mascot and informed her that she had booked her into the Conservatorium full-time, she was to have violin lessons, piano lessons, harmony lessons, all was arranged. "I was absolutely sure," Catherine told her, "that you should do music and I knew when you came back from the music camp you'd be convinced yourself!" It was true but Joan, in spite of the deep bond forged between them over all her growing years, found the lack of consultation rather overwhelming.

In fact, she did request a change of violin teacher, preferring a man to the woman teacher Catherine had arranged. It seems that she must have been aware of the strength of her own personality, for she felt that a woman might not have enough influence over her. So, over the next years, she settled down to the discipline of two rehearsals each week with the Conservatorium orchestra, excellent piano lessons with Laurence Godfrey Smith, which she enjoyed immensely, ('I owe him a great deal,' she says thirty years on) and violin lessons from Haydn Beck. She found Beck a wonderful teacher and with him learnt 'the Bach E Major Concerto, a very nice Beethoven sonata, lots of Handel sonatas and other fine things.' Friendships with her brother Alastair's colleague, Peter Harwin, family friend Tim Yates, and on-going musical evenings at *Harpenden* filled her life to overflowing. Peter soon found himself in love with her, but this was not to be, for he could not persuade her to think of him as other than a friend.

Meanwhile Elizabeth, three years her junior, had been a decidedly recalcitrant pupil at PLC and, as we have seen, was supported by Catherine who went into battle on her behalf with the headmistress, Miss Knox. "She's a good child at home," Catherine insisted. "What is wrong with the school?" She demanded to know why there were negative remarks, not only against academic subjects, but others. "*Dressmaking: Weak!*" she exclaimed. "That's extraordinary! Elizabeth and her friend, Janie Lemann, spend their Christmas holidays making their own dresses. And very pretty dresses indeed." She was in no way deterred to find that her offspring was not inclined to the discipline of 'drafting patterns' as required at school. The long-suffering headmistress finally suggested, quietly, that as the school seemed unable to do anything for Elizabeth, it would perhaps be better if she were to leave. Catherine conferred with her young daughter and discovered that she would like nothing better; she had always enjoyed her ballet classes at Turramurra and declared she wanted to take up ballet full-time. So, in triumph as it were, Catherine removed her from PLC, found the one full-time ballet school in Sydney and sent her there.

Alan was appalled. He had envisaged architecture as a career for Elizabeth. She had patiently helped him with his yacht designs; he had observed her with the delightful Janie (one of his 'gems') industriously working at their dress designs. No doubt it seemed to him that she had only to transfer these activites to the architectural sphere and there was a highly satisfactory career for her. He frowned upon ballet as a pursuit. "Oh well," said Catherine, "it's what she wants." In this absolute support for the children in whatever bent they might have, and wish to follow, Catherine was certainly remarkable. Alan saw that argument was pointless. Furthermore, they must both have remembered their fruitless attempts, ten years before, to persuade the 15-year-old Charles to continue with academic studies. Elizabeth, though never imagining herself to have his kind of potential, was quite as single-minded and self-willed. Well, so be it. But in the light of later events, it seems clear that Alan determined, from this point, to keep a close watch on the long-term well-being of this much loved child of his in her chosen career.

The Frances Scully Ballet School was tucked away in the old Palings building at the back of George Street, not far from Wynyard, where Elizabeth alighted each morning. She was as happy as the day. "That old building had a fabulous atmosphere," she recalled. "An old pulley lift, sounds from everywhere of singing lessons, sopranos running up scales, people practising all kinds of instruments. I loved everything about it, and the teaching was good."

She had just completed a year, when a crisis occurred in Joan's life, and in the life of all those doing advanced studies in violin at the Conservatorium — their well-loved and revered violin teacher, Haydn Beck, decided to return to England. The only other person Joan knew of, from whom she would want to learn, lived in Adelaide. She wrote to Charles for advice. It was succinct. "For goodness sake, if you're going to go away from home to study, there's only one place to go, and that's London.'' Catherine thought that made very good sense and when Elizabeth asked whether she might go also to study ballet at Sadler's Wells or wherever possible, the seal was set upon it. "Russian training's the best,'' said Catherine, "we'll find a Russian Ballet School in London.'' Alan did not demur, Neil was working and studying; Alastair was on his way home from Cambridge and would look after the twins who were now at Sydney Grammar. So, early in 1952, the three set sail in an Italian ship for Europe, a few weeks' vacation in Italy, then London and 'the furthering of the girls' careers.'

They could hardly have had a more stimulating person to give them their first glimpse of Europe than their much travelled mother, so deeply versed in and appreciative of everything European. They arrived in Naples in February and it was so freezingly cold that the girls' ardour was somewhat dampened, but not even the cold wind blowing off Vesuvius reduced Catherine's enthusiasm as she explained to them in exuberant detail the lifestyle of those touchingly stilled citizens of Pompeii. She hired a car and drove them all over the country, which *was* exhausting, although she knew her way around Rome and Florence, Padua and Siena. It was not until they reached Venice and had three delightful days moving about by vaporetta and gondola that she managed to send off a postcard-photograph to Alan. It must have been reassuring for him after the long silence to see the three, all smiles, in a gondola on the Grand Canal, to be told how 'successful so far' everything had been, and gratifying to have the brief missive signed 'love C.M.' In her element, away from the clash of personality which afflicted them, and with the close bond of family, the phrase no doubt came naturally to her. It is pleasant to think of Alan driving in to *Harpenden* and its household of men on one of those hot

Catherine with Joan and Elizabeth, Grand Canal, Venice, 1952

February evenings, after a hard day's theorising in his newly appointed role at the NSW Electricity Commission, and receiving this small but rare signal of affection.

In London, there was a joyous reunion with Charles and meeting with Judy and their two infants. It was then decided that Joan would take lessons from the distinguished violin teacher, Frederick Grinke. Catherine booked her in at once and she began the intensive study and practice necessary to enable her to audition for the Royal Academy of Music. They moved to a flat closer to the centre of London, and Catherine then made enquiries on Elizabeth's behalf.

She discovered that the best course would be to enrol her at the highly recommended Legat School at Tunbridge Wells which had produced, among others, Moira Shearer, famous for her role in the film *Red Shoes*. It was run by the gifted, if somewhat eccentric, Madame Nadine Nicoleva Legat, former *prima ballerina* of the Marinsky Imperial Ballet, St Petersburg, and widow of the noted Russian teacher and *premier danseur* Nicholas Legat, former professor of the Class of Perfection at the Imperial Ballet where his pupils had included Fokine, the great Nijinski and Anna Pavlova. He and Madame Legat (his second wife) were with the Moscow State Theatre of Opera and Ballet after the revolution and in the 1920s left Russia, with the permission of Lenin, and set up a studio in London. Legat was then asked to join Diaghilev and the *Ballet Russe* in France; he subsequently opened a studio in Paris and trained many of the famous dancers of the day, then moved once again to London where Sir Robert Helpmann was one of his students. After Legat's death in 1937, Catherine

Madame Legat at Tunbridge Wells

learnt, Madame Legat had taken over the school and at the outbreak of war moved to Buckinghamshire and subsequently to the small town of Tunbridge Wells in Kent, where she made boarding school facilities and general education available in addition to ballet and music. Another extra was yoga, of which she was a firm devotee, and the pupils of the school appeared regularly on BBC television in a programme presented by Sir Paul Dukes, then one of the leading exponents of yoga in the U.K. Madame Legat was also the author of an excellent textbook, *Ballet Education*. It all sounded eminently satisfactory and they would go down to Kent at once, Catherine decided, and ask for an interview. Elizabeth was, of course, ecstatic.

On the morning they arrived at the school, Madame Legat was still in the throes of her yoga exercises. The secretary, who had found her standing on her head in the corner of her room, at which point she was never to be interrupted, asked her nephew, Andrew Briger to interview them; his parents lived at the school and he often advised his aunt on business matters. It so happened that he was in the throes of confronting a personal crisis in his own life, in the shape of a broken engagement to one of the teachers at the school, and he went down reluctantly, with his mind far from concentrated on the 'Australian lady and young girl' he was to interview. He saw 'a plump lady and a fair-haired girl' and thought 'Ah yes, they'll think *here's another Moira Shearer*' and he began somewhat distractedly answering Catherine's searching questions, wishing he were anywhere but there. Since it was a mixed school, there would be the question of young boys she commented. Were the pupils supervised? He went through the gamut from this to 'And where is the laundry?' before his aunt appeared and he was able to make his escape to deal unhappily with his shattered romance. There is no doubt that the formidable Madame Legat and Catherine at once recognised each other's metal. The interview went well and Elizabeth was booked in forthwith.

She settled in quickly and became a keen pupil, as determined to make a success of her dancing as she had been to cease academic studies during her intractable days at PLC in Sydney. A diversion, other than visiting the teashops in the town (members of the ballet school were objects of great curiosity to the locals), was to spend an hour, together with one or two other students with the charming, diminutive Madame Briger, the former Comtesse Zenaide Soumarokov-Elston, and absorb the atmosphere of old Russia which her apartment breathed. She always received the girls very warmly, gave them tea, and particularly liked to talk with those who, like Elizabeth, were very far from home. She had led an extremely sheltered life herself — she had 'never crossed a street alone' — and loved to hear about their adventurous young lives. She was as charmed by these fresh, eager students as they were by her — her gentle accent, the little hats she wore even in her apartment, the reminiscences they were able to draw from her as they admired an icon or a painting or a fan, any of the objects so redolent of her former life. They also drew her forth on 'dear Kolia' (Nicholas Legat), his days at the Imperial Ballet and then in Paris where visitors to her apartment had included rising young stars among his pupils, such as Markova, Danilova and the Irish Pat Dolin. Elizabeth relished it all and became a frequent visitor.

She met again Madame Briger's son, the handsome young man with the strong French accent, who had seemed rather distant when she had come with Catherine for her interview. Andrew, she now learnt, was partly qualified as an architect and worked for a month at a time with a firm in Wales, came back to London 'to have a good time', and returned periodically to Tunbridge Wells where he also had several clients. She found that he was an extremely lively and interesting person to talk to, while for his part, he liked her direct straight-forward attitude to every topic discussed, it was 'most refreshing'. He was also astonished and not a little impressed as were the inhabitants of the town generally, at an incident which occurred about this time.

Elizabeth was walking through the common at Tunbridge Wells one morning when she saw a man severely maltreating and beating a child. With the memory of her own blissfully happy childhood no doubt welling up in her, together with outrage at the brutality, she grabbed a large stick and whacked the offending man across the back with it. "There was a summons," Andrew recalled, "the man was in fact abusing his own child, and the child was taken away from him. The magistrate thanked Elizabeth — but he also asked would she mind dealing with a situation like that more gently in the future please!" It was a situation reminiscent of her brother Neil's swift and practical reaction to injustice suffered by the young and defenceless. Andrew laughed at the recollection of the fierce Elizabeth and the mildly rebuking magistrate. From his 31-year-old heights at the time, he began to find this 16-year-old Australian girl very companionable indeed and also greatly valued her friendship with his mother.

Meanwhile, Joan had approached the august portals in Marlyebone Street, passed her audition and been admitted to London's Royal Academy of Music where she was fortunate enough to have as teacher Robert Masters, leader of the Robert Masters Quartet and later a colleague of Yehudi Menuhin. Two wonderful years lay ahead for her, in both musical experience and in the friendships she made.

"Once I was in London," she recalls, "I felt that somehow I was happier than anywhere else. I had been brought up by my mother to think that the most beautiful things in the world were all to be found in Europe. She used to say that the essence of Australian beauty was not the same as the essence of the beauty to be found in Europe — just no comparison between the two. Everything European was, *ipso facto*, marvellous. Standards were much higher, everybody's manners were much better, everybody spoke much better, all the different cultures and languages and traditions of the different European nations all made for a very much more interesting way of life. And England was part of this. She talked a great deal about it. Everything that happened over here was more important than things that happened in Australia. And so I became imbued with the idea and I felt somehow that I was at home." Catherine's much travelled youth — 'Civilisation at last!' her father had exclaimed to his 11-year-old as their ship steamed into the Mediterranean — was certainly the basis for this, but the indoctrination, for Joan, was to prove a two-edged sword.

Catherine stayed for some months at the London flat, enjoying herself but keeping an eye on the initial progress of the girls, and during the Royal Academy's summer vacation took Joan to Austria. Charles and Judy

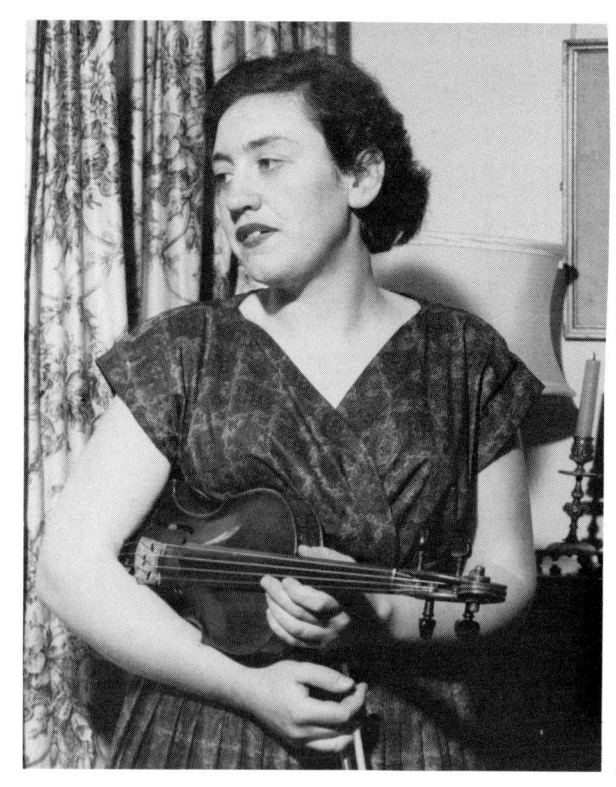

Joan, as young violinist

accompanied them, and he was able to intersperse some research on 18th century music in Vienna with their tour by car round the spectacular Austrian Alps, beauty spots such as Lake Konstanz, and several days in Salzburg for the Festival. "It was all very exciting," said Joan. "Also having Charlie with us, very amusing." He had lost none of the high spirits they had missed so much when he left Sydney and he was obviously delighted at the close companionship with Catherine again and Judy's *rapport* with her and with Joan. He was in very fine form indeed and it was a memorable holiday for them all.

It was capped for Joan by a magic week with her mother in Paris. Catherine managed to talk away French resistance to *les Anglais* over coffee and *croissants* at breakfast, snacks at cafes along the Champs Elysees later in the day and good red wine with *cordon bleu* meals at night. They visited the Louvre, the opera and Versailles. They knelt together in Notre Dame and Sacré Coeur, they leafed through old editions at the bookstalls on the Left Bank, gazed at the city from the Eiffel Tower and took a boat trip on the Seine — everything possible in one crammed week. Back in England, Catherine went swiftly to see how things were with Elizabeth and talked with the redoubtable Madame Legat again, a woman, she realised, who was as outspoken as herself. She received a favourable report. Besides, Elizabeth's happiness was visible.

Catherine returned home in September, satisfied that both girls were now receiving the tuition and impetus they needed — and she was right. She had gone about launching her fledglings with imagination and flair. As a mother she seems somehow to have had a larger than life quality. She was not only giving and creative, in a very vital way, but had an intuitive grasp of the needs of her children, trusted them, urged them early towards independence and was quite devoid of possessiveness and dark inhibiting moods. Unfortunately, her intuitive understanding did not carry over into her relationship with Alan; she was wholly insensitive in the manner in which she undermined his role with their family while revelling openly in her own. But if she was a difficult wife, she was a mother *par excellence*.

Joan missed her badly. She had made many good friends in London, was an invited guest at recorded broadcasts and concerts made by Charles with the BBC Concert Orchestra of which he was the director, and often saw him, together with Judy and their two daughters, but continued, nevertheless, to miss Catherine. She wrote her long letters with every detail of her daily life and discussed all the matters that most concerned her, such as her decision to become a Catholic and the instruction she was now receiving in the process. She was, as she freely admitted, still very dependent on her mother for this sort of communication. Elizabeth was much more independent and also much less given to verbal expression, either in person or on paper. It is doubtful even if she put pen to paper when a major crisis occurred in her young life in her second year at the Legat School.

Andrew Briger, back on one of his periodic visits to Tunbridge Wells, was walking through the main hall of the school one afternoon when from the dining hall, normally empty at that hour, he heard the sound of someone weeping and went to investigate. There he found his young friend, the 'Australian girl' crying her eyes out. She had an injured knee, it was very swollen and she had not been able to dance for weeks, she told him through her tears. She'd been having treatment and today the doctor had told her she would have to give up ballet — and she'd come all the way from Australia to do the course. "Go and see my aunt," Andrew advised her sympathetically. "She's unconventional, she'll take you to an osteopath and see if it can be manipulated." Elizabeth did just that, the limb was jerked expertly back into place and that was the end of her knee trouble. This created another bond between them and when, in November that year, his mother fell ill following a severe attack of asthma, and they were both sitting comforting her, he felt he could ask Elizabeth to stay while he went off about some necessary business. She stayed until Andrew's father returned from his music teaching at the school. Madame Briger died in her sleep that night. She had been very precious to Andrew, and Elizabeth had stayed with her, spoken with her, after he had. This was a deep bond indeed.

Several months later, early in 1955, feeling very restless about his somewhat piecemeal career, he came to a sudden decision and went to tell Elizabeth the unexpected turn of events. They had talked a good deal over the two years and she knew that he had been to school in Paris, later in London and had done his course in architecture at the London

Polytechnic, had two subjects still to complete and had never bothered to do them, since he lacked incentive in the jobs he had to date. He'd just gone along enjoying life; his mother's death had made him take stock of himself. His close friend, Michael Bentine, one of the original members of the Goon Show, with whom he had done some children's television, was now in Australia, with his family, doing the Tivoli circuit, was currently in Melbourne, and had asked him to come out and join him. He knew of Andrew's frustration and restlessness and felt there was more opportunity for him in Australia. He wouldn't hear of a refusal and had paid his fare on the *Oronsay*. So he was going to Australia! Elizabeth laughed. He had joked about Australia so much she found it hard to believe that he was going to settle there.

She reminded him that, up till now, her country had been for him simply 'a pink blob on the map at the other end of the world that had a bridge over a river somewhere, produced soldiers with turned-up hats who fought well but were terribly undisciplined, cricketers and tennis players, and where you'd be likely to find kangaroos hopping in city streets and sheep all over the rest of the place'. This 'colonial' version, though exaggerated, was in truth about all he did know of Australia and her laughter filled him with misgiving. As they said goodbye, she told him that if he went to Sydney (he was going to Melbourne), he must look up her parents and she gave him their address. He rolled the word on his tongue as he went off — *Turramurra* — difficult even to pronounce. Everything would be like that. His heart sank. And it sank even further when he stood in the purser's lounge of the *Oronsay* and looked at the map of the world on the wall. Australia *was* right down at the bottom, it was no joke at all. His European blood curdled; he felt quite sure he was going into outer space.

In London, Joan too was packing her bags. She had completed her studies — A.R.C.M. and L.R.A.M. — and was leaving to take up a teaching job in Oxford. Her life had been very eventful. She and an old university friend of Alastair's, had fallen in love but her religion, which was very important to her, proved a stumbling block. She broke off the affair, was very unhappy for a time, and after her graduation was particularly grateful and glad to spend Christmas with Charles and Judy and their delightful young daughters whom she knew well by now. Since parental responsibility remains as constant in the more rarefied artistic circles as anywhere else, she had been glad during the year to 'babysit' the youngsters on occasions so that Judy could get to an opera or concert to hear Charles conduct. Christmas in the small family circle was very cheering, with the giving and receiving of gifts, Joan's being 'lovely records' which she 'could never have afforded'.

Now it was Oxford and the well-known school for girls, Hedington. She settled in at once and loved everything about the life. The job itself was rewarding for she proved a naturally good teacher, she also found immediate accord with two colleagues, Margaret Bailey (Director of Music) and Rachel Sheila, both of whom were to become lifelong friends. She also appreciated the atmosphere generated by the university, the many people of similar interests, and the concert round. She found herself in demand as a violinist, played frequently in the operas and concerts which were produced regularly in the town and the surrounding districts, and thoroughly enjoyed life.

Meanwhile Elizabeth, towards the end of her course, went with a young Swiss fellow-student, Christa Studer, to Switzerland for a holiday. They found that auditions were being held in Berne for positions with the *corps de ballet* in the Swiss National Ballet and decided to audition. "It was such a lovely theatre, we thought we'd just try for fun," said Elizabeth. "I really don't know where we got the courage from! Probably because there were two of us and we gave each other confidence." Her friend, of course, spoke the language so that also facilitated matters. To their astonishment, they were both successful. It was particularly surprising in Elizabeth's case because the Swiss are reluctant to employ people of other nationalities and are very rigorous in the matter of working permits. But the fact that she had to go off to the police station and renew her permit every fortnight, although annoyingly time consuming, was nothing to the joy of finding herself in a professional company, dancing, and experiencing all the excitement, tensions and heightened emotions of stage performance.

"It was a small *corps*, we all took turns, and I don't think it was a very outstanding ballet company," she said with her customary disarming candour, "but it was a beautiful theatre." She wrote in similar vein to her parents. Catherine was delighted and did not quibble at her setting up flat with a similarly youthful friend — after all, Christa's parents lived in Switzerland and would no doubt keep an eye on them. Alan was altogether unhappy at the prospect. He missed her badly, but also felt that

Elizabeth, in Berne, 1956

she herself would be much better off in Sydney. However, he bided his time. Let her feel her wings for a while yet.

As Andrew's friend Michael Bentine had foreseen, he had found a choice of interesting jobs available in Australia. He and the Bentines were now in Sydney and he had opted for a firm, Leighton Irwin & Co. whose manager had also trained at the London Polytechnic; they were engaged in hospital design and construction. He found himself accommodation of sorts at Point Piper — 'a room which had been a storeroom to a large house, divided by a masonite partition — the maid and her lover had the other half, and the boiler house was directly underneath!' He enrolled at the University of Technology (now the University of NSW) to complete his course and was made to feel very much at home by 'a very friendly bunch of young students'. He spent weekends alternately with Michael and Clementina Bentine and their children who were as close as his own family to him, and with Leighton's English manager, John Goodings and his wife who had befriended him. Then the Bentines left for England and it was almost like losing an arm. Often lonely now, he thought suddenly of the Mackerras address.

Catherine's distinctive voice answered his phone call. She invited him to dinner, and when the day arrived drove him around French's Forest in her little blue Hillman and told him how much, by comparison, she loved Europe. That evening at *Harpenden* they played the opera, *Boris Godounov*. "You speak Russian of course, you must translate for us," said Catherine. It was no easy task. "Thank goodness I could do some of it!" he laughed at the thought of that instant challenge on his first acquaintance with this *ménage extraordinaire*.

Next, Alan Mackerras appeared at his office in the city and invited him to go sailing with him. He was told to meet him at The Spit, bring his own sandwiches — and 'nothing you have to throw into the harbour, like peel'. Andrew wondered what was ahead of him. As it turned out, it was a magical experience, never in all the years to be quite recaptured. There was a stiff south-easter blowing. "Bonzer day!" said Alan and set *Antares* into the wind. It was Andrew's first day out on the harbour and he never forgot it. "Alan was a magnificent sailor," he said, "and *Antares* was really a racing boat. We just raced on the harbour that day, the water sprayed round us, flowed round our faces, we got soaked, and it was absolutely marvellous — I've been out many times since, with him and with others, but I've never had such an exhilarating experience again."

He wrote to Elizabeth in Berne and told of his remarkable initiation, both at *Harpenden*, where he was often invited again, and aboard *Antares*; she replied and said how much she was enjoying her independence as well as the ballet. So they remained in touch.

Elizabeth did indeed love the European lifestyle, and although she had baulked at learning another language earlier in her career, now took it in her stride. It was essential for her to learn to speak German and she proceeded to do so. Joan came for a visit and stayed at the flat. The two sisters visited the coffee shops of Berne together, ate delicious continental cheeses and cakes and agreed, without equivocation, that Europe was the place for them. In 1956, however, at a turning point in his own career,

Alan had other ideas, particularly for his younger daughter, and set about implementing them.

He went over by ship, contacted Elizabeth, and took a train to Berne. At the time of his arrival there was a performance and she was unable to meet him, so he went straight to the theatre. They met at the stage door, Elizabeth already made-up and in costume. He was appalled at the heavy layers of stage make-up on her young face but nothing could take away from his pleasure at seeing her. "Well, I'll just have to kiss you, even with that dreadful muck all over your face!" he exclaimed. After the performance he told her that she must resign as soon as possible and come home, at least for six months; she could return to Europe later if she really wanted to. He had arranged for Joan to come from Oxford and they would all go on a tour of Switzerland together. He would not take no for an answer. Alpine country, they knew, was one of his chief joys.

Joan saw her father in a different light during the few weeks they had together. He was clearly resigned to the fact that she had become a Catholic, talked to her about her teaching job in Oxford and was glad that she was so happy. Amongst the Swiss Alps and lakes she found him relaxed and companionable. "We went to the tops of the mountains together and did little trips on the lakes and I got on with him much better at a personal level than I ever had before," she commented. "I'd always been aware of loving my mother more than my father, but now he seemed reconciled to us having our own ideas and views and we were able to talk about anything and I felt that I did very much belong with him as well." When away on his own, yet again, as he had done with Charles, he was able to establish a new positive relationship with one of his family. He admitted frankly to the girls that he felt that their mother had had too strong an influence on them in regard to everything European being better than everything Australian, and pointed out that as Elizabeth was not yet 20, it was better that she return and make up her own mind. Elizabeth posted off a card to Andrew Briger with this news and said that she would like to see him. At least there would be somebody who realised just how hard it would be for her, and to whom she could talk. Joan argued happily enough with her father on the theme of Europe versus Australia — she had no intention of returning.

"So," said Elizabeth, "Dad dragged me back home." She could not have been more reluctant and boarded the ship, the *Moreton Bay* — or as she and Joan had nicknamed it, the *Moreton Bay Fig* — with a bad grace. She was aware that she was not *prima ballerina* material but luck had been with her, she had made a very satisfying niche for herself, and she continued to brood about the wrench it had been to leave her life in Europe and resign from the ballet.

Her heart must have lifted a little when they steamed through Sydney Heads, and it was good to see her mother and brothers again. At *Harpenden* they were as lively and noisy as ever, but she could not help feeling restless and unhappy. It seemed to her that she had left independence and freedom behind. In retrospect, she feels that her father's action in ensuring that she as least give herself a chance to find a fulfilling life in her own country, and amongst her own family, was eminently sensible. It took several months, however, to acquire this view. Somewhat unaccountably, she did not hear from Andrew Briger, and gathered that he had lost interest in keeping up their friendship. Catherine invited 'interesting young men' to their musical gatherings and Elizabeth went out with one or two but her heart was not in it. What was she to do at home? She did not intend to stay long, therefore there was no point in trying her luck with any of the Australian ballet companies. She and her longtime friend, Janie Lemann, who at that time was finishing a course in Design at the East Sydney Technical College, used to meet frequently after Janie's lectures and take themselves off to the old Kashmir Restaurant and coffee shop at Kings Cross.

"It had all those Rosalind Nortons, weird murals all over the wall, witchcraft and so on," said Janie. "For Elizabeth it was a bit of Europe which she was missing badly — she didn't fit in with the normal Australian youth at all. She'd done a lot since she left school. She was much more mature than me, but we still did seem to have a bit in common." They did indeed.

Then a phone call came from the man who was for her, of course, the very personification of all that she had left behind in her three years in Europe. Andrew Briger had moved from the oddities and rigours of his Point Piper boarding house to a more comfortable one at Randwick, mail had not been forwarded as directed, and he had only just received her card. He asked her to dinner and found a ballet film to take her to afterwards. Life in Sydney suddenly assumed another dimension.

Soon also, Elizabeth and Janie managed to get fill-in jobs as nurses' aides at the John Williams Children's Hospital at Wahroonga and tore their hearts out over young polio patients. Fortuitously, Andrew Briger was designing new nurses' quarters for the hospital. The matron there, Matron Worth, a forceful but charming character, took a liking to her unusual young aides, heard about the friendship between Elizabeth and the architect, saw that the two suited each other, and aided and abetted the obiously budding romance by concocting numerous messages for Elizabeth to take to him. They found the opportunity to chat and had much to recall — Tunbridge Wells, his mother and father, Madame Legat and her yoga friend and mentor (and probably, they surmised interestedly, her lover) Sir Paul Dukes, godfather to Andrew, and one time head of the British Secret Service in Russia in the hectic days following the revolution. They also had to catch up with each other's subsequent experiences, hers in Berne, his in Sydney. When they went out together at weekends, he was invited to stay overnight at *Harpenden*. But a friendship only it remained for several months for he had to overcome diffidence on several scores.

Just how did Alan and Catherine — and the whole rather terrifying family for that matter — really feel about him? He was 15 years older than Elizabeth, not yet qualified, and had very little in the way of worldly goods to offer her. Inevitably, he found that his feelings dwarfed these considerations and one summer afternoon by the harbour, 'with the ferries to Manly going by like gondolas', he told her so and asked her to marry him. And so it was agreed.

They went in search of Alan. He had just come in from sailing and had the sails spread on the lawn when Andrew, 'all on nerves' end', approached him. He was terribly fond of his daughter, he told him, wanted to marry her, and he'd like to have the family's permission to do so. "Yes, yes," said Alan. "Help me with the mains'l, will you?" It was typical of him, and perhaps, as well, with the instinct born of his special love for his daughter, he had foreseen it. In any case, Andrew realised, as he stretched the mains'l taut, her father approved and the sparing words were not indicative of his real feelings. He was greatly relieved, and also found that Catherine was agreeable — provided, she said, that they wait till later in the year to marry, since Elizabeth was not yet twenty. In the interim, spurred by Mackerras scholarship on all sides, Andrew put his head down and emerged with credits that year in the additional subjects he was studying and qualified in architecture.

The pair were married in September of '57 in the Russian cathedral at Strathfield, with choir and full regalia in the beautiful ceremony of the Orthodox Church. Near disaster occurred when a candle carried by Elizabeth caught the sleeve of the robed officiating priest and was averted by an alert choir boy who, not faltering in ceremony, swiftly kissed the priest's hand, then put out the small blaze. The clan gathered later at *Harpenden* where the 18-year-old Colin, of whom Elizabeth was particularly fond, had provided a light-hearted talking piece with his present — a

Elizabeth and Andrew (Briger) with bridesmaid Janie Lemann glimpsed in background

shining metal rubbish bin — as the unlikely centrepiece of the exquisite gifts, and the redoubtable 90-year-old Uncle Willie Creagh delivered, with undiminished vigour, the main speech. The pair then drove off in Alastair's car for a week in a snowbound chalet in the fastness of the Snowy Mountains.

Among the wedding guests had been that much valued family friend, Dr John Parkinson, and it was to a small terrace house of his at Paddington that the pair returned. Andrew received his Diploma in Architecture, Elizabeth started a small ballet school nearby, and the two took up their life together.

Some 18 months later, in Oxford, Joan was amazed to find her mother 'suddenly landing out of the skies as it were'. Catherine had made her impetuous decision to fly to South Africa when she learnt that Charles was to conduct the Cape Town Municipal Orchestra for a season. Spurred by the enjoyment both she and Charles had from the visit, and also with a question mark in her mind about Joan, she decided that 'England was really more or less on the way home'; she would return that way and see her daughter. It seems certain that with Elizabeth returning, reluctantly, to Sydney and then settling happily, she had begun to worry that she had unduly influenced Joan to make her career in England.

As usual she came straight to the point. "You're having a marvellous time here," she told her, "and I think England is absolutely wonderful — but I think you should come home." Joan was astonished at this and they discussed the matter at length. "If you stay here," said Catherine, "you'll get stuck in this nice school — in a rut. You'll probably never meet anybody you want to marry, and you'll be a schoolmistress all your life. Come back and do a university degree as a mature student." It was a devastating argument to put forward, and somehow Catherine had a habit of proving to be right on all important matters. With a very heavy heart indeed, Joan decided to take her advice.

At the end of 1959, she said goodbye to all her friends and with the quite drastic feeling that she was about to cut herself off from civilisation, returned to Australia by ship as an 'assisted migrant'. She had been away for a good six years, and was surprised at how easily she was able to take up the threads again. She had three highly satisfactory years at Sydney University studying music, history and Italian, made more friends, often visited Elizabeth and Andrew and the two baby daughters they now had, Gabrielle and Christina (the Brigers were by this time living at *Balvaig*), and generally became thoroughly involved in life in Sydney.

During the latter part of her university course, Alastair, who was then Master of the Lower School at Sydney Grammar, mentioned that they had a new music master at the school, were wanting to 'start up some strings', and suggested that she make an application to join the music staff, part-time, and teach the violin. She did so, was appointed, and later also conducted classes in violin teaching, the first person in Sydney to undertake this. She found the music master, Graeme Hall, very pleasant to work with. He was a thickset fair man who, although he was not tall like her brother Colin, somehow reminded her of him. The *rapport* grew and a summer music camp at Armidale University brought them closer together; they both worked on a performance of the Monteverdi Vespers and enjoyed the friendship and help of Dorothy White who was there as a tutor. Joan graduated and soon after they announced their engagement. Graeme was not a Catholic but very tolerant on the subject and they had the great bond of their music.

It need hardly be said that Catherine was delighted but Alan also was extremely pleased. When Graeme had sought him out, in the time honoured manner, to ask his permission, he was in the throes of making a cupboard in the back garden workshed where he spent many satisfying hours. "I'll just finish this," said he, "then we'll go inside for a sherry . . . " He had continued to grow closer to Joan, for both were now very much involved in academic pursuits. In fact, strongly encouraged by Catherine, Joan had undertaken an honours degree and was doing a thesis for her M.A. on the history of violin bowing in the 18th century which required some 'extraordinarily interesting research'. Alan's pride in her is evident in the photograph of her on his arm on her wedding day in September, 1965.

There are a number of independent recollections of that occasion, which seems to have been a particularly happy one. Peter Harwin recalls complimenting Catherine on 'the loveliest dress he'd ever seen her in — a rich, drab-mustard-lace — and the beautiful cross she wore with it'. The camera also records her sharing a high-spirited moment with that other magnetic personality, Alan's brother, Ian Mackerras, while Nancy Phelan had an earlier impression reinforced — that of Ian and his fellow-scientist wife, Jo, as the most satisfyingly married pair ever.

Joan continued teaching and finished her thesis, the main thrust of which was that in the performance of 17th and 18th century music, the variety of bow in use at that time produced a better result than a modern bow. She examined instruction books on violin playing published in Europe from 1695–1831 in an attempt to discover more about the techniques of that era and the gradual change to modern bowing techniques. Her thesis, which she entitled, *The Art of Bowing, An Enquiry into the History of Bowing Techniques in Violin Playing from c.1675 – c.1842*, was regarded as very good indeed. It was the first time that material of this kind on violin playing had been correlated and examined in Australia, and Joan had imported for the purpose quite an extensive amount of microfilm material from Oxford, Cambridge, Paris and Bologna. As so often happens, whether it be Darwin and Wallace or many other less exalted cases, at the same time as she undertook her research, which she hoped would result in original work, a similar project had been undertaken, in this case by an American professor, David Boyden. "Unfortunately," said Joan, "his book, *A History of Violin Playing*, appeared just a few weeks before my thesis was completed and presented to the university in March 1966, so it did not seem very original." In fact, it was a considerable achievement, and she had some subsequent correspondence with the American professor.

Meanwhile, a crisis occurred in the Music Department at Sydney Grammar School where Graeme was music master and Joan teaching violin. As we have seen elsewhere, the headmaster appointed, after Colin Healey resigned in 1965, was an Englishman, Peter Houldsworth. Arriving at a time of rising nationalism in Australia when Australians

Joan, with her father.

Catherine with Ian Mackerras at reception at Harpenden.

wanted their own countrymen appointed to significant administrative positions, Houldsworth made matters worse by his high-handed attitude. Very much a product of the English Public Schools system, he made many disruptive moves, though usually, as Alastair commented, 'with the best of intentions'. The Music Department, in which a string section was now flourishing, was running very smoothly and more and more students taking up music as their extracurricular activity. It was not surprising then, that when the headmaster brought out from England a musician who had impressed him there and placed him over Graeme Hall, there was strong reaction. The newcomer, Peter Seymour, was indeed very gifted and was to become an innovative and inspirational force in the expanding music scene at Sydney Grammar before moving on to the wider musical sphere in Sydney, but the appointment at the time was made in a very ill-considered manner and raised the hackles of many members of staff.

Graeme himself felt that he had been placed in an impossible position, as did Joan on his behalf. Of all the Mackerrases, she was probably by temperament the most likely to be stirred to swift action by a happening of this kind. With feeling running high, they decided to take a year's leave of absence, travel in Europe where Graeme could gain further experience, and then come to a decision. Many colleagues urged them to stay but they had made up their minds and set off forthwith.

They stayed for some time at Grenoble in the south of France, Joan taught violin and Graeme taught English at the Lyce Mounier (a large boys' school, where they were given a flat) and at the same time he studied French at the University of Grenoble. It was in Grenoble that their first son, Bartholomew, was born.

Catherine made another of her dashes across the world to see her grandson and to be present at his christening in the historic baptistry in Florence where the great Dante had been held as a babe at the same font in 1265. Revelling in the event, she insisted, with Joan, that although it was no longer the practice, the service be read in Latin. Peter Harwin, who was on study leave in Europe, and to be god-father, recalled the whole lively occasion, "Charles's wife, Judy, was there too — she was my co-godparent — and it was hot, 100 degrees. The priest had to rush away and get a copy of the Latin — he'd forgotten where he'd put it. But we had young Barty done in Latin, then Catherine gave us a lovely party at an air-conditioned hotel and shouted us all champagne." So, with her usual flair, Catherine launched the Halls on their family life, and herself set off with Peter for Charles' villa at Elba, there to gaze at the Mediterranean, indulge her passion for Italian straw hats, majolica pottery — and discussion.

The Halls had by now both resigned their positions at Sydney Grammar School and decided to move to England to live. Graeme had been imbued as strongly by his parents (both born in the U.K.) as had Joan by Catherine, that everything in England and Europe was more culturally rewarding than in Australia, so it is not hard to see, under all the circumstances, how they came to this decision. Catherine had the virtue of never interfering in the lives of any of her family after they married and she did not at any time try to influence them to return to Australia. With her prescience, however, there is little doubt that she must have felt that their action in severing links with Sydney Grammar and the educational scene in Australia, where the Mackerras family is so broadly based, was somewhat precipitate. It is possible that she realised that, with Joan, she had perhaps overplayed her hand in regard to the advantages of England and Europe. They would, of course, be happy there and that was the positive thing.

Graeme became Director of Music at a State Grammar School in the lovely cathedral city of Norwich and they settled there for some years. Their other three sons, Drostan, Ambrose and Sebastian — names redolent of their mother's consuming interest in music and history — were all born in Norwich, but the four are now growing up in Suffolk where Graeme is Director of Music at Woodbridge School, not far from Aldebrugh. It is an independent school set in wooded parkland — a Victorian building with modern classrooms — and of the 640 boys and girls more than half learn an instrument and there is a music staff of 25. He took over when the Music Department was somewhat run-down and has worked energetically, through many trials and tribulations, so that the school — a separate music school was built and opened by Sir Peter Pears in 1977 — now boasts three orchestras of varying sizes, two choirs, a wind band and several recorder groups. In 1977 he was appointed an examiner to the Associated Board for the Royal Schools of Music which takes him periodically all over England.

As the children have grown, Joan has taken on a major role among the music staff at the school and is Head of Strings, helps coach the Chamber music and takes sectional rehearsals for the Ogden Chamber Orchestra which tours in Europe. She enjoys the intellectual stimulus and, like her husband, finds the English music scene rewarding but does miss her family and friends, in spite of visits made each way.

All the Hall children play a musical instrument and Drostan is an outstanding young violinist. His mother considers that he is much better than she was at the same age and wishes her own mother could have lived another decade to hear him play, particularly some of the concertos she and Catherine played together at *Harpenden*. Drostan takes part in Master Classes at the Aldebrugh Festival each year under such people as Ruggerio Ricci and Norbet Brainier, and has done since he was 14, and each week his father drives him across country to take lessons with Joan's former teacher, Frederick Grinke. Judy Mackerras heard this young nephew compete for the Menuhin prize at 15. "He didn't get it, but he was amongst the finalists, he's very good," she commented. "I don't know whether he's going to be a knock-out soloist, but he's a very talented boy." The Mackerras musical gift seems indeed to have come to light again in green Suffolk. Meanwhile, in 1982, Alastair Mackerras invited Drostan and his brother Ambrose to come to Australia and meet their cousins.

In the intervening years, much had happened in the lives of Elizabeth and Andrew Briger. In the mid-1960s he became a partner in the architectural firm with which he had been associated for some time and it became McCauley, Conran & Briger. He was particularly interested in town planning and often lamented Sydney's lack of a Champs Elysées and of pedestrian malls. In 1965, his brother-in-law, Malcolm Mackerras, then a research officer for the Liberal Party (the Askin Government had just won office in NSW), was looking at possibilities of changing the city boundaries to give the party at least some chance of breaking the stranglehold that Labor had had on the Sydney City Council for the past 17 years. Malcolm learnt that one of the anti-Labor organisations was the Civic Reform Association and that they were looking for professional candidates to stand for office. "Here's your chance," Malcolm told him, "you're always talking about city planning and Sydney's lost opportunities, come and talk to these people!" The upshot of this was that Andrew stood for election that year and worked very hard, although there was little chance of winning with the city boundaries as they were.

Elizabeth was not particularly interested in municipal politics but if Andrew wanted to have any real say in town planning it was necessary for him to become an alderman, and since she thoroughly approved of his ideas for the city, she helped as much as she could. This involved distributing a huge bag of leaflets into the myriad letterboxes of Fitzroy Ward which stretches from Potts Point to Surry Hills. This she did, accompanied by her two small daughters (who naturally wanted to stand on tiptoe and 'help' push them in . . .) and since it was summer and she was heavily pregnant, this was no small feat. As expected, it was to no avail on this occasion, but Andrew's keenness and the general support he had been able to muster, led to the Civic Reform Organisation asking him to form the Darlinghurst City Group, of which he became chairman.

In 1966 the Brigers' third daughter, Nicola (Nicky) was born, and Catherine and Alan came to live in the lower flat at *Balvaig*. Although they lived independently, Elizabeth naturally wanted to do as much for them as she could and life was exceedingly busy. Three years later, their family was complete with the arrival of their son Alexander (Alex). The same year Andrew was elected to office as an alderman of the Sydney City Council, and as chairman of the City Development Committee, he initiated the work on the first (1971) City of Sydney Strategic Plan which, in identifying the problems of the city, set the guidelines and policies for its future development. As Chairman of the Steering Committee he was appointed Liasion Officer between the City Council, the Planning Consortium, Ministers, Public Authorities, community and business organisations and threw himself into town planning projects aimed at the beautification of the city. He and Alderman Leo Port, well-known throughout Australia as a specialist panellist on the ABC-TV programme, *The Inventors*, initiated in the Council the concept of the Martin Place Pedestrian Mall. They became known for a time as 'the terrible twins' for they had to combat the strenuous opposition to the project by various Government Departments and Labor Party aldermen.

The then Lord Mayor, Nick (now Sir Nicholas) Shehadie was strongly behind the plans, and his wife Marie was also enthusiastic. Elizabeth found them both very congenial and it was at dinner at the Shehadies, with talk focussing on the projected Mall, that the Brigers met that vital theatre personality, Robin Lovejoy, and his wife Patsy. He was then director of the Old Tote, and also had the beautification of Sydney very much at heart. "I remember coming in with bits of advice and offering to rustle up demonstrations and get students with flowers and have a spring carnival for Martin Place!" he recalled. For the Brigers, and Elizabeth in particular, this was the beginning of a much valued friendship.

The planning and persuasion finally came to fruition and the Mall into being. "As I stood in Martin Place, opposite the GPO, with Leo Prrt and Nick Shehadie, immediately following its closure to traffic," Andrew recalled, "I felt it was probably the most fulfilling day of my life." He now began planning, with added zest, other streetscape projects, and at much the same time, Elizabeth felt the need to expand her own activities.

She began a course in business administration and was in the throes of this when Andrew was invited to accompany the then Lord Mayor, David (later Sir David) Griffin, on an official visit to Moscow and Leningrad as guests of the Moscow Soviet. It was interesting from every angle and also his first opportunity to see the Soumarokov-Elston's palace, his mother's home in Leningrad in Russia's pre-revolution days. It proved as rewarding as expected and one of the official highlights was the meeting he and David Griffin had with the 'Chief Planner' of the present day city of Moscow.

Now, the opportunity for which Elizabeth had been looking unexpectedly presented itself. Her longtime friend, Janie Breden (formerly Lemann) had become highly qualified as an interior designer. Janie was on holiday with the Brigers at Merimbula on the New South Wales coast when a call came from the then Director of Historical Buildings with the National Trust, David Earle, asking her to return with all speed to Sydney and plan their entire move to new headquarters. It was the first major job she had been asked to do. She found the new premises to be 'a wonderful old building, the old Fort Street Girls High School near the Observatory where the Trust still is', and met the challenge so well that other offers followed. Elizabeth finished her business course and joined her, part-time, on the administrative side, Andrew was able to put more work in their way, and *Janie Breden & Partner — Interior Design*, at Potts Point, soon became a thriving business. During these years, the flexible hours allowed Elizabeth to try her wings but also ensured that she was there in the morning when the children left for school and reassuringly at home when they returned in the afternoon.

About this time, she also had the big responsibility at *Balvaig* of the care of Alan and Catherine in their last years. This was not made any easier by their unfortunate incompatibility. It had come as something of a shock to Andrew to discover that Catherine and Alan's marriage was far from happy, for it had never been apparent to him in the earlier years. He continued, however, to have an excellent relationship with each of them and noticed that, although living at such close quarters, neither ever interfered in the life of the Briger household or offered advice, unless sought. He sometimes called in the early evening for a sherry and talk with Catherine whom he found warmly responsive.

He had often commented to Elizabeth on her own Scottish lack of demonstrativeness, and by now, having observed the phenomenon of Alan and his 'gems', and experienced his long and pleasantly cosy chats with Catherine, which frequently ended, as he was taking his leave, with his arm about her responsive shoulders, it occurred to him that undemonstrativeness was not a salient characteristic of either parent but a product of their incompatibility and had to some degree, therefore, been

224   *Scholars and Gentlemen*

unconsciously absorbed by their family. He has never agreed with what he calls *le sang-froid Britannique* and has made a point of encouraging a display of affection with their own children. Elizabeth, defending her own Scottishness, told him, "We feel deeply, we don't need to show our feelings." This was so, and the important thing was that she had instinctively inherited her mother's facility for picking out and fostering the varied talents of her children, developing a companionship with them, yet spurring them to independence. Catherine herself was now known to all her grandchildren, with great fondness, as Austra, the name given to her by Charles and Judy's children to distinguish her from their English grandmother. We will look later at the special relationship which grew between her and the Brigers' eldest daughter, Gabrielle.

In 1975, there was strong rivalry between Andrew and Leo Port when both stood for the Lord Mayoralty. Elizabeth had no particular liking for Leo, although recognising his interesting European background; she regarded him from the beginning as something of an opportunist and so it proved. Andrew disliked the lobbying and behind the scenes machinations necessary in the political process, failed to follow up some oblique approaches made to him, and when it came to the point, Leo was elected Lord Mayor (by a majority of one) and Andrew, Deputy Lord Mayor. After the positions were confirmed, they buried the hatchet and worked well together.

There was a great deal of deputising also and that year, at the invitation of the United States Government and PAN AM, Andrew and Elizabeth

Elizabeth meets the Queen, Andrew (Deputy Lord Mayor) looks on. Lord Mayor Leo Port is glimpsed on right. Sydney, 1956

attended meetings of Mayors, Deputies and their wives from various capital cities of the world in New York and San Francisco, as part of the bi-centenary celebrations of the two cities. It was a particularly interesting trip for Elizabeth, as she had heard much from her father over the years of the United States, of his liking for the people, and of the friendly communication of American scientists with him. She also found a bond with the informal, straight-speaking Americans and Andrew did not have the problem on official occasions there with which she sometimes presented him in Australia.

With Royal visitors or on vice-regal occasions in Sydney, Elizabeth has consistently refused to do any 'bobbing or bowing'. Whether the Queen or any of her relatives, or representatives such as Sir Rodin Cutler, Sir Zelman Cowen or Sir Ninian Stephen have, over the last decade, noticed an independent wife of a Sydney dignitary who did not perform the customary bobbing and bowing, is doubtful, particularly as Elizabeth invariably found them very charming to talk with, was very much at ease herself and likely to proffer an invigorating remark or two rather than the usual pleasantries. It is certain that many Australians would emulate her in regard to the extreme formalities if given a choice, and probable that by the turn of the 21st century the curtseying and bowing custom will have been dispensed with. On the subject of Royal visits Elizabeth is amusing. "I have nothing against the family," she says, "but I really do wish they'd stay at home — they cause so much disruption, to traffic, everything." Andrew, a much more formal person in public life, does not agree!

The four young members of the Briger family were now all at private schools and with fees soaring, Elizabeth's business involvement and contribution to the household exchequer was of vital importance, as was her ability to conjure in a couple of days near enough to 'model' dresses for one or other of her teenage daughters or herself. Now, they faced all at once a crisis in Andrew's career.

Things had really gone very well for him up to date, she felt. This was the man who had imagined that he was going 'into outer space' when he set out for her country. Australians had taken him to their hearts. He was Deputy Lord Mayor and Chairman of the Planning Committee of their major city. Suddenly, they discovered very forcibly the adverse side of politics. Leo Port, as Lord Mayor, faced allegations of impropriety, and although Andrew was in no way involved in the matter, he belonged to the same group within the Council, and in 1977 was not re-elected to his position of Deputy Lord Mayor. "All the political guns were suddenly aimed at me," he said, "it was one of the worst periods of my life, a dreadful trauma, and Elizabeth was a tremendous support."

In the midst of it all, they were cheered by official recognition of Andrew's services to Local Government, for he was appointed a Member of the Order of Australia in the Australia Day Honours List in 1977 and at much the same time awarded a Life Fellowship of the Royal Australian Institute of Architects.

Meanwhile, tension continued to mount within the City Council. Leo Port had contracted a viral illness, accusations and sensations followed one upon another. Andrew defended him in Council on one of the more minor matters which had been blown out of proportion. He and Elizabeth visited him in hospital, aware of the seriousness of his illness, and upset by the victimisation to which he was being subjected.

The ALP were attacking, the CRA in disarray. On the day on which media persecution reached a peak, with a condemnatory article and a caricature splashed on the front page of a leading newspaper, Leo Port died. It was almost as though he had been hounded to death. "The allegations had been basically trivial," said Andrew. "We were appalled at the whole thing. It was a period of extreme stress for both Elizabeth and me."

Before discussing Elizabeth's own career, it seems appropriate here to look briefly at the two important projects she was particularly pleased to see Andrew complete in 'his final years as a Sydney Alderman and Chairman of the Planning Committee — these were the Circular Quay Mall and the Dixon Street Mall in Chinatown. The first is familiar to the tens of thousands who visit Sydney every year and head inevitably towards the harbour and the ferries at Circular Quay; the Mall has enhanced everyone's pleasure in this focal Sydney area and given the opportunity for more leisurely pedestrian use. The Dixon Street Mall was more difficult to accomplish for it was necessary to have the co-operation of the very divergent sections of the Chinese community and persuade them to work together for the project. Andrew managed to do this and as a group they made a substantial financial contribution to the construction of the colourful ceremonial archways at each end of Dixon Street which enclose the Mall and give it its distinctive flavour.

In 1980, Andrew was chosen Lord Mayoral candidate by Civic Reform and Elizabeth and the family helped in the campaign. It was, however, an uphill battle, for the Wran Government, anxious to end the CRA reign in the city, had removed from the electoral role some 10,000 business voters, the basic support of the Civic Reform group. These tactics resulted in a Labor victory. It was a bitter disappointment for Andrew, for he had hoped, as Lord Mayor, to implement further streetscapes and plans for the city.

Elizabeth, for her part, was not sorry to say goodbye to the municipal political scene and the endless series of functions it entailed, but was happy for him when, much about the same time, the Royal Australian Planning Institute awarded him its highest distinction, the Sidney Luker Memorial Medal, in recognition of his 'notable contribution to town and regional planning in Australia.' She felt that it was well deserved, and summing up his 11 years chairmanship of the City Development and Planning Committee, remarked, "I think he changed the face of Sydney."

Her own career, as a partner in *Janie Breden & Partner — Interior Design*, had now become very rewarding and satisfying and also important financially, with the younger members of the family still at secondary school. The firm now carries out projects not only in Sydney but throughout eastern Australia and in South Australia. Janie, as the interior designer, feels that it is particularly advantageous that the partnership should be divided in expertise as it is — Elizabeth manages the administrative side — and they have gone ahead in leaps and bounds. The projects undertaken are numerous and diverse and include the interior design and fitting out of the professional and commercial offices of

Andrew Briger confers with Janie Breden & Partner — Interior Design (Janie and Elizabeth)

architects, town planners, doctors, solicitors, accountants, developers, Real Estate and Advertising Agencies, restaurants and taverns, town houses and flats from Surfers Paradise to Sydney. There is further variety with sports centres and domestic houses, including a mansion in Vaucluse which they enjoyed, and the challenge of designing the Renal Unit at Royal Prince Alfred Hospital.

In one of those time-gap fulfilments which sometimes happen — Alan had envisaged a career in architecture for Elizabeth in her youth — she is currently in the throes of a part-time architectural drafting course at Sydney Technical College and doing extremely well. "It will enable her to visualize things three-dimensionally," said Janie, who thinks it an excellent move. The two are as close friends as ever, able to relax as well as work together, and as with most long-term Mackerras friends, music is a bond. In light-hearted moments at a party, the pair have been known to kick off their shoes and improvise some uninhibited choreography — an allegory in dance so to speak — to that favourite of both, Mozart.

Balvaig has naturally become the family Mecca in the last decade, for not only do the Brigers live there but Alastair, who has the downstairs flat, while Charles has his quarters there when conducting in Australia. Neil, Colin and Malcolm invariably stay *en route* to seminars or elsewhere, as do their children when birds of passage. It is now round the Briger table that the family gather and it is Elizabeth who, like Catherine for so many years, prepares the meals and looks after the sojourner. "It's so often the women who hold the families together," commented her long-standing friend, Robin Lovejoy. "The Mackerras brothers have had this support all the way through. The interesting thing too, in this family so strongly oriented towards dominant male, is that although Elizabeth is a rather shy person — she does not give her friendship easily and never pushes herself into the public eye — her presence is always quite a definite statement. She does not pale in the room when her ebullient brothers are around, but makes a contrast to them and gains in some way by her very difference. She radiates a kind of stillness, a kind of immediate magnetism." This admixture of reserve and confident presence is very much part of the Mackerras make-up, and the latter, stemming from their background, is an attribute shared by them all.

With such a busy life, Elizabeth has formed the habit of giving Sunday lunches to keep in touch with her friends, and many personalities from the world of the arts in Sydney have at one time or another gathered round the Briger luncheon table on a Sunday. When Charles is in Sydney he invariably enjoys these occasions — 'a great *bon vivant* and very entertaining' Andrew describes him — and Elizabeth invites some of his old acquaintances. Among them often was Robin Lovejoy, [11] one of those with whom he used to forgather at the Conservatorium in the early days and who later met him in London at Sadlers' Wells when he was producing La Bohéme and Charles was conducting there. "The real business at Elizabeth's lunches starts after the dishes are cleared," said Robin.

Robin Lovejoy seated beside Elizabeth at Balvaig (farewell luncheon party for the Brigers' daughter Christina, who was leaving for Europe). Back (l-r): Janie Breden, Andrew Briger and Christina.

---

11. Robin Lovejoy died on 14th December, 1985.

"People stay on and talk round the table, which I love. It's far the best way to have conversation — round the table with a glass in hand!" One can hear the strong chorus of assent from those of like mind and habit everywhere. Robin and his theatre-minded wife, Patsy, also formed a lasting bond with the Brigers' daughter, Christina, at one of the luncheons. "A delicious girl," said Robin. "We got into a deep philosophical conversation and afterwards she always referred to me as her *guru*."

The Brigers' son Alex, a student at Sydney Grammar, is particularly close to Alastair who knocks punctually on their door at 7 a.m. each weekday and drives him to school. Alex is learning violin and sounds of practice are just part of the music that soars throughout *Balvaig*, upper and lower flats, whenever there is a Mackerras or Briger at home. Joan observed this when she flew over as one of the 'surprise' guests when Charles was the focus of the television programme, *This is Your Life*, in 1979. It was good to find herself in the middle of the family circle again. They, in turn, found that she was still the decidedly forceful character of *Harpenden* days, frequently taking the role of stirrer in their wide-ranging talk as Catherine had so often done, and they were amazed at her increasing physical resemblance to their mother.

Elizabeth was glad to see Andrew's interest, outside his architectural practice, turning again to the arts in the 1980s. He became a director of the Australian Theatre for Young People, and in 1981, at the invitation of his former Sydney City Council colleague, Sir David Griffin, who was now vice-president of the Australian Elizabethan Theatre Trust, he became a director of the Trust and in 1982, on the resignation of Sir Ian Potter, the 'music-loving stockbroker and financier' who had given many years of service, he was appointed chairman. The same year he also became chairman of the NSW branch of the Order of Australia Association and Elizabeth finds that she enjoys the functions associated with it.

His chairmanship of the Australian Elizabethan Theatre Trust naturally involves attending first night performances, often exciting occasions, as when the magnificent Bolshoi Ballet visited Australia, but she is invariably outspoken in her criticism if a performance falls below standard, as was the case in one given by the visiting Royal Ballet Company just after Andrew took office. He was somewhat embarrassed, but soon there was a series which very much made up for it. A press headline ran, *The Mackerras Connection, Planning the Trust the Briger way*, with the comment — 'When that magnificent company from the People's Republic of China, *The Peking Opera*, comes to our shores . . . courtesy of the Australian Elizabethan Trust, Andrew Briger, the Trust's newly-appointed chairman, will find a ready-made mine of specialist expertise in one of his five famous brothers-in-law.' After enumerating them, it went on to point out that in this case the consultant would be Colin Mackerras, Chairman of the Modern Asian Studies School at Griffith University, Queensland, and that his writings included *The Rise of the Peking Opera 1770–1780*. Elizabeth was delighted to see something of Colin at *Balvaig* in the following weeks for his presence somehow lightens her heart and the children are also fond of him.

The need to sell the spectacularly different, stylised opera to an uninitiated Australian public was considerable, and Colin gave explanatory lectures preceding the tour in the various Australian capitals, and the Trust's lively and resourceful PR man, Andrew McKinnon, who found the new chairman's 'very professionally developed understanding of the value of promotion' a godsend, moved in advance from city to city. The tour of *The Peking Opera*, with enchanting folktales such *The White Snake* and acrobatic, martial-arts style performances such as *Yentang Mountain*, was an outstanding success and the 56 members of the Jiangsu Opera played to full houses throughout Australia.

Elizabeth has heard much discussion over the last few years as to the direction the Trust will take in the future and in what way it is likely to diverge from its present essentially entrepreneurial role. It has been formative in the performing arts in Australia since it was set up by Hugh Hunt 30 years ago. The AETT then administered theatre, opera and ballet and subsequently launched NIDA (National Institute of Dramatic Art), the Old Tote, the Australian Opera and the Australian Ballet Companies and much else besides, and it is felt that it now needs a fresh impetus. The Brigers' friend, Robin Lovejoy, played a vital role throughout, and those interested in theatre will recall his direction of the Elizabeth Theatre Trust Players, and the wide repertoire he presented not only in Sydney but on tour in other States. More recently Robin Lovejoy became a member of the Trust's board and commented, "It is a good thing that we have Kathleen Norris as the new Chief Executive Officer. A new image is needed. We are in a state of flux and must continually remind the government and the public that we are here, ready to operate, the most available flexible instrument for carrying out any theatrical activity for the mutual benefit of the country. The Australian content programmes can be strengthened, but it must not be the tail that wags the dog . . . We can establish more links with NIDA, we can move in many directions. It is good that we have Leonard Teale on the Trust board. We need more practising professionals on the board, who know and understand show business — I don't care whether they represent circuses or whether they represent Shakespeare — and then we will go forward." This is a strong statement by the man most equipped to give it for he was a dominant force in our theatre for forty years.

These things form part and parcel of Elizabeth's life, she and Andrew are inextricably bound up with the performing arts in Sydney and there is nothing closer to her heart than the musical aspect of it. She gives practical and enthusiastic support to Sydney Grammar's burgeoning young musicians and is delighted that their son Alex, who plays in the *Alastair Mackerras Orchestra*, is now even considering music as a career. He was spurred to serious interest in the violin by the visit to Sydney of his gifted English cousin, Joan's son, Drostan. The pair did some busking together with their violins and were able to renew their friendship when Alex visited England with the school orchestra. We turn then from Elizabeth's life in Sydney to a final glimpse of that of her sister Joan in Woodbridge, England.

Joan continues in her role as Head of Strings and coach in Chamber Music at Woodbridge School and recently wrote a textbook, *Sight-reading for the Violin*, which is now due for publication. She and Graeme and their four sons have also formed a sextet and give concerts both locally and for music festivals. Joan plays violin and viola, Graeme, piano and harpsichord, Barty, 'cello and piano, Drostan, violin, Ambrose, violin and double bass, and Sebastian, recorder. One wishes Catherine could see and hear them. The Halls have made their home, *Cherry Tree House*, into a musical haven and in their music room is to be found a 'square piano' of 1806 vintage, and a Georgian music stand beside the constantly used grand piano. Drostan, who plays in the National Youth Orchestra of Great Britain, has recently been invited to become a member of the Britten Pears Orchestra and his future looks bright indeed.

As in Sydney at *Balvaig*, or at Charles' home in London, so at *Cherry Tree House* in Woodbridge, there is always a bed for a wayfaring Mackerras, and Joan was delighted recently to have Elizabeth's daughter Nicky to stay, and Alastair also, on his way home from Cambridge. Unfortunately she has not seen either of her twin brothers since she herself came to Sydney for *This is Your Life* in 1979; Colin's journeyings are now usually in China and Malcolm's in the USA. Since none of them correspond in the way they once did — though Neil sometimes keeps her up to date — she does feel a little out of touch and she was glad when Graeme made a trip home in 1985 and returned with snippets of news and impressions.

She is always, as Alastair commented, 'frenziedly busy', and although she enjoys her family, does feel 'rather fettered', as she remembers her mother once did, at the constancy of 'churning out meals for all these hungry people'. At the same time, she never ceases to be grateful that Catherine urged her always to the higher qualifications which have resulted in her very satisfying teaching career. She and Graeme have become

Joan and Graeme with their family, (l–r) Drostan, Barty, Sebastian, Ambrose. Woodbridge, England, 1984

addicted to current affairs television programmes of an evening and she is never short of contentious talking points for discussion which she continues to enjoy either in the school staff room or by their own fireside.

The links between Joan and Elizabeth, their homes and their offspring, whether in Suffolk or in Sydney, are as firm, if sometimes frustratingly distant, as the cultural bonds between our two countries. And each in her different way, finds fulfilment in music, that truly *sphere-descended* Muse, and like their brothers, would agree with all the praises ever sung to St Cecilia.

Chapter 8

Colin

In 1957 Colin was an exuberant outgoing student in the Arts Faculty at Sydney University but not at all sure which way his career was headed. Exceptional results at Sydney Grammar in modern languages had determined his final choice of subjects and to his study of French and German, he added Music, a lifelong love, and Modern History. His twin Malcolm began the same year, following his own specific bent as a part-time student, and they cheerfully went their separate ways as the family invariably did.

"I was passionately interested in the languages," Colin recalled, "and in German literature and German music. But it wasn't clear where it was going to lead. I didn't know whether I wanted to work in a university — I just knew I was interested in things intellectual."

The same applied to his close friend, John Sheldon, with whom he was delighted to find himself converging as a student again, for John had also gone up to Sydney University that year and had opted to do classical languages. The two had been friends since their days at St Aloysius College where the young Sheldon had stayed to complete his secondary education while Colin went on to Sydney Grammar. They had renewed acquaintance at concerts in their mid-teens and subsequently developed the habit of visiting each other's homes to listen to music together, graduating from G & S, through Italian opera to the complex harmonies of Wagner and Beethoven. John in fact had so much in common with the Mackerrases as a family that he came to regard *Harpenden* as a home away from home. Catherine was particularly drawn to him, for not only was he a gifted student who loved to talk with her, but he had been born and bred a Catholic and she found, as a convert herself, that he was able to contribute something to her understanding of Catholicism when they discussed the subject — which was frequently.

Catherine had had a profound influence on Colin in this regard. He had accepted her strong arguments on behalf of the Roman Catholic faith, had attended services consistently, and had resolved for some time to become a member of the Church when he reached 18, the age of self-determination on which his parents had agreed. Accordingly, with John as his sponsor, he now did so. Strangely, and yet perhaps inevitably in his case, this made his life very much more complicated.

As always during first year at university, or among students anywhere at that age, there was much questioning and argument on the verities. Colin began to find some gaps in the theological reasoning he himself put forward. He was 'confronted with evidence that didn't quite seem to tally' and also other value systems which were presented with as much force and conviction as Catherine presented hers. He found himself arguing with a highly intelligent and sensitive young student, the budding poet, Geoffrey Lehmann, together with other very articulate people whose views were diametrically opposed to his own and he and John became friends with the group. Colin remained invincibly high-spirited and good-humoured, peppering and prefacing his comments, Lehmann recalls, with 'Our Lords' and 'Mother Church's attitude' when metaphysics or morality were under discussion. Nevertheless, he became haunted by serious doubts and this inner conflict began to prey on him. He had, after all, just made a public vow of faith.

"I was very disturbed and unhappy," he said, "I wanted to have a simple and total belief and yet I couldn't quite reconcile that — looking at it with hindsight — with intellectual honesty. I wouldn't have put it in those terms then, but that's what it was." He found that the best antidote was to go to Mass daily. Accordingly, and confiding his misery to no one, he bicycled off each morning at 6 a.m. to church at Pymble, and there, immersing himself in the ritual, he endeavoured to preserve the spirit of his belief and resolve his unwanted doubts.

John concluded that he was simply passing through an excessively devout phase, and their student life proceeded. Contemporaries included two who were to have a close association with another of the Mackerrases, these were the young John Howard (studying Law) and poet Les Murray (gearing himself to edit the university magazine *Honi Soit*) so that the standard of debate and discussion about the campus must have been lively to say the least. It also ranged to music; John and Colin discovered that Geoffrey Lehmann was a Beethoven addict and knew his Wagner, preferring the former because, he argued, he had 'more intellectual range'. They took up the battle cry, for they considered these musical greats to be of equal stature, and each day for one whole semester chose a snatch of music from each composer which would not be easy to distinguish in style, Colin then hummed the notes to Geoff and called on him to identify the composer. Lehmann, who remembers Colin as 'a remarkable character, very confident, physically big and with a rather highish voice', recalls this episode of his undergraduate days with some triumph for he did not once falter and unerringly picked his Beethoven.

Colin is indeed 'physically big', being the tallest of the Mackerrases and, like most of them at one time or another, his large frame could probably have done with some trimming. But they took their cue from Catherine. Life was for living, she decreed, and since, in their view, this automatically meant that music and discussion took precedence over exercise or sport as relaxation, the latter were lucky to be fitted in at all. The semi-camping holidays which Alastair arranged at his house at Kiama followed this pattern but also allowed for beach and bush walking as well and Colin and John joined the groups there during vacations in May and December with enthusiasm. Alastair remembers lively debates that year and Colin putting forward left-wing political philosophies, while John Sheldon recalls his exuberance in their multifold activities with some nostalgia. It was, as it turned out, to be Colin's first and last year at Sydney University.

When they were at Kiama in December, a phone call came from Catherine. She had just seen a paragraph in the morning paper advertising scholarships in Oriental Studies and the Chinese and Japanese languages at Canberra University College (then attached to Melbourne University). Would he be interested? He had done extremely well in modern European languages, why not think of oriental languages? "They're live-in scholarships, you'd have all your board and lodging paid at Narellan House," she told him and left the thought with him.

It was an extraordinary bolt from the blue. For serveral days he turned it over. His mother had always looked at things through European glasses and was not remotely interested in Asia herself. Why had she started him thinking along these lines? She was an historian, of course, therefore perhaps she saw Australia's future becoming increasingly tied to that of Asia? He knew that she was very ambitious for them all and wanted a good career for him. She must see this as a real opportunity. Gradually also, the idea of learning two entirely different languages took hold of him.

"Do you know," he said to John, "I think I'll try it. It'd be interesting to learn Chinese." He applied, won a scholarship, and in doing so changed the whole focus and direction of his career. In retrospect, one can only think of it as something of a *coup* for Catherine.

He admitted to them all frankly that he was going to miss everyone badly in Canberra, and Catherine and John drove down with him to make the move less of a jolt. In fact, as the weeks wore on he felt more isolated than he had expected. It was a difficult year altogether, not only tackling the languages, making new friends and acclimatising generally, but continuing his lonely inner battle with the theological doubts which had beset him.

Again each morning he bicycled to Mass, and continued to do so quite literally at the crack of dawn through the biting Canberra winter and there wrestled with his problem. It was not only a question of theology; other aspects of Catholicism worried him. He found 'a sort of dichotomy' between the approval of fleshly things in terms of good food, wine and fellowship, and the repression of the sexual side. He saw that Catherine was thoroughly imbued with this attitude and was 'somewhat puritanical in matters relating to sex' — as was he himself. He began to wonder if this, in fact, might be harmful. He does not seem to have formulated his ideas fully on the subject at the time, nevertheless, the question mark was there. But if, as he has said, 'the process of moving from belief in a religion like Catholicism to not believing in it is a very slow and traumatic one', he realised at the time that he must cease tearing himself apart over it. He put his doubts away, was greatly cheered by several visits from Catherine and John Sheldon who drove from Sydney to see him, and gradually became absorbed in undergraduate life at the College.

His habit of walking about the campus from point A to point B with an operatic aria or orchestral theme bursting unselfconsciously from his lips had been observed by fellow-students, as also other evidence of Mackerras eccentricity. "Who is this Marilyn Monroe?" he enquired at breakfast the morning the world was abuzz with the news that life had become too much for the most publicised sex symbol of the day. They laughed and accused him of belonging to some sort of sub-culture. He took their raillery in his stride and his naturally confident, outgoing personality began to assert itself. In 1959, by which time he had decided that he liked and wished to continue with the study of the Chinese and Japanese languages and with Far Eastern History, he was elected president of the Students Association and an executive member of the Newman Society. He also began to notice a strong-minded, fair-haired, exceedingly pretty fellow student, one Alyce Brazier, with whom he had been on nodding acquaintance in German class at Sydney University.

Alyce was from Euchareena in western New South Wales and her upbringing as one of a family of four on a country property, combined with her academic talents, made for a direct, forthright person with whom Colin found it easy to relate. They now saw a great deal of each other and, she startled and challenged him as a student by beating him that year in Japanese. They found that they often shared a tendency to take up the cudgels for the left in political argument and when student parties were being organised and he made such remarks as "Oh, the women provide!" and "You're wearing slacks?!" she was amused at these relics of ultra-conservatism and upbraided him accordingly. He was enormously good company on these occasions, enlivening bus trips by singing anything from *The Mikado* to *Iolanthe*, word perfect, and spurring others to sing snatches with him. She, in her turn, was not only lively and a decidedly challenging fellow-student, but outspoken and had no qualms in pointing out unpalatable things, such as the fact that yoghurt and other 'health foods' would be the solution to the shedding of his few extra pounds. He identified with this directness and her positive attitude generally, being well accustomed to these attributes, and invited her to *Harpenden* during vacation. By this time, of course, they had fallen in love.

Catherine seems to have immediately recognised a kindred spirit in Alyce and the two got on extremely well. At the same time she formed a good relationship with Alan, talking quietly and separately with him, perhaps with an understanding which sprang from Colin remarking to her once or twice, in regard to the noisily exuberant household at Turramurra, 'Oh my poor father, I do feel for him!' She was also small and very pleasing to look upon and there seems no doubt that in Alan's eyes she gave every indication of swiftly becoming 'a gem'.

As well as the various members of the family, Colin made sure she met John Sheldon and one or two other close friends. John, who had been the closest, was naturally a little wary. He liked Alyce at once but wondered if she was rather too intense and hoped that she had enough of the Mackerras brand of tolerance and humour. In fact, she became a frequent visitor at *Harpenden*, for in order to get to her family's property at Euchareena during vacations, it was necessary to pass through Sydney and Catherine always welcomed her in her usual warm way and invited her to stay a few days. Alyce has a vivid recollection of Charles' first visit home in 1960 and the entire Mackerras family together in the kitchen, 'all singing G & S at the top of their voices, taking different parts', and clearly having a wonderful time. They must surely have seemed an extraordinarily gifted and uninhibited brood and it says something for her own confidence that at the not very considerable age of 20, she appears to have been in no way overwhelmed by them and fitted into a comfortable observing role.

Colin and Alyce both graduated in 1961, by which time Canberra University College had become part of the Australian National University. They promptly announced their engagement and Catherine arranged for Colin to have his share of her father's estate in order to go to Cambridge and do a further degree. Alastair had been in touch with several dons and Fellows at St John's College whom he had known in his years there, and Colin was duly admitted; he registered to do an M. Litt., a two year research course. Alyce stayed in Canberra for the time being to do an honours course at ANU. "So," said Colin, "we had to kiss and correspond."

His first year at Cambridge was probably, emotionally, the bleakest of his life. Although his good friend John was also there, and at the same college (he had arrived several months earlier and so was able to introduce him to the friends he had made), Colin himself had to live in digs outside the college, and as might be expected in the circumstances was very lonely. But the main cause for unhappiness was extremely unexpected. He found that his work in classical Chinese was not up to the standard his tutors had expected and they were quite scathing on the subject. For Colin this was devastating. He was used to topping courses and shining scholastically in what had come to be the Mackerras tradition, and to have his work actually looked down upon was quite traumatic. He had chosen to do his

Colin and Alyce at Turramurra, 1961

dissertation on the Uighurs, savage Turkic tribes and warlords who rose to power on the Mongolian steppes (744–840) and his major sources were the Tang dynastic histories. "I did find great difficulty at first," he admitted. "I worked very hard and spent most of my time in the Cambridge University library." Afterwards, the dissertation began to fall into shape.

Meanwhile, whenever he could, he visited his brother Charles, wife Judy and young daughters, Fiona and Catherine, at their home in London, became very fond of the children, and went to concerts and operas at the Festival Hall and Covent Garden. Charles was often surprised at evidence of Colin's very extensive musical knowledge and ability, the two really came to know each other, and altogether the Charles Mackerras household at Southgate was a home away from home for him at a time when he was most appreciative of it.

As he progressed with his thesis, tracing Uighur power structures, battles, rebellions, *coups d'etat* and evidence of violence which sometimes penetrated as far as China's main cities, he found that the Chinese used two age old methods of 'keeping the ferocity of peripheral peoples at bay'. Not only was trade vital, such as Chinese silk for Uighur horses, but the arranging of diplomatic marriages between Chinese princesses and threatening warlords, in this case, the powerful Uighur khagans. Diplomacy succeeded so well on occasion that when the Emperor's eldest son, Li Shu, commanding Chinese forces in the north east provinces in 757, was beset by rebel troops and a fierce battle raged for the major city of Changan, near the junction of the great Yellow River with the Wei, he was able to gain the support of the Uighurs, who with a small force of 4000 cavalry swooped down from a mountain stronghold, 'took the rebels by surprise and won the day for the government'. Colin comments, "Once again a small number of Uighurs, had proved decisive in a battle involving huge numbers of men. The sources speak of 100,000 severed heads lying about the plain." He does not advice accepting this figure at its face value but notes that the number of killed must nevertheless have been large.

He was particularly interested to explore the manner in which these fierce warrior people, at the height of their power in the 760s, had adopted the Persian-based religion Manicheism. It was this facet of their life which had initially prompted him to work on the Uighurs, for he had developed an interest in the subject when in Canberra. He found that Manicheism had spread to Asia through Persian traders who travelled and settled as merchants and 'carriers of art and new religions in many parts of Central Asia, the steppes and China'. The aspiration of the founder, Mani, a Persian of the third century, was not to interfere with Christianity (although he presented himself as Advocate, or Comforter, and, like Jesus, had 12 disciples) but to convert Asian countries. The religion had appeal for both the philosopher (St Augustine was said to have been influenced by it) and the masses, and seems to have developed from Zoroastrianism, while drawing also from Buddhism and Gnosticism.

Colin commented in his dissertation, 'Mani believed in two opposing principles, good or light, and evil or darkness, the second of which was assisted by the material world and especially the human body. He taught that time should be viewed in three phases . . . man existed as body and spirit only in the middle phase and it was his duty to abstract himself from all matter. This would help bring on a great cleansing process which Mani believed would usher in the third phase. When that time arrived, those who had succeeded in freeing themselves from the material world would live in the region of light, those who had failed in that of darkness. Mani's religion was led by a stratified clergy, termed *'the elect'*, of whom celibacy and fasting were required. The laymen were allowed to marry and eat normally but were expected to be fairly abstemious and generous in giving alms.' It was a strange paradox that the warlike Uighurs, who, during the period of his study (744–840) had become 'masters of the steppes', should also have become Manichees and been the only east Asian empire to adopt Manicheism as a state religion. He had researched and brought to light this central fact in the meagre Uighur and Arab sources available and then discovered, when co-relating it with the Chinese texts, that not even the greatest Chinese historian, Sima Guang, had mentioned the matter at all.

Noting the imbalance of this and other aspects of the Chinese texts, he concluded, 'A general point of the utmost importance concerning these and almost all other Chinese historical works, is that they are completely centred on China.' He went on to add, 'It is not surprising that the Chinese sources should be deficient in this way, since Chinese Confucian historiography was aimed at the moral edification of future *Chinese* administrators and therefore regarded foreigners as a mere sideline.' Yet, 'the relative lack of any other sources' in the study of these remote people, makes Chinese texts the 'basis of our knowledge', and he found, in the work of Sima Guang, in particular, 'copious isolated reference to Uighur history', with 'datings so precise, style so coherent and clear' that they were of immense value to him overall.

As he was in the midst of this formidable scholarship, Alyce, who had completed her honours course at ANU and had then taught for a few months in Japan, arrived in Cambridge and, of course, it was a case of *let joy be unconfined* for the two young academics. Alyce took a job as a librarian and they made plans for their marriage. Alyce, who had belonged to the Church of England, had decided the previous year to convert to Catholicism. Colin himself, in view of his own crisis in belief and of his absence overseas, was not likely to have influenced her, but she had two close friends, both of whom were Catholic and had been at ANU with her, and it seems that they were the decisive factor. She also has something within her own character which appreciates positivity and that, it will be remembered, was one of the main arguments put forth by Catherine when comparing Catholicism with that she termed the 'wishy washy' Protestant version of Christianity. In any case, the decision was happily made and Alyce also clearly felt that it would smooth their future path together.

Malcolm, in Sydney, aware that the marriage of his twin brother was soon to take place, decided to take six months leave and make the mandatory Mackerras migration to Europe at this time so that he could also play the role of bestman. He and Colin are far too idiosyncratic and individual to have had any sort of twin dependency, and that was made even less likely when they diverged in classes during their Sydney Grammar School days, but they were close enough for Malcolm to feel a need to be there — as it was possible to arrange it.

Colin and Alyce, London, 1962

Charles offered his home in London and also gave the bride away. So, it was top-hats and cutaways for the three brothers, a charming gown for Alyce, and they were married by Monsignor Gilbey, the Catholic chaplain at Cambridge (whom Alastair had known well), at a small church in Southgate not far from Charles and Judy's home. John Sheldon, who was then teaching in the Midlands, came down for the wedding as did friends from Cambridge and there was a plethora of cables from Australia. Charles, who has a wickedly accurate ear and memory for the unusual juxtaposition of voices, recalls Colin's pleasant accents that day sounding 'very Australian' as he repeated his vows after this 'terribly, terribly upper-class English gentlemen!' (An interesting thought for those amongst us whom might still be under the illusion that educated Australian sounds much the same as educated English.) Of course it was a delightful, high-spirited occasion with everyone in top form, and it cannot have been easy for the two to return soon to Cambridge, Colin to the rigours of his thesis and Alyce to temporary librarianship.

During the five months he now had to finish his dissertation, he and Alyce went frequently to London, usually at weekends, for operas and concerts, rushing away without dinner to catch the train, sometimes staying overnight with Charles and Judy, which was a great boon, at others, when Colin felt it necessary, returning to Cambridge the same evening. "That was often," said Alyce, "and I remember the agony of trying to catch that train, and then, after the performance, standing and waiting for a bus home to Cambridge — which never seemed to come. But we still went down!" Colin's musical interests and knowledge had, in fact, become known to the dons.

He completed his thesis, himself laboriously typing the whole 355 quarto pages — they were now living solely on Alyce's salary as a librarian —

and presented it. It was assessed by the then Professor of Chinese at Cambridge, Denis Twitchett, and accepted. He immediately started sending off applications for post-graduate work to various American academic institutions and waited impatiently for replies. At the same time Professor Twitchett approached another Cambridge don, Dr Laurence Picken, an authority on East Asian music, in regard to Colin's career. He told him he felt that Colin was 'not cut out to be a straight historian and might find some historical topic in Chinese music more congenial' and suggested that he might study Chinese music with the doctor on some sort of professional basis.

Before discussing his several months work with this gifted man and the friendship which developed between them, it is important to look at the change of attitude which occurred in the Chinese Department at Cambridge regarding Colin's abilities as a scholarly historian. A few years later, as a direct result of his dissertation on the Uighurs, he was asked to contribute a chapter on the subject to the *Cambridge History of Inner Asia*, one of their prestigious history series. "I was very, very pleased to be asked," he commented. "I took out a great deal of the analytical stuff about the Uighurs themselves, as distinct from their relations with China, re-wrote it and sent it in." He also revised and re-wrote the full thesis and it was published (ANU Press) under the title: *The Uighur Empire, According to the T'ang Dynastic Histories*.

Meanwhile, increasingly worried by his financial position, and bitterly disappointed to receive negative replies to his applications in the United States, he began study with Dr Picken in early Chinese music. There was immediate accord between them. 'A lovely man' is his description of his tutor, while Dr Picken himself, now retired, recalls Colin's 'sunny disposition and the mop of golden hair that matched it'.

Dr Picken had written two of the chapters for *The New Oxford History of Music* (1957), one on Chinese music, the other 'on the little that was then known' of the music of Mongolia, Tibet, Korea, Japan, Burma, Thailand, Indonesia and the islands of the Indian Archipelago. There was still enormous scope for research so that he was delighted to have Colin to study with him and suggested that he work on 'a little fourteenth century monograph' on Chinese music, which he proceeded to do.

Nevertheless, he felt himself to be very much at the crossroads, and one morning, walking down the street in Cambridge, he met a friend who told him with some excitement that he was off to teach English in Peking. He learnt that in the People's Republic of China, right at that time, Premier Zhou Enlai had started a campaign to upgrade the teaching of foreign languages. Zhou Enlai had earlier lived abroad, in France, spoke several languages himself but invariably used interpreters, and had found on a recent trip to Africa, while in one of the countries of French Africa, that he had occasion to correct his own interpreter. He therefore decided to take steps to improve the speaking of foreign languages in China and bring in large numbers of teachers. He made contacts in countries with whom the PRC had diplomatic relations (Australia was not yet one) and in the United Kingdom one of the people contacted was the Cambridge author, Joseph Needham, then in the throes of his vast work, *Science and Civilisation in China*, and he, it seems, had begun to pass on the information to those students known to him. Colin immediately asked how he could go about applying and subsequently went off with all speed to London to interview the PRC's *Charge d'Affaires* there. He and Alyce, who was now expecting a child, were both accepted and appointed to teach at the Peking Institute of Foreign Languages and were requested to depart as soon as possible. It was stipulated that, in view of Alyce's pregnancy, they must fly and not go by rail.

The three months pregnancy was also the source of some apprehension to the pair themselves. They knew nothing of conditions in China, and Alyce felt 'far from calm' at the prospect of having her baby there. Would they even have modern obstetrics? Colin was somewhat reassured by the *Charge d'Affaires'* insistence on the flight. If that sort of care was to be the pattern, then all should be well, and he was altogether excited and uplifted by what he realised at once was 'a quite extraordinary break'. It was indeed a turning point in their lives.

"It was a sad day for me when Colin revealed that he would be departing for China," Dr Picken commented. "The work he was doing here was just nearing completion. Though the invitation to teach in China had such important consequences for his development, it also meant that the work he did with me was never published! This remains very sad because while it is the case that an American Chinese, Professor Rulan Chao Pian, transcribed the music in the monograph some years later in a book on *Song Dynasty Musical Sources and Their Interpretation* (Harvard University Press), no one has ever translated the Chinese text that accompanies the melodies — tunes for poems from the anthology known as *The Book of Songs*, compiled perhaps in the fifth century BC, as well as tunes for hymns of the Confucian rites." It is surely a measure of the exigencies of his career and the direction it has taken that Colin has not paused to finish this infinitely worthwhile piece of scholarship, for he remains devoted to Dr Picken and has always kept in touch with him.

"Going to China made a big impact on me," Colin recalls, "not only because it taught me so much about China but also because it taught me that if one door closes, another, and often one leading to much better things, will open." There is no doubt that in the mid 1960s, after his rejection by United States colleges and institutions, where many scholars went, the appointment to China, where 'very, very few went at that time', was such a case, and for most of us a parallel could be found somewhere in our lives. He set off then, full of zest, like Ulysses on his Odyssey, and so it was to prove, for on subsequent journeyings in the far flung provinces of China he came to know their many cities and peoples and to learn their ways.

All the foreign teachers working in Peking in 1964 lived in a large compound of flats called the Friendship Guesthouse and ate communally in a big restaurant. They had time always to get to know and make friendly contact with the people they taught, for straight after breakfast they were able to leave for the Institute and a small group of cleaners came to make beds and tidy rooms. Alyce went to the large, well-equipped hospital for the usual tests and checks which pregnancy entails, and found that obstetrical practices in Peking were just as in western countries. She had concentrated on Japanese, was not yet fluent in Chinese, and since the doctors and nurses spoke only Chinese or Russian, a fellow teacher from the Institute accompanied her on these visits and acted as interpreter.

In the early hours one morning in the following February, midwinter in Peking, and with the first snow falling, Colin called a taxi and took her to the hospital, where, to the pleasure and delight of the staff as much as themselves, their first son Stephen was safely delivered. The married teachers at the Institute all had their wives, small children and babies with them, and to each infant an 'ayi' (auntie), the name by which Chinese children call all women other than their mother, was allocated. To them came 'Comrade Wang', whose own four children were grown and at school and who lived in a flat nearby. "We loved her, she was a person of great gentleness and personal dignity," Alyce told an interviewer in Sydney a year or so later. When she herself returned to teaching after the permitted 56 days' leave (she had worked up to the time of the birth) their 'ayi' came for 8 hours a day instead of four, had a great deal to do with the rearing of their small son, and was boundlessly patient and loving.

Colin took an initiative at this time on which much of his future scholarship was to rest. The teaching contract at the Institute was for two years, and wishing to follow up the start he had made with Dr Picken at Cambridge in learning something of Chinese musical history, instruments used, and styles evolved, he found that the most accessible and widespread form of which he could make a study was in the music basic to Chinese drama, in particular, that of China's most famous form of theatre, Peking Opera. He therefore visited theatres whenever and wherever he could,

Stephen with 'ayi', Peking, 1962

and his study subsequently became directed to the performing arts generally, set in the context of Chinese cultural and social history, rather than to music specifically.

He attended not only those theatres recommended by officialdom, where large audiences could be expected, but also sought out and went alone to performances in the 'small playhouses in the back alleys of Peking'. Also, on various holidays over the two year period, and taking Alyce with him whenever possible, he visited as many as 20 cities within a reasonable distance of Peking, went to festivals and country fairs — there were many open-air and teahouse performances — with the object of making an independent assessment of the works being performed and to discover just how Chinese audiences of the 1960s were adapting to the 'revolutionising' of the classic themes of the stylised musical dramas which had been part of their lives for centuries and had featured emperors and kings, beautiful maidens and courtesans, good and wicked judges, scholars and soldiers, clowns and ghosts. Romanticized stories, and folk tales, martial arts and comedy were an intrinsic part of them. He himself regretted what looked like being the passing of an art which he considered 'one of the most perfect ever devised' and seeing revolutionry dramas such as *The Red Lantern* and *The White-haired Girl* replacing traditional ones such as *The Cross Roads Inn* and *The Palace of Eternal Youth*. A love duet from the last mentioned opera is transcribed—

> Hand in Hand we wander among the flowers,
> Past the cool pavilion,
> and past the wind-blown lotus,
> which trembles on the lake.
> I love the calm of these planes
> which form such deep green avenues.

While there is a moving little song about the cold north wind and a young girl exploited and raped by a horrible landlord in *The White-haired Girl*, signifying 'how much suffering the masses must go through', a more typical verse occurs in *The Red Lantern*, whose characters were involved in the war with Japan—

> I burst with anger when I think of the foe!
> Repressing my rage, using every trick to get the code,
> Hatoyama has killed my granny and dad!
> Biting my hate, chewing my rage
> I force them down my throat,
> Let them sprout in my heart.
> I'll never yield, I'll never retreat,
> No tears shall wet my cheeks,
> Let them flow into my heart,
> To nourish the bursting seeds of hatred.
> . . . Just wait, you villain Hatoyama!

"The Communists understood the impact on the mind of popular opera and music," Colin commented, for he had very soon found that the most significant aspect of Peking Opera, which had grown from the many regional theatres, is that, unlike the comparatively elitist opera of the West, it is a mass form of art. "You put people up on the stage who fulfil certain characteristics — they're noble, or patriotic, or loyal to the CCP, or, with the negative image, they're selfish, disloyal, traitorous and so forth. Audiences identify with them — I do or don't want to be like *that one*." He attributes some of the success of the CCP (Chinese Communist Party) to this method of spreading their ideas and doctrine to the great mass of the people, for it was consciously done and put forth as part of 'Mao's thought'. Art and literature, Mao said, were legitimate means of propaganda and must be used as part of the process of transforming society.

One of the biggest anti-revolutionary forces in China and other Asian countries, Colin believes, is fatalism. "The idea that everything that happens is ordained by fate — if there is a famine and a million people die, then it must be accepted — that sort of reaction was something which also had to be countered," he said. "It was one of their biggest problems." He was very impressed by the positivity the CCP leaders had managed to inject and there was no doubt in his mind, from direct personal experience in observing the voluntary attendance of great numbers of ordinary people in the smaller, obscure playhouses, that the revolutionary dramas had taken hold of their imagination and were to a considerable degree responsible for this.

Fortunately, from the beginning of their stay, he had haunted the Peking bookstores and bought a large collection of books on the classic operas, on music, on cultural and social history which were to be invaluable to him

Colin with his students, Peking Institute of Foreign Languages, 1966

over the years, as were some classic opera recordings he managed to acquire. This was as well, for under a new ruling in 1965 their sale was prohibited.

This change of policy was the result of a power struggle among the CCP leadership which involved a determination never to suffer again the humiliations inflicted on China by foreign domination in the past, of which such things as the ceding of territories (e.g. Hong Kong to Britain in 1842) had been a part. There was a fierce surge of nationalism, a drive to reinforce Mao Zedong's [7] ideology, and the PRC's own sovereignty within the communist world; it was led mainly by Mao and his wife, Jiang Qing and aimed chiefly against the President of the PRC, Liu Shaoqi, who was thought to be a revisionist. There was greatly increased hostility to both the Soviet Union and its ideologically, technologically and militarily aggressive role, and to the United States which had just introduced ground troops in the Vietnam war, had a two-China policy (recognising Taiwan in the United Nations, to which body mainland China had not yet been admitted) and had not established diplomatic relations with the PRC. It is not possible to try to unravel here all the tangled political and diplomatic developments but the whole process resulted in internal victory for the Maoists and culminated in the Cultural Revolution in 1966.

Meanwhile, the performance of all classic drama, as an unwanted appendage of the past, ceased. Colin discussed the situation with a middle-aged Chinese friend, who had been brought up during the Kuomintang under Chiang Kaishek. In his opinion, the classic theatre was one of the necessary casualties of revolution. "Besides," he said, "my children have no use for those old dramas. What relation do they have to the young people of China today?" Nevertheless, it seemed to Colin a sad departure from tradition.

When travelling outside Peking, whether it was to one of the people's festivals, such as that held each May at the former Summer Palace of the emperors — a place of beautiful pavilions and halls with courtyards set around a splendid lake — or to fairs in the countryside, Colin made contact and spoke with the Chinese people and developed a strong feeling for them. At the same time, he had not forgotten his friend Dr Picken, and wherever he went he kept an eye out for children's sound-producing toys, bought them, and sent them to him in Cambridge. "I owe to his devotion this unique collection," said Dr Picken, "and they are now the property of the University's Museum of Archaeology & Ethnology, together with the rest of my ethnic musical instruments. He also purchased for me a large zither — a splendid modern instrument with steel strings on which my pupils used to play when we first began to reconstruct the music of the Tang Court here in Cambridge. That too is now in the Museum."

As he worked and went about in this way among the Chinese people, Colin began to have a new feeling of freedom. There were no churches,

---

7. Mao Tse-Tung. Pinyin romanization, as above, is now used by Sinologists for Chinese names and terms. In the case of Peking — now Beijing — the former spelling has been retained in this text in order to avoid confusion.

of course, and it was not possible to continue religious observances, so that the burden of keeping up the appearance of the faith from which he had been so traumatically moving, left him. It is probable that his foray into comparative religions during his recent study at Cambridge, together now with the major impact that China, the Chinese people and the evidences of their ancient civilisation had made on him, strengthened his intellectual attitude, but, in any case, he began quietly to analyse the restrictions he had felt with some aspects of Catholicism. Principally, he found, they were sexual. "There is the feeling that has been quite strongly bred into the Catholic Church that there's something immoral about sex," he commented frankly. "It's not of course the Catholic Church's doctrine, which quite specifically states that it is not immoral, but it is so hemmed about with circumstances in which it is not immoral, that it leaves the feeling of immorality. I think that does set up a dichotomy from which it is quite difficult to escape. I know my mother had it. And I had it quite strongly. I've come to think that's a very harmful thing. One likes to think one has escaped from it — but in psychological terms one probably never does." This forthright statement, dealing as it does with significant complexities, central to most and relevant to all, seems to be one with which many could identify.

Politically, both he and Alyce now identified themselves with the left. It seems that although they themselves, or at least Colin, up to this point, had not felt aligned one way or the other, the impression they had given in discussion in the family circle in Sydney from the time of their student days at ANU (Canberra), was that of support for socialistic principles and ideals. They certainly had now become quite radical in outlook — apart from the fact that Alyce held fast to Catholicism — and the events they witnessed in Peking in August '66, as the Cultural Revolution came into force, made an indelible impression on them.

The CCP Central Committee met and adopted resolutions guiding the progress of the Cultural Revolution and a major aspect was the formation of the Red Guards, which was announced at a rally in Peking of over a million people. This militant move, so clearly supported by the Chinese people, was both impressive and deeply disturbing. To satisfy their need for sovereignty and a powerful independent voice in the world, China would now take whatever extreme measures were deemed necessary. At the same time, the struggle to overcome poverty amongst the predominantly peasant population which had been at the root of the whole revolutionary movement must be continued. It had been made more difficult by Mao's simultaneous direction, a most unfortunate and mistaken one, to increase and multiply, for over four-fifths of China's 400 million people live a hand-to-mouth existence in rural areas. Trade in essential foodstuffs, such as wheat, must somehow be kept up, and the clash of militancy with this essential trading would create a gigantic problem. Peking was now a most uncomfortable place indeed for Europeans to find themselves and most left of their own accord.

It happened that the Mackerrases had just reached the end of their two year contract at the Institute of Foreign Languages in Peking. They had developed much accord with the Chinese people, identified with and admired their ideological struggle, and were in no hurry to get a berth on the first available ship home. Colin wanted particularly to see Lushan, a beautiful mountain resort in Jiangxi Province where the CCP often chose to hold a meeting, and Alyce was prepared to stay in Peking with their small son for an extra month while he did so.

Their sympathies were now very much with the resurgent people of Asia. On the voyage home Alyce noticed that Colin frequently argued against the escalation of the Vietnam war and American intervention; he was totally convinced that the Vietnamese people should be left to pursue their own fight for independence. She herself, hearing of the horrendous casualties in Vietnam, and 'seeing parallels with the history of the national liberation struggle in China', was similarly moved.

Colin had applied in advance to the Department of Far Eastern History at ANU and been appointed Resident Scholar. But first there was an exciting reunion and a week in Sydney with the family whom he had not seen for nearly five years. Catherine and Alan were very soon to move to *Balvaig*, so it was the last time the family gathered at *Harpenden*. It was good to catch up with Neil and his family, Elizabeth and hers, and to listen to some Wagner with John Sheldon and Alastair, with whom that music has always remained a bond for Colin. There was, as can be imagined, an avalanche of talk and Neil was particularly interested in their views, but could not be persuaded away from the DLP and its attitude that 'expansionist Communist China' was a threat to Australia. However, as always, discussion remained tolerant and unheated. The Mackerrases could hardly have been more politically diverse at this time, for Malcolm was a member of staff of the Liberal Party and had been transferred to Canberra where Colin and his small family were now headed. They were to see him quite regularly.

Colin's purpose as a Research Scholar was to collate his material and write his Ph.D. thesis on the development of the Chinese regional theatre and the rise of the Peking Opera in Manchu China from the 16th to the 19th centuries. It was a formidable task, entailing the unravelling of many difficult Chinese texts, and three very solid years work lay ahead. "He has enormous concentration," Alyce remarked. "He can force himself to do things when he doesn't feel like doing them — and it's constant. He works all the time." At this time, she could not help envying him his freedom to do so.

She was soon to have their second child, a daughter Lucy, while two years later their second son, Martin, was born. Life in Canberra was also something of a 'culture shock'. She had been occupied in academic pursuits the whole of her adult life, but now there was no *ayi* to help look after the infants — not even creches or kindergartens — and she had to become fully, for the first time, a housewife. Then there was the atmosphere of the place itself. Most Australians find Canberra a city they prefer to visit rather than live in, a place of birds of passage politicians and circled sedateness which barely relates to the vital, grass-roots feeling of the various state capitals. Alyce found it suburban. "I had to go to luncheons and we both had to go to dinner parties where people really didn't talk about anything," she commented. "Or what they did talk about wasn't very relevant when the situation in Vietnam was so bad and we'd come from China and were aware of what was going on in the rest of the world."

Nevertheless, while Colin pored over his texts, she tried to organise her life so that she could have at least one undisturbed hour a week to work on a textbook on Asia which she and a group based around ANU had decided to write. She undertook the section on Japan, but found that it was the hardest thing in the world to keep her precious hour intact. It would be a long-term project indeed.

Meanwhile, Malcolm was a regular visitor and they thoroughly enjoyed the visits paid them every so often, and always separately, by Catherine and Alan. Catherine had undertaken research at the National Library on her grandfather's life, but found time also to talk, to mind the children, and to sit and spoon feed an infant while relating incidents of her own early youth. Alyce discovered, amongst much else, that coddled eggs were a daily must for small children in the first years of the 20th century, but to her regret learnt nothing of Catherine's own brood when young. "She was egocentric," Alyce commented, "but so outgoing and generous and supportive with it. A wonderful mother-in-law." Catherine was constant in this for it was a tribute she had earned 15 years before from Charles' wife, Judy.

The leopard, of course, does not change his spots, and Alan also came into his own as he had when staying, alone, with the Charles Mackerrases. He was relaxed and chatty with Colin and Alyce in Canberra and the former recalls one discussion, in particular, he had with him on one of his visits. Alan was very pro the American policy in Vietnam, as also, he knew, was Malcolm, and Colin argued with his father against it. "Well, one of these days", said Alan, "we'll get Malcolm to marshal all the arguments for it and you can marshal all the arguments against it. And we can decide which is the most valid." Alan clearly felt that quiet, rational argument would resolve anything. "Father was very old-fashioned," Colin commented. "Very charming in some ways, and the older I grew the more sympathy I had for him. I don't know whether he ever realised it." Perhaps he did, for he made these visits at reasonably regular intervals and must therefore, with his sensitivity on the subject, have felt very sure of his welcome.

The most tempestuous and exhausting visitors they had were, predictably, Neil and his family. Colin and Alyce enjoyed political discussions with them, and continued attempts to wean Neil from his allegiance to the DLP, but he and Elizabeth and their children were usually *en route* somewhere and invariably wanted to get away at 4 a.m. Alyce recalls rising one morning at that hour in the Canberra cold to get them off and inquiring whether they would like toast or porridge or eggs for breakfast. They settled for all three. Then there were farewells, voices making smokey spirals in the frosty air, and a return to the littered kitchen! Its hectic disarray must have reminded Colin forcibly of *Harpenden* days.

It should be mentioned here that about this time, in 1968, he finally decided to leave the Catholic Church. He was no longer able to believe in its tenets and therefore felt, as a matter of intellectual honesty, that it was the only thing to do, and has 'so far, not regretted that decision'.

As he proceeded with the work for his doctorate, tracing the rise of the Peking Opera, he established that it was a combination of music and techniques which derive from several of the 300 or so forms of regional theatre. "In Suzhou," he explained, "very near what is now Shanghai, there arose in the 16th century an aristocratic form of theatre called *kunqu*, noted for its slow moving elegance. This form spread throughout China and contributed to the Peking Opera. All the original forms were mass popular theatre. Late in the 18th century, actors moved from Sichuan in China's south-west to Peking to celebrate the Emperor's birthday, and after that time actors came from other parts of China in groups. It was this successive wave of actors which ultimately gave rise to the Peking Opera."

In his treatise, he focused substantially on the social aspects of the regional and Peking Opera and discussed how great clans in the countryside used theatre as part of their family celebrations and how operas became an integral part of popular festivities generally. One fascinating feature he discovered in the Chinese sources was the predominance of the theatres along the thriving interregional trade routes. Since the principal means of transportation was the boat — China's lakes, rivers and canals abounded in trading vessels of all sizes — and 'by far the most important thoroughfares in the country were the Yangtze River and the Grand Canal (Yunhe) in the southern Jiangnan provinces', that was where the rich merchants who traded in everything from salt and grain to silk, cotton and porcelain, demanded theatres for their entertainment and also wanted the styles to which they were accustomed in their home towns. They used to gather, 'arrange the construction of high stages and invite actors to sing and dance all night' (the sources for this sort of information were many and varied, one, Chunxiang Zhuibi, providing the above).

Another interesting aspect was the very lowly status of actors. They were regarded as similar to slaves according to the law and barred from any social advancement. Economic problems due to overpopulation led to more and more peasants selling their children for a limited period and to the phenomenon of boy-actors as prostitutes. Colin noted that 'the sources abound in references to love-affairs between scholars and actors and suggest strongly that an adult homosexual seeking a partner would be able to find one among the xianggong (actors)'. These young people had to master highly stylized acting techniques and singing, and for a brief time lived colourful and interesting lives, as did the eunuchs at court who were also trained in acting techniques.

In unearthing all this material, he also came upon some interesting footnotes to history. In 1793, he noted, 'when pressures had begun which were to lead to the era of China's humiliation at the hands of the Western powers', the first British ambassador in China, Earl George Macartney, was received at court by the Emperor Qianlong at his summer residence in Jehol, to discuss the expansion of trade (Canton was the only Chinese port open to commerce with the outside world at the time). Macartney refused to follow the Chinese custom and kowtow to the Emperor and compromised by an obeisance similar to that made before the King of England. The request was refused, and a similar mission in 1816, headed by a descendant and namesake of the famous William Pitt, suffered a similar fate. When officials were sent to teach Pitt the kowtow, he flatly refused to learn it, was declared arrogant, not even admitted to the imperial presence, and 'the mission was a fiasco'. Colin records this temporary diplomatic triumph of the Chinese over the British with some satisfaction. Just 25 years later, following the Opium War of 1839-42, the next Manchu emperor was forced to cede the island of Hong Kong to the victorious British, together with 'an enormous indemnity' and to open four more Chinese ports, amongst them Shanghai, to foreign trade.

At this time in Peking, teahouse theatres, where audiences chatted and drank tea together during performances, were much frequented, while 'popular opera' was forbidden at the court of the Manchu emperors. However, the demand amongst courtiers for this form of theatre grew, eunuchs were trained to act, and finally when their numbers were insufficient, highly qualified actors were admitted. The prejudice against bringing 'the vulgar Peking Opera' and members of the city troupes 'to the imperial presence' was overcome, and although there were various vicissitudes and temporary banning, the opera was finally taken up and given a permanent position at the court by the Empress Dowager Cixi in the 1880s. She had a magnificent three-tiered stage built at the Summer Palace and used herself to overlook every detail of performances, 'sending to the stage one of her eunuchs to transmit her Imperial commands as to the speaking of certain lines or the using of certain postures.'

So the highly stylised Peking Opera, as it is known to-day and has been viewed on tour from the PRC by Australian and other Western audiences, grew to maturity. Colin's work was published in 1972 by Claredon Press, Oxford, under the title *The Rise of the Peking Opera, 1770-1870, Social Aspects of the Theatre in Manchu China* and forms a detailed and absorbing account. In Cambridge, Dr Picken noted, probably with a little disappointment, that Colin was in the process of becoming an historian rather than 'an ethnic-musics man', for the publication was 'more concerned with the social history of the origins of this genre of Chinese music, than with the music itself'. He concluded his comments with the interesting remark, "I personally have a great regard for his book on the rise of Peking opera. It displays so convincingly that the Marxist view of the origins of the genre is wholly false." Meanwhile, in Canberra in 1969, his thesis gained for Colin his Ph.D. and an academic appointment.

The head of the Department of Far Eastern History at ANU, Professor Wang Gungwu, who had come from Malaysia only the previous year, was one of those to assess Colin's work. "It was excellent," he said. "I thought he was very well qualified in his work on the Opera, in his knowledge of music, in the theatre and drama generally. His scholarly work, his ability to dig out very obscure facts from very difficult texts in the classical Chinese over a range of materials in social and cultural history, which is the background to the Peking Opera, was outstanding. I was able to offer him one of the first two appointments I made after my arrival." So Colin became a Research Fellow in Chinese Cultural History at ANU.

The other appointment made by Professor Wang, as charming and friendly a man as one could meet, was that of the well-known expert on PRC politics, Dr Stephen FitzGerald, who was a friend and contemporary of Colin and had been working in the Department of International

Relations at ANU. "Stephen FitzGerald submitted his thesis about the same time as Colin," said the professor. "It was on the political side and it was also excellent. In his case, we offered him a job for his knowledge of contemporary Chinese policies with the historical background of the earlier part of the 20th century. They were two parallel appointments, but in very different fields — one for contemporary history, the other for cultural history. Both proved excellent choices."

This must have been particularly satisfying, for Professor Wang was following in the footsteps of that distinguished Sinologist Professor C. Patrick FitzGerald, whose historical works on China are so widely known and appreciated both inside and outside the academic world. A book in his honour was planned, to be entitled *Essays on the Sources for Chinese History* and Colin was appointed one of the editors and also undertook the compiling of the complex index. This, together with the rewriting for publication of his two dissertations (on the Uighurs and the Rise of the Peking Opera), and the major ongoing work of researching and writing a volume on the Chinese theatre from 1840 to modern times, must have tested even his capacity for work.

Certainly, about this time, the members of Colin's wider family circle and close friends sometimes wondered if the price paid for his all consuming scholarship were not too high. He seems not to have noticed that his small children were 'wild and undisciplined, kicked holes in walls, scribbled on things' and generally went unchecked. Alyce, herself geared to scholarship, does not appear to have been unduly worried by their unruliness or perhaps she just gave the unequal battle away. Catherine refrained from comment, but broke her rule of non-intervention in regard to an eye defect of one of the children, for although she knew that they had received medical advice against an operation in both Peking and Canberra, she felt strongly that further expert opinion should be sought. Whether it was the stress of daily existence and the arrival during the next year or so of their two youngest children, Veronica and Josephine, or simply that Colin and Alyce were satisfied with the opinions they had already received, the matter was not pursued further. Catherine, for once, remained critical. Yet they were very caring parents and Malcolm, calling on occasions, was astonished to find Colin changing a wet infant with practised hand — something he was never to get round to himself when marriage and fatherhood overtoook him, which they were soon to do.

In 1971 there was much political ferment and discussion in the press and the community at large about Australia's relationship with communist China. The Vietnam issue was losing much of its divisiveness as U.S. and Australian involvement there drew to a close, and the question now being asked everywhere was, *'Should we move towards recognition of Mainland China?'*

There were signs from China itself of a retreat from the initial excesses of the Cultural Revolution. The popular Premier Zhou Enlai was aiming at moderation and away from isolationism, and working towards recognition of the PRC by as many nations as possible and its substitution for Taiwan in the United Nations as representative of the Chinese people. The wheat trade with China was of increasing importance to Australia and the Liberal Prime Minister McMahon and National Party Leader, Doug Anthony, were well aware of the fact and wished to proceed, cautiously, and without offence to the United States, towards normalisation of relations. However, it was the Labor Party, in opposition, led by Gough Whitlam, which took the initiative. He headed an ALP delegation to Peking in May, 1971, taking with him, amongst others, Colin's colleague, Stephen FitzGerald, as adviser and interpreter. This was all highly controversial, and the whys and wherefores of the Cultural Revolution and PRC policies became a matter of great public interest. Colin and another Sinologist from ANU were asked to conduct a seminar on contemporary China at Young, a flourishing country centre in western New South Wales.

The Mackerras family friend, John Goldrick, was then a magistrate on circuit and at that centre. "The honest burghers of Young," he said, "were very keen to be informed. It was freezing but they turned out for this seminar. It was fascinating, but I couldn't quite work out whether Colin did or did not approve of the Cultural Revolution." Colin was, in fact, very unsure himself at that time whether the leadership of the CCP had not gone too far with their militant, repressive policies; for not only had there been total censorship of literature and all the traditional arts but large-scale internecine clashes and bloodshed, as instanced in factional fighting in Wuhan, capital city of Hubei province and an important strategic centre. It was time, he felt, for more moderation in the achieving of revolutionary objectives.

Fortunately, this was at hand. The U.S. President Nixon and Secretary of State Kissinger had been pursuing diplomatic overtures with Zhou Enlai, the PRC was subsequently admitted to the United Nations in October 1971, while Nixon announced in July of that year, to a world somewhat stunned at this reversal of global policy, that he would visit Peking before May '72. In Australia, when the Labor Government came to power in November of that year, Whitlam immediately followed up his earlier initiative, and after some swift diplomatic moves, conducted in Paris, announced the establishment of diplomatic relations between the PRC and the Australian Government, together with the acknowledgment that the PRC was the 'sole legal government of China' and the removal of our diplomatic representative from Taiwan. The first result was the release of the controversial journalist, Francis James, and a feeling of goodwill thereafter began to emerge among the Australian people towards China. Stephen FitzGerald was appointed Australia's first ambassador to the PRC, while Colin, in May — June 1973, now a Senior Research Fellow at ANU, was able to make, for research purposes, his first visit there since 1966.

Based in Peking, he found that his movements were much more restricted than they had been previously, and this despite the new warmth in relations between the two countries — Prime Minister Whitlam and entourage were to visit in a few months and receive a personal welcome at the airport by Zhou Enlai with 100,000 workers, students and children lining the streets to give him 'a stormy welcome'. It would seem nevertheless that the CCP's basically suspicious attitude towards Europeans in their midst had become deeply ingrained. However, Colin obtained interviews with people such as 'Xifan, a high level cadre for the section on literature in the People's Daily'. He had been struck by the regrowth of interest in traditional forms and themes in art and had observed at one exhibition in Peking of the industrial arts 'that classical themes outweighed revolutionary by a considerable margin'. Commenting on this to the Chinese journalist, he asked if the revival of traditional theatre might now also be a logical step, and was told that 'some classical pieces had already been shown to selected visiting dignitaries and would probably be performed publicly again in due course'.

Colin had been commissioned by a Singaporean publisher to write his third major work (which directly involved his current research) and it was to be published under the title, *The Chinese Theatre in Modern Times, From 1840 to the Present Day*. At the crucial moment, the publisher became bankrupt. Colin found this to be a blessing in disguise for he quickly found a London publisher, Thames & Hudson, established an excellent relationship with that firm, and the book was published in 1975. It contained not only fascinating material about famous actors, musical theatre, and Chinese musical instruments, with an abundance of evocative illustrations, but much basic social history and a number of extremely interesting first-hand incidents of life in and around Peking in the mid-1970s.

Meanwhile, back in Canberra in the second half of 1973, the next major formative event occurred in his life. He was offered a chair in Modern Asian Studies at Brisbane's about-to-be-formed second university, Griffith, at Mt Gravatt. The offer came from Professor John Willett who, together with Ted (now Sir Theodor) Bray, retired chairman of Queensland Newspapers Pty Ltd, had been planning its foundation, at the State Government's request, over the previous 18 months. "We led the initial planning team," said Professor Willett, "and since we had only a very, very general instruction from the government, we had an opportunity to think about what it is that ought to go into a university starting in the 1970s." Both he and Sir Theodor had very strong views on Australia's relationship with Asia and were agreed that one of the priorities would be to establish a School which concentrated on modern Asia, 'particularly that set of people to the north of the country, that is, Japan, China and the Malay peoples'. They decided that fully a quarter of the first courses at the University would go into Asian studies, and Colin, with his reputation as a Sinologist, was one of the first people approached. He accepted the appointment at once — Alyce rejoiced at the opportunity for him — and took it up the following year, when this truly Australian landscaped-based campus, with cool modern buildings set in natural bushland on the hillsides of Mt Gravatt on Brisbane's southside, was ready for its first occupants.

During 1973, Alan, after a prolonged illness, died, but not before he had been told of this son's appointment, and signified his happiness, which made Colin's heart glad for he had strong regrets at not having established a more satisfactory relationship with his father earlier in his life. Catherine, making her last visit to them in Canberra a few months later, took the opportunity, which she felt singularly appropriate, to give Colin something which he has treasured ever since. This was an original edition of a book written by their illustrious ancestor of mathematical fame (of whom we have spoken), Colin MacLaurin (1698–1746). He was the youngest professor ever to be elected to a chair and admitted to Bericharle College, Aberdeen, at the age of 19 in 1717, and in 1725 was made Professor of Mathematics at Edinburgh University on the recommendation of Sir Isaac Newton, and also a Fellow of the Royal Society. The book, entitled *An Account of Sir Isaac Newton's Philosophical Discoveries* was published from Colin MacLaurin's manuscript papers in 1748, two years after his death, by one Patrick Murdock. Somewhere on the flyleaf is also inscribed, 'Brearcliffe' which was Catherine's middle name. The 20th century Colin (Catherine had undoubtedly chosen his two names, Colin Patrick, from this historical circumstance) packed the precious volume with the greatest care for its journey with them to the sub-tropics.

Others were sorry to see the Colin Mackerrases head north, particularly Malcolm's wife Lindsay, who, like Alyce, was from western New South Wales and had established a fond and easy relationship with her. At ANU, Professor Wang regretted losing a Senior Fellow but at the same time 'applauded John Willett's enterprise in planning a School of Modern Asian Studies — the only one of its kind in the country'.

So, at the relatively young age of 34, Colin became a Foundation Professor at Griffith University and built a house in the same kind of natural bush setting in which the university itself stands. This home is at Capalaba, some kilometres further out of town, and he left the choice of schooling for the family to Alyce with whom he did not wish to precipitate the sort of difficulties which had grown between his own parents. The children were brought up in the Catholic Church at her insistence, but she decided on an admixture of State and Church schools. Each of the five, when he or she grew old enough, took up a musical instrument, ranging from the piano to the cello, oboe, clarinet and bass guitar, so that the native Queensland eucalypts and acacias in the Mackerras neck of the woods ring as resoundingly with music as did the poplars and liquid ambers at *Harpenden* in Colin's own youth.

He found that he enjoyed university teaching and the contact with students very much indeed, and in the course of administrative work, formed a close bond of friendship with the Vice-Chancellor, Professor Willett. At Griffith they had the usual hurdles of a second university to face, principally, the idea amongst prospective students, their families and employers that it is 'second best'.

"I think this university has done very well against that persistent Australian pattern," Professor Willett commented. "You find the same thing in Sydney with the University of New South Wales, and in Melbourne with Monash — and that's been established for nearly 25 years. Here, the Modern Asian Studies School has astounded me. I thought that we'd be really lucky to average 70 students who would be prepared to take that course — which has the requirement for them to study one of the difficult Asian languages. But we've taken them by their hundreds, every year except '79 and '80 — and it happened in the School of Science too — when there were dangerous stories about in the press and schools, exaggerated talk about graduate unemployment, an oversupply of teachers for schools and colleges and universities. School leavers were being urged to go and get a job and were being told that there was no value in going on to higher education. It was quite wicked — it resulted in a hopeless shortage of teachers in Queensland." Fortunately, most of that group of possible tertiary level students, after a couple of years in the work force, felt the need themselves to do a university course and many went in the direction of Griffith University and Modern Asian Studies, which is now a very big School, averaging about 600 students.

"Some of these are top-rank, some are middle level performers," said the professor. "How well this second group does depends on the quality of the teaching and their own internal motivation. Motivation goes back to the teacher and that's where Colin is enormously important . . . If you take a group of, on the face of it, not brilliant students, and get them to achieve to the topmost of their ability, that's what a university's about . . . The pursuit of excellence is the taking out of students everything they've got in them. And that's what Colin's good at — he's a first-class teacher in every sense."

Apart from the historical forces at work, it does seem to be one of those pre-ordained things that a university with one of its specialties in the area in which Colin was highly qualified should have been founded at this time, for he had so many teaching years ahead, and, within him, a great deal to give to the young in a teaching role. When varying student standards were being discussed, he said, "Care should be exercised in mentioning that subject. I love them all." He undoubtedly means it, and the feeling, it seems, is reciprocated. One young Griffith postgraduate, off to take up a scholarship in Japan, commented, "He's really loved by the students. He goes into the Common Room and chats with them and spurs them along. He knows every student's name within a fortnight." One thinks immediately of brother Alastair.

In spite of divergence in matters political and on religion, these two brothers have a number of characteristics in common — tolerance, in argument and in practice, a generally benevolent attitude — and the engaging peculiarity, which has persisted over all the years, of singing or humming aloud from their vast musical repertoire. "It's really when their attention is not fully on the conversation — that's when the singing comes out!" commented the perceptive John Willett with his quiet smile. "Colin at the table or a dinner party is terribly funny . . . " Whether it was Brahms or Beethoven at the root of his amiable distraction, he and Alyce certainly appreciated the Willetts' hospitable table. Jean Willett, before her husband's retirement, was well-known for the friendship offered, not only to her husband's senior colleagues and their wives, but to junior ones as well.

Alyce taught Japanese and other subjects at St Thomas More College in their first two years in Brisbane, then Chinese at the Brisbane Boys' Grammar School for several more, until there were graduates from Griffith who could 'take over'. Then, with two Chinese friends, she started work on something she had wanted to do for some time, which was the compilation of a textbook for teaching Chinese.

From the time he arrived at Griffith University, Colin undertook a major long-term project, apart from his ongoing volumes on the performing arts in China, and this was a comprehensive chronology of events in modern China from 1842 to the present day. It was to be a huge 8 years' task, during which time the Australian Research Grants

Committee provided some assistance, appointing a Research Assistant, Robert Chan, to work fulltime on the project at Griffith for 2 years. But that still left Colin with 75% of the necessary research and work to do himself. How much did his own specific studies since 1964 help in the task?

"Enormously," he says. "Although there isn't much about theatre in the chronology, I used mainly Chinese sources, and grasp of Chinese general history helped greatly in compiling it and understanding the interrelationship of events." This was just as well, since the chronology, to be presented in two sections, was to cover major political or general incidents — military or civilian, foreign or domestic policy — on left-hand pages, and on the right-hand, six categories under the titles, Economics; Official Appointments, Dismissals, Resignations etc; Cultural and Social; Publications; Natural Disasters; Births and Deaths. A daunting prospect for which he was surely going to need all his disciplined reserves.

Meanwhile, during these years, there were other interesting developments and journeys to China, when possible accompanied by Alyce and one or other of the children, so that each could experience something of the country which means so much in the lives of their parents. They have all stood and gazed out over the Great Wall; they all now know Peking and its special atmosphere, where ancient grandeur lives side by side with unpretentiousness. They have ridden bicycles on the wide boulevards where there are so few cars, where small ponies and donkeys still bring loaded carts of produce into the city's centre, and where small brick thatch-roofed cottages often sit improbably between buildings and you are likely to turn a corner and come upon some wonderful carved gateway or other mark of the old distinctive civilisation.

In 1977, a practice was begun at Griffith University whereby a delegation is taken to an Asian country from the School of Modern Asian Studies — 'especially to socialist countries which are not so easy to visit as the others' — and places of interest in that country are visited as a group; this is of great practical benefit to both staff and senior students. Colin organised and led the first one — to China. He had a work in progress on contemporary aspects of the performing arts and was interested during this visit to hear tunes from the popular *geju* (sung opera), *Red Guards of Honghu Lake*, being broadcast constantly and whistled and hummed by people in the streets. This was an early revolutionary opera which had been banned during the reign of the 'gang of four' because of the portrayal in it of a former revolutionary hero of whom they disapproved. During another visit the following year, Colin learnt from the leading actress in the opera that during the Cultural Revolution she had been severely persecuted, forbidden to perform, shut in a dark room and had her life threatened. There could hardly be a more striking instance of the fact that the performing arts are seen by successive PRC leaders, whether radical, moderate, or revisionist, as a major vehicle for the spreading of ideas and as representative of desirable or undesirable behaviour for the populace. Fortunately an element of humour is usually present.

It is interesting that both Professor Wang of ANU and Professor Willett at Griffith, have compared traditional Chinese operas and dramas with the television 'soapies' of Western countries — a reflection of lifestyles. Colin certainly became aware on successive visits to China that film and television would soon overtake the traditional performing arts in the cities, gradually in the villages as technical facilities became available, and also be used by the government 'as a legitimate propaganda vehicle'. He visited a number of cinemas in Peking and devoted a good portion of his next work to the subject.

Returning home via Sydney and calling at *Balvaig*, he was distressed to see Catherine's severe deterioration in health. His sister Elizabeth was also clearly worried about her. He sat and talked for an hour with Catherine and it was indeed to be the last time, for she died a few weeks later. Like all the family, he was glad for her sake that there was not to be a protracted illness such as their father had suffered. He and his mother had always been close and he never ceased to be grateful for her instinctive perception and quick action in pointing him so unexpectedly to the career which he found so fulfilling.

Later that year he was invited by the State Department, Washington D.C., to be an International Visitor and call on people of like interests in Washington, New York, Cambridge (Massachusetts), New Haven (Yale University), Chicago and Madison (Wisconsin) and Honolulu. Like his father 50 years before, he found American professors very stimulating in discussion, very hospitable, and enjoyed visiting their universities and cities. The last port of call, Hawaii, was the most interesting of all. "I found at the University of Hawaii," he recalled, "the best specialist on Asian theatres in the U.S. It was a great joy to me to establish contact with them, and the highlight of my trip."

Also, like Catherine some years before, he decided that England was practically on the way. In London he had seen his brother Charles in his role as Director of the English National Opera, in Suffolk visited his sister Joan, and in Cambridge his old friend Dr Picken who described his visit and their talk as 'a rare pleasure for me in my retirement'. It seems to have been a particularly good thing that he made this trip, for other than two brief visits to the U.S. for conferences in the '80s, he has not since been able to direct himself to anywhere other than China and Asian countries, so all consuming is his interest in them.

On his return, he immediately took part in seminars and lectures on the Chinese Exhibition — a display of artifacts which was one of the first cultural exchanges between China and Australia and made such a big impact on the community. At the opening in Sydney he was delighted to meet, for the first time, Gough Whitlam who astonished him, as they walked about discussing which province this or that object came from, by also displaying knowledge about his own MacLaurin family history. The former P.M., who is interested in Australia's distinguished families as well as general history, was aware not only of the eminent Sir Normand MacLaurin and his contribution to university, business and political life in the early part of this century, but also of that earliest musician in the family, Issac Nathan, and his arrival on our shores in 1841.

At Griffith University in 1979 another important development in Colin's career took place. He was appointed Chairman of the Modern Asian Studies School. "Chairmen of Schools here," said Professor Willett in

1983 not long before his retirement as Vice-Chancellor, "are not elected. They arrive out of a very curious process in which I talk to the senior members of the teaching staff of the School. We canvass and talk about the possibilities of who might do the job. As a result . . . Colin was appointed, although many of us had a bit of reservation as to whether he would prove to be an effective manager . . . He turned out to be idiosyncratic — not a routine bureaucrat — but effective. The Schools are in fact mini-universities, they run their student group, do all their own academic planning, run their own budgets — Colin's got a budget of 1½ million dollars. He consults his colleagues — often too much . . . and sometimes drives you to desperation, but he's an effective, conscientious and sometimes very imaginative manager. He gets things done and he takes the School with him which is important in a flat, non-hierarchial organisation like this university."

He added wryly, "Colin also battles amongst a lot of hungry colleagues who'd strip the Modern Asian Studies down to its last professor if they could! His ways of fighting are not some of the more aggressive ways, but he fights, and with a degree of success too . . . I've seen quite a lot of spit and fire out of him. If you cross Colin you can raise quite a whirlwind — not that you'd want to very often."

At the end of Colin's first term, the Vice-Chancellor approached the Modern Asian Studies staff again for suggestions and they were of one mind — to persuade Colin to serve another term. He agreed (two terms are the maximum allowable in succession) and has recently completed the six years, proving in the most practical of all ways, that he does not live entirely in a world inhabited by classic Chinese texts and characters.

"As you probably gather," said Professor Willett, from his retirement, "I seriously appreciate Colin — as a friend, a colleague and as one of the co-founders and co-managers of Griffith. I was very strongly criticised for having 'left-wing mavericks' in professorial chairs, but he has never been anything but fair-minded."

We are, however, anticipating. There were a number of interesting highlights in Colin's life from '80 to '85 — publications, visits and study leave in China, and, as well, events celebrating the 10 years of the resumption of Sino-Australian diplomatic relations which involved unprecedented numbers of the Australian community. We will touch, briefly, upon each.

He visited China early in 1980 and spoke with many 'cadres' involved in film production (65 films had been produced the previous year) and in 1981 with theatre specialists, which gave him excellent material for his work *The Performing Arts in Contemporary China*. It was published not long afterwards and focuses on the years 1976–80, telling of the predominance of revolutionary themes in the traditional operas and their likely decline in favour of film as Chinese society and the economy become modernized. He discusses several of the 65 films recently produced, such as the love story *Little Flower* which tells of the heroine's sufferings during the 'gang of four' era and is strikingly different from Western films in that bodily contact between the lovers remains absent. He finds the films technically excellent; for instance, one based on the life of a musician is compared with 'Ken Russell's superb *Mahler* of 1974 on the career of the famous

Colin with theatre specialists, China, 1981.

composer'. The English publishers have presented the book most attractively and the illustrations are very fine.

A small item for Colin, but of particular interest to those without specialist knowledge, is his contribution on Chinese music to the delightful series put out by the Curriculum Development Centre, Canberra, on *The Musical Cultures of Asia* about this time. It is accompanied by a tape which includes items from the famous revolutionary operas such as *The Red Lantern* and *The East is Red*. It contains some exquisite melodies, while the text explains much about Asian music which to most Western ears is enjoyable only in small amounts. One discovers that the feeling of a certain sameness and repetitiveness is due to their more frequent use of the pentatonic scale (represented on the piano by the five black notes) than is usual in Western music, which is based mainly on harmonies through the various scales. The increasing admixture of Western instruments with the Chinese is deplored by musical purist, Colin, while both he and John Willett found the Isaac Stern film, *Mao to Mozart*, decidedly patronising. "It is ethnocentric," Colin commented, "in that everything is based on the assumption that the West should teach the East. I don't accept that assumption."

Interestingly, Professor Wang Gungwu like the majority of Australians, to say nothing of the Shanghai audience, thoroughly enjoyed that film. It should be mentioned, however, that the excellent Larry Sitski ABC programmes, *Journey Through the Musical Highways and Byways of China*, do meet with our purist's approval as being 'just right for an intelligent and sensitive Australian audience'.

A renewal of acquaintance with Gough Whitlam, who was at Griffith University to lecture on Korea in 1981, was a particular pleasure. (Mr Whitlam, on that occasion, referred to Colin as his 'favourite Mackerras' and recently, commenting from Paris, remarked that he feels 'ideologically closest to the Mackerras at Griffith'). The following year saw the publication by Thames & Hudson, London, of Colin's major work, *Modern China: A Chronology from 1842 to the Present Day*.

This is a truly extraordinary work which had never been attempted before, and the last 4000 of the printrun were sold to a Californian publisher. Colin was anxious to get the book into print quickly, as a reference work, and seems to have inadvertently given the full copyright to the publishers. Their Brisbane representative, Geraldine Pestorious, comments, "This wonderful man was not particularly interested in the hardback $60 edition, he wants a paperback out so that his students can buy it!"

The trouble seems to be that, due to the complexity of the work, a paperback could not be produced for much less than the hardback — that is according to this firm of publishers. As they hold the copyright, Colin is not able to negotiate with others, and since he poured a fair proportion of his heart's blood into compiling the text over a period of 8 years, it is little wonder that he feels very frustrated that his students, and those in other Australian cities and other parts of the world, are unable to purchase copies at a reasonable price.

In the second half of '82, during which time the Commonwealth Games were being held in Brisbane and Griffith campus was taken over by athletes from around the world, Colin decided to take study leave. He perhaps

Colin and Alyce, Peking, 1982

could have been helpful to many overseas non-English speaking sportsmen, but wherever there is an undue emphasis on sport, Colin would prefer to be elsewhere. As John Willett remarked with a smile, "It's very good that sporting teams are not the major agent of social change in China!"

In any case, Colin and Alyce, together with their two youngest daughters, left for Peking and took up residence at the Central Institute for Nationalities — this is rather a misnomer for it takes about 50 minutes by bus, which Colin used frequently, to the central government area, while Alyce and the two girls got about by bicycle. His special purpose was to study 'Minority Nationalities', and in fact at the Institute there were Uighurs, Manchus, Mongolians and others, and some American, Japanese, Korean and one Italian student but, other than himself, only two scholars, one Japanese, one American. It was an extremely productive six months, and he made three major trips out of Peking — one into the grasslands of inner Mongolia, visiting the old city of Datong *en route*, a second to North Korea (unusual for Westerners to travel there and therefore particularly valuable), and a third to Urumqi in Xinjiang in the far west of China.

Alyce was able to accompany him as far as Datong on the first trip and they had some respite from his data gathering and interviewing in a visit to the famous Buddhist caves there. "Very beautiful, very ancient," he commented. "There are large 5th century Buddhist statues which are quite marvellous."

One of his impressions of China during this time was that of a collapse of morale among the youth of the nation following the markedly revisionist policies of CCP leader Ziaoping Deng and the pragmatic Premier Zhao Ziyang who had been denounced during the Cultural Revolution as a 'revisionist' and had now achieved prominence again. "There is a general collapse of belief in the system," Colin remarked. "If you spend years trying to instil views and then tell them that revolution is not great, if you put up a leader like Mao and then take him down, you're likely to get a bit of confusion among the people." He feels that this is compounded by the fact that China is a poor country and cannot substitute for the former idealism even a higher standard of living for the young. "So," he said, "you get this collapse of confidence, you get scepticism. And I think that's a very sad thing for the Chinese." On the other hand he is impressed with the rate at which literacy and the overall standard of living have risen and feels that they are dealing in the only way possible to stabilise population growth, which is the one child per family ruling.

There are, however, quite serious social problems attached to it. "The most important," he says, " is not so much that of the 'spoilt child' but the question of infanticide, especially female infanticide — because the people want sons. It's very wicked, disturbing and distressing." In spite of which, he thinks the one child per family edict is absolutely necessary if disastrous famines in the future are to be avoided. As it is, China feeds one-quarter of the world population with one-seventh of the world's arable land.

Colin had a positive impression of North Korea. "For one thing," he said "I don't think there's any crisis of youth there or any crisis in the system. There are very good social services, it's a very beautiful country, and it's much more prosperous and much cleaner than China. The people are a great deal better off in material terms." His main qualification about the country is the intense propaganda system, centred round an extreme leadership cult, in which credit for everything is given to one man, the leader, Kim Il Sung, but he still remains impressed by all that has been accomplished there.

Before their return to Australia, Colin and Alyce and the two small girls managed to make a weekend trip to the former summer residence of the Manchu Emperors in Chendge. "A lovely place of palaces and beautiful temples like those of Tibet," said Colin, but found that even he was glad to breathe again the scent of gum trees when they reached home.

A journalist from *The Australian* interviewed him at his home in Brisbane and the paper ran an article entitled *China 'dramatically different'* with comments by him as 'one of Australia's foremost China watchers'. He had certainly earned this reputation. Apart from work on his own specialty for an American publisher, he was also now in the throes of co-authoring, with Griffith colleague, Edmund Fung, a work on 'Australia's Policies Towards the People's Republic of China since 1965'.

The Prime Minister Malcolm Fraser had just made another successful journey to Peking to mark the 10th anniversary of the Australian *rapprochement* with China and now scored something of a diplomatic *coup* by persuading Chinese Premier Zhao Ziyang to visit Australia. This was to take place in April '83, and already arranged were two major cultural events to 'promote understanding and friendship between our two peoples'. These were the visit from a traditional Peking Opera Theatre (the Jiangsu Company), to tour Australian capital cities from February to April; and the exciting Entombed Warriors Exhibition, a display of seven terracotta warriors and two horses from one of the great archaeological finds in history at Xian in central China in 1974 — the buried lifesize terracotta army of 7500 warriors and horses at the entrance to the mausoleum of Qin Shihuang, First Emperor of China who died in 210 BC.

Colin was naturally deeply involved in both these cultural events and was the first speaker at an International Conference held in Sydney to coincide with the visit of the Peking Opera. The overall title of the seminar was *Chinese Theatre in the Twentieth Century*, which could hardly have been more relevant to him. The community generally was fired by the spectacular programmes, and the tour was booked out. An excerpt from the revolutionary drama *A Battle of Wits* seemed to typify the point made by Colin consistently in his written works — the integration of the performing arts and society. *The Jade Bracelet* was charming and delicate and full of lively characterisation, *The White Snake* a brilliant piece also, displaying the universal feeling for the mystic and the equally universal single-mindedness of anyone driven by love, but at the same time some wonderful acrobatic skills of a specific Chinese character; and *Yentang Mountain* was a *tour de force* of the whole intricate art with amazing masks and costuming.

It must have been singularly gratifying to Colin to find this form of theatre, on which he had spent so much scholarly work, accepted so enthusiastically by culturally-minded fellow Australians. The Entombed Warriors Exhibition had an even more widespread appeal and Australians in their thousands queued at the capital city galleries to see this magnificent display of extraordinarily lifelike figures from another age. The individuality of the warriors was palpable — a kneeling bowman looked quizzical, a standing crossbowman was thoughtfully making a point — and the Mongolian ponies looked as though they might break into a gallop at any moment. As Queensland art critic Dr Gertrude Langer commented, in urging people to go and see it, and she was not given to hyperbole, "The impression is simply stunning . . . and the appearance of the figures is enhanced by a quite magical theatrical display . . . Spaces of the gallery have been transformed to recreate the atmosphere of the pits, which is supported by wall-size color photographs printed on canvas showing where warriors were placed 2200 years ago; computer-controlled light-changes spot the figures in the darkness and make them appear to breathe . . . " Ancient China certainly lived again.

Colin had seen the figures *in situ* in Xian on several occasions and was asked to give an introductory lecture at the Queensland Cultural Centre on their historical and social background. He is a fine academic lecturer (one student was heard to say to another after a class of his on colonial rule in Indo-China 'How's that for inspiration?') but on this occasion did not seem particularly at ease with a general audience. One art lover, who knows nothing of China, proclaimed herself 'more confused' at the broad canvas he covered, while an academic present remarked 'splendid'. It would seem to be a trap for academics to speak to their colleagues and pitch a lecture above, or in some way not strike the right lively note with, a non-academic but informed and interested audience.

A little later he was delighted to welcome to the Modern Asian Studies School at Griffith colleagues from the Peking Foreign Languages

Colin with colleagues from Peking, on campus, Griffith University

Institute's English Department, Professor Liu Chengpei and Mr Zhang Zhongzai, to teach classical Chinese to Honours students for a three month period. So the cultural exchange was continually expanded.

In October '83 there was much talk of politics in the Mackerras household at Capalaba, with the Queensland State Election on hand following the highly controversial Liberal Party debacle. Alyce manned the local polling booth on behalf of the Labor candidate and Malcolm appeared on the scene from Canberra in rumbustious vein, publicly brushing with Colin's political *bête noir,* Premier Bjelke-Petersen, all to no avail, as the latter swept back into power.

Before the year was out there was better news for Colin. The University of Hawaii Press published, in good time, a work which he had edited and to which he had contributed several chapters: *Chinese Theater: from its Origins to the Present Day*. The major conclusion of this volume is that 'theater as propaganda played an important and broadly successful role in unifying the Chinese against the enemy during the war against Japan . . . Similarly, it has continued as a vital and also broadly successful mechanism in securing integration since 1949.' This book, with more aggressive American publishers, had done very well indeed. Quite astonishingly, the prestigious *Cambridge History of Inner Asia* (Cambridge University Press), to which Colin had contributed a chapter on the Uighurs some fifteen years before, has not yet seen the light of day. This is due to procrastinating academic contributors who, as a breed, are the bane of Colin's life.

He and John Willett (who had just retired as Vice-Chancellor at Griffith University and was succeeded by Professor Roy Webb from Melbourne)*now co-led another delegation to China. It was a memorable few weeks for a number of people, including Queensland's State Librarian, Lawrie Ryan, who referred to it as 'an absolutely fascinating experience'. They visited various provinces as a group (often facilitated by having the recently retired Vice-Chancellor of an Australian university with them), went to Peking Opera performances, saw such things as jade being manufactured as well as less exotic objects and all, with the exception of one disgruntled Englishman, found the trip enlivened in numerous ways by Colin's even-handed affability and exuberance. Lawrie Ryan was particularly struck by his musicianship, recalling with amusement his trying to fix a 'key' for the loud hum of turbines at a power station, and he has an indelible memory of him 'singing Mahler on the Great Wall of China!'

In May 1984, Colin was one of those named by *The National Times* as being amongst *Australia's Top 50 Thinkers*. The four compilers remarked that this list was 'unashamedly arbitrary as any such exercise must be'. There were two broad criteria for inclusion in it, viz: those presently teaching in Australian universities, and with international reputations for their work in Australia. A cross-section of academics were asked whom they considered the best in their own field and the names which cropped

---

* Sir Allan Sewell is now Chancellor of Griffith University.

Professor Willett and his wife Jean, Grand Canal, Wuxi

Colin questioning neighbourhood committee in Wuxi on vital matter of birth control.

Professor John Willett and Colin with the Head of China Travel Service in Nanjin at a grand dinner given in their honour.

Colin and others watch rehearsal of opera company

Lawrie Ryan (back left), Colin (partly obscured back right) and others with cast of Jiangsu Opera Company after performance

up most frequently formed the basis from which the list was chosen; nominations were also checked with experts from outside universities. It is interesting that Brisbane's 'second' university, Griffith, should have produced three chosen by their peers throughout the country, and it was good to see, beside household names such as Manning Clarke, Sir Mark Oliphant and Dame Leonie Kramer, those of Griffith's Andrew Field (School of Humanities) and Nancy Viviani (School of Modern Asian Studies) as well as Colin. It was a tribute indeed to all three. There seems no doubt, in regard to Colin, that his *Modern China: A Chronology from 1842 to the Present Day*, referred to in *The National Times* article as 'one of the definitive texts on contemporary China' consolidated his international reputation as a Sinologist.

That year he co-led a delegation from Griffith to Vietnam and they travelled from one end of the country to the other. He had previously visited only Saigon, and then for a few weeks on his way to Cambridge in 1962 when it was under the old regime, so that it was an extremely interesting experience. Unfortunately, he is not very optimistic about its future. Although the country had been unified since 1976, he found the south more prosperous than the north but even then the whole country 'much poorer than other socialist countries in Asia'. He was struck by 'apathy and lack of enthusiasm everywhere, particularly in the south, and the number of beggars everywhere'. The country also has a serious population growth problem, while the draining and continuing war with Kampuchea increases the country's 'reliance on the Soviet Union'. It does seem that this war-torn country has suffered disproportionately as a battleground for ideologies.

About this time Colin was working, with two colleagues, co-authoring and co-editing a volume on *Marxism in Asia* and impatiently awaiting the release by University of Queensland Press of his joint work with Edmund Fung on *Australia's Policies towards the People's Republic of China, 1966–82* which they had entitled: *From Fear to Friendship*. This duly appeared mid-1985 and received a qualified reception from critics who, while noting in one way or another its 'left' bias, nevertheless acknowledged it as the first comprehensive publication on the subject and therefore its value as a reference book. For the non-specialist, who is interested to learn of the political convolutions, the intricate interweaving of ideologies and pragmatism, basic trade and self-interest, and the flashes of statesmanship which illumine power and party politicking and brought the two countries from suspicion and mistrust to very good terms indeed, the book makes good reading. One need be only temporarily deterred by some of the introductory comments, such as '1966 saw the launching of the Great Proletarian Cultural Revolution', and by an over-emphasis in the introduction generally on Australia's 'siege mentality', and 'obsession with external aggression — first of Japan, then of Indonesia and then of communist China', which is said to have 'bordered on the irrational'. Overall, the dissection of events, policies and personalities takes hold, particularly in the earlier chapters where Australian political figures come to life and we see Anthony coping manfully with a conflict of ideology and wheat sales, Whitlam making his meteor-like appearance, and Fraser, waiting in the wings, ready to seize upon relevant power factors and consolidate the Whitlam *rapprochement* with China.

At the same time as Colin worked on these latest volumes, Alyce, with whatever time was available from her household of seven, worked with two Chinese friends, Peter Chang and Yu Hsiu Ching, with support from the Australia-China Council, to complete the first of a series of secondary school text books for the teaching of Chinese, entitled: *Hanyu*. Australia has proved a world leader in the teaching of Chinese, so that a series of this kind should prove extremely useful. Alyce also spends some time with a ecumenical peace and justice group known as *Action for World Development*.

In June '85, as Colin reached the end of his two three year terms as Chairman of the Modern Asian Studies School (he was succeeded by the Vice-Chairman Professor David Lim), and was looking forward to a year's study leave to be spent mostly in China, he felt the time had come to organise a top-level conference on China-Australia relations and thereby, through meeting together and delivering representative papers and points of view, strengthen the growing ties. Professor Hugh Dunn, former Australian ambassador to China, who had recently joined the staff, got plans under way and acted as convenor. Coln spent the last few weeks in his spacious office, where the plateglass seems to invite inside the sloping bushland surrounding it, very busy in this transitional period as Chairman, but gave what assistance he could. Professor Dunn invited Premier Sir Joh Bjelke-Petersen, recently returned from a trade mission to China, to open the conference.

It was held in mid-July in Brisbane's winter sunshine which lived up to its reputation, crowning the hundreds of flowering wattles to be seen on all sides at the Griffith campus and producing pleased expressions on the faces of delegates, most of whom were from colder climes. Speakers included Mr Huan Xiang, of the Chinese Academy of Social Sciences and director of the PRC's International Affairs Research Centre; Mr Nie Gongcheng, Chinese Ambassador to Australia; Sir Gerard Brennan, of the High Court of Australia; Professor Allen Whiting, of the University of Arizona, whose work *China Crosses the Yalu* is regarded as a classic; Sir Leslie Price, Australian Wheat Board Chairman; and many distinguished Australian government, mining and banking respresentatives.

As at most conferences, delegates found as much information and interest from discussion with colleagues between times as from the addresses. John Willett was a vitally interested observer, as was Professor Wang Gungwu of ANU and many other former Canberra colleagues with whom Colin was able to renew acquaintance. Colin himself delivered a paper on *Australia-China Political Relations under Hawke* and spoke of Prime Minister Hawke's visit to China and the return visit to this country of the CCP's Secretary-General Hu Yaobang, and of complex policy matters which involve both countries' relations with the Soviet Union, together with the very vexed question of Kampuchea. He concluded that 'friendship between nations proceeds from how they perceive their national interest at the time — and so it has to be a changing condition'. American Professor Whiting, commenting on China's present policies, is of the opinion that two-thirds of the population has not sufficient education to cope with the government's plans of organising coastal Chinese towns as international trading centres, but does predict that its 'open door policies will stay at least into the 1990s'.

"It was a successful conference and I think we all learned a great deal from each other," said Colin. "On the other hand, I left the conference less optimistic about the future of Sino-Australian relations than before it, because I don't see enough basic goodwill towards China in the business community, which is where goodwill matters most."

Professor Wang Gungwu, commenting on the subject, said, "The Australian community has been slow to absorb the graduates of Asian Studies Schools. We have been slow to wake up to the fact that in our neighbourhood in South East Asia there's a lot going on. The countries are really developing very fast and we ought to have people who can take advantage of that and work together with them and help themselves in the process. The opportunities are out there." It is to be hoped that more Australian business leaders will become aware of this fact before the 80s are out.

In spite of this, Colin set out in good heart for the first three months of his year's study leave, which he spent in China's most populous province, Sichuan, as Australian Scholar at Sichuan University where he did further work on China's minority nationalities, in particular, the Tibetans. He is currently at the Peking Foreign Studies University, where he has been invited to deliver a series of 15 lectures on *Western Images of China*. "The scope is broad," he said, "going from Marco Polo to the present, and including Western Europe and the U.S. It covers people of various ideologies, including Christians, Marxists, liberals and conservatives." It sounds a thoroughly daunting undertaking and it is little wonder that during the few months he had back in Australia with Alyce and their family from December '85, he consistently burnt the midnight scholastic oil.

The final impression of this *present day* Marco Polo, attested by family, colleagues, students and detached observers alike, is that of a giving man, who wears his abilities and scholarship unassumingly, has promoted understanding between this country and China, and is endowed with a grace of spirit which lightens that of others.

Chapter 9

Malcolm

Since political analysis is something which interests almost everyone, whether they survey the national scene from Adelaide or Alice, Broome or Ballarat, Weipa or Wagga Wagga, Malcolm, whose subject it is, is undoubtedly the most widely known of the Mackerras family in this country. As a natural corollary, aided and abetted by a tendency he has had to precipitate statement, he is also the most widely criticised.

In spite of this, on election nights, as results unfold on the television screens of the nation, a sizable proportion of Australians stay tuned to his pronouncements. Sometimes right, sometimes wrong, invariably outspoken, frequently contentious, he is found to be both entertaining and knowledgeable, and when results are actually established he is notable for his swift pinpointing of the most interesting of the new statistics.

We shall now unravel his career, observe how his single-minded obsession with the political scene developed, assess his contribution, and discover where criticism has been deserved, or undeserved.

Malcolm's precocious exchange with Prime Minister Menzies when he and Colin, as 12-year-olds, attended a political meeting with their brother Neil, has already been recorded, and the fact that it was Neil's study of election figures which first stimulated Malcolm's interest in such things. It should also be mentioned that in their Sydney Grammar School days, with Colin a year ahead and scholastically brilliant, Malcolm was often asked if he was envious of his twin brother. His reply was always in the negative and he meant it. He didn't mind when Colin carried off 'about 20 prizes', because he himself won the debating prize. Colin certainly had a number of choices ahead of him but he was as yet unsure which direction his career would take, whereas Malcolm already had a driving ambition to involve himself in politics. He was also 'actually better at some things' — the best example of this being sport, for not only did he do some sailing with his father, but played a reasonable game of tennis. In short, he felt in no way undermined by Colin.

"People wouldn't believe me when I told them this," he commented. "It was as though I had a *duty* to be envious of Colin! I just wasn't. Colin and I got on fine." So much for sibling jealousy. It was simply not part of the Mackerras make-up and a great deal of credit must go to Catherine for imbuing in them this confident, independent attitude.

She and Alan now decided that Malcolm should take a job and do a university course part-time. Accordingly, a job was sought, he joined the staff of BHP as a Student Cadet and began evening classes in Economics at Sydney University, majoring in government. For the following three years at BHP, he worked side by side with the present Corporate Treasurer of that company, Graeme McGregor, who has followed his subsequent career with interest and comments, "BHP Sydney office in those days was a major training ground for commercial trainees (who were) attending university at night. Competition was intense, with each trying to achieve the necessary break to start up the corporate ladder of success . . . Malcolm did not fit the mould and few of us saw him as a serious contender . . . It was obvious that his interests lay elsewhere and he was a fount of knowledge on anything political while most of his colleagues had outside interests more similar to those of others in their late teens. I remember that he earned our repsect for his knowledge on one occasion when we were reading newspapers over a sandwich lunch and there was mention of some obscure by-election in England. Malcolm immediately quoted the swing necessary for the seat to change parties and one doubting colleague took the trouble later to check the previous election result to prove that he was right . . . " His particular bent then was very clear.

At the same time, he was achieving good results in his university course and in the third year, at Student Union debates in the evening, met the full-time law student, destined for the upper echelons of politics, John Howard. It was an acquaintance which, given the vital interest of each in the political scene, was soon to grow. Malcolm had continued to be interested in the Liberal Party and was not influenced by his brother Neil's switch of allegiance and his role in the formation of the DLP, or by Catherine's support for that party. In late '59, he resigned from his Junior Cadetship at BHP and was appointed an Assistant Research Officer at the Federal Secretariat of the Liberal Party at their New South Wales headquarters in Ash Street, Sydney.

He worked frequently with the State Government Liberal Party member for Earlwood, Eric (later Sir Eric) Willis, who had ahead of him 10 years as Deputy Leader and Minister for Education in the Askin Government, and a brief period as Premier. "Malcolm and I became interested and worked together on various figures, such as redistribution of boundaries," said Sir Eric. "We'd do all the figuring as to what effect it was likely to have on the electorate if a boundary was changed from here to there, whether it was going to make it better or worse from a Liberal point of view. We did a lot of calculating of this kind and I think that although his interest in politics preceded this, it was where he generated a great deal of his interest in political statistics." This was true and it was the beginning of Malcolm's specialisation in that area.

Meanwhile, he enjoyed getting to know his brother Charles in 1960 on his first trip back to Australia in 23 years. He had previously seemed to him a shadowy figure whom he hardly knew, but from this point on, he began to appreciate and like him. Malcolm saw quite a lot of the family generally during these years, for Alastair and Joan were both living at home at the time and the former had just built his holiday house at Kiama which they often visited, joined sometimes during university vacations by Colin and Alyce. Their friend Jeremy Nelson (now a colleague of Alastair at Sydney Grammar) recalls some youthful exuberance on Malcolm's part on one memorable occasion when the clan was gathered there. He had mixed some cocktails and the normally abstemious Malcolm, like many impulsive innocents before and since, indulged excessively in the pleasant-tasting, innocuous-looking concoction. When Catherine later learnt that he had regaled them by rolling down the lawn reciting the names of railway stations and electorates before passing out, it was the undeserving mixer of the cocktails and not her youngest born who found himself 'very much in her bad graces'!

In marked contrast to his apparent overall confidence, Malcolm seems to have been inherently shy and inhibited with girls he met at work or university or parties. This of course he cloaked with lively talk, but the young are very quick to sense any deep-seated awkwardness or unease, and he had a certain earnest eccentricity of manner which compounded this. It was to be a few years yet before he met someone who appreciated and understood these things.

At *Harpenden* he shared their musical evenings when he was not at university classes or an election meeting, and like the rest of the family is able to recognise and sing snatches from the major symphonies and operas, though this knowledge does not go 'anywhere near as deep as Alastair's or Colin's'. On one of Charles' earlier visits home, when Malcolm walked in and immediately identified a Czech composer, he said to him interestedly, "Tell me, Malcolm, are you musical or aren't you? You must be — you just recognised that Janacek!" He was gratified but is aware of his limitations. He has a special appreciation of the ornamentation which Charles uses in some of his interpretations, and on Christmas day invariably plays the *Schwarzkopf Christmas Album* which contains some exquisite examples of it. But he does not collect records to any great extent, nor does he pause in the headlong pursuit of his career to listen to music, except at the wheel of his car when he stays tuned to the station where there is classical music, but even then 'only when parliament is in recess'!

In his early twenties, Malcolm, like Colin, though perhaps not so intensely, suffered withdrawal symptoms and doubts about Catholicism, which he had also embraced. Living at home, he was particularly conscious of the effect his 'lapsing' would have on Catherine. About this time he met again the young John Howard, who was by then a solicitor and also actively involved in the Liberal Party. The two saw each other frequently at the headquarters in Sydney where Malcolm worked, became friends, and this was one of the subjects on which they talked.

"Malcolm and I used to have lunch together at the Civic Club which was in the same building as the Federal Secretariat of the Liberal Party," John Howard recalled. "We had many interests in common — politics, especially psephology, the electoral statistics, and we also talked a lot about comparative religion. It's an association which has endured for a long time. I like him. He's a very black and white sort of person — very much like his mother." This last observation was prompted by the fact that he used to have dinner with them sometimes at Turramurra, and was very interested to hear Catherine's forcefully expressed opinions. As others before him, he came swiftly to the conclusion that she was 'a very, very strong lady' and her husband 'a much quieter man'.

In 1962 Malcolm graduated, was promoted to Research Officer, and the following year took six months leave of absence to travel in Europe, look into a matter on behalf of Amnesty International (the newly founded organisation in which he had become extremely interested), and attend Colin's wedding. While staying with Charles and Judy in London, he resourcefully looked up the parliamentary lists to see if there happened to be an Australian-born MP who might care to show him personally over the House of Commons. There was, and he had an interesting few hours there, together with the Charles Mackerras's two young daughters whom he took along. He had some difficulty getting a visa for East Germany to make his inquiry on behalf of Amnesty, but managed to visit East Poland where Charles was conducting, and went on with him to Czechoslovakia for another few weeks, so that it was altogether a very rewardng six months.

He returned in time to assess possibilities, calculate swings and write speakers' notes for the early election called by Prime Minister Menzies for November, 1963, in order to face 'international crises', which included a call for military aid from the beleagured South Vietnam Diem Government. The first promise from Canberra of state aid to private schools, and the P.M.'s barbed reference to the faction-torn but policy dictating ALP Federal Conference as the '36 faceless men', were also contributing factors in the Menzies-McEwen Coalition Government winning back 10 seats from the Calwell-Whitlam led Opposition and Malcolm had a field day with the figures.

In Sydney he continued to see a great deal of John Howard, who had by now been elected to the State Executive of the NSW Liberal Party, and over the New Year Malcolm asked him out sailing. It was a pleasant change for Alan to have one of his offspring interested enough to ask a friend out sailing on *Antares* — though Elizabeth's friend Janie Lemann and other of his 'gems' sailed sometimes — and they went out on several later occasions. Malcolm's relationship with his father does seem to have been on a quite positive basis — probably from the days when he had evinced interest in both power stations and astronomy — and he was somewhat mortified to receive a curt answer when he confided in him that he had decided to cease being a practising Catholic. "Have you?" said Alan dismissively, and went on with what he was doing. He had clearly suffered too much over the whole matter and simply did not want to discuss it further.

In 1964 Malcolm made several trips to Canberra to compile data for the Liberal Party, and at the half Senate election in December of that year found himself in the Central Tally Room scrutinising figures beside Prime Minister Menzies, with whom he had had his memorable exchange as a schoolboy over just such an election. The following year he jumped at the chance of a transfer to the national capital. His sister Joan had just married and, at 25, he was the last of the clan to leave home. He relished being close on hand to the major political scene but at the same time was afflicted with the same loneliness that both Alastair and Colin had felt when leaving Sydney and the family circle. A hostel in Canberra was a very bleak

Menzies (in background, Dame Pattie), Central Tally Room, Canberra, 1964

substitute for *Harpenden* at the end of a day, and at weekends decidedly miserable. He was glad to have the Ian Mackerrases to visit every so often. His uncle and scientist wife — Aunty Jo as the Mackerrases called her — had resigned from the Queensland Institute of Medical Research [8] and were now working as Research Fellows at the CSIRO in Canberra. Malcolm greatly admired his uncle, in particular, his adventurous streak and his swift volunteering to be 'in the thick of things' in both World Wars; he drew him forth on these subjects on Sunday afternoons and heard some lively stories about the camaraderie of those days which finally spurred him to join the CMF.

"I also felt it was a reasonably useful thing to do because I was in favour of Australia's involvement in the Vietnam War at the time," Malcolm commented, adding with his customary frankness, "and furthermore we used to go on camps so it gave me something to do at weekends." He was certainly the only offspring of Catherine and Alan Mackerras ever to evince an interest in military matters. At the same time, he was instrumental, with several others, in forming the Canberra branch of the non-politically aligned Amnesty International, and undertook the presidency of the group for a number of years, working towards the release of specific 'prisoners of conscience' in diverse parts of the world. He recalls,

---

8. Dr Ian Mackerras, director QIMR 1947–61, 'retired, leaving the Institute with a well-established world reputation for research of the first rank'. (K. R. Norris, *Historical Records of Australian Science*, Vol. 5, No. 2 Nov. 1981)

in particular, the Greek girl, Eleni Vougari, and a Brazilian named Batista, a Russian, Levitin and an African, Ncumbe. The great satisfaction of working for the organisation is that it offers help irrespective of class, colour and creed, and in spite of frustrating instances of 'getting nowhere', its policy of bringing to public attention serious cases of injustice achieves many tangible results.

In the second half of 1966, Malcolm was delighted to have Colin and his family take up residence in Canberra — Colin as a Research Scholar at ANU — and before the year was out he applied for a new position himself. It had been a lively few months with a Federal election in November, won in a landslide by the Holt Government, the campaign having centred on the Vietnam issue and the Holt slogan 'All the way with LBJ' — and some new domestic policies were implemented. One of these was the formation of the Commonwealth Department of Education and Science, headed by the Government Leader in the Senate and Works Minister, John Gorton, who decided it would be advisable to appoint a Research Officer to his staff in the education area. Malcolm was one of those who applied and since Senator Gorton had met him a number of times at the Secretariat, both in Sydney and Canberra, and been 'impressed with his knowledge and enthusiasm', he chose him for the job.

Malcolm began work for the Senator in February 1967; ten months later Prime Minister Holt went for his fatal surf at Portsea and in the resulting political upheaval, John Gorton was elected to fill his place. Malcolm continued to work for him in the first two months of his Prime Ministership, while the procedure of a by-election and Mr Gorton's transfer to the House of Representatives took place; when the new Ministry was formed, former Army Minister Malcolm Fraser became Minister for Education and Science, appointed his own staff, and Malcolm lost his job. He and Mr Gorton had got along reasonably well, though Malcolm did not have the impression of having the *rapport* with him that he had expected. This was undoubtedly due to the inherent and unexpected stiffness within his own seemingly extrovert personality which could hardly have been more removed from Mr Gorton's relaxed style. Nevertheless, the Prime Minister wrote him a very substantial reference, recalling his favourable impression of him from 1961 onwards and making particular mention of his 'grasp of detail, especially of a statistical nature', and of his 'helpfulness to members of Parliament interested in the Commonwealth's role in education.'

This enabled Malcolm to get immediate employment as Senior Economic Research Officer with the Associated Chambers of Manufactures. He spent just under two years there, during which time he launched himself into publication and the public eye. In 1968 there was a massive redistribution of Federal electoral boundaries throughout Australia — only 5 of the 125 House of Representative seats to be contested in the forthcoming election remained unaltered — which meant that all previous election figures were now unreliable and inaccurate. As ACT journalist, Jonathan Gaul, commented in *The Canberra Times*, 'Assumptions which have applied about "safe" and "swinging" seats since 1955 for the politician, candidate, party worker, journalist, political scientist or simply the interested private citizen are no longer valid.' It was the perfect opportunity for Malcolm to capitalise on his expertise in this area and he seized it.

His book, *The 1968 Federal Redistribution,* published by ANU Press, providing the new figures and assessments, was brought out in good time for the 1969 Federal election, was favourably reviewed, and became the form guide for the election. On the crest of the wave, he stood for preselection as Liberal Party candidate for the ACT, but was unsuccessful. He decided to confine his ambition to becoming 'the top election expert'. How was he to go about this? Clearly, the best way to do it was to become known on television. Accordingly, he asked for an appointment with the Controller of ABC TV News. "I told him he should take me on as a commentator," he recalled, "and he did."

Malcolm predicted, in print, that the Gorton Government would be returned but with its majority reduced from 38 to 5. He found himself on the ABC News panel in the Central Tally Room on election night with James Dibble, Michael Willesee and John Power. It became clear during the course of the night that he would be only one seat out in this forecast and he was elated.

During this election he also had the opportunity to talk in depth with visiting British election expert and Fellow of Nuffield College, Oxford, Dr David Butler, who influenced him profoundly and to whom he 'owes a big intellectual debt'. It was at Dr Butler's suggestion that he decided to broaden the base of the publication he planned to precede the next Federal election, and to show statistics as far back as 1958, thereby enabling him to draw more comprehensive conclusions.

Now he was really on his way, and he saw that the next step was to qualify as an academic and spend all his working hours in his chosen field. He therefore applied for an appointment in the Department of Political Science at ANU to research his Ph.D. and at Christmas 1969, was able to give his parents, by then at Rose Bay, the good tidings that he was to become a Research Scholar at the university where his brother Colin was already a Research Fellow in Far Eastern History. He had chosen for his study, *The Role of the Candidate in the Electoral Process in Australia.* It was all very satisfying; he had not done so badly for the 'non-intellectual' of the family.

He asked his friend John Howard to dinner at *Balvaig* during that vacation to celebrate and they discussed, as ever, Liberal Party matters. "John was then a young lawyer looking for a seat," Malcolm recalled, "and we discussed the various electorates and possibilities." During the year the two also saw each other at meetings, for Malcolm was elected to the State Executive of the Liberal Party as respresentative of Canberra and Southern New South Wales.

He had long since moved from his hostel, tried sharing a house with friends, and had now moved to a flat. Observing Colin and his family, and the pleasant, separate visits of Catherine and Alan to that household, he decided it was high time he got married. Quite recently, Colin had introduced him to a contemporary of his from Sydney University student days, the poet Les Murray, who was then working in the Prime Minister's Department, and Malcolm formed a friendship with the ebullient Les and his wife Valerie. He felt very comfortable and at ease with them and now sought their advice on the matter of girls and courtship.

"Malcolm," says Les Murray, with some affection, "is an eccentric. He's also a genuine innocent. The most innocent of the Mackerrases. Nearly everything I know about him is something that Valerie and I chuckle about. Like when he decided he'd better get married. He thought it should be laid out like a battle command. 'At what stage do I present roses?' he asked us, and 'At what stage should the goodnight kiss start?' We tried to convince him that a mechanical scheme like this wouldn't work. . . "

However, it was something which he had to find out for himself. At one point he was endeavouring to make a 'battle plan' of this kind work when the girl, who had been in Canberra, returned to Holland. He mentioned to Catherine that he was interested in this girl, and since she had been hoping for some time that he would marry, she promptly gave him a return air fare to Amsterdam. When he arrived, the girl was sensible enough to know that he was not really in love with her, so he used the ticket to visit Northern Ireland where, in Belfast, he survived both the sudden bombing of a building just in front of him in the street *and* admitting to the Rev. Ian Paisley when attending a service at his church that he had just previously been to Mass in the Catholic Church on the Fall's Road! Fortunately a change of luck was coming his way.

Meanwhile, he decided that although he had been elected to the State Executive of the Liberal Party for 1970–71, he would not renew his membership of the party when the office expired since, as a political scientist, he felt it was better not to be actively involved in one party, and to be seen to be bi-partisan in approach (one also suspects that he was becoming susceptible, as was half the nation, to the persuasive, principled idealism of Leader of the Opposition Whitlam). At the same time, he got into the habit, in confident Mackerras fashion, of approaching all the major political figures well before an election and discussing the situation with them. Thus he had long conversations with such personalities as Gough Whitlam, Malcolm Fraser (then Defence Minister), Doug Anthony (newly elected Leader of the Country Party), Jim Killen (later Sir James, then Minister for the Navy) and other prominent politicians, gleaning much valuable information.

He also consulted those of his friends whom he considered had some political *nous* and conducted straw polls. Les Murray remembers many such sessions. When in Sydney, Malcolm sought out people like John Sheldon for an 'outside' informed opinion and at the ABC, where he frequently called, he would buttonhole whoever looked likely. At the same time, he compiled his figures for his forthcoming book, detailing results from all the Federal elections since 1958, made assessments and developed his 'two party preferred system' from ideas evolved in his conversations with the British expert, Dr Butler.

The political scene in Australia was particularly volatile at this time — the McMahon Government had replaced that of Gorton, the looming Whitlam presence was being felt, and it was possible that an early election might be called, thus ruining the market for Malcolm's meticulously researched work. He wondered on occasions whether he might even abandon his project, and would probably have done so if it had not been for the consistent encouragement he received from Associate Professor of Political Theory at the University of Sydney, Professor Henry Mayer, and Peter Cullen, a Canberra lobbyist, and Don Aitken of the ANU.

It was in this somewhat fraught state that he went to a party at a friend's home in Canberra and his eye fell upon a dark-haired girl with a charming smile, one Lindsay Ryan. Conversation flowed pleasantly with her. He discovered that she was a member of staff of the Department of Defence and had just returned from a trip overseas. He invited her out, and they began seeing a great deal of each other. Lindsay hails from Cootamundra on the south-west slopes of New South Wales and has about her a certain balanced sensibility which many country people have, stemming no doubt from the recurring exigencies of their disciplined lives. When Malcolm introduced her to Les Murray, a bush boy himself, the poet at once recognised the 'delicate webbings' of this quality. He also saw that this was the girl Malcolm had been waiting to meet. "He'd finally met someone with a sense of humour," he remarked. "She was the best piece of luck he was ever going to have. She understood him straight away, and recognised his good sides and his good points — of which he has many."

He put the finishing touches to his book; *Australian General Elections,* in February 1972 and Angus and Robertson brought it out very briskly just two months later. It was a resounding success. The statistics he produced on the 1958, 61, 63, 66, 69 elections proved his major point — the efficacy of measuring the possible swing by concentrating on a 'two party preferred vote', that is, Lib-CP/Labor, and assessing the share of each in the preferences of the minor parties in the previous election and their notional share in the forthcoming election. As in his previous book, he made his assessments on what he considered 'safe seats' (requiring a swing of 10% or more to lose), 'fairly safe' (requiring 6-9.9%) and 'marginal' (requiring 5.9% or less). The book also contained an electoral pendulum which he had devised and adapted from a British device known as a swingometer (we will discuss the pendulum further, for it was to become his trade mark), electoral maps, the origin of the name of each seat, observations on the nature of swings, tables of aggregate party support throughout the country, a guide to predicting results and the many factors, including Gallup Polls, involved. The newspaper *Nation Review,* referring to him in the ironic fashion it had adopted as 'our very own psephologist', summed up the work with the comment, 'Mackerras has done all the sums that nobody else has ever got round to in Australia . . . the dedicated election watcher cannot be without it.'

This year Malcolm also became actively interested in New Zealand elections. He attended a Political Science Conference in Wellington and amongst the psephologists gathered there met Nigel S. Roberts, an academic from the University of Canterbury. He found that the New Zealander shared many of his ideas on political analysis, and since the two-party preferred system could be applied very satisfactorily in that country, they decided to work together on data and a pendulum for subsequent elections there.

The word psephologist was at that time in general use — it has been largely abandoned since for the more pronounceable 'political analyst' —

and is derived from the Greek, *phesos*, a pebble used in ancient Greece for voting. 'Man is by nature a political animal', Aristotle had observed, and 2000 years later, at the other end of the world, it was still proving so. Malcolm's book sold very well, and like most pundits, he was predicting a Labor victory for December, 1972. All his activities over these years contributed to his progressive work as a Research Scholar and formed part of the basis of his Ph.D. thesis which he hoped to complete after a further year's work.

Meanwhile, in June, Malcolm and Lindsay announced their engagement. The latter had run the gamut of the somewhat daunting family in Sydney and come through with the qualifying remark from Catherine that she seemed 'rather guileless'. Lindsay thinks she probably was at that time, but it was not very wise of Malcolm to repeat the remark to her. When he saw her reaction, he said, "Well, so what? It simply means without malice." It was a rather uneasy start to her relationship with the family. A very different impression was made with the Sydney friend Malcolm was most anxious for her to meet. This, of course, was John Howard, who had himself married that year, and there was immediate accord between the two couples, which has remained.

In September, Dr David Butler arrived in Australia for the election watching process and commented in an article in *The Australian* that the Mackerras book on the forthcoming election was 'absolutely indispensable'. Malcolm's cup was full and he began telling people exuberantly that the book was as important to those interested in the election stakes as a racebook to a Melbourne Cup punter!

Wedding arrangements for October were now under way and it was decreed that the men in the bridal party were to wear morning dress.

"Righto, Malcolm," said Les Murray, who was to be bestman, "claw hammer coats and striped pants. Are we going as far as top hats?" They were. Lindsay, a church-going Presbyterian, was barely consulted as to the church in which they would be married. "It must be Catholic," said Malcolm, "otherwise it would upset my mother." Accordingly, he went ahead and also arranged for Neil and Colin to take part in the service, thereby making something of a family affair of it. It did not occur to him that Lindsay's parents might have some feelings on the matter, which in fact they had. It was a case of history repeating itself, for Lindsay's mother, of Scottish origin, had married a member of a Catholic family, Bill Ryan, over whom she had agonised when, as a young army sergeant in 1942, he had been one of the first Australian troops over the Kokoda Trail. This had put differences in religious doctrine in their true perspective at the time, but she knew the difficulties and was not happy about the wedding arrangements. Lindsay herself spoke with both the Catholic priest who was to officiate, and her own Presbyterian minister, and it was simply agreed that she would not 'stand in the way of any children of the marriage becoming Catholics if they so chose'.

Les Murray, himself a Catholic convert, enjoyed the whole occasion — even his own blunder. "I didn't know that the best man has to speak about the bridesmaids," he recalled. "I thought I had to propose the toast to the bride and I did. I proposed her in very sincere tones — and the poor girl blushed . . . " He was however, well aware that he had to read

Poet Les Murray proposes the toast to the bride, Lindsay

telegrams, for Catherine and Alan and Malcolm had all approached him separately, and asked him not to read any doubtful ones. They need not have worried, there were none of that ilk, but a great many from the folk down at Cootamundra. The *pièce de résistance* was one from Gough Whitlam which read: *Congratulations. Hoping the two-party preferred system will work as well matrimonially as psephologically.*

Lindsay had serious doubts in the first few weeks if it would. So obsessed was Malcolm with matters political that their honeymoon — 'to the electorate of Forrest in Western Australia' — had all the ingredients of a disaster or a British comedy script, depending on how you viewed it. Since Malcolm had not packed so much as a toothbrush to take with him, an efficient groomsman, Canberra friend Stuart Wilcox, volunteered to drive to the flat with them and briskly pack. Lindsay waited outside in the car 'for about two hours' while the pair rummaged frantically around the place looking for clean clothes, only to find an accummulation of laundry bags awaiting the washing machine and dry cleaner. An old khaki drill outfit, which didn't fit any more, remained. Malcolm squeezed into this and emerged, cheerfully clutching the laundry bags. He felt sure his bride would deal with them. She averted her face and declined. They dropped them off at *Balvaig* and by the time they boarded the train for the great stretch of the Nullabor, they were barely on speaking terms. Malcolm looked so absurd in his bursting at the seams khaki and was so irritatingly unconscious of the fact, striking up election chat with everyone on hand, that Lindsay went off to the other end of the train to get away from him. In Perth, where he had failed to make a booking, they were forced to stay in a 'dreadful, sleazy boarding house'. Lindsay spent the money her mother had given her for eating out at restaurants, buying clothes for

Malcolm who promptly rushed out saying that he had to 'see Charlie Court and a few other politicians and journalists' and suggested that she go and lie on the beach!

She did meet the charming Sir Charles Court and several others but Malcolm continued to perform unpredictable vanishing tricks at the very mention of a new political name and she was despatched to the beach with a book much too frequently. He returned on one occasion particularly pleased with himself after an interview with a Channel 7 reporter, who, as it turned out, was Brian Burke, currently Premier of Western Australia, but Lindsay was by then far too angry with him to even look at the programme. During their journeyings in 'the electorate of Forrest' in the south-west of the State, although the wild flowers and scenery lived up to their reputation and trips to Cape Leeuwin and the Albany Whaling Station were interesting, Malcolm proved hopelessly uncompanionable, being far too busy extracting from all the locals in sight their opinion of the sitting Labor member.

"My friends were astonished to get so many letters from me on my honeymoon," said Lindsay. "I was reading Somerset Maugham's *Of Human Bondage* and I told them it was just too appropriate — here I was, saddled with this dreadful, eccentric man . . . " When they arrived back in Sydney she discovered that he had yet more politicians to see, so she flew home to Canberra alone, more than half convinced that her remarks to her friends had a dismaying element of truth in them. "A total disaster," she says of their first few weeks as man and wife. But a smile is not far off, for with notable tolerance, she managed to salvage the pieces and they have a very stable and happy marriage. Election times remain her least favourite.

Malcolm's 1972 election forecast — that the Whitlam-led Labor Party would win government by 'a majority of about eleven' — was again, as in 1969, only one seat out, for the majority was nine and he was particularly glad to have predicted correctly that the previously Labor-held seat of Forrest in W.A. would go against the trend and return a Liberal. The following year he contributed an interesting article to the Henry Mayer edited volume *Labor To Power*, to which Neil also contributed, and pointed out that the Australia which put Labor into office was the south-eastern section stretching from Tasmania to south-eastern Queensland and listed the many reasons why, in his opinion, South Australia, Western Australia, the Northern Territory and outlying Queensland had not followed suit. In a volume of the prestigious British journal, *Political Studies*, Malcolm's New Zealand colleague Nigel S. Roberts, in an article entitled: *The Roundabout Swings of Australian Psephology* commented on his *Australian General Elections*, concluding, 'Psephologists owe a large debt to Mackerras'. But as so often, when the sailing seems smooth, there were some unexpectedly rough seas ahead.

As though to foreshadow these things, Malcolm was brought up with a jolt by his father's illness in 1973, the distressingly long course it took, and his death in August of that year. He and Lindsay made a number of trips to Sydney to his bedside and Malcolm observed, more strongly than ever before, his mother's lack of sympathetic support for his father during his last months. He commented to Lindsay that he now agreed with Neil's quote from The Mikado, 'Matrimonial devotion did not seem to suit her notion'. He felt sad for his father. On the other hand, Lindsay had now developed a good relationship with Catherine and it was to become closer still in the following few years.

Lindsay's burgeoning harmony with the family was a little disturbed a few months later. They had driven down for the opening concert of the Sydney Opera House, at which Charles conducted the Sydney Symphony Orchestra in a Wagnerian programme and the soloist was the fine, but very large Swedish singer, Birgit Nilsson. At a party after the concert Lindsay shared the general euphoria. Wearing a lovely, new full-skirted gown on which Catherine had complimented her, though it probably did emphasize her then pleasantly rounded contours, she overheard Charles chuckling with Elizabeth, "Malcolm's brought us his own Birgit Nilsson!" The bubble of excitement and pleasure vanished. Young and vulnerable, she was naturally hurt and it took her some time to feel at ease with the family again. Elizabeth later inadvertently helped to heal this wound by extending the warmest and most caring hand when Lindsay's father was desperately ill in hospital in Sydney. Such are the hazards and rewards of any spirited family life, and the Mackerrases were no exception.

During this period, Malcolm brought out a statistical reference book, *New South Wales Elections* (ANU, 1973) which gave figures from 1959 and dealt with the effect on the electorate of the current redistribution, while the following year was both formative in his career and one of crisis for him.

In January 1974, he applied for a position as Lecturer in Government at the Royal Military College, Duntroon, went before an interviewing committee and was appointed for a three year period, tenure, or permanency, being conditional upon his obtaining his Ph.D. A few weeks later he completed his thesis: *The Role of the Candidate in the Electoral Process in Australia*, in which he argued that being a long-term sitting member was not a particular electoral advantage. Colin and several other academics looked through it for him and felt that it was a sufficiently in-depth dissertation on the subject to be acceptable.

The Head of the Department of Government at Duntroon, Professor Brian Beddie, was on leave at the time of Malcolm's appointment, but he had met him and knew his work. The professor's deputy Dr Hugh Smith, who had been one of those to interview Malcolm, made it clear that the department 'certainly expected that he would get his Ph.D.' In the event, it was rejected. It was a severe blow to Malcolm — and very surprising to the senior staff at the College. "I hadn't read it," Dr Smith commented, "but it's the sort of area where you can get quite divergent views in the academic world, that is, on the value of this kind of study. It happens also in my own field of international relations. People who do the more quantitative studies, figures and so on, often find their work very strongly criticised by others — and I think that's what happened in Malcolm's case."

Since the permanency of his position was very important to him and hinged on his getting his Ph.D., it was clear that the only thing to do was to tackle it again. He changed the title to: *Incumbency as an Electoral Advantage* and spent most of his nights during the following year working on and

Malcolm at time of appointment to staff, Duntroon Military College

developing various aspects of it. Meanwhile, other events crowded in, and his spirits soon rose.

He met and found a great deal of *rapport* with the highly articulate Huw Evans of ABC's Current Affairs television and radio programmes, who asked him to go on his list of interviewees for *am* and *pm*. The fundamental difference between ABC Current Affairs Division to which *am, pm*, Notes on the News, Nationwide and Four Corners belong, and the News Division, which, as well as the news, runs election night coverages, is that the former relish those who are prepared to speak out boldly, make surmises and conjectures, while the latter want certainty, and surety. Malcolm, with his propensity for 'sticking his neck out', was clearly going to be much more useful to Current Affairs and so it proved.

A half Senate election was due in May and he spoke on the various programmes as to the effect on the electorate of the controversial happenings — the appointment of Queensland DLP Senator Gair as Australian Ambassador to Eire for one — which preceded it. He was then galvanised into frenzied activity when Prime Minister Whitlam secured a double dissolution following obstruction to an Appropriation Bill in the Senate, and it was necessary to make a full assessment, a new electoral pendulum, and estimates of swing for an election of both Houses of Parliament. By election night he was in a high state of excitement and already convinced in his mind that Labor would go back.

He took his seat with John Power and Ken Begg on the ABC News panel in the National Tally Room and his conviction increased as the votes started coming in. At 9.30pm he said so, prematurely awarding the victory. The former Prime Minister, John Gorton, was consulted and asked to comment on Malcolm's statement. He said, "No, it's too soon. There's going to be a swing about half past ten. They may not get back. Certainly it will be a lot closer than Malcolm thinks." He was right, a fact which soon became apparent to viewers round the nation. In the Tally Room itself, Malcolm then clashed with Liberal supporters in the back gallery who began heckling him. This was anethema to ABC News. Furthermore, the swing was marked, the election became a cliffhanger, and Prime Minister Whitlam was not able to claim victory until 11 days later and with a reduced majority. Malcolm admitted to the ABC that he had made an error of judgment, but defended himself by saying that he preferred to err on the side of liveliness during elections, and be wrong occasionally, than to make 'bland, boring and totally obvious statements'. They did not agree and he lost his job as one of their election coverage panel. It was a severe blow, particularly given his continuing role in their Current Affairs Division.

His friend Les Murray, who had witnessed the controversial programme from his Sydney home, made the general comment, "Malcolm's only got one fault in politics, he goes off half-cocked." Some agree with this, others do not. Huw Evans comments, "I'd rather have somebody who is prepared to say, on the basis of all available evidence at this time on this day, I would suggest *that* is the most likely outcome, which is what Malcolm does, rather than have somebody who is only having five bob each way. Of course, people love to be able to point the finger and say, 'I told you so'. To some extent going on television exposes him. I admire him for having the guts to say what he thinks. He's a forthright person — it's a good healthy quality." He was to interview Malcolm on diverse matters, polemical and political, over the next ten years, and have no cause to change his mind.

Malcolm and Lindsay had made their home in a leafy avenue at Campbell (near Duntroon), one of Canberra's neatly ordered suburbs, and Lindsay was particularly sorry to see the Colin Mackerras household move to Brisbane for she had found a natural affinity with Alyce. Since they were very dissimilar in most respects, she attributes this to their country background and their normal interest in each other's families and doings which she found lacking in the seemingly remote, career-oriented Mackerras siblings. Catherine of course, was *very* different and came to stay with them frequently about this time, for she was researching material on her grandfather, Sir Normand MacLaurin, at the National Library. She developed a special fondness for Lindsay and even considered at one point moving to Canberra to stay permanently with them. It was an alarming thought, for other than Ian Mackerras of whom she was very fond (his wife had died in 1971), the only friend she had there was, paradoxically enough, Lindsay's Presbyterian minister, the Very Rev. Hector Harrison, who often called and the house then rang with amiable theological dispute. However, talk of staying soon ceased. It was now learnt that Lindsay was to follow in Catherine's own footsteps and become the mother of twins, and the house would certainly be ringing with very different sounds which Catherine, with deteriorating health, was no longer equipped to face.

Malcolm made a brief trip alone to England to study the British elections before 1974 was out, and the following year was one of the busiest he had ever known. It was a great joy when, in June, after the days of anxiety which invariably accompany a twin birth, Lindsay was safely delivered of

Malcolm and Lindsay with their twin sons, William and Patrick, 1976

two small sons. They were named William and Alan Patrick (to be known as Patrick) after their grandfathers Ryan and Mackerras, and in due course were baptised by the Rev. Harrison. No one mentioned the baptism to Catherine but Lindsay felt sure she would have understood. Malcolm joked with his friend Les Murray that he had 'named one son for William of Orange and the other for St Patrick' with the idea of keeping both sides of the family happy. The next six months must have been very testing, for although delighted with his sons, Malcolm had multiple tasks on hand and was of little practical assistance with them. It is little wonder that he dedicated the book upon which he had now embarked, '*To my wife Lindsay for her help and tolerance of psephology*'.

He had taken some time from his thesis to prepare a comprehensive pre-election statistical reference book, for 1975 was a period of political turmoil in the nation's capital. The Labor Party, plagued by the Khemlani affair, was lurching from one crisis to another and the Fraser-led Opposition clearly aimed at precipitating an early election. Malcolm worked exceedingly hard to keep abreast also with his other commitments, which included the completion of a paper with Nigel Roberts on *The Utility of Swing in the Analysis of General Elections in New Zealand*, with an electoral pendulum as a guide to the November election there, and he then managed to make a swift trip across the Tasman to study the swing to the National Party which they had predicted.

Meanwhile, on the Australian political scene a financial deadlock approached as a consequence of the Opposition's refusal to pass the Budget Bills in the Senate. In an article in *The Canberra Times*, Malcolm forecast the possibility that the Whitlam Government could be dismissed by the Governor-General, Sir John Kerr, declaring that in his view it was the only proper course open to him — the one other political scientist in Australia to make a similar statement was Dr Paul Gerber of Queensland University. Within weeks of the dramatic event actually occurring, Malcolm's book *Elections 1975* was published. It carried detailed analyses of the 1974 and earlier elections, the full Kerr statement, a number of assessments of the situation, including a combined commentary from Laurie Oakes and David Solomon, and was extremely useful to all those involved in the ensuing bitterly contested campaign. Malcolm had no problem finding alternative television networks to the ABC keen to have his commentary on election nights and finally settled for Channel 10, though on this occasion he made his lively contribution from Channel 7 and recorded the sweeping Liberal-Country Party victory and the beginning of the formidable Malcolm Fraser's 7 year reign as Prime Minister.

There was now the vital matter of Malcolm's thesis, on which hung the tenure of his position in the Department of Government at Duntroon. Over the past year he had continued to work on the second version, *Incumbency as an Electoral Advantage,* and had had many discussions on the subject over morning coffee with a senior colleague, dedicated Canberran and friend, David Daw. He had read the first version of the thesis and the comment on it, and advised Malcolm to spend more time in proving his point of view rather than asserting it as a fact. "Once Malcolm's thought things through and reached a conclusion," said Daw, "you can discuss it till you are blue in the face and he won't change. He needed to be very careful and painstaking in the way he presented his conclusions and we all told him this. If you're writing a book for the market, you can do what you like in a sense, but with a thesis you've got your examiners to think of and how they will receive it."

However, Malcolm felt certain that he was spelling out sufficiently his main premise and his reasons for concluding that being a long-term sitting member was not a particular electoral advantage. Disregarding what seems in retrospect to have been very sound advice, he completed the thesis as he had planned and presented it confidently. All are agreed, including David Daw, that he was extremely unlucky to find yet another board which viewed it unfavourably. In each instance, in 1974 and '77, there were a number of assessors who approved his dissertation and had they sat on either board in a different combination, it would have been passed.

An incisive word on the matter from a detached observer seems appropriate. "Malcolm's chosen discipline does have problems," Huw Evans commented, "but no greater than some of the other social sciences where disciplines have been developed. Basically, the problem stems from the viewpoint held by people with a more classical or old-fashioned academic training. You're applying mathematical calculations to what is in many ways a subjective subject . . . you're trying to draw inferences which trespass into highly objective political evaluation. But from my experience of some of the fields of study to which doctorates are so readily allocated, one can't but be surprised that somebody was not prepared to give Malcolm a go. In any field where you approach a subject honestly, with integrity, with discipline and with perception, irrespective of whether it yields up the pot of gold at the end of the rainbow, if you process the information with those qualities, I think that you deserve some sort of recognition." Few would not agree with this, however, the unfortunate second rejection remained.

It was a serious setback for Malcolm, but, as his colleagues observed, though upset, he took it well and 'pressed on regardless'. In other words, when the University of New South Wales, which administers Duntroon, now required that his position be declared vacant and advertised, he simply applied for his own job, putting forward as strong a case as possible, well aware that there were 'three Ph.D.s' among the applicants.

"There were quite a number of candidates," said Dr Hugh Smith, deputy head of the department, "and they were all interviewed, amongst them, of course, Malcolm. He got his own job back, and in those circumstances, he was appointed permanently. Not getting the Ph.D. was a worrying period for him, but in the end I don't think it will seriously affect his career." A very pleasant Englishman with a sense of humour, Dr Smith added with a smile, "As a colleague it's good to have someone around who's as lively and enthusiastic as Malcolm. The enthusiasm is the important point. He loves what he's doing and communicates it to his students. And I think they're quite pleased to have someone who's a TV analyst — he's a bit different!"

So Malcolm survived this mortifying reverse in his career, having retained his job and, importantly, the affection and respect of his colleagues. "What you see is what you get," said David Daw. "Malcolm's very genuine, no masks, no cover, no role playing. He just gets a little bit trying round election time . . . "

Lindsay, who had witnessed the countless hours poured into the thesis, was vastly relieved to have the whole issue over and done with. She knew that his heart lay in political analysis, that he was not particularly ambitious as an academic — security for his family had been his whole object in studying, and now that was achieved, she was simply glad that he had emerged from his trials with a positive attitude. He could get on with lecturing his large class of first year cadets in Australian politics, his second year students in American politics, enjoy the teaching and the tutorials round the large oak table in his book-lined, map-hung room at the College without underlying worries. There would, she knew, be controversy and drama to spare in the continuing saga of elections, by-elections, State and Federal, and in New Zealand, to say nothing of the American and British elections which he watched like a hawk. She herself, now that their twin toddlers were not quite such an overwhelming handful, had undertaken some editorial work with ANU Press and was finding it a necessary and satisfying stimulus.

"Lindsay is very tolerant and good-humoured about Malcolm," Dr Smith remarked with a gleam of amusement himself, for they often shared a quip or two over his foibles. He now managed to salvage from his thesis and capitalise upon one of the most interesting conclusions he had drawn, namely, 'that the proposition that women candidates lose votes' is totally false. He wrote several articles on the subject and something like a campaign got under way.

His first article, in *The Australian Quarterly*, in September, '77, drew attention to the fact that 'while 50% of voters are women, only 4% of legislators belong to the female sex'. Why? Because, he found, women have traditionally been conditioned not to take much interest in politics and do not stand for election in proportion to their numbers; there is prejudice against choosing women candidates for winable seats, and they are rarely chosen for safe seats; there is the expectation by women that they will be discriminated against; it is supposed that women candidates lose votes and that women do not vote for women. However, he noted that parties do seem to be more prepared to put women into upper houses than lower houses, women constitute 8% of all upper house members, but only 1% of lower house members. It was clearly a rich field to explore. "Then," he said, "various women's groups started quizzing me, and I organised a seminar."

He was able to explode the myth that 'women candidates lose votes' by analysing several Federal election results. He proved, for instance, that the ALP's Joan Child, the only woman member of the House of Representatives from 1974–75, won a higher percentage of the vote than any man Labor had fielded in that electorate, and that when she lost her seat in 1975 in the national swing against Labor, she still gained a higher percentage of the vote than most other Labor candidates across the nation. He continued his battle on behalf of women parliamentarians over the next three or four years (the cause considerably helped by the election of Conservative Leader, Margaret Thatcher, as Prime Minister of Great Britain), and in 1979 was quoted in the mass circulation *Australian Women's weekly*, surrounded by photographs of Kathy Martin, Ann Forward, Ros Kelly and Yvonne McComb, as saying, "It is time women were selected for safe seats." Finally, after the 1980 election, he made a careful analysis of the results in this particular regard (there were 8 women in the Senate, four Labor, three Liberal and Flo Bjelke-Petersen NCP, three in the House of Respresentatives, all on the Labor benches, including once again, Joan Child), and was quoted thus in the *Sydney Morning Herald* the following May: "The evidence seems to me to show that it makes no difference whether a candidate is a woman or a man . . . Women will be elected when parties select them for safe and winable seats." The editorial noted that, commendably, 'the current Federal Parliament . . . has more women members in it than any other since Federation. The imbalance between male and female parliamentarians is untenable and this movement towards redressing it may be one of the most significant political developments of the last few decades. It is certainly long overdue.' Malcolm can be said to have contributed in some small measure to it.

Meanwhile, developments in his own career had also taken place in the latter part of the '70s. He began writing regularly for that national institution *The Bulletin* and an early article, *Wran's a winner — now or later*, in May 1976, after the cliffhanger State Election but before the results were determined, was a good start. He forecast that Neville Wran would be able to form a government, that there would be reform of the Legislative Council and a redistribution based on one-vote-one-value would be accomplished over the next five years, that the former Premier Sir Eric Willis would be in a precarious position, and that the parliament would not last its full term, all of which were correct, and concluded, 'New South

Wales has entered an unusually interesting period in its political life and it does seem safe to forecast the entrenchment of Labor . . . '

From this time, his electoral pendulum, with the assessed swing, has been published in advance of each State and Federal election by *The Bulletin*, is a recognised feature, and has indeed become his hallmark. It must have been satisfying to Catherine in the last year or two of her life to see the pronouncements of her youngest born in this journal which had featured cartoon and comment on the parliamentary role of his great-grandfather, Sir Normand MacLaurin, before the turn of the century, and later, articles by his grandfather Dr Charles MacLaurin, reviews of his work, and her own literary reviews. Now it was Malcolm and politics once more.

We should pause here to give a brief explanation of the pendulum and its pre-election use, for as the present Leader of the Opposition, John Howard, remarked, "It's the first thing you look at. It's become an essential tool of the political trade." Assessed on the two-party preferred system, it ranks the seats in order of their safety, Liberal-Country Party on one side, the Labor Party on the other, and at the base, the marginal seats, which are placed according to the results of the previous election, and show how much an overall swing from 1% to 6% will have upon the result of the forthcoming election. The swing in consecutive elections is never uniform, but the deviations invariably cancel themselves out, so that the number of seats changing remains the number that would change in a uniform swing.

We include in our text, by way of illustration, the pendulum compiled for the 1980 Federal election. It will be seen that the median seat, towards which the arrow points, is Fadden (Lib. Qld.), which means that it is the middle seat in terms of party strength at the previous election. Fadden ranks 63rd out of 125 whether you begin at Bradfield (top left) and finish at Sydney (top right) or vice versa. After all preferences had been distributed in Fadden, the 1977 result was 56% for Liberal's Don Cameron and 44% for Labor's Clem Jones, Therefore, in the 1980 election, Labor needed a swing of 6.1% to win Fadden. On a uniform movement Labor therefore needed a 6.1% swing to win the election. In order to use the pendulum, you make your own guess at the overall two-party preferred vote for the coming election, calculate the swing by subtracting that guess from the distribution of the vote in the previous election, and by applying it to the pendulum, you find the amount of swing which you consider is needed.

Before looking at the ramifications of that election, we must touch upon the range of activities undertaken by Malcolm in the latter part of the '70s which were to become part of the continuing pattern of his life. New Zealand holds a special place in his affections, he enjoys the challenge of the different, smaller electorate, of meeting the people and the politicians, of producing a pendulum and commentary on elections there, of conferring with his knowledgeable friend, Nigel Roberts. He finds the whole democratic process absorbing.

He also became a regular speaker on the excellent ABC programme: *Notes on the News*. "He's forthright," remarked Huw Evans, "and that

THE ELECTORAL PENDULUM (1980)

Electoral Pendulum, 1980

makes him very useful in terms of the media." A glance at copies of Malcolm's broadcasts in 1979 confirms this at once.

His topics ranged from the much debated question of the possibility of Australia becoming a republic, to the contentious issue of abortion, to American elections, to the treatment of dissidents throughout the world, whether in Russia or Indonesia, and the role of Amnesty International. He has very definite views on all these subjects and sums them up forcefully. Looking objectively at pro and anti-abortion arguments, he concludes, 'I do not share the widespread criticism of Right to Life's tactics. In a democracy any group of people are entitled to question candidates on their attitudes . . . involving legislation that may come before Parliament. They are quite entitled to campaign for the defeat of candidates who will vote against their views. Those who hold opposite views should try to counter rather than condemn the campaign tactics of Right to Life. Similar campaigns were conducted in the 1978 U.S. Congressional election, the 1978 New Zealand election and the 1979 British election.' Thus he puts it in perspective.

Perhaps his most interesting comment, however, was on republicanism in Australia. We find him open-minded on the proposition then being put by that most prominent of its advocates, Gough Whitlam, that we follow the lead of Commonwealth countries such as India and change status from monarchy to republic while remaining within the Commonwealth, but thoroughly opposed to the view, adopted by others, of a change from essentially parliamentary to presidential-style government similar to the U.S.A., where the President is able to appoint members of his Cabinet from the entire range of personnel available anywhere in the country. He summed this up: 'In my view, since ministers make political decisions they should be professional politicians and thus trained to understand the political consequences of their decisions. While . . . the presidential system provides a far greater pool of executive talent our parliamentary system gives something more important, namely a greater likelihood that ministers will have political experience . . . authority and an ability to work as a team.'

He then pointed out that in his view the major defect of the American system lies in the extraordinary difficulty in removing a President (in 190 years only one American President has been forced to resign mid-term, by contrast in only 80 years, 8 Prime Ministers have done so in Australia) and argued: 'When Richard Nixon quit the Presidency in August 1974, many saw his decision as a triumph for the American system. True, it did show that a real threat of impeachment could force a President out. I would have thought, however, that Nixon should decently have resigned ten months earlier when he dismissed the Watergate special prosecutor. The public outcry which that dismissal caused would have been enough to topple an Australian Prime Minister immediately. The inflexibility of the American system delayed the President's deposition by ten months, during (which) the nation went through a wholly unnecessary ordeal.' His comment concluded; 'The greatest challenge to democracy in the last fifth of the 20th century will come from the accelerating pace of technological and social change. In this situation we need a responsive and flexible system of government. In a world which fears the shortage of energy it is difficult to enthuse about a situation in which President Carter can put forward sensible plans for the conservation of energy only to find them stalled by Congress.' These are the sort of assessments he continues to make on Current Affairs programmes which do much to refute the widely held notion that he is a lightweight devoted almost exclusively to statistical analysis.

Before the year was out the household at Creswell Street was made complete with the birth of a daughter, Ailsa, who delights all their hearts, and with the new decade Malcolm turned his attention to the preparation of a book, *Elections* 1980, another comprehensive guide similar to the one he had published in '75, for the Federal election due towards the end of 1980.

This time he included a comment on the increasing importance of the Gallup Polls by an expert on the subject, Bill Maley, who, in an interesting article, made the vital point that these surveys 'provide an estimate of voting intention at the time of the survey rather than a prediction of the ultimate outcome of the election', since many factors, from late swing and undecided voters to 'feedback' (some people vote largely on the basis of expectations of how others will vote, so that you may get a 'bandwagon effect' or an 'underdog effect'). Malcolm noted, in the section accompanying the pendulum he prepared, an increase in the number of marginal seats and commented: 'increased electoral volatility make the outcome of future Australian elections more difficult than ever to predict'.

This was only too true and it is a pity that he did not stay with his original prediction, made in this book, *Elections* 1980 and published a few months before the October election, viz, that there would be a 4% swing to Labor, and the Fraser Government would be returned with its majority reduced to about 19 seats (a loss of around 15 seats). This was close to the final result (majority 23, seats lost 13). However, in the month before the election he vacillated wildly in his predictions, with the ever changing Gallup Polls, which did indeed indicate a very volatile electorate. In his *Bulletin* article in mid-September he stayed more or less with his original prediction (Fraser Government victory of 13 – 19 seats), two weeks later when Gallup Polls showed a decisive swing to Labor, he changed his tune and thought that the Government would be defeated. A week later he was in a state of 'great uncertainty' and vacillated between a narrow Government win and a 23 seat Labor victory.

The fact is that the electorate *was* very uncertain and *was* gearing itself for change, but being essentially conservative, took another three years to bring that change about. Malcolm was simply caught up in this vortex and would have been infinitely wiser to remain silent. But that, of course, was not in his nature. His reputation as a pundit suffered badly in consequence, for he was so spectacularly wrong on this occasion that he played into the hands of critics, his predictions became something to joke about, and everyone forgot that he was more frequently proved right than wrong.

The Department of Government at Duntroon has never quite lived down a visit paid to them at this time by journalist, Stephen Downes, of *The Age*. The Royal Military College is overall an impressive place. The entrance, resplendent with regimental badges and Rising Sun leads

Malcolm and Pendulum (by courtesy of The Age)

through a poplar lined driveway to the famous parade ground, lovely old Duntroon House, a fine modern chapel and the main college buildings set in pleasant grounds. There is then a severe falling away. 'The Department of Government,' the journalist observed, only too accurately, 'is a small temporary looking building in a forlorn and windy corner of the campus. A corridor runs the length of the structure like a backbone . . . doors slam shut . . . there is a crash . . . the whole building shudders . . . Malcolm Mackerras, the king of psephological swing, has a room (there).' He continued in this satirical vein and while giving him credit for his achievements, in particular, the electoral pendulum, the inference to be drawn throughout is that of Malcolm as a lightweight entertainer rather than a serious analyst. The article contains such phrases as 'Election time is his Spring . . . he flits about in the flame of the national media . . . but like any moth his hour is brief and superficial.' There were also some gratuitous comments describing him as having 'the appearance of an outer-suburban grocer', with his 'short ginger hair . . . white striped shirt, nondescript slacks' and so on, which Lindsay found very trying for she had never been able to persuade Malcolm away from his total indifference to clothes.

"He showed us all that article," said David Daw, who is still capable of wincing at the mention of 'forlorn and windy corner'. "I'd have hidden it. It was awful. But it was also compulsive reading!" Unfortunately, it did tend to set a pattern and he became fair game for all. He accepted this cheerfully enough, for he had weathered worse storms and knew that there was necessarily an adverse side to being in the public eye, which he frankly admits enjoying.

He was much more perturbed at some fairly widespread questioning of the accurate working of his electoral pendulum, which in fact worked perfectly, deviations in the swing cancelling themselves out. The pendulum had indicated that Labor would need a 6% swing of the two-party preferred vote to win, and when, on election night, the term 'swing' was used in reference to the Labor primary vote which was running 7% ahead of 1977, it caused confusion among many who failed to take into account a sharp decline in support for the minor parties, which left the net movement between Lib-N.P. and Labor at only 4%, and therefore 2% short of that needed to topple the Government. British expert, Dr David Butler, in Australia observing the election, was quick to point this out in the following *Current Affairs Bulletin*, and also commented, 'The system worked in its familiar and predictable way. A 4% swing in the preferred vote produced a net switch of 13 seats from the Government to the Opposition which was almost exactly what would have been expected from the Mackerras pendulum. Five seats that would not have fallen to Labor on a uniform swing were won by them. But 6 they should have gained on a uniform swing were not won. The one freak result was Labor's loss of Riverina. The predictability of the system does not depend on total uniformity but only on variations more or less cancelling each other in a random manner. This happened again in 1980. Yet again, the Mackerras pendulum worked well.' Malcolm also no doubt slept well after this authoritative confirmation of something which he himself knew to be true.

Other events were soon upon him, amongst them the Franklin Dam referendum — he was very caught up in this, having travelled to Tasmania and journeyed along the tranquil far reaches of the Gordon River which he fervently felt should remain undisturbed — and he also covered for the first time a Tasmanian election, in May '82, correctly predicting a Liberal win; but it is not possible here to cover all Malcolm's activities.

It is important, in the overall context, to pause instead and discuss the opinion of some of Australia's elder statesmen and prominent political figures on the value and effectiveness of political analysis. Gough Whitlam comments, "It's very valuable. Malcolm Mackerras has done a pioneer job — played a useful role. He analyses individual electorates and that is useful. Before the war Australia was homogeneous, now it has diversified and this has a geographical basis. He examines aspects of the way people vote in various regions and the changing Australian population has meant that political analysis has a geographical basis. So it is valuable to examine it in this way."

On the other hand, Malcolm Fraser remarks, "Politicians make mistakes if they take too much notice of political analysts — or of newspaper editorials. But Malcolm's electoral pendulum works reasonably well." Former Liberal minister, Sir James Killen, comments "The forecasting of elections is very dear and near to the heart to all practising politicians. What is likely to happen? There are a number of criteria available, but the final judgment is, in my view, substantially a subjective one. And that's where the difficulty comes in. It's not everyone who has the knack, the art or the gift, call it what you will, of being impartial and being able to control personal prejudice with respect to a gathering of objective facts and that's where Mackerras has proved exceptional because he's managed to do just that . . . You hear people say 'Only 1.1% swing is needed to win such and such a seat' — and they've worked it out on the pendulum he's put together. Furthermore, he studies not only Federal elections but State elections as well — and that's a very broad field. To be able to say what's likely to happen in a Victorian election, to master all the facts, all the elements that go into an election in that State, and also in New South Wales, and Queensland, is a difficult thing because there are so many different factors. In general terms, his forecasts have been fairly accurate. If I could be as accurate in picking a programme at Eagle Farm tomorrow, as he is in picking an election, I'd be immensely cheered!" Malcolm lived up to this comment early in 1982 when three of his horses came home in quick succession — correct predictions on the Lowe by-election (Federal), the Drummoyne by-election (NSW) and a very close pinpointing of results in the Cain Government's victory in Victoria.

When asked to comment on political analysis and Malcolm's role therein, Australia's present Foreign Minister, Bill Hayden, who knows and has a high regard for Colin in the Asian Studies field, commented, "Malcolm Mackerras is known to me because of his involvement in a very narrow field of electoral statistics. It is my understanding, although I cannot vouch for it, that the political pendulum system, reputedly evolved by him, is in fact directly derived from overseas. While his work represents 'mechanics tools' for politicians, frankly it is of about a level of accomplishment fairly commonly adopted by a wide range of politicians with a background of varying academic qualifications."

It has already been stated that Malcolm derived the idea of a pendulum from a British device known as a 'swingometer', but the concept of reducing all election statistics to a two-party preferred vote was developed by him, as was that of having a chart of marginal seats. "Earlier Australian political analysts had naturally thought of both those things," said Malcolm "so I do not claim that they are 100% original but others did not develop or pursue them to their logical conclusion."

To complete the assessment from both sides of the political fence, two MHR's well-known to Malcolm were approached, Manfred Cross (Labor, Brisbane), and Don Cameron (Liberal, Moreton). The former, it seems, did not have time to spare from the busy political round to comment, the latter remarked, "Malcolm is a blend of uniqueness in his own right . . . he has elevated to professional status the art of analysing, predicting and presenting Australian politics . . . the Mackerras pendulum is now such a part of the Australian political system that in the centuries ahead when people seek the origin of the name, it could well be the instrument which unearths a remarkable 20th century Australian family." Given the ubiquity of the political scene, it seems entirely possible that the archaeologist's trowel may chance first upon evidence of Malcolm's works!

In 1982 he had the opportunity to examine firsthand the American political system and in June, at the invitation of the American Ambassador and under the auspices of USICA's International Visitors' Program, attended a Multi-Regional Project on *The American Governmental System* which began with a week in Washington 'to bring together leaders from overseas and the United States . . . and provide an overview of the structure . . . and dynamics of the U.S. political process'. It did just that, and he met many politicians, public figures and media representatives in the process, and with a number of other delegates visited cities in Arkansas and Oregon.

Like his father and Colin, he was very impressed with the erudition and warm co-operativeness of his American colleagues and was delighted later that year to be honoured, together with Canberra's Chief Electoral Officer, Keith Pearson, with an invitation from President Reagan to attend a *Conference on Free Election* (convened by the United States Dept. of State and other instrumentalities on the President's initiative) in Washington in November that year.

This was by far the most stimulating conference he had ever or was ever likely to attend, with distinguished speakers from France, Germany, Spain, Turkey, India, Brazil, Venezuela, Japan, the Philippines, Thailand and a dozen other countries, including of course, Great Britain and Canada, with papers ranging from *Elections in Developing Countries*, and *Establishing Free Elections against a predominantly non-demoncratic background*. The keynote of the conference, spelt out earlier by President Reagan in an address to the British Parliament, was 'to foster the infrastructure of democracy'. It was a resounding success in terms of exchange of ideas and Malcolm returned with a deeper knowledge of specific problems, of the whole democratic process and 'a feeling for America and American politics' which he has since, he feels, been able to pass on to his students.

This peripatetic year of Malcolm's made life rather lonely for Lindsay and the children, but there were also some highlights. Amongst them, was having John Howard (then Treasurer in the Fraser Government) and his wife Janette to dinner at Creswell Street. Canberra was *en fête* at the time for the opening of the National Art Gallery and it was altogether an occasion. She continues to meet a number of interesting people, either with Malcolm or through her work with ANU Press, such as the writer, Blanche D'Alpuget, who has become a friend — and she remains one of those who would not exchange the serene pace and space of Canberra for any other city, except at election time when the fever abroad is personified in Malcolm. Then she likes to keep to herself.

There was now another Federal election ahead. In current Affairs sessions with Huw Evans in the second half of '82 Malcolm predicted, as the economy went from bad to worse and Bill Hayden's approval rating in the polls jumped remarkably, that Prime Minister Fraser would not bring forward the election due at the end of 1983. He was wrong. He was also incorrect in predicting a win for Labor in the Flinders by-election but commented soon afterwards in an article in *The Bulletin* 'On behalf of the people of Australia, the people of Flinders have delivered an ultimatum to the Labor Party: Change your leader or lose the 1983 election. The speculated 1982 general election was in all probability Opposition Leader Bill Hayden's last chance to become Prime Minister. Australia's next Labor Prime Minister will be Bob Hawke — in 1983 or in 1986.' Mr Fraser set the election for March '83 and Malcolm promptly remarked that the Prime Minister would 'go down in history as the turkey who called an early Christmas'.

This election was one of his successes in forecasting. He remained consistent in his prediction of a Labor victory throughout, becoming even more certain when Bill Hayden stepped down and Bob Hawke assumed the ALP leadership. In the tense National Tally Room on election night, Mr Hawke and other political leaders manned one of the two panels at Channel 10's booth, while the analysts, David Butler, Laurie Oakes, Malcolm and others, sat at the other, using a newly designed CSIRO Predictive Computer in which Malcolm had great faith. At 9.10 p.m. the computer figures predicted a 21 seat ALP victory and Malcolm himself 'a labor landslide'. The computer was very close and Malcolm proved right as the Labor Party swept in and Mr Hawke assumed the Prime Ministership with a majority of 25.

Next morning, amongst the election headlines in the *Sydney Morning Herald* was an article, accompanied by a photograph of Malcolm standing by the Channel 10 booth, and comment from political journalist, David Dale, which concluded, 'The night also restored Malcolm Mackerras's reputation as an election picker. As the result looked more and more like his original prediction, Mr Mackerras kept getting up from his chair behind the 10 desk and beaming out over the crowd towards the tally board. He looked so proud you felt like leading the crowd in three cheers.' He was, in fact, checking tally board figures with computer figures. It was hard to win.

Malcolm checks figures Central Tally Room, 1983 (by courtesy Sydney Morning Herald)

Nevertheless, he enjoyed the questioning and queries with which many interested election watchers plied him in the following weeks. About a fortnight after the election, his brother Charles, who was then in the midst of his second year's season as Chief Conductor of the Sydney Symphony Orchestra, was in Canberra with the orchestra. "I asked Malcolm and Lindsay to come back to my room after the concert for a drink," recalled Sir Charles, "but Malcolm got surrounded by all the members of the orchestra — 'I want to talk to you! You said so and so!' I just slithered into the background." Sir Charles also commented on Malcolm's outspoken remarks about leading political figures. "I was surprised after the things Malcolm said about him that Mr Fraser would even talk to me. He comes to all the concerts and so does his mother — and they were both very charming to me." It is certainly a pleasant attribute of the music-loving former P.M.

In October that year, Malcolm went to Brisbane to comment on the forthcoming Queensland election. There had been unprecedented drama over the Terry White affair and the Premier Joh Bjelke-Petersen's controversial handling of it, manoeuvring to force the resignation of the 7 Liberal Ministers, the whole Liberal Party debacle, and the Premier's seizing of the opportunity to campaign for sole government by the National Party. There was widespread criticism and controversy within the State itself — 'Joh must go', 'He's gone too far this time', and similar comments were heard frequently. He was being hard pressed by the media, and the day before the election that former doyen of Australian political journalists,

Elgin Reid, had a large feature article in the *Courier-Mail:* END OF JOH BJELKE-PETERSEN ERA. Malcolm arrived similarly convinced and was met by Colin, who was no doubt thinking along the same lines. He then went off to talk with political scientists from Queensland University and other very well informed people on the local scene. They reminded him of the deep-seated, widespread support for the Premier throughout the State which he criss-crossed so frequently and patently cared about, but he did not listen to their cautionary advice. Instead, he went on television and forecast a resounding defeat for the redoubtable Joh (now Sir Joh) Bjelke-Petersen, who later that night replied that Malcolm would 'end up eating crow'. He in turn replied, again on prime television time, "It's the Premier who will be eating crow."

As everyone is very well aware, the Premier confounded all his critics and won government for the National Party with a swing of 12% and remembered to remark as he left the tally room to join triumphant supporters, "This Mackerras will have to wipe the egg off his face." Malcolm, looking somewhat distrait and sitting on the same panel as John Barton and Mike Walsh (impassive on this occasion), nevertheless quickly assessed figures for viewers and picking up the pieces of his credibility as well as he could, commented, "I was utterly wrong, but this is a lesson in the importance of leaders — the vital importance in the role of a leader." He returned to Canberra considerably chastened, but it was another of

Malcolm and Colin, Brisbane 1983

those occasions, which his colleagues at Duntroon have observed from time to time, of his being quite immovable and impervious to advice once he has thought things through and made up his mind. It is a quality which seems likely to stay with him — with both good and bad results.

A month later, the long-standing Federal member for Moreton, Sir James Killen, resigned. "One of my favourite politicians," Malcolm commented, "He did the right thing, he waited awhile after the Federal election to resign — and they don't all do that, McMahon didn't, Snedden didn't. Killen is not only articulate and amusing — but he's straight. He's loyal, he wasn't just thinking of his superannuation." He was glad to see the former member for Fadden, Don Cameron, whom he regards as 'a very good campaigner', contesting the seat and *The Canberra Times* headlined his prediction of 'an easy Liberal win', quoting his comment that 'the slaughter of the Queensland Liberals in the recent State election has no relevance in the Moreton by-election'. There would, he said, be a swing to Cameron of around 4%. He also contended that history was on his side, for in the 3 by-elections in Liberal-held seats under a Federal Labor Government since World War II (Parramatta '73, Wannon '83, Bruce '83), none have fallen to Labor. He was right; Don Cameron won with a 3% swing and Malcolm's own spirits were swiftly restored by his forecast.

He now put his mind to the matter of Constitutional Reform and the complicated issues involved in the proposed referendum being put forward by the Hawke Government. It is not possible to pursue these in detail here, but he delivered several astute and very straight-shooting addresses (*Notes on the News*, ABC), condemning the proposal for Simultaneous Elections as 'the most dishonest ever put to the Australian people . . . its purpose is not to give the people benefit of joint elections for the two Houses . . . (but) to give more power to the Prime Minister and to weaken the independence of the Senate'. He commended the non-Government Senate majority for their principled stand in voting to insist on an amendment to the Referendum Bill, knowing that their action 'would give a short and medium term advantage to the Labor Party', and enable it 'to use the existing constitutional arrangements to justify an early election'. He himself thought an early election justified, not for the reasons put forward but in order to bring together the House of Representatives and half Senate election which had been thrown out of kilter by former Prime Minister Fraser's calling of an early election in 1983. As is now very much a matter of recent history, there was a major redistribution, and the early election took place in December '84. A somewhat bemused electorate voted at the same time on the referendum proposals on Constitutional Reform (both were defeated), the Labor Government, which had been 'odds on' for the first time ever, was returned with a proportionately reduced majority — Malcolm and many other pundits had predicted a gain — and the Opposition Leader, Andrew Peacock, unjustly hounded by the press, went down in a bravely fought campaign which won him general admiration.

A subsequent sidelight was an interview Malcolm had with Richard Carleton on an ABC Current Affairs programme in which he commented, "In 2 months we shall see that Labor would have had 4 more seats if it had not been for the huge informal vote." This, of course, was due to the difficulty people found in coping simultaneously with the referendum questions, and makes one wonder how Constitutional Reform is ever to be efficiently implemented.

Malcolm has now been appointed a Senior Lecturer at Duntroon and has resigned his presidency of Amnesty International in Canberra while still undertaking some 'Embassy work' on their behalf. He is also invited to the British High Commission on the eve of elections to make commentaries on British elections as results unfold, and continues to predict, with a good measure of success (in spite of the Queensland setback), every Australian State election as it occurs.

He covered, for example, the tightly fought Victorian election in March '85. His electoral pendulum, featured as ever in *The Bulletin*, showed Monbulk as the 'litmus test' electorate, indicating that a 3.2% swing would be necessary to unseat the Labor Government, and his accompanying article predicted, correctly, that Premier Cain would 'face a tussle for the upper house', would fail in his objective of winning a majority there (which would have put his party 'in a position to abolish the Legislative Council'), but that his Government would be re-elected. And so it transpired. It is little wonder that Malcolm becomes increasingly fascinated with the continually evolving democratic process.

Later in the year, he watched the tense struggle for the leadership of the Opposition between Andrew Peacock and John Howard and the latter's unexpectedly swift victory which saw commentators such as Richard Carleton confounded. It is clear from continuing tensions within the Liberal Party on economic policy and the leadership, that the ultimate judgment as to which will make the better leader remains uncertain.

The years ahead look extremely interesting for those whose *raison d'etre* is political analysis. It is instructive that ABC News Division has now reversed its 1974 decision, fallen into line with Current Affairs and asked Malcolm to cover the 1986 Tasmanian election, aware no doubt, like its clear-sighted Huw Evans, that his outspoken commentary enlivens television election coverage. John Howard, discussing his pronouncements, remarked, "They're always very entertaining and his knowledge of statistics is unrivalled. I don't always agree with his predictions, but whoever does in politics?"

Canberrans generally regard Malcolm as 'a character' which, in the Australian vernacular, is praise indeed, and Lindsay has learned to live happily with the idiosyncrasies of her particular Mackerras.

He has made a worthwhile and original contribution to political analysis in this country, a fact which is recognised by English, New Zealand and American colleagues alike. He could be said to have carved his own highly individual niche in Australian politics.

Chapter 10

Catherine and Alan (II)

As the family at Turramurra diminished, Catherine was able to devote more of her considerable talent and energies to writing and at the same time Alan's career took an unexpectedly satisfying turn. Life entered a new phase for each, but as ever, it was separate, not shared. It had become more of an effort for them to present a united front, but the days were too full and busy to dwell upon the fact.

Catherine had never allowed her literary talent to languish completely. Throughout the 1950s, articles with her strongly individual flavour appeared again in the pages of *The Bulletin* as they had done in the 1920s. Now she wrote as well for the *Catholic Weekly* on a range of subjects which covered literature, history, theology, music and art, and also did some reviews for the music journal *Canon*.

She had lost none of her touch. Discussing the paradox of this 'materially-minded' generation's appreciation of the paintings of El Greco and the music of Bach, she concludes, 'Surely there is still hope for a generation that has come to revere the most profoundly Christian of musicians, the most purely spiritual of painters.' Describing the surgery of her great-grandfather, Dr Charles Nathan, which survived into the first decade of the 20th century she wrote, 'There was the horsehair and mahogany examination couch which was too high to climb unaided; and a tall pair of antiquated scales, all black and white, most beautifully made, on which I longed to stand, but was forbidden. I did not dare to open the glass front of the great, massive bookcase, through which there shone the gilded titles of well-bound surgical handbooks from a day long past.' So the dark recesses of that room are conjured — and the gleam of instrument, kidney dish and starched white sheet.

Reviewing a newly released Wagner recording, she states authoritatively: 'When Wagner first wrote the words for *The Ring*, he was under the influence of the Oedipus Rex of Sophocles; later he discovered Schopenhauer, whose disciple he remained. Many of us who admire Wagner's music, reject his confused philosophy . . . '

She declares the performance [9] of *Die Gotterdumerung* (Act III) 'in some ways excellent, on the whole disappointing' and makes her major point:

---

9. Boston Symphony Orchestra, soloist, Eileen Farrell, conductor, Charles Munch.

'To me the luckless heroine of *The Ring*, who has to suffer the disadvantages of both humanity and divinity, is never more human than in her frenzied abandonment of life; and I do not think that Farrell sufficiently emphasizes (this) . . . It is when Brunhilde has ceased to sing that the orchestra is most unsatisfactory. I hear little attempt to realise the poignancy of the *Redemption Through Love* motive as it soars above the solemn chords depicting Walhall dissolving in flames; nor does Mr Munch gather together the threads of the great complex Tetralogy into a majestic final consummation. He has, in fact, made his climax too early . . . ' Turning to the excerpts from *Tristan and Isolde* she finds, 'It is better, the orchestra distils something of the very essence of the Romantic spirit, which is the Prelude . . . ' The whole review indeed distils something of the essence of Catherine herself; it is little wonder that she was so often able to hold a drawing room audience in thrall.

Nevertheless, up to this time, although she had always wanted to write a comprehensive work, it had not been possible. Now she was urged to do so by Alan's cousin, the well-established writer and her own very good friend, Nancy Phelan. The friendship between them had grown, despite the age gap (Nancy was still at School when Catherine was thirty and the mother of two) for they had the same unusual literary background, were both Anglophiles and had much in common. She commented. "When my sister and I were little, our grandmother told us such riveting tales, I remember someone saying, 'The Creagh children talk about Abraham and Isaac and the Kings and Queens of England as if they lived next door!' Catherine was brought up like that too. She treated characters from history

Catherine at Harpenden, 1960

and literature as real people. She would say suddenly, out of the blue, 'That expression on Queen Victoria's face when she was listening to music, you know . . . '. It gave her conversation a marvellous feeling of life. And I'd always admired her writing. I often told her she belonged more to the 18th than the 20th century. She had the grand manner, there was a stately 18th century elegance in her writing — like Gibbon. She didn't have any imaginative ability in the creative sense. When she said to me, I think I'll write a book on my family', I always replied, 'Why don't you? Why don't you?' And so she began the one on Isaac Nathan.''

Nancy, very much the vital connecting link in the family, also has recollections of one of Alan's visits to her home at Mosman after Saturday sailing, and of her husband, Peter, who was in the process of adding yet another adapter to a power point, saying with alarm, ''For goodness sake, don't let Alan see this!'' Alan overhearing this was vastly amused.

Alan's outstanding ability as an engineer seems to have been in his keen grasp of theory and abstraction, the gift of elucidating these things and applying them in practice. His ambition never matched his ability. His colleague of early Sydney Municipal and County Council days, Tom (T.J.) Keating commented, ''He was never interested in status, just deeply interested in engineering and he was possibly the ablest engineer the Council ever had, certainly one of the very best.'' This opinion is shared by another early and younger associate, John Sproule (currently System Development Engineer at the Electricity Commission of NSW). Both men noted his natural ability to teach, and the latter remarked, ''He loved seeking simple explanations, going back to fundamentals, and enjoyed helping young people — and their company as well.'' Alan had also enjoyed the role of lecturer at the Worker's Educational Association and the NSW branch of the British Astronomical Association for a very long time, and the family had often noticed how frequently his advice was sought by their young friends.

In view of these things, and the very important fact that Catherine, with the personal magnetism which characterised her, had assumed the teaching role in their own household, it is not as surprising as it may seem that when a sudden opportunity in this direction arose, Alan seized it.

One cold, clear day in June 1957, he was at work at the Electricity Commission on a special investigation into transmission which he had under way, when his old friend, David Myers, at that time Dean of the Faculty of Electrical Engineering at Sydney University, phoned and asked if he knew of 'some bright young man' at the Commission who might be prepared to join his staff. The professor told him that he and his colleagues felt there was a need for someone with more extensive practical experience of theoretical aspects of engineering than they at present had. The upshot of this was that Alan called back an hour later and said, ''What about me?'' So it came about that he gave up his career at the Electricity Commission and was appointed Senior Lecturer in Electrical Engineering at the University of Sydney.

Professor Myers attended his first lecture and it quickly became obvious to him that Alan had made his decision because of his love of teaching. ''I was most impressed,'' he recalled, ''by his ability to present his subject in rigorous but readily understandable terms. That first lecture also produced its moment of humour. Alan made a statement which was in contradiction to what I had told the students earlier. This caused great hilarity — but he swiftly pointed out that we had been dealing with the subject in quite different context." So Alan set out on the path which was to bring him the greatest satisfaction.

Towards the end of the year when Russia launched its first satellite, Professor Myers noticed that 'press reports, purporting to be scientific, were either incorrect or misleading', and he felt that this state of affairs should be rectified. "What was necessary," he said, "was a short publication, couched in understandable terms, so that students who had studied mathematics to a reasonable level could share the excitement of the exploration of space. I thought at once of Alan Mackerras." Within several days of being approached on the matter, Alan had ready a text and diagrams for a pamphlet entitled: *The Role of the Satellites*. Dr Harley Wood, NSW Government Astronomer, and well-known to Alan, wrote a preface, and it was published soon afterwards by Shakespeare Head Press.

This booklet, explaining the orbit of Sputnik I, is absorbing even for those not mathematically inclined, and was widely read and appreciated. Alan clearly enjoyed compiling it and permitted himself a light-hearted moment in the course of the text. In summing up one aspect, he stated, 'On the assumption (then) that there is no atmosphere, a satellite close to the earth's surface would have a periodic time of 84 minutes', and added, 'if Puck tried to "put a girdle round about the earth in forty minutes" he would have to attain a velocity at which he would fly away from the earth never to return. To keep him in his orbit a force over four times as strong as gravity would be required. Presumably the explanation is that, being a fairy, he could defy the laws of nature.' It is interesting that in spite of the lack of normal communication between himself and Catherine, he continued to ask her, as in their early years, to 'check his English' before publishing a paper and did so with this small but still valued publication. It is an indication of just what might have been if Catherine had been prepared to mine, rather than close up, that which still existed between them.

It was clear that Alan's image in the academic world was far from that of the somewhat austere, withdrawn figure he presented at home. Professor Myers left Sydney before 1960 for a Canadian university and when he returned was appointed Vice-Chancellor of Melbourne's La Trobe University and therefore drifted out of touch with Alan, but remembers that a number of students formed the habit of staying behind to talk to him after lectures, even when in danger of missing their subsequent one. "I believe that many students who attended his lectures and his laboratory classes over a period of years were greatly influenced by him and profited from his extraordinary ability to teach," he commented from his retirement in Melbourne. "Alan was also very sympathetic to the underdog and went to great lengths to help those who were struggling with their course. He was extremely popular with the students and with colleagues, and his advice was constantly sought. Some of the best ideas in academic life come from informal discussions over a cup of tea or coffee and I remember many pleasant chats of an informal nature with Alan and others which led to interesting lines of work being followed up." Sir John

Madsen (Emeritus Professor, Electrical Engineering) and Professors Hugo Messerle and Frederic Evans were among those with whom this interchange of ideas often took place. There was also a lighter side and everyone enjoyed Alan's role as umpire in the annual cricket match between staff and students.

"His decisions reflected his personality," said Professor Myers. "They always seemed to favour the side that appeared to be losing at the time — and dark glasses helped him in reaching these decisions." A younger colleague mentioned to Alan's nephew, Dr David Mackerras, that the joke was extended on one occasion when the students borrowed a dog from a nearby resident, rigged it up as a guide dog for the blind and in addition to the dark glasses, equipped Alan with a cane and he 'tapped' his way on to the field.

Everything about university life expanded Alan's personality — the teaching role, the quiet exchange of ideas, the camaraderie. None of this surprised his old friends such as Tom Keating, who had never observed anything of the dour Scot about him and still kept in touch. One of Alan's special subjects was Engineering Economics and this friend recalls in the first years of Alan's university appointment, when he himself had just completed a comprehensive study on the costing of conversion of some major plant in Sydney from 'direct current to alternating current', coming upon a paper which Alan had prepared as a lecture on *Engineering Economic Choice* and he wished profoundly that he had 'had the benefit of it beforehand'.

Among the students in Electrical Engineering at this time was John Hooke (later Chairman and Chief Executive AWA Ltd.) who delighted Alan by winning the University Medal. He and several other students also began sailing with him. With John it was the beginning of a friendship which, like that established many years before with John Wilson, was to be lasting and important to both.

Sailing had always been Alan's means of self-expression and escape from tensions at home and now, with other pent-up frustrations released, life

Alan at Harpenden, 1960

seemed altogether to have taken a turn for the better. Although his relationship with Catherine had deteriorated, that with members of the family, as long as they were not *en masse*, had mellowed. Elizabeth, safely removed from the European stage, was settled happily in Sydney with husband and infants, Joan was home again and taking a degree at university, and the careers of the five boys were either established or being established. It was particularly gratifying to have Alastair appointed Master of the Lower School at Sydney Grammar and to have Charles back periodically to conduct in Australia. He also made several trips himself over these years — one to Norway and its sparkling fjords filled him with joy — and to cap these things, his brother Ian was now with the CSIRO in Canberra and they were able to see more of each other. In his later years he was finding much real fulfilment.

Catherine, apart from reigning over the smaller family circle at *Harpenden*, had made another of her frequent dashes to Europe, and in London spent many satisfactory hours at the British Museum and the Jewish Museum unearthing background material for her biography of her ancestor, the musician and composer, Isaac Nathan. Home again, she and Nancy conferred frequently, and unless the latter herself was on one of her journeys abroad to Europe or Asia (Catherine frowned upon the latter — 'Darkness comes from the East' she warned her!), she was at the other end of a phone in Sydney to give advice as Catherine plunged into the actual writing. They also shared some pleasant weekends at Alastair's house at Kiama where writing was interspersed with delicious meals, a bottle of wine, and for Catherine, the occasional small cigar which she had taken to smoking.

Everything about Nathan's career provided her with material on which she was extremely well-equipped to write — there was a plethora of eminent early 19th century English personages, a voyage by clipper to Australia, and the early attempts to develop a musical culture in Sydney. In view of the outstanding musical talent of the present generation of Mackerrases, it is interesting to look briefly at Nathan's career — the first professional musician to settle in Australia — for it is to him that the strong musical gene can undoubtedly be traced. Catherine tells us that she had 'long determined to perpetuate the memory of this exotic ancestor' and she proceeded to do so with relish.

At 20, Nathan was chief assistant to the famous Italian singing teacher Corri in London and could 'compose sentimental songs by the dozen' for his pupils to sing. He was elegant, good-looking, highly educated and his Jewish birth was no detriment to him in Regency London. He was soon appointed singing master to Princess Charlotte, only child of the Prince Regent and with royal patronage his carcer as a teacher was secure. More was needed if he were to make his name as a songwriter. 'The musician had only recently emerged from the status in which he wore a nobleman's livery, as Haydn and Mozart did,' Catherine commented in her work, ' . . . and Isaac Nathan shrewdly realised that he needed the collaboration of a distinguished poet.' He approached Walter Scott (not at that stage titled or generally known as the author of the Waverley novels) and asked him to write the verses for 'a considerable number of very beautiful Hebrew melodies of undoubted antiquity which he had selected. Scott

Isaac Nathan (from portrait by unknown artist), London, about 1815

declined, with his custmomary modesty, not thinking himself adequate to the task.'

He then approached Lord Byron. Catherine quoted in full 'the monstrously servile and flattering letter, typical of that age of grovelling sycophancy' with which he made the request. It succeeded. Of the 26 poems which the celebrated poet wrote for the melodies, the two most familiar to us today are the exquisite *She Walks in Beauty like the Night* and that school anthology favourite *The Destruction of Sennacherib*. Riding high on the wave of his great good fortune, Nathan launched the *Hebrew Melodies* in London concert halls with the famous singer John Braham, large audiences attended, and 'critics raved in unmeasured terms as much over the music as over the verse'. Catherine makes no bones about the fact that Nathan was much inferior as a composer to his eminent collaborator.

It is not possible to follow here all Nathan's fluctuating fortunes in England. The peak of his career was undoubtedly the occasion in 1815 when, on the same day, he was visited by Walter Scott, and subsequently himself visited Byron (whom he idolised) to tell him that Scott regarded him as 'a wonderful genius'. The perceptive Byron, speaking in terms of literature and ahead of general opinion, replied, 'Then, Nathan, you have been visited by the greatest man of the age' and went on to extol the Waverley novels. The following year Byron left England in disgrace. Nathan's fortunes took a downward turn. In the early years of Victoria's reign he found himself in disfavour with Lord Melbourne, and in spite of a well received *History of Music,* eventually succumbed to the then prevalent scourge of artistic circles in London and fell into debt.

He migrated to Australia in 1841, via the fully rigged sailing ship *York* with his second wife and children and the offspring of his first marriage, including his son, Catherine's great-grandfather, Dr Charles Nathan, who gave up his practice in London to accompany him. They formed the greater part of the 23 cabin passengers aboard, and there was a full complement in 'the wretched steerage' — cargo included a stud bull and four elegant carriages. The ship tied up at Campbell's Wharf (Circular Quay), Sydney Cove. Already, Catherine noted, 'the noble lighthouse topped South head, there were fishing-huts and farmlets around Watson's Bay; otherwise, save for a mansion, a villa or a cottage here and there among the universal gum-trees, the shores of Sydney Harbour stretched in native wildness to the water's edge.' It was a sombre sight to Nathan's English eyes. Within weeks, however, he was organising his first concert.

The *Sydney Morning Herald* referred to him as 'our celebrated new Colonist' and the clergy of St Mary's Cathedral, who had earlier encouraged some excellent amateur musicians, asked him to arrange an *Oratorio* to celebrate 'the grand opening of their new organ'. Nathan scraped together an orchestra of 26 (he and Charles and two of the Nathan girls formed a vocal quartet) and the concert included fugues from Mozart and Beethoven Masses and portions of the Messiah, and, of course, selections from the Hebrew Melodies. There were 800 people present, which seems a remarkably good audience from a population of 40,000. So Nathan's music making in Australia began. He developed a strong interest in the chants of the Aborigines who still performed corroborees in the vicinity of Sydney, and was the first to take down the aboriginal call 'coo-ee' in its several variants. He included one chant, *Koorinda Braia,* in which 'a whole volley of contrapuntal coo-ees accompanies the song', in one of the many concerts he gave at Sydney College in the room which is now known as the *Big Schoolroom* at Sydney Grammar School of which the old College forms part.

If, in terms of the contribution made by Charles Ives, known as the Father of American Music, it seems extravagant to class Nathan, as Catherine did, the 'Father of Australian Music'[10] he certainly laid the foundations on which others were to build. At 74, he was killed when alighting from Sydney's first horse-drawn tram in Pitt Street in 1864. Catherine's biography, entitled, *The Hebrew Melodist,* was published with the assistance of the Commonwealth Literary Fund by Currawong Publishing Co. in 1963.

She complained to Nancy that Alan was not interested and did not read it. This was part of the complexity of his feeling towards her. He was in fact proud of her writing. Venetia Nathan (Nelson), travelling by train with him from Turramurra one morning, was astonished when the first topic he broached was Isaac Nathan and Catherine's biography. The various branches of the Nathan family in Sydney had found her obsession

---

10. *The Macquarie Book of Events* lists him as such.

with Isaac over these years something of a trial, and imagined that Alan, of all people, would have gone out of his way to avoid rather than court the subject.

By 1966 all the family had left *Harpenden* and it was decided that Catherine and Alan would move from the big empty house at Turramurra to the lower flat at *Balvaig*. Alan was very much against the move. It was quiet and relatively peaceful at Turramurra, he could take his dog, *Marco*, a beautiful Labrador, for long and pleasant walks; he was very attached to the district, it suited him. Catherine wanted to move, her Persian cat Pushkin would present no problem, and the family thought it advisable. So Alan's wishes were over-ruled. He was never happy there but he continued to find great satisfaction in academic life and had recently lectured at a Winter School for post-graduates held at the University of Queensland and his nephew Dr David Mackerras (Senior Lecturer in Electrical Engineering there) found him 'completely in his element'.

Catherine had been engaging a series of typists to cope with her literary output. She was extremely clumsy with her hands and had always said, "Oh well, one has to have a mind above buttons!" when she found it impossible to sew on missing ones; typing was quite out of the question. She had just completed her memoirs, or strictly speaking the account of her conversion to Catholicism, which, she made clear, had its origins early in her youth. The work, which she entitled, *Hitherto*, was never published in full, but sections of it dealing specifically with her 'search for truth', were published in the *Catholic Weekly*. The original manuscript is held in the Mitchell Library and makes fascinating reading, for in order to dissect her rebellion against the agnosticism with which she was surrounded in her youth, she tells of life at 155 Macquarie Street with her grandfather Sir Normand MacLaurin in the Edwardian era, her journey to Europe with her parents during World War I and the interesting medical and literary career of her father, Dr Charles MacLaurin. A significant omission when discussing her own student days at Sydney University, is any reference to the strong intellectual exchange and companionship she enjoyed with Alan there. Again later, when dealing with the effect the Great Depression had upon her when she was a young wife and mother at Vaucluse, she mentions Charles, Alastair and Neil as infants, but does not refer to Alan. The only reference to him at all is an oblique — 'I was unable to be with my father in his last days for I had married the year before and was living with my husband in Schenectady, New York'. This total exclusion of her husband diminishes the work, for although essentially an account of her spiritual journey, she brings all other central figures abundantly to life.

Since she was writing for publication, it is probable that her motive in omitting Alan was that of not wishing to make public the deep divisiveness her conversion had caused. But it would have been entirely possible to convey their early intellectual accord, the falling in love, and the fact that several years after marriage, when she became a Catholic, Alan was not prepared to change his views. The avoidance of this vital matter, leaves the feeling that she probably suffered quite a strong sense of guilt. When discussing her parents in these memoirs, and her consciousness of always coming second in their affections, she remarked, 'Few in my experience

Nancy Phelan, Sydney, about 1968

are the women who are perfect wives and perfect mothers too.' She was well aware where her own strength lay.

There is a charming scene in the garden of the old home where Nancy and her husband now spend most of their time at Lawson in the Blue Mountains, which reveals Catherine at her most beguiling, a friend and companion *par excellence*. Nancy's husband had necessarily to remain at their Potts Point flat in those days, and she used to take Catherine with her sometimes for a weekend at Lawson. The house is on the mountainside with a lovely old garden, big trees and shrubs and in the summer they used to sit out on the lawn, under the stars, with a bottle of wine and Catherine would recite poetry. It was a magic setting for Shelley and Keats and Milton and Catherine's voice resounding with one or other of their timeless verses, as from *Il Penseroso* —

> To behold the wandering moon,
> Riding near her highest noon,
> Like one that had been led astray
> Through the Heav'n's wide pathless way;
> And oft, as if her head she bowed,
> Stooping through a fleecy cloud.

"It was quite lovely," said Nancy. "Catherine had the most wonderful memory and loved the classics. I shall never forget those evenings with her."

One wishes that Catherine had, as well, shown some interest in Australian poets and had made the acquaintance of her Sydney contemporary, Kenneth Slessor, and others whose poetry also holds its splendours.

Her next major project was a life of her grandfather, Sir Normand MacLaurin. Since he had been an important figure in many spheres — a room in the Union building at Sydney University is named for him, he was known in the business world as the *Scottish Banker*, and as a parliamentarian was an opponent of Federalism — a great deal of research was necessary and it was several years before the actual writing was commenced and typists began to come and go once more.

Alan was delighted in 1969 at Alastair's appointment as Headmaster of Sydney Grammar School and again when he married and brought into their lives four step-children whose company he particularly enjoyed. Alastair's step-daughter, Frances, loved sailing and went out many times with her newly acquired grandfather. She became Alan's favourite 'gem', and he relaxed his rule to the extent that Monte Carlo biscuits were allowed aboard *Antares*.

John Hooke had continued to sail with him and was now more or less a permanent crew member. Alan still moored his boat at the old John O'Rourkes' shed at The Spit, painted her an oatmeal-egg colour although everybody else painted theirs white, refused to have an engine in the boat because he was a purist and wanted to enjoy sailing in the traditional sense, and had a cup of tea after sailing instead of joining in the conviviality at Middle Harbour Yacht Club. He was nevertheless the one who was called upon if anything had to be solved or decided. He wore an old white towelling hat and amused John by saying every time they went out, "Oh well, I'll either wear my even more disreputable clothes or my slightly less disreputable clothes . . . "

Alan at the tiller, with Alastair's step-daughter, Frances Edwards

He also has a memory of a Christmas dinner to which Alan invited him just before the family left Turramurra. Catherine and Alan sat at each end of the table. "Everyone was talking in small groups," he recalled, "on literature round Catherine, law round Neil, architecture with Andrew and politics with Malcolm, and all at the tops of their voices. Alan just sat at the other end listening." He realised from that day how much Alan needed his peaceful weekend sailing, and over the years completely changed his view of him. He had initially had the image of someone who had really only made a medium success of his life. Later, he saw it differently. "He'd inspired generations of young people," he said, "either in sailing or at university and had really been enormously successful. Not so much in a material sense as in a total sense. I had a great respect for him — and he was a splendid companion."

It is sad to think of him, silent, in the long white room at *Balvaig* with Catherine, of his avoiding having lunch with her, and taking his dog *Marco* for walks along the narrow footpaths of New South Head Road or the marginally wider ones in the side streets leading down to the harbour. He was never able to settle at the house at Rose Bay. In 1971, when Charles and Judy were in Australia and staying with Alastair and Sue at Mosman, Judy arrived one day with a cooked chicken and hot rolls for lunch. Catherine and Alan sat down with her and both exclaimed, "How nice!" She reminded them that they could always have it that way if they wished. It was unfortunately much too late to improve the situation.

In that year, Dr John Wilson, the family friend in whom Alan had instilled a love of sailing, returned to live in Sydney. He again went out regularly with him and found that *Antares* had sailed so well she had had her handicap increased each season. Alan himself was then responsible for handicapping. "After a race," John recalled, "I have seen him patiently listening to angry skippers of the Middle Harbour fleet, arguing their handicap. His reply was always, 'Ah well.'" It would certainly have been hard to continue antipathy at that rate.

In 1972 Ian's son, David, was in Sydney and went to see Alan who showed him over the university and looked extremely hale and hearty. Elizabeth and Alastair, who saw most of their parents, felt the same way about him. He had reached retirement age at the university but still participated in a series of lectures there on Astronomy, under the auspices of the Department of Tutorial Classes and the WEA.

Elizabeth's eldest daughter, Gabrielle, had now become close to Catherine, often shopped for her and sometimes had dinner with her grandparents. She was just approaching 14 and found the silence between them hard to cope with. The only conversation she recalls is the announcement by Catherine that the meal was ready and her grandfather's reply, "Oh, dinner ready? Good." He would sit down to the steak and chips or salad, with which both had a glass of red wine, and return to his room immediately afterwards. It was then time for Catherine's after dinner sherries and cigar and a request to Gabrielle to put on *Iolanthe* or *The Mikado*, while she relaxed and chatted. Of the two, even to her young eyes, her grandfather appeared much the fitter. In fact, Andrew Briger, who kept his excellent relationship with both, can recall his father-in-law about this time, lean and fit as ever, climbing up the mast of his boat to make a repair as though he were forty.

Within months, Alan's very cruel fate overtook him. He suffered a stroke, was paralysed on one side, and it was the beginning of a long drawn out ordeal from which he never recovered. The responsibility for his care rested chiefly on Elizabeth, for even if Catherine's own health had not begun to fail, she was clearly not the one to assist. He made valiant efforts to do what he could for himself and even went out in the boat several times with John Wilson and John Hooke. They used to lift him into the dinghy, then onto *Antares*, lash him into a corner of the cockpit and 'under his instructions sail around the Sunday fleet'.

He now only had the use of his left hand. At home Gabrielle and her sister Christina tried to help him with a model sailing ship on which he had been working. The girls had no talent for this — pieces got lost and glue got everywhere. They saw his misery and ran into Catherine. Intricate manual things of that kind were beyond her. "Why waste your time on those stupid things!" she said impatiently. "Put on the Mikado and pour a glass of sherry . . ."

Ian came down to see him and Alastair was often with him as his disability increased. And so the nightmare continued. Eventually it was necessary to go to hospital. He chose the Scottish Hospital at Paddington, for it seemed a suitably frugal place, but it made Elizabeth's heart ache to have him there. She visited him twice a day, while the various members of the family called whenever they could. Catherine went quite regularly for some time but seemed to realise that her presence irritated him. Nancy was overseas and received letters from her full of pity for him but discussing the misfortune in a strangely detached way, as though he were a character she was looking at from afar. Nancy is convinced that she began to see him more clearly and fairly, and she certainly wished she could be more helpful, but knew that 'all she could do was pray for him — which she did.'

The news of Colin's appointment to Griffith University was brought to Alan and the words "Colin's a prof . . . " were amongst the last he managed to utter before he lost the power of speech, as were those in a request to John Wilson to care for his much loved boat.

"It was a slow and desperately cruel thing," said Elizabeth, "it went on month after month. All he could do was write with his left hand — slowly. He couldn't even swallow. He couldn't move his eyes — but his brain was just as active. Alastair used to sit with him and do mathematical problems. He'd start off an equation on a piece of paper and Dad would do the next stage and they'd do this until it was completed." And so the mathematical minds continued to meet.

Ian Mackerras, who had been desolated some eighteen months before by the loss of his wife, came from Canberra several times to be with Alan and also communicated with pencil and paper. Ian himself was about to retire because of a disability with his hands which made intricate dissection impossible. "When the amplitude of one's shake exceeds the size of the specimen, it is time to give up!" he told Alan. So the two brothers, who had shared a lifetime of interest in the sciences, remained close to the end.

Catherine at Balvaig, 1972

*Her favourite granddaughter,
Gabrielle Briger*

Clouds gather for Alan

He died in August 1973, just a few months before Charles was to arrive to conduct the opening concert at the Sydney Opera House. The whole agonising and protracted illness had bitten into Elizabeth's heart and there was real grief in the family now. This is probably the reason why none of his sons could bring themselves to accompany Andrew, John Hooke and John Wilson when, at Andrew's suggestion, they buried his ashes at sea from *Antares* off North Head where he had known such enjoyment and shown such skill as a single-handed yachtsman. Later, a service was held.

Catherine was filled with conflicting emotions, dazed and bemused. It is probably a measure of her underlying feeling that her own health deteriorated greatly from this point. She was moved by the tributes to her husband from Sydney University and from Dr Harley Wood, his longtime friend and associate, who, after writing a full account of his achievements in engineering, astronomy and yachting in the Sydney bulletin of the British Astronomical Association, said to the family, "The most difficult thing to convey is the affection in which he was held by so many people and the way in which we all relied on his wisdom when anything difficult was being discussed."

John Wilson thought of him as 'a celtic seed from the old country binding firmly the soil of this'. It is an interesting concept and true if one thinks of the qualities Alan inherited from his Irish and Scottish forebears. He had a Scottish reserve. He was also frugal and somewhat over-correct. From the very upright Irish Creagh family he inherited an unwavering integrity and loyalty — so strong that never at any time did he criticise Catherine, within or outside the family — and from the Creaghs also came his real and quick sense of humour. But above all he was Australian. Unlike Catherine he did not hark back to 'the old country' and find everything that was good there. He was content to be Australian. He felt deeply about this country. "He was a key figure in my Australia," John Wilson commented, "not only as the father of a remarkable brood, but also in his character. He contributed significantly to nation building and on a big scale — but without self seeking." And that goes to the heart of the matter.

Elizabeth, after the long ordeal she had shared with her father, now worried about Catherine. She was not able to get about as she used to, was very much overweight but had no intention of curbing her enjoyment of life, of food and wine, or of changing her now very sedentary habits. Gabrielle spent as much time as she could with her, and a young Yugoslav girl was found to come in by day. Alastair came always to take her to Mass on Sundays and friends such as John Parkinson and Peter Harwin found her as vital and interesting as ever.

Janie Breden came to stay for a few weeks and found her warm and affectionate, drawing her to the window to look at a sunset over the harbour as enthusiastically as she had experienced the same joy in her youth at 155 Macquarie Street. She had almost finished the biography of her grandfather, Sir Normand, but tired of it and Alastair resolved that one day he would complete the task. She was badly upset when Neil, with a flourishing practice at the Sydney Bar, left and went to Moree, but she was not to know the outcome of that. Overall she took great, though not overweening, satisfaction in her family's achievements and was delighted by their marriages. "I know that I have been extremely fortunate," she told Hazel de Berg when interviewed in 1974 for National Library records. And she had.

A night at the opera remained one of her special joys. Gabrielle remembers well the ritual it entailed — the setting out of the freshly cleaned gloves, the opera glasses, and the early dressing for the occasion. But most of her days were spent sitting in her favourite chair in the drawing room, with her cat Pushkin on her lap, Alan's dog Marco at her feet and reading biography or history. Nancy returned from abroad, visited her frequently and invariably found her thus.

"I'd come in through the French windows," she recalled, "and even as I bent to kiss her, with no greeting at all, she'd look up over her glasses and begin a conversation as though we were already in the middle of one — 'And now they say poor George III wasn't mad after all!' — anything from Wellington to Tolstoy and the Old Testament." The point was that she knew Nancy would understand and there was no need to waste time on small talk. They had many delightful lunches together, prepared by the little Yugoslav girl, and always shared a bottle of wine — the greater portion to Catherine since Nancy was driving. Then it was back to the black chair, the somewhat bad-tempered fur-shedding Pushkin, the aged Labrador and coffee. The room, Nancy felt, in spite of the beautiful rugs and antiques and *bibelots*, always remained homely and comfortable. And of course the conversation would proceed with some wonderful *non sequitur* from Catherine — 'But don't you think Schubert was the saddest?' "It was wonderful," said Nancy with some nostalgia, "people from history and music and literature just lived in that room."

Catherine spoke of the humiliations of old age, and they often talked of life and death, though Nancy would not allow herself to become involved in theological argument. On mortality, Catherine's comment was, "No matter what you do, it's the briefness of life here that's so sad." Conversation frequently centred round the poets and composers who had died young. "She spoke as though they were young people she had known," said Nancy, "yet she was not depressing. I think she liked a bit of romantic melancholy, in fact she would admit it. Under all her intellectual coverings, she was a romantic at heart."

Early in 1976, Alastair's wife, Sue, took her to England for a few weeks. In London, Charles and Judy arranged for her to be at a hotel near them, for she could no longer manage their stairs. The highlight of her week there was to see Charles conduct the centenary performance of her favourite G & S, *The Mikado* at the Savoy Theatre. They had several weeks with Joan and Graeme down in Suffolk. "Graeme loved my mother," said Joan, "and always enjoyed her visits, but this time we were very saddened at the way she had gone down hill. We knew that we wouldn't see her again." She spoke for them all.

In fact Catherine had only another year. When she returned, it soon became necessary for Gabrielle to help her dress in the mornings, cook dinner and help her to bed at night. "She was a wonderful woman" said this young granddaughter. "My friends used to love being with her and hearing her talk. The only time I didn't see a smile from her was in the last few months when she wasn't able to do anything for herself." She still enjoyed reading history by day — Joan of Arc and Queen Victoria were favourites — and at night Gabrielle often read detective novels to her, usually Agatha Christie, sometimes Dorothy Sayers. Elizabeth and Alastair were now frequently with her, and the memory of their father's long illness was always in their minds. It was a deep anxiety.

Nancy came frequently to share lunch and remembers Catherine's last greeting to her as she came through the French windows and bent to kiss her. "Did you know," she asked, looking up from her book, "that poor Nelson begged Hardy not to let them throw him overboard after he died? Imagine throwing Nelson overboard! Don't you think it was pathetic? So modest." There was to be nothing again quite like these hours spent with Catherine.

She remained lucky to the end. The first weekend in February was a particularly pleasant one for her. On Saturday night, Gabrielle and two of her friends had dinner with her. "Later, after the mandatory glass of sherry," said Gabrielle, "she read some history to us and seemed very much at one with everything." The following night, Alastair came, as always, to take her to Mass. Afterwards, at dinner, she discoursed at length on Moses. He put her to bed about 8.30, and in the morning Neil's daughter, Helen, who was staying with her, found her propped in bed with her glasses on her nose and the book she had been reading — *The Queen and Mr Gladstone* — lying on her chest. She had died an hour or so before.

The family gathered for the service at St Mary Magdalene church, Rose Bay, and the putting to rest of their mother at Waverley Cemetery in the MacLaurin family vault with her grandparents and the sad little coffin of their only daughter, Harriet, who lived just a few days, and with her own parents. It was a calm and beautiful day, the sky as blue as the dazzling, shimmering sea, and there was no sadness. She had had a wonderfully fulfilled life. She had escaped a lingering illness and died most peacefully. Her children and grandchildren were moved as they walked through the vault and then stood high on the cliff looking out over the great expanse of sea. There was something quite wondrous about that place, as Catherine herself had found so many years before.

Strangely, at *Balvaig*, her cat Pushkin wandered away and was never to be found. Her favourite black chair by the window is where Alastair now reads and listens to his music. He is a loved and central family figure, just as Elizabeth fills her mother's role. Colin and Malcolm often pass through, Neil sometimes and recently Joan's husband was there. They all look forward to the vitalising visits of Charles who will be with them again in the bicentenary year. When the family dog barks and disturbs a conversation, Alastair says, "Peace! Dad wouldn't like you!" All have come to understand and appreciate their father more over the years. His telescopes are at the Observatory at Sydney Grammar's Preparatory School at St Ives, where the constellations can be observed more clearly. In the classrooms at College Street, Sydney, and at Woodbridge, England, the lecture rooms at Griffith University, Brisbane, and at Duntroon Military College, Canberra, Alan's teaching ability and pleasure in students appear again in his sons and daughter.

Balvaig remains the gathering place, the heart of the family, and the warmth and brilliance which Catherine radiated in her life, is still its living pulse.

Index

Aboriginal Legal Service, 188-9, 193-200
Adcock, Dr David, 67, 80
Age, The, 190-1, 292-4
Aitken, Don, 278
Aiton, Douglas, 190-1
Amadio, Neville, 74, 105, 117
Amnesty International, 273-4, 301
Andre, Peter, 107-8
Angus, Professor, 31
Anniversary Day Regatta, 16, 63
Anthony, Doug, 252-3, 277
Aprahamian, Felix, 100-1
Australasian Post, 104
Australia — China Council, 267-8
Australian, The, 263
Australian Ballet Company, 120
Australian Broadcasting Commission/Corporation, 85, 90, 102, 106, 111, 116, 155, 222, 260, 276-7, 283-4, 289-91, 300-1
Australian Elizabethan Theatre Trust, 229-30
Australian General Elections, 278-81
Australian Labor Party, 10, 28, 46, 153, 174-5, 182-7, 226, 253, 273, 277-8, 281, 283-5, 288-97, 300-1
Australian Music Centre, 98
Australian National University, (Canberra University College), 235-7, 248-55, 257, 268, 275, 278
Australian Opera Company, 115, 123, 155, 230
Australian Women's Weekly, 288
Australian Worker, The, 28, 30

Bailey, Sir Harold, 126

Bailey, Margaret, 211
Baker, Dame Janet, 106, 113
Barton, Sir Edmund, 138
Barton, John, 299
B.B.C. Concert Orchestra, 92, 96-8
Beck, Haydn, 203-4
Beddie, Prof. Brian, 282
Begg, Ken, 283
Bell, Alistair, 143-4, 149
Belloc, Hilaire, 35
Benson, John, 163-4
Bentine, Michael, 211, 213
Bentine, Clementina, 213
B.H.P., 271
Billing, R.W. (Reg), 136, 138
Bjelke-Petersen, Sir Joh, 265, 268, 298-9
Blyth, Alan, 112
Bray, Sir Theodore, 254
Breden (formerly Lemann), Janie, 71, 85, 204, 215-6, 223, 226-8, 316
Breden, Janie & Partner, 223, 226-7 Interior Design
Brennan, Sir Gerard, 268
Briger, Alex, 163-4, 229-30
Briger, Andrew 207-30, 312-16
Briger, Christina, 216, 228-9
Briger, Elizabeth (formerly Mackerras), 53, 59, 63, 65-6, 71, 78, 81-7, 96, 104, 118, 130-2, 155-6, 158, 164, 198, 202-32, 248, 258, 282, 307, 313-16
Briger, Gabrielle, 216, 224, 313-18
Briger, Zenaide, 207, 210 (former Comtesse Soumarokov-Elston)

Brinkman, Jan, 66, 68, 73
Brisbane Boys Grammar School, 256
British Astronomical Assoc. (N.S.W. Div.) 33-4, 78, 87, 304, 316
Britten, Benjamin, 98, 109
Bryant, Robert, 161
Bulletin, The, 8, 38-9, 162, 292, 297, 301-2
Burke, Brian, 281
Burns, Monsignor Ian, 126
Butler, Dr David, 276-7, 279, 294, 297
Buttrose, Charles, 116
Byrne, Mother Lua, 202
Byron, Lord, 308

Callas, Maria, 119
Cambridge, History of Inner Asia, 241, 265
Cameron, Don, 289, 296, 300
Canberra Times, 275, 285, 300
Cardus, Neville, 97
Carleton, Richard, 300
Catholic Weekly, 85, 302, 310
Central Institute for Nationalities, Peking, 262
Chan, Robert, 257
Chang, Peter, 267
Chauvel, Sir Charles, 76
Chicago Symphony Orchestra, 111
Child, Joan, 288
Chinese Communist Party, 245-7
Chinese Theatre in Modern Times, The, from 1840 to the Present Day, 254
Chinese Theatre, From its Origins to the Present Day, 265
Civic Reform Organisation, (Sydney), 222-6
Clarke, Manning, 265
Clarke, Peter, 196, 198
Climpson, Roger, 117
Cole, Senator George, 176
Conference on Free Election (Washington U.S.A), 296-7
Corelli, Franco, 119
Country Party (later National Party) (see Liberal-C.P. Coalition)
Court, Sir Charles, 281
Covell, Roger, 116, 122
Cowper, Sir Charles, 137
Cowper, Sir Norman, 32, 137, 144-6, 148-50, 154
Cox, Edward, 137

Craggs, Charles J., 61-2
Craig, Dr Gordon, 32, 35, 39
Craig, Helen, 32, 42
Cranko, John, 93-5
Cranswick, Canon (later Bishop of Tasmania), 20, 22
Creagh, Albert, 16, 20, 22, 32-3
Creagh, John, 33, 75
Creagh, Lillian 16-17, 32-3, 59
Creagh, Louisa, 16-17, 20, 22, 33, 59
Creagh, Patrick, 16-17, 19-20, 22, 50
Creagh, William John, 4, 16, 20, 22, 45, 75, 217
Croal, Sally, 12, 26
Croal, Thomas, 2
Crouch, Graham J., 154-5, 165, 168
C.S.I.R. (later C.S.I.R.O.), 51, 274, 297, 307
Cullen, Peter, 278
Cultural Revolution, 247, 252-3, 267
Czech Philharmonic Orchestra, 89, 105, 122

Dale, David, 297
D'Alpuget, Blanche, 297
Davey, Jack, 72, 104
Daw, David, 286-7, 294
Dawson, Peter, 97-8
de Berg, Hazel, 104, 316
de Burgh, Una, 82
Deer, Sir Frederick, 83
Deisendorf, Dr Walter, 62
Democratic Labour Party, 174-6, 181-7, 248-9
Dent, E.R., 136
Dibble, James, 276
Dodgson, Patrick, 198-200
Dodgson, Mackerras & Co., Solicitors, 199
Downes, Stephen, 292-4
Dunford, John, R., 179
Dukes, Sir Paul, 207, 215
Dunn Prof., Hugh, 268

Earle, David, 223
Edwards, Frances, 143, 312
Edwards, Rev John, 31, 39, 46, 50, 58
Edwards, Dr Stephen, 143
Edwards, Dr Tony, 143, 153
Elections 1975, 286

Elections 1980, 292
Electricity Commission of N.S.W., 74, 83-84, 206, 304-5
Elkins, Margreta, 122
Elkins, Professor, 195
Elms, Lauris, 122
English Chamber Orchestra, 98, 110, 119
English National Opera, 113, 115-16, 258
English Opera Group, 98-9
Entombed Warriors Exhibition, 263-4
Essays on the Sources for Chinese History, 252
Evans, Prof. Frederic, 306
Evans, Huw, 283-4, 289-91, 297, 301
Evatt, Justice Elizabeth, 172, 202
Evatt, Dr Herbert Vere, 24, 133, 174

Fairfax, John, 137
Federal Redistribution, The 1968, 276
Field, Prof. Andrew, 267
Fifield, Elaine, 94
Fitzgerald, Prof. C. Patrick, 252
Fitzgerald, R.D., 138
Fitzgerald, Dr Stephen, 251-3
Foster, Gordon, 61
Fraser, Malcolm, 263, 267, 277, 285-6, 292, 295, 297-8, 300
Freehill, Hollingdale & Page, 173-4
Freeman, Cardinal, 187-8
Freeth, Sir Gordon, 182
Frobel House (Kindergarten Training College), 4-5
From Fear to Friendship: Australia's Policies Towards The People's Republic of China 1966-82, 263, 267
Frost Dr (U.S. Astronomer), 43
Fung, Edmund, 263

Gair, Senator Vincent, 176, 182, 283
Gameley, Doug, 107-8
Gaul, Jonathan, 275
Gielgud, Sir John, 111
General Electric Company (U.S.A.), 38-40, 44
General Electric Review, 44-5
Gerber, Dr Paul, 286
Gilbey, Monsignor, 126-7, 240
Godfrey Smith, Laurence, 203

Goldrick, John, 59-60, 68, 130, 172-3, 175-6, 178-82, 188, 196, 253
Goldsbrough Orchestra, 98, 100
Gonski, David, 143, 151, 160
Goodings, John, 213
Goosens, Sir Eugene, 76, 95, 120
Goosens, Leon, 73, 76
Gorton, Sir John, 182-3, 275, 277, 283
Granowski, Helen, 82, 202
Griffin, Sir David, 223, 229
Griffith University (Qld), 229, 254-69
Grinke, Frederick, 206

Hall, Droston, 221, 230-1
Hall, Graeme, 141, 217-31, 317-8
Hall, Joan (formerly Mackerras), 53, 58-60, 65-74, 76-8, 81-7, 96, 104, 118, 126, 130-1, 139, 141, 154, 202-32, 258, 271, 273, 307, 317-8
Hanyu, 268
Hamburg State Opera, 109-11
Hanson-Norman, Aubrey, 139
Hardie, Kevin, 131
Hardy, Thomas, 35
Harewood, Lord, 111, 113
Harewood, Countess, (formerly Patricia Tuckwell), 111
Harrap, Brian, 126
Harrison, Rev Hector, 284-5
Harwin, Peter, 86, 138-9, 143, 146-7, 156-60, 168, 203-4, 218-20, 316
Hawke, Robert L. (Bob), 297, 300
Hayden, Bill, 295-7
Hazelwood, Donald, 105, 115-16, 120-2
Healey, Colin, 128, 130-1, 134-6, 139-41, 218
Hebrew Melodist, The, 307-9
Heinze, Sir Bernard, 74, 203
Helpmann, Sir Robert, 88, 206
Hempel, Professor, 201
Herbert, Xavier, 171
Hicks, Ian, 184
Hirst, Professor, 165
Hodge, Margaret, 9, 12, 27
Holt, Harold, 182, 275
Hooke, John, 306, 312-13, 315-16
Hope, Justice R.M. (Bob), 174, 177-9, 189-90, 197
Horne, Marilyn, 111, 123

Houldsworth, Peter, 140-1, 144-5, 160-1, 218-20
Howard, John, 234, 272-3, 276, 279, 289, 297, 301
Hu, Yaobang, 268
Huan, Xiang, 268
Hughes, W.M. (Billy), 83
Hurwitz, Emanuel, 100
Hutchinson, Louise, (formerly Wilson), 28, 58, 195

Inson, Graeme, 158
Institute of Engineers, 45

James, Francis, 253
Janacek, Leos, 90-1, 94-5, 101-2, 109, 113, 116-9, 122
Jones, Clem, 289

Kaishek, Chiang, 246
Kane, Senator Jack, 176, 182
Keating, Thomas J., 62, 68, 304, 306
Keene, Rosalind, 106-7
Kerr, Sir John, 180, 285-6
Killen, Sir James, 277, 295, 300
Kimber, Beryl, 74
Kim Il Sung, 263
Kings School, The, 68, 132, 159, 162
Kirby, Justice Michael, 190
Knock, Rodney, 86, 133, 149
Knox, Dorothy, 87, 204
Kramer, Prof. Dame Leonie, 267

La Trobe University, 305
Lady and the Fool, The, 95-6
Lancaster, Osbert, 94
Landlord & Tenant Practice & Procedure in N.S.W., 174, 177-9
Langer, Gertrude, 264
Laverty, Piers, 149-50
Lawes, Dr Frank, 67, 83
Lawrence, Sister Mary, 104
Leavis, Dr F.R. 159
Lee, Joy, 163-4
Legat Madine Nicoleva, 206-10
Legat, Nicholas, 206-7
Legat Ballet School, 206-7, 210
Legge, Walter, 100
Lehmann, Geoffrey, 234
Leighton, Irwin & Co., 213
Liberal-C.P. Coalition, 83, 174, 176, 182-4, 252-3, 273, 278, 288-90, 292-4

Liberal Party, 83, 174-5, 222, 248, 271-8, 288-90, 296-301
Liebermann, Rolf, 109
Lim, Professor David, 268
Lindsay, Lionel, 22-3
Lisner, Charles, 93
Liv, Professor Chengpei, 264-5
Lockhart, Justice John, 158-9, 168
Lockington, S.J. Father W., 50
Lockwood, Douglas, 106
London Symphony Orchestra, 98, 106
Lovejoy, Robin, 222-3, 227-30
Lumsdaine, Keith, 133

McCauley, Connan & Briger, 221
McGilvray, Alan, 138
Mackerras, Alan,
  childhood and schooldays, 3-4, 17, 19-22, 27
  at University, 28, 32-7
  family life and career, 53-87, 98, 104-5, 115, 130-2, 139, 141, 153, 202, 204-6, 213-16, 218-19, 222-3, 236, 248-9, 271, 276, 281, 285, 302-3
  career as academic and last years, 304-319
Mackerras, Alastair, 46-8, 53-60, 63-72, 76-8, 81-7, 95, 104, 115, 118, 125-170, 198, 200, 217, 221, 227, 229-231, 237, 248, 256, 271-3, 307, 310, 312-8
Mackerras, Alyce, (formerly Brazier) 236-269, 272-3, 284
Mackerras, Catherine (formerly Maclaurin)
  childhood and schooldays, 1, 3-5, 8-16, 22, 24-27
  at university, 28-32, 34-37
  early years of marriage, 328-52
  family life, 53-88, 96, 102-105, 115-116, 126-7, 130-3, 139, 141, 146-7, 153-5, 171-3, 175-6, 180, 183, 190, 195, 202-10, 213, 218-224, 233-6, 248-9, 258, 270-3, 276, 279-282, 284, 289
  as author and last years, 302-318
Mackerras, Sir Charles, 44-48, 55-69, 72-77, 88-125, 133, 152, 154-8, 162-3, 197-8, 200, 204-11, 220, 224, 228-9, 238, 240, 258, 272-3, 282, 298, 307, 310, 313, 317-8

Mackerras, Prof. Colin, 53, 64–6, 74, 78, 80–81, 84–7, 102–4, 116–7, 122, 132–3, 138, 142, 154, 182, 198, 201, 216–7, 227, 229–231, 232–270, 272–3, 275–6, 279, 284, 299, 315, 318
Mackerras, Dr David, 63–4, 80, 105, 121–2, 152, 198, 306, 310, 313
Mackerras, Elizabeth (see Briger)
Mackerras, Elizabeth (formerly Connolly), 172–198
Mackerras, Elizabeth (formerly Creagh), 4, 16–20, 32–33, 56, 75, 105
Mackerras, Hilary, 82
Mackerras, Dr Ian Murray, 4, 17, 19–22, 27, 32, 38–9, 51–2, 64, 73, 75–6, 80, 105, 116–7, 138, 158, 163, 218–9, 274, 284, 307, 315
Mackerras, Joan (see Hall)
Mackerras, Lady Judith (Judy) (formerly Wilkins), 88–124, 152, 154, 197–8, 206–11, 220, 224, 238, 240, 273, 313, 317
Mackerras, James Murray, 16–20
Mackerras, James Taylor, 16–18
Mackerras, Dr Josephine (formerly Bancroft), 38–9, 80, 105, 274, 284
Mackerras, Lindsay (formerly Ryan), 187, 255, 278–301
Mackerras, Malcolm, 53, 64–6, 77–87, 102–4, 116–7, 133, 185, 187, 190, 221–2, 227, 231, 239–40, 248–9, 252, 265, 270–301, 312, 318
Mackerras, Neil, 47–8, 56–60, 64–8, 76–83, 87, 104, 115, 118, 130, 171–201, 227, 248–9, 279, 281–2, 310, 312, 316, 318
Mackerras, Neil & Co (Solicitors), 195
Mackerras, Sue (formerly McCubbin/Edwards), 143, 145–8, 153–6, 317
McGregor, Graeme, 217
McKinnon, Andrew, 230
MacLaurin, Anne (formerly Croal), 1–5, 13–4, 34–5, 39–42, 44, 57–9
MacLaurin, Dr. Charles, 1–5, 9–14, 22–32, 34–5, 39–42, 76, 122, 125, 138, 289, 310
MacLaurin, Prof. Colin, 14, 128, 254–5
MacLaurin, Donald, 10
MacLaurin, Lady Eliza (formerly Nathan), 5–10, 131
MacLaurin, Brigadier-General Henry Normand, 10, 24–5, 76
MacLaurin, Hugh 10
MacLaurin, James, 128, 168
MacLaurin, J.B., 10
MacLaurin, Sir Normand, 5–8, 10–2, 14–6, 24, 131, 150, 258, 284, 289, 310, 312, 316
McLean, Douglas, 106–7, 111
McLean, Pamela, 106–7, 111
McMahon, William, 183–5, 252–3, 277
McManus, Senator Frank, 176
McNicoll, David, 162
Mace, Ralph, 111
Maddison, John, 181
Madsen, Sir John, 305–6
Maguire, Justice Hugh, 172–3
Maley, Bill, 292
Manchester Guardian, 113–4
Manning, Alan, 175–6
Mannix, Archbishop, 174
Mao, Zedong, 246–7, 262
Marxism in Asia, 267
Martindale, S.J. Father W, 49
Masters, Robert, 208
Mayer, Prof. Henry, 185, 278, 281
Melbourne Symphony Orchestra, 107
Melville, Sir Leslie, 78
Melville, Tony, 78, 126, 128–9, 132
Menuhin, Hebzibah, 203
Menzies, Sir Robert, 64, 83, 133, 140, 148, 270, 273–4
Messerle, Prof. Hugo, 306
Metropolitan Opera N.Y., 111
Middle Harbour Yacht Club, 55
Miller, Prof. John, 128
Mitchell Library, 310
M.L.C., 6, 171, 173
Modern China: A Chronology fron 1842 to the Present Day, 256–7, 261, 267
Monash University, 193, 255
Moore, Lyle, 140
Movement, The, 174–5
Mudie, Michael, 89, 95
Munro Jnr, Lyall, 194
Munro Snr, Lyall, 191–3, 198
Murray, Les A, 234, 276–7, 278–80, 284
Muset, Father Alfred, 64, 68
Musical Cultures of Asia, The, 260
Myers, Prof. David, 45, 61, 304–6

Nathan, Dr Charles, 6-7, 100, 131, 137, 302, 309
Nathan, Isaac, 9, 85, 258, 304, 307-9
Nathan, Ted, 131
Nation Review, 278
National Aboriginal Conference, 191
National Civic Council, 175
National Party, (Qld), 298-9
National Times, The, 112, 189, 265-7
Neate, Kenneth, 92
Needham, Joseph, 241-2
Nelson, Jeremy, 81, 150, 161, 168, 272
Nelson, Venetia (formerly Nathan), 81, 150, 309
Newcombe, Harriet, 9
Newington College, 132
New Philharmonia Orchestra, 106
Newton, Sir Isaac, 255
Nicholson, Sir Charles, 137
N.I.D.A., 230
Nie, Gongcheng, 268
Nilsson, Birgit, 115, 282
Norris, Kathleen, 230
Norris, K.R., 274
N.S.W. Election, 282

Oakes, Laurie, 286, 297
Observer, The (London), 94
Oliphant, Sir Mark, 265-7
Order of Australia Assoc. (N.S.W Branch), 229
Ormandy, Eugene, 69, 74
Outterside, Bob, 162

Packer, Leo, 69
Parkes, Henry, 137
Parkinson, Dr John P, 47, 69-70, 82, 117, 126, 129, 131, 145-6, 217, 316
Paterson, A.B. (Banjo), 138
Peacock, Andrew, 300-1
Pearson, Keith, 296
Peking Foreign Studies University, 269
Peking Institute of Foreign Languages, 242-7
Peking Opera, 244-6, 248, 250-1, 263, 265-6
Pekarek, Rudolf, 105
Pennicuick, Ramsay, 61
Peoples Republic of China, 241-8, 251-4, 257-8

Performing Arts in Contemporary China, The, 259-60
Pestorius, Geraldine, 261
Phelan, Nancy (formerly Creagh), 16, 32-3, 38, 45, 55-6, 75-6, 80, 105, 180, 218, 303-4, 307, 309-11, 317-8
Phillips, F G (Sandy), 68-9,
Picken, Dr Laurence, 241-3, 246, 258
Pineapple Poll, 93-4, 101, 106
Plodr, Eva (formerly Hustoles), 91-2
Plodr, Frank, 91-2
Port, Leo, 222-6
Potter, Sir Ian, 229
Power, John, 276, 283
Prague Academy of Music, 89-90
Prague Symphony Orchestra, 105
Prerauer, Curt, 90
Price, Sir Leslie, 268
Prokhovnik, Prof. Simon, 122

Queensland Institute of Medical Research, 80, 158
Queensland Lyric Opera, 117
Queensland Symphony Orchestra, 105-7
Qing, Jiang, 246

Ramage, Judge Malcom, 188, 190
Reynolds, Justice R.G. (Ray), 176
Rise of the Peking Opera, The, 1770-1870 Social Aspects of the Theatre in Manchu China, 251
Ritchie, Bill, 131
Roberts, Nigel S., 278, 281, 285, 289
Role of the Satellites, The, 305
Rollo, Jack, 83
Roman Catholic Church, 10-3, 40-2, 46, 49-52, 72, 81-2, 89, 102-4, 127, 183, 186-8, 233-5, 247, 249, 272, 310
Ross, Bob, 150, 152, 166-70
Royal Academy of Music, 206, 208
Royal Institute of Architects, 225
Royal Military College, Duntroon, 282, 286-7, 292-4, 300
Royal Philharmonic Orchestra, 106-7
Royal Sydney Yacht Squadron, 16, 98
Ryan, Bill, 279, 282, 285
Ryan, Lawrie, 265-6

Sadler's Wells Ballet & Theatre Ballet, 89, 92-93
Sadler's Wells Opera, 88-9, 92, 96, 101, 107, 111-3
Santamaria, B.A. (Bob), 174-5, 186
Schwarzkopf, Elisabeth, 100, 272
Segal, Phillip, 195, 198-200
Sewell, Max, 195
Seymour, Peter, 141, 155, 163
Shaoqi, Liu, 246
Shawe-Taylor, Desmond, 95-6, 100, 109
Shehadie, Sir Nicholas, 222-3
Sheila, Rachel, 211
Sheldon, John, 86, 102, 138, 141-3, 146, 150, 156-7, 160, 167-8, 171, 233-6, 248
Shirley, (School), 9
Shore, (School), 64
Sitski, Larry, 260
Smith, Dr Hugh, 282, 287
Solomon, David, 286
Spiegl, Fritz, 96
Sproule, John, 74-5, 84, 304
St. Aloysius College, 51, 56-9, 77, 89, 172, 233
St John, Edward, 180
St Johns College (Cambridge) 125-6, 165-6, 237
St Thomas More College, 256
Stacey, Brian, 117-120
Stevens, Ron, 106-7
Street, Sir Kenneth, 138
Street, Sir Lawrence, 163
Stromberg, Dr (U.S. Mathematician), 43
Studer, Christa, 212
Sunday Times, The, 100, 109
Swan Alan, 131, 138
Sydneian, The, 133-6
Sydney Conservatorium, 61, 66, 68, 73, 203-4
Sydney City Council, 222-6
Sydney County Council (Electricity Undertaking), 38, 45, 61-2, 74-5, 304
Sydney Grammar School, 1, 6, 22, 28, 51, 61, 68-70, 83-4, 128, 130-70, 217-21, 229-30, 233, 270, 272, 307, 312
Sydney High School, 161-2
Sydney Morning Herald, 34-6, 66, 116, 122, 163, 167, 184-5, 297-8, 309
Sydney Opera House, opening season of, 115, 153, 189, 282, 315

Sydney Symphony Orchestra, 73-4, 76, 88, 105, 115, 120-2, 162

Talich, Vaclav, 89-91
Tancibudek, Jiri, 90, 92, 106
Teale, Leonard, 230
Te Kanawa, Kiri, 117
Thames & Hudson, London, 254, 261
Thatcher, Margaret, 288
Times, The London, 111-113
Tipping, Mother Borgia, 50-1, 67, 72, 172
Tucker, Norman, 89, 94
Turnbull, Malcolm, 131, 141-4, 151, 160
Twitchett, Prof. Denis, 241

Uighur Empire, The, According to the T'ang Dynastic Histories, 241
University of New England, 217-8
University of New South Wales, 195, 213, 255
University of Queensland, 286, 310
University of Queensland Press, 267
University of Sydney, 6-8, 15-6, 24, 28-9, 34-5, 61, 76, 80, 105, 136-7, 171-2, 233-5, 304-6, 310, 313, 316

Van Otterloo, Willem, 115-6, 120
Van Pragh, Dame Peggy, 93
Verbrugghen, Henri, 31
Victorian State Opera, 120
Vienna Philharmonic Orchestra, 99, 115
Vienna State Opera, 119
Viviani, Nancy, 267

Walsh, Mike, 299
Wang, Prof. Gungwu, 251-2, 255, 260, 268-9
Webb, Prof. Roy, 265
Weigall, Albert, 132
Welsh National Opera, 123
Wentworth, William, 136
White, Dorothy, 85, 202, 218
White, Sir Thomas, 95
Whiting, Prof. Allen, 268
Whitlam, Gough, 153, 182, 185, 253, 258, 261, 267, 273, 277, 280-1, 283-6, 291, 295
Whittaker, Doug, 107-8
Willesee, Michael, 276
Willett, Jean, 256, 266

Willett, Prof. John, 254–62, 265–8
Williams, Vaughan, 97
Willis, Sir Eric, 174, 271
Wilson, Dr Harold, 66, 202
Wilson, Dr John R.E., 66, 78–80, 306, 313, 315–6
Wilson, Kate, 69, 147, 153
Wilson, Margaret, 66, 202
Windeyer, Sir Victor, 34, 136
Wood, Prof. Arnold, 28–9, 34
Wood, Dr Harley, 45, 305, 316
Wooley, Prof., 137
Wootten, Justice Hal, 180

Workers Education Assocn (W.E.A) 78, 304, 313
Wran, Neville, 288–9

Yates, Tim, 85–7, 142, 162, 203
Young, Peter, 126, 128, 138, 151, 167–8
Yu, Hsiuching, 267

Zhang, Zhongzai, 264–5
Zhao, Ziyang, 262–3
Zhou, Enlai, 241, 252, 253
Zioping, Deng, 262